D1376429

LIBRARY
Gift of
The Bush
Foundation

FURTHER LETTERS
OF MRS GASKELL

MANCHESTER
UNIVERSITY PRESS

FURTHER LETTERS OF
MRS GASKELL

edited by John Chapple & Alan Shelston

MANCHESTER UNIVERSITY PRESS
Manchester & New York

distributed exclusively in the USA by St. Martin's Press

Copyright © John Chapple and Alan Shelston 2000

While copyright as a whole and of all editorial matter is vested in John Chapple and Alan Shelston, copyright of all other material belongs to the respective authors and institutions as acknowledged, and no editorial or documentary material may be reproduced wholly or in part without the express permission in writing of both authors and publisher.

Published by Manchester University Press
Oxford Road, Manchester M13 9NR, UK
and Room 400, 175 Fifth Avenue, New York, NY 10010, USA
http://www.man.ac.uk/mup

Distributed exclusively in the USA by
St. Martin's Press, Inc., 175 Fifth Avenue, New York, NY 10010, USA

Distributed exclusively in Canada by
UBC Press, University of British Columbia, 2029 West Mall,
Vancouver, BC, Canada V6T 1Z2

British Library Cataloguing-in-Publication Data
A catalogue record for this book is avalaible from the British Library

Library of Congress Cataloging-in-Publication Data applied for

ISBN 0 7190 5415 x *hardback*

First published 2000

07 06 05 04 03 02 01 00 10 9 8 7 6 5 4 3 2 1

Typeset in Bembo
by Koinonia Ltd, Manchester
Printed in Great Britain
by Bookcraft (Bath) Ltd, Midsomer Norton

PR
4711
.A4
2000

071901-6156K8

THIS BOOK IS DEDICATED TO

KATE CHAPPLE AND DOROTHY SHELSTON

BY THE EDITORS, WHO BEST KNOW THEIR VALUE

ELIZABETH GASKELL TO EMILY SHAEN

'moreover Mrs Wordsworth sent me a letter of Branwells
to Mr W. & altogether it was dreary work,
looking over, correcting, interweaving, &c &c &c'

CONTENTS

ACKNOWLEDGEMENTS

J. A. V. Chapple thanks the Leverhulme Trust for awarding him an emeritus research grant. Alan Shelston thanks the Humanities Research Board of the British Academy and the University of Manchester for enabling him to take research leave in 1998–9.

We are particularly grateful to the many generous owners and custodians of Gaskell letters (see pp. 297–9 below) for allowing us access to them and for giving us the benefit of their special knowledge. We are also greatly indebted to Elizabeth Gaskell's descendant, Mrs Trevor Dabbs, Professor Arthur Pollard, who initiated this editorial project, John Geoffrey Sharps, former President of the Gaskell Society, and to Joan Leach, its Secretary. Stephen Gill, who found a number of new letters in America, presented us with the results of his research.

One of the pleasures of undertaking a project such as this is to find how generous in spirit the academic and wider community can be. This is particularly true of our contacts with the staff of the various libraries that we have visited most frequently: Manchester Central Library, The John Rylands University Library of Manchester, The Brotherton Library, Leeds University, Hull University Library and Cambridge University Library.

Specialists, colleagues and friends in several countries have also drawn Gaskell letters to our attention and helped us greatly with their responses to particular queries. They include Janet Allan, Caroline Arnaud, J. G. Baldry, A. S. Bell, Benedikt Benedikz, Yvonne L. Barwick, Christopher Bolger, Dr Ralf Breslau, W. H. Brock, John Cantrell, John, James and Christopher Chapple, R. J. Childs, Paul Chin, Stephen Colelough, Marjorie Cox, Richard Cowley, Gill Cowper, Robert Craig, Ute Dietsch, Ann Dinsdale, Professor Angus Easson, Professor K. J. Fielding, Shirley Foster, Dr E. G. Franz, Ian H. C. Fraser, Pam Godman, Ruth Green, Jeanette Griswold, Geoffrey Head, Professor Alain Jumeau, Mrs Portia Holland, Edward Holland CBE, Niall P. Kearney, Elizabeth Kemp, Julie Khan, Silke Koch, Aldona Kucharska, Anthony Laude, Dr Bernhard Lauer, Christine Lingard, George Low, Ann Mahoney, J. C. Maxwell, Joyce Meakin, Michael Meredith, Ruth Meyerson, Charlotte Mitchell, Professor Sylvère Monod, Mrs Marie Moss, Christine Nelson, Max Nettleton, Margaret Norwell, Richard Ormond, Charles Parish, Miss C. L. Penney, Professor Arthur Pollard, Richard Renold, Christopher L. Ridgeway, Major C. D. Robins, Professor Michael Rose, Professor Don Roy, Margaret Sarosi, Professor Frank Shaw, Dorothy Shelston, Christopher Sheppard,

Michael Silverman, Mary Siner, Celia Skrine, Professor Peter Skrine, Margaret Smith, Susanne Stark, David C. Sutton, Sylvia Tynan, Jenny Uglow, Anna Unsworth, Alexander D. Wainwright, Dr Ian Walker, Professor R. K. Webb, Frank Whitehead, Professor M. D. Wheeler, N. E. Willis, Derek and Celia Witney, and Professor Philip Yarrow. We have received so much help over the years that we fear names may have been omitted. If so, we apologise sincerely.

INTRODUCTION

In 1966 *The Letters of Mrs Gaskell*, edited by J. A. V. Chapple and Arthur Pollard, was published by Manchester University Press. Mrs Gaskell had always had a reputation as a sympathetic and vivacious correspondent, and a number of her letters had previously found their way into print. Jane Whitehill's edition of the correspondence between Mrs Gaskell and Charles Eliot Norton had been published in 1932, and earlier studies like Mrs Ellis Chadwick's *Mrs Gaskell: Haunts, Homes, and Stories* (1910, rev. 1913) and Elizabeth Haldane's *Mrs Gaskell and Her Friends* (1930), drew on the correspondence that was available to their authors, as did critics like A. Stanton Whitfield, G. DeWitt Sanders (both 1929) and A. B. Hopkins (1952). The 1966 volume brought together over a thousand letters, many of them newly discovered. It revealed Elizabeth Gaskell as one of the great letter-writers of the Victorian period, and it rapidly became the foundation of the remarkable growth of her literary reputation in recent years.

It was conceded by the editors of the 1966 volume that their search could not be complete and one of the consequences of their work was that more material rapidly came to light. As letters came into the salerooms they were acquired by universities, many of them in the United States, eager to reinforce their special collections; Gaskell manuscripts were sought after by private collectors, and letters by her were discovered in the files of other literary and historical figures where they had not been detected before. The Location Register of Literary Manuscripts at the University of Reading revealed yet more sources, while the increasing interest in Victorian material generally ensured that this activity was sustained. Meanwhile biographies by first Winifred Gérin (1976) and then, much more substantially, Jenny Uglow (1993), and the work of scholars like John Geoffrey Sharps, Edgar Wright and Angus Easson, together with an increasing number of critical studies, confirmed the reputation of Mrs Gaskell as a Victorian author of far greater variety and accomplishment than had previously been recognised. Feminist criticism, initially slow to follow the pioneering lead of Aina Rubenius (1950), made its mark in the 1980s, for example in the full-scale studies by Patsy Stoneman and Hilary Schor, both published in 1987.

For all these reasons we have decided that it is an appropriate time to gather together all of the letters that have come to light since 1966 in a single volume, in order to make the record as complete as it now can be. Significant absences identified by the 1966 editors remain: we have uncovered few new family letters and the holy grail of any letter from Mrs Gaskell to her husband continues to elude the seekers.

In *Cranford*, in the chapter headed 'Old Letters', Miss Matty burns the love-letters of her own mother and father: 'She said ... that it seemed as if it would have hurt her to allow them to fall into the hands of strangers, who had not known her dear mother, and how good she was, although she did not always spell quite in the modern fashion' (*Cranford*, ch. 5). Exactly the same might have been the thoughts of Meta Gaskell, when the more intimate letters of her mother were so destroyed, those to Catherine Winkworth as early as 1883 or before. But just as we were completing this supplementary volume a set of previously unknown letters addressed to the Gaskell family governess, Barbara Fergusson, discovered entirely unpredictably in a sale of family effects, arrived on our desks. Undoubtedly we shall again be overtaken by material that has not so far surfaced, or that we have overlooked. Nevertheless we believe that the material as we have collected it here substantially extends the 1966 volume and undoubtedly represents a valuable new source for Gaskell studies.

~

The letters printed in this volume come from all stages of Mrs Gaskell's adult life. Perhaps the most exciting discovery, in that they come from a period of her life of which we had little direct knowledge until now, are the five letters she wrote before her marriage to her Newcastle friend, Harriet Carr. Another recent discovery, a single letter that she wrote, we think to the same correspondent, a quarter of century later when both were married, supplements the sequence. As a young woman the then Elizabeth Stevenson stayed in Newcastle at the home of her relation, the distinguished Unitarian clergyman William Turner: the letters to Harriet, written first from Birkenhead and then from Knutsford, date from the period immediately following this visit. In one of them the unattached Elizabeth jokes about 'knowing of forty-three couples engaged – couples, not single people': by the last of them, written in August 1832, Harriet too is engaged and she herself is 'in the middle, or rather I hope, three-quarters through the bustle of wedding-gowns', since, 'I am to learn obedience the 30th of this month' (p. 19).

These letters remind us that, as with many of the writers we refer to as 'Victorian', Gaskell's formative years were in fact pre-Victorian, not so much by their reference to the coming Reform Bill and to the cholera threat of the early 1830s as by their lively chatter about lists of music to be copied and books to be read, and about balls, engagements and subsequent weddings. We are as close here to the world of Jane Austen as to that of the Manchester minister's wife. The high spirits of these letters, clearly written with some regret for a social life that she has been deprived of since leaving Newcastle, come close to presenting their writer as the 'little giddy thoughtless thing' that her Aunt Lumb is supposed to have called her, and they remind us that Elizabeth Stevenson's adoption of her later role in life must have involved a considerable effort of personal adjustment on her part. In the much later letter to Harriet, now Harriet Anderson, she remembers the 'terrible headaches' that her correspondent had suffered in those early days, and reviews the course of her life since then. She now has, she says, 'a capital helper in my husband, who has an admirable knowledge of language; and an almost fastidious taste as to style'. (She is working on her *Life of Charlotte Brontë*.) Then, in describing her children, she unexpectedly reveals that she had given birth to a 'little son', born at some point in the late 1830s between her second and third daughters, who died 'while yet a baby' (p. 156). The editors of *Letters,* following earlier biographers, referred to 'six children, of whom four survived' (*Letters*, p. xiv). This at least might have been thought to be final. But in fact, like the progeny in Wordsworth's poem, they were seven. The child referred to here is in addition to her son Willie, who died while less than a year old, and to the stillborn child she lost in 1833. It is the first time that his existence has been specifically documented.

The death of Willie Gaskell of scarlet fever in 1845 was a sorrow that we know was never forgotten. To her cousin, Fanny Holland, Mrs Gaskell wrote in 1847, 'I don't believe even heaven itself can obliterate the memory of that agony' (p. 00). Present when he died, in addition to his mother and the eleven year old Marianne, the Gaskells' eldest daughter, was the governess, Barbara Fergusson, who has until now been a shadowy figure. We learn in the same letter to Fanny Holland that she is no longer considered to be suited to the upbringing of the Gaskell girls, but the circumstances of Willie's death created a bond that was not easy to break. This is confirmed by the letters to Barbara Fergusson herself, where Mrs Gaskell recalls 'that most mournful week of watching' (p. 00), and in which she is addressed more as a friend and confidante than as a young, paid employee. In two of them Fergusson is actually addressed by a nickname 'My dear Daddy', while Mrs Gaskell insists, 'Don't be mine "very sincerely" again there's a good girl', and signs herself 'Ever your very affect friend' (p. 00). She expresses, as if to an equal, her concerns about such domestic matters as William Gaskell's diet, and the complications caused by the unwonted pregnancy of Annie, her cook, who has been deserted in her hour of need by both her mother and her seducer. As a mother and an employer Mrs Gaskell thus had direct experience of a problem that she was to allude to several times in her stories, and most famously of course in *Ruth* (1853).

A further contribution to our understanding of Mrs Gaskell's household at a later point in time is made by the letters to her long-standing friend Mary Green, wife of Henry Green, minister of the Brook Street Unitarian chapel at Knutsford. The family structure of the Greens was very similar to that of the Gaskells: they too had four daughters, each of them slightly older than their Gaskell equivalents; the youngest of them, Isabella, then aged five. Mrs Gaskell had described her to Barbara Fergusson as 'a little abomination' (p. 30), but this might have been a temporary lapse. As they grew up the Gaskell and the Green children often exchanged visits. although it is noticeable that Isabella does not figure in later letters. There was also an only son, John Philip, who cannot but have reminded Mrs Gaskell of her own loss. Mary Green was a friend 'to open my mind to' (*Letters,* p. 45), as she once wrote to another such intimate, her sister-in-law Nancy Robson. The wives of the two ministers had a considerable amount in common, and the twelve letters which we print, dating from 1852 to 1864, are evidence of an affection reinforced by these shared experiences. During this period the children on each side grew into adulthood, and parental anxiety is a recurrent theme.

Philip Green would seem to have had some difficulty in finding his feet before leaving for a legal post in India in 1860; even worse perhaps, he had by then become a Roman Catholic. (We remember the extreme concern of the Gaskells themselves, at one point, that their daughter Marianne might be tempted by Rome.) Her sympathy for the Greens at the moment of Philip's departure is typically heartfelt – 'I am quite sure no one that I know of ever needed our sympathy, but what we gave it with true hearts' – and she does her best to reassure her friends. As she says, however, 'I do not think he has an idea (when had children ever!) of how much you suffer at the prospect of separation' (p. 00). When for her part she announces the engagement of Florence to Charles Crompton, it is clear that the feelings of parents are as much at issue as the plans of their children: 'as you may fancy … we were all a good deal upset by the event of last week … at first I was more surprized than pleased, as I knew nothing of him' (p. 251). When she informs Florence Nightingale of Florence's marriage, she still describes her as 'my little daughter' (Florence was then twenty-one) and continues, 'This parting from a child *stuns* one; and it is very strange and difficult to turn back to the home-life and feel that she will never be there as before – as one's own *possession*' (p. 258).

It is safe to say that Mrs Gaskell operated at a high level of anxiety where her daughters were concerned. The letters to Mary Green are very much concerned with the responsibilities of wives and with the social lives of daughters; they also refer intermittently to the problems posed by Mrs Gaskell's writing, as for example in her anxiety about the reception of *Ruth*, and the demands on her time made by the travelling involved in research for *The Life of Charlotte Brontë*. In 1850 Mrs Gaskell famously observed that she had a 'great number' of 'mes' – that is, separate selves – and that she always had difficulty in reconciling them (*Letters*, p. 108). The decade that followed was one in which the demands made upon her increased on every front, with a corresponding intensification of the conflict between the various competing dimensions of her life: 'such a strain upon one's powers of doing, saying & being', as she puts it when she is suddenly called upon to accompany 'the girls' to a Hallé concert and 'Mr Gaskell is too busy to chaperone them' (p. 142).

The connection with Florence Nightingale reminds us of Mrs Gaskell's strong commitment to philanthropic activity. There are a number of references to her in *Letters*, including a long account to Emily Shaen (*Letters*, pp. 316–321), for which we now have the manuscript source. This letter was written from Lea Hurst, the Nightingale home in Derbyshire, where in 1854 Mrs Gaskell completed the writing of *North and South*. But there were no original letters to Florence Nightingale available in 1966: in this collection we are able to print five which confirm their regard for each other. Florence Nightingale was one of a number of figures with whom Mrs Gaskell shared both compassionate and intellectual interests; thus, at the time of the cotton famine, she writes to her friend to enquire whether unemployed cotton-workers might be suitable to be trained as nurses. In her next letter she reveals that she has sent her a copy of *Sylvia's Lovers* ('nothing could have made me more pleased … than to know that it had given *you* one hours enjoyment') and that she is reading Nightingale's own writings in return (p. 257).

Her philanthropy was invariably prompted by the individual case. She writes to the secretary of the Royal Literary Fund, Octavian Blewitt, for example on three occasions about the situation of Mrs Davenport, an authoress and resident of Knutsford, who has fallen on hard times (e.g. pp. 49–50), and she seeks help from Richard Cobden for Thomas Wright, the Manchester prison visitor, whom she has befriended. She asks Cobden also whether he might use his influence to obtain employment at sea for 'an orphan-boy … brought up as a pupil-teacher [his] health broke down, partly from hereditary tendency, partly from … employment and over-study' (p. 278). A sequence of letters to the Christian Socialist John Ludlow details the case of Mrs Glover, wife of a bookseller from Bury, who has contracted cancer, and for whom she seeks urgent medical attention. Conventional medicine having failed she asks his advice about the possibilities of mesmerism, rejecting out of hand 'that terrible Dr P. Smith' (p. 97) … 'about whose *wilfulness* in operating when there was no hope I heard stories which amounted to absolute cruelty' (p. 95). As our notes indicate, Smith was a pioneering surgeon with a high reputation for the care of his patients: this is an interesting example, perhaps, of a woman's reaction to the increasingly scientific tendencies of patriarchal Victorian medicine.

The involvement with Ludlow, whose practical politics appealed to her, develops into lasting friendship. Later she visits him at his home in Wimbledon and consults him about his experience with the Working Men's College when her husband is about to embark on a similar venture in Manchester. She had no inhibitions about calling on her friends when she felt that specialist knowledge was required: thus she seeks 'a little *gratis* law' from Ludlow, to help a working man who has invested unwisely in the Chartist Land Scheme (p. 162), and 'a little *law*-knowledge, *gratis*' from Mrs James, wife of a distinguished judge, to enable her to intervene in the case of a young girl who is suffering from the behaviour of her deranged father (p. 120). To read letters like this is to be brought close to the darker realities of Victorian domestic experience, never more so perhaps than in the account Mrs Gaskell gives of the last hours of John Nicholls, the promising son of two members of the Cross Street congregation (pp. 203–5). Rarely can a Victorian death bed have been so graphically described.

The urgency of the writing when the distress of individuals had attracted Mrs Gaskell's attention can convey the human dimension of larger public events. To Ludlow again, in 1857, she writes of 'our terrible Indian anxieties'; the reference is to the death of her friends, Colonel and Mrs Ewart, in the massacre at Cawnpore (p. 177). Later Indian anxieties would focus upon Meta's precipitate engagement to a widower with two children, Captain Hill. At home she was to be troubled by the cotton famine of 1861–4, a period when a sharp decline in the trade cycle, combined with the consequences for the Manchester cotton trade of the war in the United States, led to extensive unemployment and social distress in the cotton districts. Actively involved in relief measures, Mrs Gaskell enlisted the help of yet another of her young lawyer friends, Vernon Lushington. She fears that the termination of the Civil War will only make matters worse for it will depress the Indian markets: 'we fear its becoming worse [i.e. the famine] … if the American war is likely to come to a speedy conclusion; so one's interests clash terribly' (p. 238). Again, her responses are practical ones: Lushington is thanked for a financial donation and informed immediately of its effectiveness, and he is told how best to disburse further financial generosity (pp. 235–8). As in the case of Ludlow, we can detect in the sequence of letters to Lushington the growth of a more personal relationship. The last of the letters to him conveys congratulations on his engagement, with a tongue-in-the-cheek request for 'an *impartial* account of one who is going to become the wife of a valued friend' (p. 266).

A capacity for generous friendship was one of Mrs Gaskell's most attractive qualities. Throughout these letters we sense the spontaneity of her affection for friends and companions new and old. Her acquaintance with a succession of American friends drew her into anxious comment on the American Civil War. A strong interest in the United States, reflected in the splendid letters to Charles Eliot Norton, reprinted in 1966, was reinforced by the visits paid by prominent American Unitarians to Cross Street and to Plymouth Grove, and by her association with American expatriates like the Wetmore Storys whom she met in Paris and in Rome. As early as 1841, to another Boston Unitarian, John Pierpont, she had confessed that 'we dare not hope ever to be ... sufficiently at large with regard to time and money to go to America, easy and rapid as the passage has become' (p. 25). Her misgivings proved well-founded, but she never lost her affection for the individual Americans of her acquaintance.

The letters to Charles Eliot Norton, first printed by Jane Whitehill in 1932, document what is generally regarded as one of the most interesting relationships, literary and personal, of Mrs Gaskell's life. This correspondence is now supplemented by the letters she wrote to Edward Everett Hale, another prominent Boston Unitarian minister, on several occasions in the early 1860s. Characteristically, Hale is regarded as a familiar friend, privy to news about the family and all of their doings. She writes in difficult times, expressing her concern at 'the sad news that you Northerners are likely to be at war when this reaches you' (p. 222). In the next letter she voices alarm at the prospect of war between England and America, provoked by the perfidy of 'the Emperor of the French' (p. 229). The American Civil War confuses her, since it produces conflicts of emotion and conflicts of loyalty. As she famously did with regard to the science of political economy in *Mary Barton*, she somewhat disingenuously pleads ignorance of what is at stake: 'I wish I could understand American politics which are *the* most complicated things I know' (p. 223). American politics were indeed complicated to English observers of the mid-nineteenth century, but through her American friends she was more than usually well-informed about the American scene.

Notwithstanding the revealing letters we are now able to print from Mrs Gaskell's early years, the bulk of the material collected here inevitably comes from the last fifteen years of her life, the period when she was most active as novelist and writer. It was the response to *Mary Barton*, and in particular Dickens's recruitment of her for the initiation of *Household Words* in 1850, that launched her literary career and effectively turned her into a public figure. The friendship with Lushington was perhaps typical of the kind of connections that Mrs Gaskell made in her later years. As her literary career developed we find her using her influence on matters of public concern; at the same time we find her drawn into the company both of influential professionals and of country house society. Thus at the Cheshire home of Mrs Caroline Davenport, whom she had known since early days and who by her second marriage was to become Lady Hatherton, she meets Amelia Harriet Strutt and

Maria James, sisters and each of them the wife of a very distinguished lawyer. At Oxford she enjoys the company of distinguished dons, while she invites the mathematician Henry Smith to stay at Plymouth Grove, expressing the hope that he 'will not be too grand a Savillian [*sic*] Professor for us poor unmathematical creatures' (p. 224). She arranges for her daughter Meta to copy a painting by Bartelomé Murillo for Lady Hatherton, lent to the Manchester Exhibition of 1857 by the collector of Spanish art, William Stirling. If not all of her correspondents are as grand as the Duke of Devonshire to whom, after a visit to Chatsworth, she sent an autograph letter of Charlotte Brontë's in response to his personal request (p. 172), many of the later ones are titled, or like Monckton Milnes, who became Lord Houghton, have acquired titles in some way. To Lord Stanhope, in 1856, she writes without detectable irony, 'We stand, each labourers on the same broad field' (p. 151). Her personal connections, via her dissenting allegiances, to the Holland and the Wedgwood families had certainly brought her into contact with social distinction at an early stage. The new contacts, however, register movement into a different sphere – not deliberately sought after, but perhaps an inevitable consequence of her talent for what we would now call networking, and an index too of the fluidity of English middle and upper class society at this particular moment in the mid-nineteenth century.

With the confirmation of Elizabeth Gaskell's reputation as one of the major novelists of the Victorian period it is the development of her literary career in the last two decades of her life which is of primary interest. Her literary reputation has traditionally fluctuated between extremes: was she best considered as the delicate provincial ironist of *Cranford* or as the sympathetic if soft-hearted chronicler of urban realities, the author of *Mary Barton*, her 'Tale of Manchester Life'? In recent years, however, there has been a much greater willingness to see her in terms of a richly rewarding literary corpus, varied in kind, in focus and indeed in quality, and not to be represented by any one individual work. Mrs Gaskell came relatively late to the writing of fiction – she was thirty-eight when *Mary Barton* was published in 1848 – but the success of her first novel led to Dickens's invitation to contribute to the opening number of *Household Words* and to the association with his periodical that so rapidly enabled her to make up for lost time. In 1853 she writes to John Forster that 'I seldom see the Household Words' (p. 87) – this at a point when *Cranford* was appearing in its pages. She frequently borrowed or begged her books from publishers, rather than buying them: the records of the Portico Library in Manchester even reveal that her husband once borrowed its copy of *Jane Eyre*. One suspects, however, that *Household Words* was a journal that she might not have borrowed either, written as it was for a new and more general readership. Later there were to be problems over the serialisation of *North and South* in its pages, and in 1855 she declared to her friend Maria

James that 'I will never write for H. W. again' (p. 123). In fact she continued to write for Dickens's magazine for as long as it remained in circulation.

During the period in which *Household Words* appeared, from 30 March 1850 to 28 May 1859, Mrs Gaskell published some twenty-five shorter items in its pages, as well as the pieces which were collected together to form *Cranford* (1851–3) and the full-length serial novel *North and South* (1854–5). *Ruth* was published by Chapman and Hall as a three volume novel in 1853, and *The Life of Charlotte Brontë* in two volumes by Smith, Elder in 1857. When *Household Words* was succeeded by *All The Year Round* in 1859 Mrs Gaskell continued to contribute stories and articles to Dicken's new periodical. However she was effectively transferring her loyalties to George Smith, publisher of her Brontë biography, for whose handsome *Cornhill Magazine* she was to write both *Cousin Phillis* (1863–4) and *Wives and Daughters* (1864–5), along with other shorter pieces. For Smith, she also published *Sylvia's Lovers*, this time as a three volume novel, in 1863.

The move from Dickens to Smith is significant in more than a literary context: for Dickens, Mrs Gaskell was writing primarily for a popular audience, while Smith's journal aimed at exactly the kind of professional and leisured middle-class readership with whom she had become acquainted in her personal life. It is worth spelling out these details – and they are not fully inclusive – since what they represent, especially as so much of her work appeared under the pressures of periodical publication, is nearly fifteen years of continuous writing on Mrs Gaskell's part from 1850 to her sudden death in 1865. In terms of literary history they reflect the move from her early moralistic 'social-problem' fiction to the provincialism – in the precise sense of the term – and the sophistication of her final work, while in personal terms they reveal an increasing professionalism about her work in every sense of the term.

In their Introduction to *Letters* the editors identified from her correspondence a number of aspects of Mrs Gaskell's literary activities that were reflected in her correspondence: her writing procedures in her various works, for example, her response to their reception and her dealings with her publishers. In all of this they detected 'increasing assurance' on her part about her work, even while she remained 'deeply conscious of its defects' (*Letters*, pp. xix-xx). In the letters we print in this volume the anxiety which for her always seemed to accompany literary production is confirmed, as in her references to the reception of *Ruth*, and to the work involved in her preparation for *The Life of Charlotte Brontë*, while our knowledge of her dealings with publishers is extended by letters to Frederic Chapman and to George Smith, about the transfer of copyrights between the two men, and to Sampson Low, her 'rascally publisher' in the 1966 volume (*Letters*, p. 531). Low, who was heavily involved in the American book trade, caused problems by his dealings with Harpers, the New York publishers, over her story *Round the Sofa.* For this reason we have decided to include two business letters written on her behalf by her daughter Meta to Charles Eliot Norton. The first of these expresses her mother's misgivings about Low's behaviour which have led her to favour a separate deal with the firm of Ticknor and Fields, but by the time of the second, 'Mr Sampson Lowe[sic] has just offered her £1000 for a tale but little longer than the one Messrs T & F bid for' (p. 197), and Low is back in favour. This was a substantial sum, and the more experienced Mrs Gaskell became in these dealings the more aware she became of her market value. According to Meta, in 1857 her mother was moved by 'what happened in 1859 about the Life of C. B.' to resolve on giving up publishing in England and 'publishing for the future in America' (p. 197). The sums she received for her final works rewarded her for abandoning this decision.

One of the more regrettable absences identified by the editors of *Letters* was that of any letters to Mme Mohl, the Parisian friend of Mrs Gaskell who entertained her on a number of occasions. We have not been able to restore this omission, but a fascinating sequence of letters found in the archive of Hachette et Cie, the French publishing company, reveals a business relationship between Louis Hachette, the founder of the firm, and Mrs Gaskell that undoubtedly originated in one of her frequent visits to Paris. In March 1855 Mrs Gaskell was asked by Hachette to recommend works by English authors for translation and publication by his company. At the same time Hachette negotiates with her about the translation of her own work. This is a key moment in European publishing: the development of the railway system had led Hachette to initiate his 'Bibliothèque des Chemins de Fer', a library series modelled on similar ventures which had been developed in England as the railway system expanded. The German publisher Tauchnitz similarly initiated his series of paperback reprints of English and American fiction at this time and while these did not involve translation, we have extracts from business letters to his firm from Mrs Gaskell. Clearly her work was successful on the continent as well as in England, and in fact all of her major novels, as well as some of her stories, were to be translated into French with at most only a few years' lapse after their English publication.

Mrs Gaskell's recommendations to Hachette broaden our understanding of the Victorian literary scene. As well as her friends Mrs Nicholls (Charlotte Brontë) and Geraldine Jewsbury, she recommends a number of lesser novelists, most of them women, although she is cautious in her endorsements. Mrs Marsh – actually a relation by marriage – 'has written about thirty novels, one or two of which are very good, three or four tolerable, and the rest forgotten as soon as read.' Mrs Gore, for her part, whose 'writings ... are about as numerous as those of Mrs Marsh', writes novels 'of the class called in England "Fashionable novels."' These, however, 'have very little plot in them, their principal interest ... consisting in a lively, spirited, epigrammatic description of the manners of lords and ladies', while Miss Mulock 'has written six or seven pretty sentimental novels, with not much power displayed in them, but with a good deal of grace and delicacy.' These comments remind us both of the care of Mrs Gaskell's literary judgement – while not as severe as George Eliot, she has little time for fictional trivialities – and of the enormous productivity of the Victorian female fictional industry. The men seem to be treated less cautiously. A new work by 'a young writer, a friend of Mr Dickens' is 'detestable': it is Wilkie Collins's early novel, *Basil*. Charles Reade's *Christie Johnson*, however, is written with 'glorious power', while *Lady Lee's Widowhood*, by the now forgotten Major Hamley, is 'very brilliant and clever' (pp. 127–8).

It is interesting that her judgement of the Brontës is again somewhat guarded. In earlier correspondence she had described Charlotte Brontë as putting 'all her naughtiness' into her novels (*Letters*, p. 228; p. 90 below), and here *Jane Eyre* is described as 'a very remarkable book' – a somewhat ambivalent comment perhaps. In the *Life of Charlotte Brontë* Mrs Gaskell drew a clear distinction between Currer Bell the author and Charlotte Brontë the suffering woman, reserving her judgment on the novels themselves. To Hachette she writes that *Shirley* is 'not so good' – as *Jane Eyre*, that is – and while *Villette* is considered 'fully equal' to *Jane Eyre*, 'the story is not so interesting.' She is not sure 'how far the French would appreciate' *Wuthering Heights*, but she considers the biographical memoir which Charlotte wrote for the second edition of Emily's novel to be 'as extraordinary, and as interesting as any of the stories she has written' (p. 126–7). Anne Brontë remains unmentioned.

Mrs Gaskell continued to correspond with Hachette, the business connection reinforced by meetings in Paris and by invitations to Hachette and his family to Manchester. She was clearly impressed by Hachette's professionalism and her early misgivings about the quality of some French translations – 'Every author of any note is anxious for a correct and faithful translation of what they do write', she says (p. 130) – were overcome to the point where she readily ceded the rights of French translation of her works to Hachette and his translators. Reviewing their work, she expresses her satisfaction. 'I am delighted with the grace and ease of the translation', she says of *Cranford*; and again, of *Ruth*, 'I was extremely gratified to find my meaning so well rendered in a foreign language' (p. 150). Further recommendations for translation of novels by her contemporaries were offered, although in 1858 she deplores the state of English fiction: 'I never knew so few good romances published ... Dickens reads aloud, instead of writing, and is said to earn more money in this way' (p. 188). If the increasing warmth of these letters confirms her confidence in Hachette, the connection with the Tauchnitz firm was also a source of satisfaction: she writes to its head as 'one ... who has always behaved so kindly and liberally to me' (p. 189).

From the first Mrs Gaskell was sympathetic to cosmopolitan influences. She was acquainted with members of the large and wealthy Manchester German business community, like the Schuncks or the Schwabes, patrons of the Swedish singer Jenny Lind and the American actress Fanny Kemble. Twice she visited Rome. She also went to Heidelberg on three occasions as well as making regular visits to Paris and discovering French as well as German provincial life in some depth, greatly extending the range of her fiction. In this collection we are able to publish a letter to the eminent German scholar, Jacob Grimm, and one also, probably, to the great historian, Leopold Ranke. Clearly her dealings with continental publishers, as with her engagement with continental writers and thinkers, did much to make up for less happy experiences at home.

Writing, however, would always be a source of strain. Her multifarious activities left her with little time to reflect upon her writing processes, at least on paper. For that reason a letter to George Smith about the composition of *Cousin Phillis* is of special interest: it gives details of an alternative ending to the story which has to be rejected because of the limitations of space imposed by its serial publication in the *Cornhill* (pp. 259–60). Some might feel that this is an occasion when economics worked to the benefit of art. Similar difficulties arise over *Wives and Daughters*, and it comes as something of a surprise to find this longest and most accomplished of her novels described by her as 'the wretched story' (p. 267). To the end Mrs Gaskell was a novelist harassed by difficulties and determined to get things right. In the last year of her life she writes again to Smith, '*Am I limited* to *16* numbers? [her underlining is doubled] I am afraid the story is getting on so slowly that I must either condense, (& spoil it,) or put more in a number, or have more numbers. But I will *try* not. I wish it was ended & done with. So I dare say you do with this letter, consequently I am ever yours most truly / E C Gaskell' (p. 267).

~

We doubt whether any collection of Mrs Gaskell's correspondence could consider itself 'ended and done with', but we hope that this volume, together with *The Letters of Mrs Gaskell* of 1966 will provide as complete a compilation as is possible at this point in time. Initially we had hoped to re-organise the letters contained in the two editions in a single complete sequence as a revised and complete single edition. However, this had to be balanced against the exigencies of publishing and the delay that this would have involved, delay which would have continued to deprive Gaskell students of easy access to the material that we have gathered here, much of it either inaccessible or quite unknown.

For the sake of consistency, but also because in a collection of correspondence it seemed appropriate to use the form by which she would have expected to be addressed, we have continued to refer to her as 'Mrs Gaskell', while recognising the reasons why this is now felt to be ideologically unsound. Invariably, even to very close friends, she signs herself 'E. C. Gaskell', very occasionally 'Lily', but only on one occasion in these letters as 'Elizabeth Gaskell'. The great attraction of Mrs Gaskell's correspondence is that it reveals her so clearly as that many-sided person that she understood herself to be: minister's wife; mother; novelist and reader of novels; traveller and teller of tales; unstinting helper of the unfortunate and enthusiastic friend of those with whom she came into contact at all levels of society. To read the letters is to gain a remarkable insight into the way such a woman lived her life in the middle decades of the nineteenth century, and into the contexts, cultural and historical, within which such a life was lived.

EDITORIAL POLICY

We print the letters in a single chronological sequence, reflecting the organisation of the 1966 edition. This separates letters to individual correspondents but makes for ease of access and comparison. We have also done our best to arrive at provisional dates for the very many letters with incomplete dates, making it clear where we are not certain of our dating. It has also seemed useful to give a brief reference within our sequence to numbered letters in the 1966 edition that it has been possible to redate, or date for the first time, in the light of much new evidence and the advice of other scholars. (These indications of revised dating, some of them very slight, follow the notes to individual letters.) As in 1966, we print letters that we have been unable to date in a final section, alphabetically ordered by correspondents. A few occasional MSS that are not true letters have been relegated to an appendix.

We confess regretfully that by dating these letters as far as we could we have failed to preserve a certain valuable quality, called to our attention by the learned editor of the letters of Charlotte Brontë:

> As I find my correspondence is carefully preserved by you, I flatter myself it is with the view of being one day presented to the public in twelve handsome octavo volumes, embellished with a portrait of the authoress, and enriched with a facsimile of her handwriting. Having this hope before my eyes, I carefully abstain from the vulgar practice of dating my letters, aware how greatly uncertainty adds to the interest. (*Memoir and Correspondence of Susan Ferrier,* ed. John A. Doyle, 1898, chapter 2)

We have been more fortunate than our predecessors, in that we have not been forced to print from unique but defective texts, often inaccurately transcribed and even censored. The 1966 editors had also to resort to poor typescript copies, arbitrarily cut and occasionally running together silently portions of quite different letters. The complete original manuscripts of many truly important letters to Mrs Gaskell's young friend 'Tottie' Fox, with one notable exception here from the collection of the late Professor Gordon Ray, have still not been found. However, the texts of almost all the letters printed below have been derived from the original holograph manuscripts. Larger groups held in this country, such as those to Harriet Carr and Barbara Fergusson, have been carefully examined and transcribed. For a number of widely dispersed letters, and for letters held in European and American collections, we have been able to rely upon photographic copies efficiently provided by the various holders.

Once again, we have attempted to preserve the flowing, idiosyncratic characteristic of the originals, making only slight or formal changes in transcription. Addresses and dates have been moved to headings and obvious postscripts printed at the end wherever they actually occur in the sources. We allow sense to dictate the order in crossed letters. Intolerably long paragraphs have been broken down and their openings indented. Addresses, postmarks and significant annotations are recorded. If no separate cover is noted, either it is not extant or such details have been taken from the outermost folded sheet of the letter in question.

Our transcriptions from manuscript are very faithful, so we have been sparing in the use of [sic]. In ambiguous cases of punctuation and use of capitals, we have adopted the most readable alternatives. Superscript letters in abbreviations have been lowered and the full stop or dash omitted after contracted forms. As in 1966, long s is ignored and there are a few standard normalisations: MA, ME, Brontë, Mr, Mrs, Dr and single quotation marks in the first instance. We employ the usual square brackets for editorial insertions, together with a few other symbols for manuscript gaps < >, deletions { } and insertions \ /.

We have supplied fuller annotation than was possible in 1966. We have not attempted to explain every reference, but have given priority to identifying personalities, publications and events we judge to be significant, and to providing information that will extend the reader's understanding of these letters in their wider context. At the end of the text we have provided a Biographical Index in which we give more information about the Holland and Gaskell families. We also include the relations, friends and acquaintances who were part of Mrs Gaskell's daily life; their names are marked with a star below. A volume index lists by page number all persons referred to in both text and notes, with correspondents and important notes indicated in bold type.

J. A. V. Chapple bears primary responsibility for the text of the letters themselves and Alan Shelston for the Introduction. The notes and other editorial apparatus have been a shared responsibility.

DATED LETTERS

ANNE BURNETT[1]

[Newcastle]
Thursday Eveng.
[c. June 1831]

I can not tell you how much I felt gratified, my dear *Anne* on my return this evening from Bensham,[2] by your very kind note, and the accompanying book which I have long wished to see. I hope I shall never require any thing to remind me of any of my kind Newcastle friends, or of the many pleasant hours I have spent here, but as a token of your regard, you may be sure I shall always value it exceedingly. Like you I very much regret our having seen so little of each other, but that little has left so very pleasant an impression that I sincerely hope should I ever come to Newcastle again, I shall have more opportunity of enjoying your society. I am sure you may always depend upon my very cordial regard, and affectionate wishes for your welfare, and happiness –

Pray thank Mrs Burnett, and your sisters for their kind wishes, and remembrances – I am looking forward with great pleasure to reading your most acceptable present when settled for the Summer at Woodside, where I hope to join my Aunt[3] the day after tomorrow – I shall often hear all about you from Anne Turner, & should you ever feel inclined to write to me, I will prove how welcome your letters will be by a speedy answer. With very kind regards to Mrs Burnett, and your sisters,

Believe me to remain
Your sincere & affectionate Friend
Elizabeth C. Stevenson

Haworth Parsonage Museum
First printed in *Portrait,* pp. 11–12. More detailed information about this period is provided in P. J. Yarrow, 'Mrs. Gaskell and Newcastle', *Archaeologia Aeliana,* 5S, XX (1992), and *EY,* which includes genealogical appendixes for Stevensons, Hollands and Turners.

1 This letter is associated with the visits Elizabeth Stevenson made to Newcastle upon Tyne, where her relative, the Reverend William Turner* (1761–1859), was minister of Hanover Square chapel 1782–1841 and a prominent figure in the town. She was by this time an orphan, having lost her mother when she was a baby and her father in 1829. Turner himself had just become a widower for the second time, and was renting a house in Clavering Place with his youngest daughter Ann (1796–1851). Amongst the members of his congregation were George Burnett senior, agent and manufacturer, and George Burnett junior. We assume Anne was a relation.

2 Though the existence of letters written by a young Elizabeth Stevenson has been asserted (see *EY*, p. 3), the letter to Anne Burnett is the earliest text that has been found to date. It was written about June 1831 and sent on her return from Bensham, a village across the Tyne now a suburb of Gateshead.

3 Mrs Hannah Lumb, née Holland (1767–1837), of The Heath, Knutsford, was the widowed aunt who brought Elizabeth up. They were to stay in Woodside, a pleasant resort then being developed across the Mersey from Liverpool, with regular steam-paddle boat services (*EY*, p. 344).

HARRIET CARR*[1]

Woodside. Brandon Street.
[Saturday] June 18. 1831.

My dearest Harriet,

Thanks be to you my lazy correspondent for at last fulfilling your promise, and writing to me. I had absolutely some thoughts of giving up my dignity, and writing first, in pure compassion to your being so immersed in London gaieties. Oh what a dissipated life you have led since this third of December last when if my memory serve me rightly, your pomps and vanities began; since when Life has been a continual waltz to you – I, in my retirement at Woodside could read you a lecture on the subject, for here I have no one to remind me of *Harriet Carr*, and *giddiness* (synonyms) but a great grey parrot the tones of whose voice I sometimes fancy resemble yours. And now having convinced you that the 'grapes are sour', I shall go on to congratulate you on your new acquisition of a sister; and from all you say of her, I have no doubt that it is a most pleasant one; I sincerely wish her, and Mr Wm Carr every happiness in each other's society and affection – *most* sincerely, for besides being your brother, I have not forgotten his patience in waltzing with the personification of the 'waves of the sea'.

The next subject worthy of notice in your letter is the Ascot Races: I think Mr Thornton deserves indeed to have a place in the next edition of 'Percy Anecdotes of Enterprize'[2] since he undertook to keep you in order. I have been at so very many races, and reviews in my long life, that I think they have quite lost their charm for me, but I should like to see the King, Queen & all the Royal family, proper and improper. In spite of my 'political principles', I can not help admiring high blood, and aristocracy. And what do you think of Paganini,[3] is he so very wonderful, as people say, and did you go into hysterics with the violence of your emotions, as I have heard of people's doing. And are you going to the Horticultural Fete on the 22nd; because I prophesy rain for that day, and advise your taking a pair of pattens in your merino bag. Remember the Fete three years ago, and be advised. In a letter I had from Louisa Holland[4] she says it is a point of dispute as to whether Mr Wm Cayley is gone to get a wife or Cholera Morbus[5] in St Petersburgh. They i.e. the good people in Park Lane have been giving what sounds like a most delightful dance, only dances always do sound delightful – but they had an excellent projector, who made capital 'flirting places' in the balcony, and Gunter, & Weippert's {flower} band, & Colville's flower show, so I think it does not signify the scarcity of young ladies they complain of.

I have just had a letter from another cousin of mine who is visiting in Yorkshire; and amongst other people she describes the Benyons whom I think you met at Harrogate, and Miss Jaques the Brandling's cousin, of whom she has seen a good deal, so I shall quote the passage for your edification, Madam – 'I had no idea the Brandlings, we used to look for at the Opera, were cousins to Miss Jaques; poor little thing, we pity her; having been accustomed to live in the family with nine cousins, and now she lives quite alone, for her father is out most of the day, & she only knows one or two families about here, and those not agreeables – she looks miserable in company, from absolute mauvaise honte, though better at the end of a visit than at the beginning.' So much for Miss Jaques, only as far as I could judge from seeing her in a ball-room, she never evinced any extreme of mauvaise honte – What did you think, mia cara? Have you heard or seen anything of the Brandlings since you came to London? Are their matrimonial projects taking effect.

I had a letter from my dear Mrs Ramsay the other day – the Doctor does not seem to have been very well. She says she has been to call on the little french bride, Mrs Wm Losh; and that she is the very least little person that ever was. *I* should be a giantess to her, so I think she must be even less than you.

Oh! thank you about that Tyrolese song – but I have copied it from my cousins book – but if you like still to overburden me with obligations to you, in the copying music line of business, you *may* (I will allow you) copy either, or both, 'Rise up, rise up Xarifa', and my dear 'Rose, thou art the sweetest flower'.[6] I think you will think I am not overburdened with mauvaise honte, whatever Miss Jaques may be. Did one of the Miss Dorriens marry a Dr Drevor-rather an odd sort of a marriage? We are so very retired here that unless I told you, how the hay crops &c were going on, & what show of fruit there is, I could send you little interesting news. So I will tell you a little London news, as I think you are so very far off Babylon that you cannot hear any of the intelligence therein. Have you heard or seen anything of Col. Murat?[7] I mean to conclude you have not, for they visit very few people in town – only years ago, when my Aunt was living at Naples, she saw a great deal of him, then Prince Achille, for he was the son of 'le beau sabreur' and Napoleon's sister Caroline – then King, and Queen of Naples – Achille Murat was then a very fine young ma<n> of 18, or 19, and a great favourite with his Uncle Napoleon; but fashions change and so do kings, and at the grand downfall of the Buonapart family, Achille had to run for his life, and never stopped till he got to the Back-settlements in N. America, where he bought 3000 acres of uncleared ground; planted cotton, and married a grand-daughter of Washington, and these two descendants of Generals, & kings, & warriors set to plant, spin, weave, & make cotton up into clothes – indeed their life from all accounts reminds one of the old distich, 'When Adam delved, & Eve span, where was then the gentleman'? for they performed the very coarsest sort of manual labour. At length Colonel Murat bethought himself that instead of sitting idly in his fields driving crows away, while the corn grew up – he would study law; and a lawyer he became, and now rides some hundreds of miles with his green bag before him, as a practising barrister in Florida. This last eventful year he and his pretty 'wee wife' have been travelling on the continent, and were so courted & caressed in Paris; quite a new scene to Mrs Murat – and they then joined his Aunt Queen Hortense, and came to England, where my cousins have seen a great deal of them. She is very simple, & has scarcely got over her notes of admiration at everything different from America, & he is 'more like Napoleon, than Napoleon himself'. Hortense is the most fascinating woman that ever was.

You{r} describe bonnets but do not go any farther with fashions. Pray complete the human figure when you next write, especially the hair. I really should like to follow Mr Dorrien's precedent and wear a wig, for I do think hair is a great torment. You see I have adopted the literary *manner* of writing as to the *matter* I cannot say so much, for I fear you have thought this a most dull letter, but as I told you before we are very very retired – going to bed I suppose at the same time that you go to parties &c &c. However my dearest Harriet don't let this prevent you from keeping up your correspondence with me, for I may, and doubtless shall improve, as wonderfully as I have done in the worsted work, which I do beautifully – avaunt Modesty – and probably nearly as well as you do the chain – which, as *Elizabeth* says you do well, I will believe.

By the bye do the Russians (peasants I mean) eat bread dipped in a bucket of sea water, stirred about with a stick; and this aforesaid bread made of rye, and the barks of trees. Pray answer this important query when you next write. I have been sending an order for a dozen ivory chains by a travelling gent – who is going to Archangel, and am expecting my gushi[?] a casha[8] daily.

Pray give my kind love to Mrs Carr, and Elizabeth – and give you

[The letter breaks off here.] I have forgotten what I was going to say, and only remember that I am

Yours ever very affectionately,
Elizabeth Cleghorn Stevenson –

I have re-opened my letter to ask you if \ you / know or hear of any one likely to want a housekeeper, if you would recommend a person who was once *nursery governess* to my cousins, & afterwards companion & housekeeper to a cousin of mine Caroline Holland who is subject to fits and consequently lives separate from her family – This person Miss Swinerhath[?] by name – is very well qualified to keep house for any invalid lady, or bachelor, or widower – she is of discreet age, and a more kind-hearted, faithful creature never was. I do not know so much of her housekeeping talents but I have no doubt that she could very well superintend a not over-large family, and in any place of trust a better person could not be chosen. She is a great object of interest to the whole family – and I will refer you to Aunt Swinton for a *referee* – in whose family she was for 12[?] years – address as newspapers say – Mrs Holland 32 Norfolk St Park-Lane

Address Miss Carr Nottingham Place Marylebone London.
Postmarks C 20 JU 20 1831; illegible.
Seal Oval, with script 'Elizabeth' written lengthways.

Brotherton Collection, Leeds University
Five letters to Harriet Carr*, first printed, and annotated more extensively than here, by J. A. V. Chapple, 'Before "Crutches and Changed Feelings": Five Early Letters by Elizabeth Gaskell (neé Stevenson)', *GSJ* 4 (1990), pp. 1–27. Together with the letter to William Turner* that follows, they throw a flood of light upon Elizabeth Stevenson's life and character in the years up to her marriage on 30 August 1832. 'Women's letters and diaries brim with commentary on the array of public diversions from which they fashioned a cultural life' (Vickery, p. 276).

1 Her father George Carr was a representative of the Branch Bank of England in Newcastle, appointed 3 April 1828 on a salary of no less than £1000 a year (*EY*, p. 340). He was a member of Turner's congregation.
2 S. and R. Percy [pseud. J. C. Robertson and Thomas Byerley], *The Percy Anecdotes*, 20 vols (1821–23).
3 Nicolo Paganini (1782–1840), composer and flamboyant violin virtuoso, played in London in 1831.
4 References throughout are to kinfolk, in this instance the family of uncle Swinton Colthurst Holland (1777–1827) and his wife Anne, née Willets (d. 1845). Elizabeth Stevenson's cousins were Edward (1806–75), Caroline (1807–33), Charlotte (b. 1808), Louisa (1810–98), Frederick (1814–60) and George Henry (1816–91).
5 Asiatic cholera was sweeping across Russia and Europe. It reached Sunderland by October 1831.

6 'Xarifa' (or Bridal of Andalla), no. 1 of Frances C. Arkwright, *A Set of Six Ancient Spanish Ballads* [1830]. 'Rose, etc.', by Thomas Moore, was also one of Mrs Arkwright's songs. See also p. 15 below; *EY*, pp. 244–6.
7 Napoléon-Achille Murat (1801–1847), son of Napoleon's sister Caroline and one of his Marshals; they had been created King and Queen of Naples in 1808. Achille went to America in 1821. His aunt Hortense (d. 1837), a step-daughter of Napoleon, lived mostly in Switzerland.
8 Doubtful reading; unexplained.

HARRIET CARR*

Woodside.
August the last. 1831. & Sep. 1st

My dear Harriet,

Matthew building a house! I thought he had house & furniture some scores of years ago when he was a 'poor *boy*', and only wanted a Mrs Matthew to complete his decorations. Are you *sure*, Harriet you are not the fair lady who 'all in good time' are going to take him, and his house and engravings – I think it was very suspicious, his unwillingness to tell me which of the Miss Carrs he liked best, and he certainly did blush to the end of his hair, thereby encreasing the 'celestial [rosy] red, love's proper hue' of his hair.[1]

Many thanks to you for your charming letter. I do enjoy your letters above any body else's, I do believe, and wish I could excite your anger a little oftener, since you say you write only to scold me. Remember every little, leetle particular about yourself, and your concerns, and gossipry, and scandal, are most welcome to me, but especially all that interests you, and Elizabeth personally, down to the uninteresting in general basons of tapioca you have at lunch – I could fancy Matthew eating tapioca – such a very insipid thing can only suit very insipid people – I have been thinking a great deal about you lately, and feeling for all your anxiety for your Petersburg friends, but now I suppose and hope I may rejoice with you, for that the terrible disease has by all accounts abated so very much.[2] I was very anxious for your last letter, and was on the point of writing to enquire and tell you how much both Aunt Lumb and I have sympathized with you. I shall be very glad to hear from you, (as soon as you can feel angry) that you are quite relieved from your anxiety.

How is little Mary-Harriet-Elizabeth? You don't know how very gay your letters sound when talking of your dissipated life in London, at least compared with my own quiet proceeding at Woodside, for the last three months[.] I suppose we shall make wings to ourselves, and fly away in the course of the next month to our real home for the 'wind's very cold, and we're very old, and my doublet is not very new, well-a-day'. We have here the benefit of the North and East winds and not a tree to shelter us.

I suppose you have heard of this terrible loss of the Rothsay Castle[3] on her road to Beaumaris. Most fortunately out of all our numerous friends, who are in the habit of passing, and repassing to Wales by water, only one with whom I had a very slight dancing acquaintance was on board, & he survived. I dined with him – on Monday at Dr Traill's,[4] but as he said he had been a hero nine times that day, I could not, much as I longed, make many enquiries as to his feelings, for having been quite insensible when taken up, he must have experienced all the sensations of drowning.

At dinner there were some people of the name of Sandbach, and I heard them very busy talking about 'Harriet T<id?>y, 'Mr Ward', the 72[?], 'Tom Tidy' &c and upon enquiry found they had known the Tidys[5] when staying at a General Dallock's (I think) near Glasgow. Did you ever hear Mr Tidy speak of them? Then they went on to talk of William Mr Turvy, who, by the bye is going or gone to pay my cousins a visit in Gloucestershire. They knew also Mrs Walker (Miss Packer.)

But the grand subject of conversation just now, here is a Bazaar; for the benefit of the infirmary, and oh! how I wish the name of bazaar, like that of MacGregor might perish for ever.[6] There is to be a Ball one of the nights, a much more sensible way of being charitable, I think. Feet versus Hands. I suppose it is to stand, or to dance for a Coronation-Ball,[7] for we are going to be shabby and disloyal, and shirk the Coronation [8 September 1831] for the Bazaar. I shall long for your accounts of the \ NC / Ball, so pray don't fail to send me one, with true & full descriptions of people, & people's dresses, and people's partners, and people's flirtations, and what people's partners said to people, & what people said to people's partners.

What is become of Marianne Reed? I think I may as well conclude or imagine you have not found out this is to be a very stupid letter, and inform you that I have nothing in the world to say not even scandal that would interest you, but I want to hear from you and therefore choose to make you pay ninepence for a sheet full of crooked writing for I cannot write straight in this literary way. I will tell you what I particularly pride myself upon though; my tails to my y's – no, that is not a good specimen but look, when I am not nervous – look and admire. Can you equal them.

We were to have had a Regatta this week but the stupid man who was to give the cups has put it off for a fortnight – and then it will probably rain, & so we shall have none. My Scrapbook, for it does not pretend to the dignity of an album, is anxiously looking forward to seeing it's pages adorned by your contributions, and I will do my best in the course of winter to draw you something, though if you consider I think it is a great proof of my love for you when I know, I can not do anything fit to be put in. I have copied a short little waltz, which is a capital one for waltzing to, for you by an opportunity – I hope you have not got it but

I don't think you have, unless very lately, for it is a very local sounding one.

And I have been studying Spurzheim on Phrenology[8] during my retirement and intend to illuminate the world in the character of {of} Lecturess soon, so completely am I convinced of it, more especially as I have the organ of causality, alias the reasoning faculty, so very strongly developed, and you know what a reasonable person I am –

How are the Loshs? Mr Losh told my cousins in town that he thought my bust[9] so very like Napoleon – Do you – Among the books I mean to read sometime, are these Memoirs of Lavalette;[10] from the extracts I have seen they sound most interesting, and as Aunt Lumb knew both Bruce and Captain Hutchinson she is desirous of reading it. Have you seen the book? What a curious account of his marriage, and how strange that such an extraordinary connexion should have produced such strong affection. I think it is probable that I shall enlighten Manchester with the sunshine of my countenance before the winter is over, when I have very little doubt I shall see your Harrogate friend Dr Fleming.

I was very much amused with a remark I heard the other day of Sophy Heywood, (Miss Anna Rankin's eldest pupil) 'I do not like Liverpool nearly so well as Manchester – it is not nearly so *nice & dirty*'. We have had several pleasant sails lately up and down this beautiful river; and I do like Liverpool and the Mersey and the accent, & the people very much. Do persuade Mr Carr to take you viâ Liverpool, and Cheshire to Wales next summer, you could take the Lakes on your road you know, and fly over to Ireland if you liked.

You never told me a bit about Mr William Carr's wedding – or where they went for the bridal excursion and how many quarrels you had to be answerable for – What do you think of my knowing of forty three *couples* engaged – couples, not single people. And apropos of marriages, I heard the other day that the beautiful Miss Fanny Brandling was engaged to the Marquis of Douro[11] – is there any truth – because, if it be, M{iss}rs Brandling has maneuvred to some purpose this season – and Mr Lister the jeweller will call me the next time I am in his shop to look at the celebrated Miss Fanny Brandling who accepted the great Duke of Wellington's eldest son –

Miss Tobin *is* the most beautiful by far in spite of Miss Jaques assertion that there was a younger sister more beautiful – I saw them all at the flower show, and admire the eldest far the most in spite of her melancholy, abstracted look. I wonder what you are doing tonight; I dare say if the truth were known you are talking of your dresses for the ball – how I should like to take a peep at you. I like the sound of your hair tied up on each side; it sounds a little bit like those portraits of Madame de Grignan, put as a frontispiece to the Second volume of Madame de Sévigné – eternal woman – how often have I begun both her and Sir Chas Grandison, and never finished either.[12]

There now good-night for if I go on I shall be asleep so sleepy am I become suddenly. I meant today to have been a very fine one that we might have had a sail, on the river, and it rains so that I do believe we might have a sail on land; for streams of muddy water are rolling down the roads. Fancy our agreeable situation – not a book but what we have all read hundreds of times – Such as odd volumes of Hume, Shakespeare, Tasso and a few old newspapers containing our latest intelligence from the political world. With an irregular, little bit of a goose, of a lady, for a post who may keep our letters for days; with rain enough to prevent Damon from going to see Pythias, much more than enough to keep any of our worthy acquaintances from coming to see us, and enliven our solitude, and then wonder if you dare that I should write so dull a letter –

I was in great hopes I should have gone to my Uncle's house in Wales[13] for a month or so this autumn but most unfortunately they have the organ of constructiveness so strongly developed, that they have taken a fancy of enlarging their house and consequently made it almost inhabitable[sic] for the present.

We were talking the other day of the quantity of crime we thought was committed up and down the world by people whom the world terms respectable and who go through life with a good character, and you would really have wondered to have heard what a terrible list we made out – especially with Welsh people. I think the Welsh gentry seem not to have progressed beyond what the English were two centuries ago. The Lord of the Manor is so completely a little king, and may do what he likes, without being questioned, for every body seems to consider justice and revenge in their own hands, and the scanty population make the crimes not be heard of. My cousin Anne, and I are intending some day to publish a book, a history of *crimes* of *innocent* people; shall we dedicate it to you – but you must commit some crime of some sort that will be grand enough to entitle you to have the part of heroine, & I will beg that likeness of you in a cloak for a frontispiece. Poison Mr and Mrs Carr and Elizabeth – I will never tell your secret – and will merely put in our book that a dear friend of one of the editors committed parricide, matricide, and fratricide, and yet moves through life with the reputation of being a very tolerably amiable person –

I wish you would tell me what books have interested you particularly lately – I have been reading Paul Clifford[14] once again and am delighted with it, as I believe I am with all Bulwers work in spite of their[sic] alleged immorality. What is become of Mrs Ramsay? It is ages and ages since I heard of, from, and about her but an echo of a{n} whisper reached me from some quarter or other that she was gone to Lowe House. You don't want a wedding present, do you for any of your friends – for here is a second Howell and James here to which we are going when it is fine to buy wedding presents for two of our friends who are going to take unto themselves lords and masters, and at this moment there is a grand dispute with regard to what the present is to be – I am for a magnificent dressing box for it is a thing I always long for, with plenty of cut glass and silver about it – but I am quite in the minority, and a timepiece is the conqueror I fear. A cousin of mine here has just had a commission to buy sixty pound worth of jewellery for a wedding present.

What do you think of this pamphlet of Gibbon Wakefield's?[15] Can any good thing come from such a polluted source. – How are the Rankins? pray remember me very affectionately to them when you see them. I am very glad to hear Miss Turner's[16] cough has left her, for I do think it is the most troublesome one I ever heard, and I used to fancy it must make Mr Turner feel very uncomfortable. Spurzheim says that the moon affects people (a doctrine I thought was quite exploded) and that if we notice most people twice a month feel melancholy, languid and ennuyé they know not why. Now I don't think it is the moon but the weather, for in damp rainy weather when the sky looks like one great patch of Indian Ink I think every body *ought* to be dull and sympathize with Nature. I enjoy a thunderstorm but a long drizzle is my abomination such as we are having today and here I cannot go to the window, and make signs to a nice kind little friend of mine to put on her bonnet, and dash and fly over to me; at least if I make signs to you I much doubt if you could see them.

The other day being in Liverpool, I thought I would get some coloured cloth to work upon for stools, a la mode of some we saw the other day: so stept into a shop to ask for some fine cloth – to my great astonishment the man quite seriously asked me if I wanted it for *pantaloons*! Did you see Mr Tidy when in town – and have you heard from or of the Headlams lately – has Archdeacon Headlam taken his daughters to that Spine Quack abroad – I do hope not. Also please tell me a little about the Collinsons when you next write. I did so like that whole family, and took quite a fancy to a really disagreeable woman the other day because I fancied her a little bit like Mrs Collinson who I do think is an angel inside and outside. Do you know that at Buenos Ayres,[17] very large combs for the hair behind are quite the fashion behind, but as they have them all from Paris, they can't afford to have one a piece, so three or four subscribe for one amongst them and take it in turns to be in the fashion – It is pretty much the case with *the* pen in this house for we have but one fit to write with amongst us, and can none of us mend one were our lives at stake – Or it is like the reign of Edward the third where some antiquary has rummaged out that one needle was the common allowance among four or five sisters, and when one tore her gown *the* needle was brought forth like the pen now – which good pen as you have probably found out is monopolized by another scribbler, so that poor I have in good sooth, sometimes one little better than a stick. How did Mr John Williamson's bachelor dinners go off. Has 'nothing come of it', to use a *pussy* expression. Worthy sisterhood of cats – where are ye – gone to form a new constellation in the heavens, and supersede the Pleiades? by the bye I think it would be a very good station to peer upon[?] the proceedings of Earth's inhabitants through telescopes.

Today is the first of September but melancholy to think upon I don't believe we have a single shooting acquaintance near here so no partridges for us. Did you ever know anything of a Mr Bingham[?] in Petersburgh – I think an officer of some description. I heard a great deal of him the other day at Dr Traills from Mr Tinne the drowned gentleman. It was a most shameful thing in the agents to that Rothsay Castle to allow her to go to sea when so completely unseaworthy: and they have since behaved in the most brutal manner.

Have you taken much interest in this Deacle and Baring cause.[18] I have; not much though, but I am very sorry indeed for Mr Baring who, they say is a man of remarkably refined delicate feelings and that his health has been seriously affected by the accusations brought against him. Besides I don't believe the Deacles statement, which has evidently contradicted itself very often, and is probably very much exaggerated. This is the only little bit of politics of power to interest me much just now – for oh! how tired I am of the Reform Bill – and my Aunt and most of my cousins, are quite anti-reformers, and abuse Lord Brougham[19] and think him superficial. By the bye, the author of Sydenham[20] has written another – Alice Paulet by name[.] Do you remember sending me Sydenham that rainy day, and an invitation to *wade* over and drink tea with you and Mr Carr,[21] and how I enjoyed it – practising the Mazurka and screaming away at 'Drums[?] done' with a voice that was much better suited to 'Sleep no more, my voice doth murder sleep'.[22]

How is Mr Waldie? uninteresting wretch that he is – and you putting me, the very worst person in the whole world for keeping my countenance opposite to the piano at Jesmond when he began 'Amore che sorgerai'. And how is Mr Dorrien, and his wig and his beautiful complexion – Now dearest Harriet do write me a long newspapery letter very soon – you may keep to my old direction, as should we be gone, my Uncle will forward it to me – Remember me very affectionately, and very kindly to Mr & Mrs Carr, & Elizabeth, and ever believe me,

Your very affect. friend
E. C. Stevenson

Address Miss Carr George Carr's Esqre Clavering Place Newcastle-upon-Tyne.
Postmark LIVERPOOL SE<P 1> 1831.
Seal Figure of runner[?] in small oval.

Brotherton Collection, Leeds University

1 This would appear to be Matthew Anderson, from a family of Newcastle Russia merchants, whom Harriet Carr* later married. See *EY,* p. 340.
2 In *James Buchanan's Mission to Russia 1831–1833* (*Works,* II, repr. New York, 1970), p. 262, there is a reference to the end of cholera in St Petersburg by summer 1832.
3 The Liverpool and Beaumaris steam-packet, a wooden paddle-ship, left Liverpool on 17 August 1831 but foundered on a sandbank at the entrance to the Menai strait in North Wales, according to *The Liverpool Mercury* for 26 August 1831. Of about 150 on board, only 23 survived. See Ivor Wynne Jones, *Shipwrecks of North Wales,* 1973, pp. 128–30.
4 Probably Thomas Stewart Traill (1781–1862), who helped found Liverpool's Royal Institution, Literary and Philosophical Society and Mechanics' Institute.
5 A Mrs H. R. Sandbach, née Roscoe (1812–52) published poetry in 1840, 1842 and 1850. In 'Elizabeth Stevenson and Harriet Carr: A Note', *GSJ* 5 (1991), Jeanette Eve identifies Harriet Tidy (1808–1873), daughter of Colonel Francis Tidy, who married Ensign John Ward on 15 October 1831 at Thorpe, Norfolk. Eve notes that Mrs Ward's literary career parallels ECG's.
6 The clan MacGregor was proscribed and barred from writing their name by James I and VI in 1603, and again by William and Mary in 1693. See also *Letters,* p. 228.
7 William III was to be crowned on 8 September, but little was done to mark the occasion in Liverpool. See *The Liverpool, Mercury,* 2 September 1831.
8 J. K. Spurzheim (1776–1832) toured Britain lecturing on phrenology in 1831. A 2nd edition of his *Physiognomical System* had appeared in 1815; a 3rd edition of his *Phrenology* in 1826.
9 Probably executed by David Dunbar in Newcastle, 1829. See *EY,* p. 386 n. 15.
10 See *Memoirs of Count [Chamans de] Lavalette,* 2 vols 1831; also, R. T. Wilson, *A Full Report of the Trial ... of Sir R. T. Wilson, M. Bruce esq. and Captain J. H. Hutchinson ... for Aiding the Escape of M. Lavalette,* 1816. The allies had arrested Lavalette, Napoleon's postmaster, during their 1815 occupation of Paris, but he escaped from the condemned cell dressed in his wife's clothes. Bruce and Hutchinson helped him reach Holland. Nothing is known of Mrs Hannah Lumb's connection with them.
11 Arthur Richard Wellesley (1817–1884), who married Lady Elizabeth Hay in 1839. The Brandlings were a prominent Newcastle family.
12 Samuel Richardson's *Sir Charles Grandison* (1754) was, like Madame de Sévigné's famous *Letters* to her daughter, the Comtesse de Grignan, published in many volumes. See Philip Yarrow, 'Mrs Gaskell and France' *GSJ* 7 (1993), p. 17, for several possible editions of the latter.
13 Uncle Samuel Holland (1768–1851) of Liverpool rented Plas yn Penrhyn, Minfford, near Porthmadog, North Wales, in 1827 and immediately began to repair and improve the farmhouse (*EY,* pp. 306–7). He married Catherine, née Menzies (1771–1847). Elizabeth Stevenson's cousins were Anne (1797-post–1852), Charles (1799–1870), Frances ('Fanny', 1800–83), Menzies (1802-?1819), Samuel (1803–92) and Catherine ('Kate', 1804–86).
14 Edward Bulwer (1803–1873), later Lord Lytton, had published several novels, *Falkland* in 1827, *Pelham* in 1828, *The Disowned* in 1828, *Devereux* in 1829 and *Paul Clifford,* the story of a gentleman highwayman, in 1830. This last suggests that the law and society rather than the individual criminal are at fault.

15 Edward Gibbon Wakefield (1796–1862) published *Facts Relating to the Punishment of Death in the Metropolis* in 1831, after three years' imprisonment for inducing a Liverpool schoolgirl to marry him at Gretna Green.

16 Ann Turner had been Elizabeth Stevenson's companion in her early visits to Newcastle and Edinburgh, none of which has yet been fully dated with certainty.

17 Charles Holland had gone to Buenos Aires from Liverpool c. 1818. Commercial success enabled him to return a rich man in 1833. He was to marry WG's younger sister Elizabeth (1812–92) in 1838.

18 A Mr Deacle was awarded £50 at Winchester Assizes against Bingham Baring, MP (1799–1864), later 2nd Baron Ashburton, in compensation for severe treatment when arrested during a riot. See *The Gentleman's Magazine* for July 1831 (101, II. 74).

19 Henry Peter Brougham (1778–1868), Baron Brougham and Vaux, supporter of the first Reform Bill to extend the Franchise, passed in 1832.

20 [William Massie], *Sydenham; or, Memoirs of a Man of the World,* 3 vols 1830; *Alice Paulet: a Sequel to Sydenham,* 3 vols 1831.

21 William Turner* lived for a short time very near the Carrs in Clavering Place. See *EY*, p. 377.

22 Cf. *Macbeth,* II. ii. 36. The songs mentioned have not been identified.

HARRIET CARR*

Knutsford. The Heath Oct 20 1831.

My dear Harriet,

I am so angry with you, you little naughty naughty thing. Have not I been looking forward all summer to your sending me some drawing by the Turners, and here comes a letter to say you have not finished it. Did you ever write copies in your young days? and so doing, did you never write 'Procrastination is the thief of time', and are you not aware, Madam, that you must have procrastinated in this instance? I have seven eighth's of a mind not to send you several songs I have been copying for you, only as I suspect it would be a greater punishment to me to take one of them for another opportunity, than for you not to receive them, I shall send them, and hope you will like them, and sometimes in singing them think of the copier. 'Isle of beauty' was I dare say one of the songs Eve sang in Paradise – it is so very old – but I rather think you have not got it – and it is a great favourite of mine. 'Quien[?] quiera' is a Spanish patriotic song[1] which was very inspiriting to the peasantry during the times of the Peninsular war. The two little german ditties are shepherd's songs *they say*; but as I don't know a word of german I leave you to find out the meaning yourself. And now having grumbled *nearly* enough, (though I dare say I shall sprinkle a little more up & down my letter) let me thank you dearest Harriet for your very agreeable clearance of the portfolio, by writing on all the scraps. I wish like you with all my heart that there were any chance of my receiving such little bitters[?][2] this winter, as I used to have last.

By the bye fancy me setting up for a Mazurka mistress. I keep my pupils at the first step however, having quite forgotten the figures, though I don't acknowledge to it. But really to keep up my credit as a dancing mistress, I should be obliged to you to send me the figures. My pupils are my cousins who are all four at home just now, though after Xmas, two I believe go to town to their brothers in Brook Street.[3] My Aunt Swinton Holland & Charlotte have been staying with us, indeed only left yesterday morning; Charlotte perfectly remembers having seen you at the Cayleys and we had a good deal of 'Cayley-talk'. She likes the present *Miss* Cayley (Maria I think she called her) exceedingly – and said she was very nearly going an excursion with her brother Edward this \ or last I forget which / summer with the Hutchinsons & Cayleys to Prussia –

I am now settling down for the winter and mean to be very regular, & quiet. The last I can not help myself in, having nothing to tempt me into dissipation but I really am glad of it for it is so very long since I was steadily settled – at home with my various books, writing materials & 'helps to learning' about me, that I feel as though I were on the royal road now. You say you have not read any interesting books lately – (I am not going to recommend Lord Edward Fitzgerald, so don't be afraid) but I have been very much interested in a little two volume book, entitled 'A year in Spain by a young American'.[4] Have you seen it? If not I think you would be very much amused by it, for it gives a very interesting account of the state of the poor Spaniards, and though told in rather an egotistical manner yet I think that makes it more entertaining and romantic. I have been reading Destiny[5] for the third time – since I came home, and now I think I have done my duty by it. You have probably by this time got Mr and Mrs William Carr staying with you and I think I can fancy how much you are enjoying it. Pray as soon as they are gone, hire some one to feed you while you are finishing my drawing, for you must not go off even for sleep, and I beg you will persuade Elizabeth to remember Mrs Norton. I do not like your [being] such a 'prophète du[sic] malheur' as to prophecy that we shall not meet again till on crutches; I always like to *fancy* my future prospects bright & happy; and worse and worse that you should imagine, (though perhaps it is natural) that our feelings would change. I was lately much struck with a sentence somewhere, or other: 'the difficulty consists not in *making* friends, but in *retaining* them'. Of the quantities of people I have liked (you used to complain of my being a 'general liker[']) during this last twelvemonths how very few I may ever see again – with regard to very many of them I should not mind, but I don't like looking forward to 'crutches and changed feelings', so will drop the subject.

This week is a gay one with us being our Sessions week – and I dare say if I went into the town I might meet two people, an<d> if so I should return and say 'How very gay Knutsford is today'– I saw the Mr Littledale (the Judge's secretary) several times in Liverpool and thought of the Assizes Ball, and Miss Marianne Read.[6] – Surely she will either be killed, or married before *this* year of mayoralty be terminated. So my likeness Miss Harriet Tidy is gone to be married. I met some girls who knew her in Liverpool of the name of Sandbach, & asked if I were like her but they say not at all.

My dear Harriet, I don't ask you to do me a drawing because that is a promise, & you *must* (Imp mood) do it – but I will promise to be a very good child if you will copy me 'rise up, rise up Xarifa'. It may be from not knowing the exact title but I can not get it. And will you ask Margaret Losh for the title (please) of her book of Mrs Arkwright's songs. I am sincerely glad to hear of your improvement of character – throw tapioca to 'Matthew' and the dogs.

I shall like to hear your opinion of *my* house at Jesmond, since mine it will be, without a doubt, and your present [(]you are a very interested creature) *when* the happy event takes place shall be even unto the half of my kingdom. I never knew such a week as this has been for marriages – no less than three intimate friends of ours are become fiancèes[*sic*] during this last fortnight, and what is even more extraordinary I am not one of the number. Since I came home I have been staying at a house of my Uncle's about six miles off, with the cousin nearest my own age, by name Susan Holland, and you cannot think how I enjoyed the perfect retirement – not a house near – We had beautiful weather – and sat out of doors all day long, going to bed *almost* with the sun, and rising with the same[;] for for my own part I was generally asleep by nine o'clock, and up by six. Except now and then, when the carriage came from Knutsford bringing letters & *meat*, and an importation of cousins for an hour, or two. I felt quite sorry when we heard that Aunt Swinton was coming, and that we must return.

I see your Hunt Ball is advertised in the Newcastle paper. How is your great toe? Still in a delicate state of health. I hope you were however able to enjoy Mr Dupuis'[?] ball, and also the Guild. Thank you for all your information about Robert Losh – Did he carry a market basket when making his purchases. I do not know if it is the weather or what, but I feel just as if I had had a tapioca luncheon, and could burst into a good fit of crying – from which charming feeling you will probably be aware that nothing bright can emanate. Wherefore I shall conclude for the present at any rate – but as Miss Turner does not go till next week, I *may* be more brilliant before that time.

Oh this windy miserable weather; I am writing near a window where puffs of wind come every now & then, & chill my intellects – You will ask why I don't move. I suppose it is my vis inertiae, and my being in a most comfortable arm chair – but I am squeezing myself up into as small a compass as I can to collect all the warmth I can – Is it not a change from last winter when I revelled in cold & east wind – and laughed at your headaches & sorrows. So Lady Clanricarde has got the *real* cholera – only has recovered. Sir Matthew Tierney & Sir Henry Halford[7] both say so, & there have been two other instances in England. I can not realize any infectious complaint really coming. In what part of Wales are the Collinsons. I hope they will rave of it when they come back. They are *not* worthy to go if they don't. Pray don't forget to send me the Mazurka figures – with very affect. remembrances to your circle especially Elizabeth

believe me my dear Harriet
yours very affecly
E. C. Stevenson

Address Miss Harriet Carr Clavering Place
Newcastle-upon-Tyne
Seal Small oval containing script Elizabeth.

Brotherton Collection, Leeds University

1 Alluded to in *Mary Barton*, ch. 17. 'Isle of Beauty', from *Songs to Rosa* by T. H. Bayly, melody by C. S. Whitmore, arranged by T. A. Rawlings. 'Quien quiere entrar commigo' is a seventeenth-century piece attributed to G. Casalotti in *Manuscript Music in the British Museum*.
2 Posibly bitter medicines as tonic. See ECG, *Wives and Daughters*, ch. 28.
3 Family of Uncle Peter Holland (1766–1855) of Knutsford and Sandlebridge, who married (1) Mary, née Willets (d. 1803, aged 37) and (2) Mary, née Whittaker (1769–1840). Elizabeth Stevenson's cousins were Henry (1788–1873), Mary (1792–1877), Bessy (1796–1886), Lucy (1800–83), Charles Aikin (1809-post–1853), Susan (1811–89) and the mysterious Arthur (1813–33). Henry became a highly successful doctor, living at Lower Brook Street in Mayfair (baronet 10 May 1853).
4 Thomas Moore, *The Life and Death of Lord Edward Fitzgerald*, 2 vols 1831; [Alexander S. Mackenzie], *A Year In Spain by a Young American*, Boston 1829, London 1831.
5 Susan Ferrier, *Destiny; or, the Chief's Daughter*, 3 vols, Edinburgh 1831. See *EY*, p. 390.
6 The judge's secretary at the criminal courts held four times a year might have been connected with Harold Littledale of Liscard Hall near Birkenhead, a friend of Charles Holland. Archibald Reed[sic] was Mayor of Newcastle during the years 1830–32.
7 Harriet (1804–76) was the daughter of George Canning and the wife of the 1st Marquess of Clanricarde. Sir Matthew John Tierney (1776–1845) became, like Sir Henry Holland, a royal physician. Sir Henry Halford (1766–1844) was President of the Royal College of Physicians.

~

Letter 1 from Knutsford to Elizabeth Gaskell redated [27 March 1832]

~

HARRIET CARR*

[Knutsford, 3 May 1832]

My dearest Harriet,

Could I, at any other time, have so long delayed answering your *most* kind letter, which gratified me exceedingly I can assure, – perhaps from feeling in a great measure, that my late negligence might have, and ought to have in justice destroyed a little bit of your interest in me. I am *very much* obliged to you, for all your good wishes in my behalf,[1] and if they are fulfilled will burn incense to Harriet Carr. Pray thank Mr and Mrs Carr and dear Elizabeth too for their kind expressions of regard.

I was much concerned on your account to see the announcement of Mr Matthew Carr's death in the paper yesterday; though I scarcely know whether at such an age, life is very desirable – I am sure dear Harriet, you will rejoice with me when I tell you my dear Aunt Lumb, is recovering very securely, though perhaps not very rapidly. Still it is a very great pleasure to compare her progress from one week to another, and to see her gaining strength gradually & surely, and at this beautiful time of the year it seems almost impossible for any one to be long ill. We have had such beautiful weather that I hope Elizabeth feels stronger, for I was sorry to hear that she did not gain strength so quickly as you could wish.

How did the 'second serving-up' of the Fancy Dresses go off?[2] I heard so much of your dresses that I do not believe one word of what you say of being unwilling to show them off again. I never knew such a year as this has been for weddings – In a family of relations of ours,[3] *this year began* with the marriage of one of the sons to a daughter of Sir James McIntoshs; His sisters were invited to be bridesmaids, & while staying at Lady Gifford's, of one[*sic*] them met with a Mr Langton (grandson of Bennett Langton, of Johnsonian memory;)[4] saw him for three weeks, and then came down to her father's house to be married to him; During *her* wedding-gaieties her brother saw a daughter of Sir Oswald Mosleys for the first time, and he has been now her husband this *fortnight*; and it's only the third of May now! Today is the marriage day of one of our intimate friends, (who by the bye has taken four suits of clothes to be married in, one for a fine day, another for a fair day, another for a doubtful day, & a fourth for a rainy day!) And the day before yesterday another friend of mine has *wedded* (for really *'married'* is becoming too common a word.)

I dined twice with Dr Fleming in Manchester, and had no difficulty whatever in recalling the 'Miss Carrs' to his memory. I received your information regarding Miss Rich too late to communicate it to him, having left Manchester. Among the various marriages I forgot to enumerate my cousin Edward's[5] last Friday, and Mr Marshall's the Saturday before, to that Miss Ledyard[?], of whom I think I enquired of you, being partly a Beverley person.

I suppose you have read Eugene Aram, so I shall not enquire after that; but have you read Mrs *Trollope's* account of the Americans?[6] It is so very amusing, and by abusing the Americans has won my heart. I don't mean abusing their more solid moral qualities but their manners, which I have always disliked. Apropos des[*sic*] bottes, have you heard anything of this famous new Opera? composed by Miss Jarvis[*sic*], Ld St Vincent's daughter?[7] They tell wonders of her musical powers – when she returned from school she had no piano, and when asked to sing, stood up in the middle of the room, *singing* a piece of music – And the Opera people have arranged her compositions, so I suppose it will soon come out at the Opera-house – it has already been performed at Ld St Vincent's private concerts.

Pray don't forget, my dear Harriet, the long-promised drawing, and remind Elizabeth that when she feels equal to it, I shall be most grateful for Mrs Norton, or any *scrap* of her doing. I hear that Mr Russel, the *great* Mr Russel[8] as Lister the Jeweller called him, is very favourably received at Gosforth. Is it true? and have you seen any more of them lately. Pray send me some Newcastle news, for it seems a long time since I had any. The last interesting intelligence I heard was that *one* of the Miss Carrs, was going to be married to Matthew Anderson. I *really* did hear this, & want to know the truth. Is it also true that Margaret Losh refused Mr S. Parker?

I am quite sorry you have broken the habit of writing in a literary style; as I always feel my own natural hand, is that of such a very commonplace boarding-school young lady. However such as it is, I hope you can decipher enough to know that I am ever

Your very affectionate friend
Elizabeth Stevenson

Pray write very soon – I have not told you anything about *our* plans because they really are very little fixed; but shd you feel any wish to hear them, you have only to express it.

Address Miss Carr George Carr's Esqre Clavering Place – *Seal* illegible.

Brotherton Collection, Leeds University

1 A reference to her engagement mid-March 1832.
2 The mayoress had given a fancy dress ball and supper at the Mansion House in Newcastle on 22 March 1832, at which Mr George Carr and the two Miss Carrs appeared in Russian costume. There was a similar ball at the Assembly Rooms a few days later, on 26 March.
3 Children of Bessy and Josiah Wedgwood II: Hensleigh (1803–91) married Frances Macintosh (1800–89); Charlotte (1797–1862) married Charles Langton (1801–86); and Frank (1800–88) married Frances Mosley (d. 1874).
4 Bennet[sic] Langton (1737–1801) was Dr Johnson's 'much valued friend'.
5 Edward (1806–75), son of Swinton Colthurst Holland, married Sophia Isaac (1813–51) c. 26 April 1832.

6 Bulwer's novel *Eugene Aram*, a psychological study of an eighteenth-century scholar-murderer, appeared in 1832. Frances Trollope's *Domestic Manners of the Americans* was another best seller in 1832.
7 Maria Jervis, daughter of the 2nd Viscount St Vincent.
8 John, 1st Earl Russell (1792–1878), was a leader in the campaign for the 1832 Reform Act. A William Russell (1798–1850) was MP for Co. Durham 1828–32.

HARRIET CARR*

The Heath. Knutsford.
August the 8th [1832]

My dearest Harriet,

Though I do not know where to address you, yet I can not delay writing any longer to thank you for your beautiful little 'forget-me-not' ring, and even still more for the kind, dear little note which accompanied it. Indeed Harriet it did not require a 'forget-me-not' from you, to make me remember you with love, and interest, and recollect all the many happy hours we have spent together. Bessie brought me some sort of a message from you, of rather old standing, saying you would write from Harrowgate and seemed surprised when I said I had not heard from you; so I thought I would put off writing a few days in hopes of having another letter to acknowledge: and I trusted that letter would tell me your health was improved and that your head-aches had at any rate in some measure left you.

I was *very* sorry to hear so very shabby an account of you. Have you ever tried a little sal-volatile in water, when so troubled with head-aches? It sounds very quackish in me, does it not, to recommend anything, and I have sometimes thought that if I did not marry, I should at any rate have one characteristic of an old maid, that of wishing to prescribe for every complaint I heard of. But in this instance I have 'derived great benefit' myself from sal-volatile, and moreover it was prescribed by an M. D in the shape of Dr Holland, so do *try* it.

I am in the middle, or rather I hope, three-quarters through the bustle of wedding-gowns, though in the opinion of some sage people, preparations for a marriage should not be *begun* before the last fortnight, and it wants rather more than that to the day, when I am to learn obedience the 30th of this month.[1] Never having received a letter from any body similarly situated, I don't in the least know how to express myself on the occasion but I fancy 'to learn obedience' is something new – to me at least it is. I have got the very prettiest bonnet for the occasion that ever was, and cannot help trying it on every time I go into my room. I smell nothing but marking-ink, and see nothing but E. C. S. everywhere.

We have been a very large party this summer, and amongst other spirited actions of our lives, got up a play; I say, '*we*' though I did not take any part in it, but I was present at all the planning &c.[2] It was the

'Rivals'; and was admirably performed really; considering that with one exception, it was the first appearance of any one on the theatre[.] Most of the performers kept up their characters during the 'drawing room' part of the evening and Lucy Holland for some days was '*great*' as Mrs Malaprop, making some really capital travesties of words.

Bessie says she showed you a likeness of a reverend C. Taylor, as being so like Mr Gaskell in answer to your enquiries on the subject. It is *very* like him, & you can not tell the comical feeling of gratitude and pleasure that came over my heart at hearing that you enquired about him. I am sadly wanting to hear a regular account of your proceedings & plans; I hope before very long this rolling and bowling world of ours will cast us together again.

When I hear of your headaches I hardly like to remind you of a certain drawing promise – but *sometime* or other will you fulfil it dearest Harriet. I have been very busy copying some manuscript duett quadrilles, which are very pretty and remarkably pleasant time, and which I intend to be dishonourable enough to send you by the first opportunity[.] They are written by a half-cousin of mine, a young Cantab, whose *sole* talent lies in music.[3]

We have not yet got this fearful Cholera among us, though it has I believe been lying in all the villages about, and the other day I heard a man coining a new curse against some one who had offended him '*Cholera seize thee*'. Whether it will become quite orthodox I don't know.

How are Mr and Mrs Wm Carr? I hope there is a prospect of a family – And Mrs Simpson – have you heard of her confinement. You will write to me soon dear Harriet I hope, as you know you can scarcely tell me anything that will not interest me, while you hardly know any of my friends even by name. Those that you do know Charlotte & Louisa Holland are living at present at Overbury, a house belonging to Merton Coll; but which is situated near Tewkesbury. The worst of it is, that the worthy heads of the college will not allow them to move a single picture, and the Hall, library & dining room are crowded with them[,] not always of the most delicate description. Did you see that account of a lady & gentleman who were struck with lightning on their wedding tour? They were cousins of Mrs Edward Holland's, a Mr and Mrs Boddington, and are nearly recovered now; but for some time it made us very much afraid of putting up a umbrella, for fear of lightning, as in their case the brass point served as a conductor, and afterwards the steel in Mrs Boddington's stays, conveyed the fluid to within a straw's breadth of a vital part in her leg.[4]

How are the Miss Brandlings going on. I want sadly to hear a quantity of NCastle news, as when I have several letters by an opportunity, each supposes the other will tell me everything, & consequently I do not hear any thing. Pray give my very kind love to Elizabeth; and send me a better account of her as well as yourself, & give my affectionate remembrances to Mr & Mrs Carr.

Ever yours very affectionately,
E. C. Stevenson

Address Miss Carr {George Carr's Esqre Clavering Place Newcastle upon Tyne.} Crown Inn Harrogate.
Postmarks KNUT<SF>ORD; NEWCASTLE AU<G> 9 183<2>.

Brotherton Collection, Leeds University

1 'The deferential utterance is not an unerring sign of a deferential spirit' (Vickery, p. 83; cf. pp. 59–60 for 'obedience' in marriage). Elizabeth Stevenson was to marry the Reverend William Gaskell (1805–84), Unitarian minister at Cross Street Chapel, Manchester, on 30 August 1832, in Knutsford parish church.
2 The children of Peter Holland would have been prominent in this amateur performance of R. B. Sheridan's *The Rivals* (1775). Elizabeth Stevenson was in Edinburgh during June 1832, when a miniature of her was painted by her step-mother's brother, William John Thomson (*EY*, pp. 371–2).
3 Edmund Sharpe (1809–76), son of the Knutsford organist and Martha, née Whittaker, a sister of Peter Holland's second wife.
4 Identified from an article in the *Lancet* of 15 September 1832, based on a report by Michael Faraday. Mr and Mrs T. T. Boddington, driving in a post chariot from Tenbury to Bromyard on 13 April 1832, were struck by lightning, which also 'cast the postboy to a considerable distance.' See *GSN* 22 (1996), pp. 4–7.

WILLIAM TURNER[*]

No 1 Dover Street[1] Oxford Road
Saturday Morning [6 October 1832]

My dear Sir,

I received your most kind & welcome letter on Thursday when we arrived here; and we have been so busy ever since that I am literally seizing the first leisure moment to write my very warmest thanks for all the good wishes expressed in it, and for the kind interest you take in me. Pray thank Anne for all her nice messages in it.

I have been so completely in a 'whirl' these two days that I feel as though I could hardly arrange my thoughts enough to give you an account of the few plans we have formed with regard to our future proceedings. Mr Gaskell has promised as soon as the *formal* bridal calls are made, to go with me and introduce me to most of the families under his care, as their minister's wife, and one who intends to try to be their useful friend. My dear colleague[2] too has promised her assistance and advice with regard to my duties. I like my new home very much indeed – for Manchester it is very countrified, and is very cheerful and comfortable in every part.

I was detained by a sore throat on the road, or else we had intended being at home last week; as it was, and we had dipped into another week, we staid a few days longer in my old home, and saw Aunt Lumb's almost daily improvement in health, spirits, and strength. She promises to come and pay us a visit very soon, and I enjoy the idea of receiving her in a house of my own, and where I can in some measure provide for her comforts, as she has so often done for mine.

I have just received on the part of Mr Gaskell & myself, a very handsome fish-slice and a very kind note from Mr James Turner.[3]

Pray tell Anne I can fully sympathise with her in the troubles of removing, for I am just now feeling so doubtful as to the success of my housekeeping, and little *daily* cares, that the very idea of a removal sounds alarming. I am very glad however that you are going to leave your present house for one so much pleasanter in situation if I remember rightly.

I have been on the watch ever since I received a very charming little note from Mrs Greenhow, for an opportunity to Newcastle by which I might answer it, and acknowledge the receipt of a very pretty pair of little glass vases for flowers. I am half tempted to write by post; it seems so long since I received them. Will you give my kind love to Anne, the Rankins[,] the Eldonites,[4] Mrs Welbank, Allhusens, Mortons & Carrs if they are returned;

And ever believe me to remain
My dear Mr Turner's very affec[tionate] & grateful
E. C. Gaskell

Postmark 6 October 1832.

Newcastle Literary and Philosophical Society

Printed in J. A. V. Chapple, 'Unofficial Lives: Elizabeth Gaskell and the Turner family', in C. Parish, *The History of the Literary and Philosophical Society of Newcastle upon Tyne*, II, Newcastle, 1990, pp 107–8.

1 The Gaskells' first Manchester address, later number 14.

2 William Turner's* daughter Mary (1786–1869) had married the Reverend John Gooch Robberds* (1789–1854), minister at Cross Street Chapel, in 1811.

3 William Turner's* nephew, James Aspinall Turner (1797–1867), MP for Manchester 1857–65. He was a noted philanthropist and an important member of the Cross Street congregation, who could yet write in 1836 that his charitable schemes should not deprive his family of 'a single comfort or convenience, or even luxury' (*EY,* pp. 379, 381).

4 Inhabitants of Eldon Square, Newcastle.

MRS MARY DARBISHIRE[1]

[Manchester,
?Christmas 1835]

My dear Mrs Darbishire,

I quite intended to call on you this morning with these songs, & to give you and Mr Darbishire our very best wishes for the Season. But I was prevented by the rain, and so I must send you them on paper which never seems half so warm & real. I had only time to copy you these two songs, as we were shopping till ½ past 4 on Friday, though we went out directly after breakfast. I had intended to have copied that beautiful 'Graves of a household',[2] but it was rather long, and they were going in half an hour when I had finished these. I am having my 3rd lonely evening this week as Mr Gaskell is gone to dine at Bank[?] Hill.

I return you Brockedon's appendix[3] with many thanks. May I beg for 'little Frank', and the Dublin Penny Magazine[4] which I will return you tomorrow without fail.

I remain my dear kind friend
Yours very affectionately
E. C. Gaskell

Address Mrs Darbishire / Green Heys.[5]
Annotation [in pencil]From Mrs Gaskell 1835

Princeton University Library

1 Mary*, née Blackmore ('aged 35', 1831), wife of Samuel Dukinfield Darbishire (1796–1870), a family frequently mentioned in ECG's letters.
2 'Graves of a Household' not identified.
3 William Brockedon (1787–1854), writer, painter, inventor (of the rubber bung). His 'appendix' is not identified by *DNB* nor *BLC*.
4 *The Dublin Penny Journal* (not *Magazine*) ran from 30 June 1832 to 25 June 1836.
5 Rural area just south of Chorlton-on-Medlock, described at the opening of *Mary Barton*.

~

Letter 616 (undated) to ?Mary Howitt now dated [?May-August ?1838]
Letter 617 (undated) to Mary Howitt now dated [?18 August ?1838][1]
Letter 16 to ?Anne Robson redated [23 December 1840]

1 Dated from its position in the *Good Words* 36 (1895) article, p. 612. The quotation immediately following, 'Faith such as the rich can never imagine ...', however, is from *Mary Barton,* ch. 6.

~

JOHN PIERPONT[1]

Dover Street,
Chorlton-on-Medlock
Manchester.
June 12th 1841.

My dear Sir,

When I look at the date of your letter I do indeed feel ashamed to think how long I have been in acknowledging it; and yet like many other things, it has not been for want of good resolutions; for hardly has one single week began since I received it, but I have determined to accomplish my purpose of answering your most welcome letter, and at the close of every week I have blamed myself for my omission. So I must shelter myself under the plea of the evil spirit of procrastination, bad as that is, rather than let you think it was in any feeling of ingratitude that I have so long delayed thanking you for your most acceptable and long hoped-for letter. And I must also tell you how highly we value the volume of poems[2] that accompanied them; how much we admire, and how truly and heartily we sympathize in the trials which called forth some of them; we want sadly to know more than the vague gleanings of reports of your distressing controversy, and struggle.[3] Though we are far separated from you and may perhaps 'see your face on earth no more', yet believe us, dear Sir, often to think of you, and feel for you with deep and respectful sympathy. We shall much like to see a copy of all the printed communications that have passed between the parties. Your poems, I am ashamed to say were many of them unknown to me, and I value the volume most highly as coming from the author. It would seem presumptuous in me I think to say how much I admire them, and what pleasure they have given me.

You blame me for not having told you of my husbands poetical talents. I do not know how other wives feel, but I have the same feeling of modesty in praising my husband that should have in praising myself. I would rather trust in full faith that others if they be worthy, w{ould}ill find out all his high and estimable qualities, that his own natural delicacy and reserve make him so unwilling to obtrude. But that you, in your far-away home may have an opportunity of appreciating him, you must allow me to send you a little volume of his 'Temperance Rhymes', which I trust you will like, and which has received approbation from high quarters on this side the Atlantic. Wordsworth addressed a letter of commendation to the unknown author, and William Howitt tells us that his wife Mary Howitt exclaimed on reading some 'This is true poetry.'[4]

We are feeling as indeed all English people *must* do, that we are at a great crisis, and that there is a great struggle going on in the matter of the Corn Laws.[5] Perhaps it may have been decided before this reaches you; if not peacefully decided, at least by agitation and distress which it is most painful to think of. The manufacturing classes around us are in very great trouble, and if it were winter the lower classes would find it almost unbearable; as it is the early warmth of the season has been a great blessing. I send you a few temperance tracts which were especially recommended to me by the revd F. Howorth, who, since you were here has married a cousin of mine,[6] and is very much interested in the Temperance Cause.

Do you know we are making preparation for seeing something of the Continent in Mr Gaskell's month of absence. We purpose going by Ostend, through Belgium, seeing some of the old Flemish towns, and sailing up the Rhine as far as Heidelberg where we hope to stay with some friends for a week or so, and thus catch a glimpse of German society.[7] I have never been out of the Island before; my husband travelled for 10 weeks with a friend in the autumn of 1839, and they went as far as Florence and Venice, passing very rapidly through France and Switzerland. I look forward with such great hopes of enjoyment to our little tour; and I leave my two little girls[8] with a very faithful nurse and in charge of one of their Aunts. We dare not hope ever to be sufficiently people at large with regard to time and money to go to America, easy and rapid as the passage has become.[9] But *if* [double underline] we ever should cross the great waters be assured we shall come to No. 18 Essex St and have a peep at any rate of one whom we so well recollect and whose conduct we so much honour.

My two little girls are still my only parental objects of interest. They are very promising both in mind and body. Our mutual friends in this neighbourhood are well and much in the same situation in which you saw them. The removal of the College from York to Manchester[10] has given an increase of occupation to some of them. Mr J. J. Tayler[11] is Professor of Ecclesiastical history, Mr Robberds of Hebrew &c. Mr Robberds is expecting the marriage of his second son[12] to take place in the course of next month. It is a very satisfactory match in every way, and he is quite deserving of a good wife. Mrs Darbyshire[13] still lives in the house where you visited her, and has the comfort of seeing her sons growing up into sensible and respectable characters. *Mr* Beard is made *Dr* Beard, (as probably you have heard,) by a German degree, procured for him by his faithful congregation, who have struggled with him side by side through *his* season of trouble.[14] Whitsun week was the week of Manchester Races when the teetotallers have a grand procession; at which time they have been usually much hooted, but this last Whitsuntide, no mark whatever of disapprobation was shown even by the rough multitude who were gathered together. This present week they are also to have great rejoicings, and some of the town-dignitaries take a part in them.

I have time for no more; my husband joins me in very kind remembrances, and with much honour & respect, believe me to remain my dear Sir

Yours very truly
E C. Gaskell.

Pierpont Morgan Library, New York

1 John Pierpont (1785–1866), reformist Unitarian minister of Hollis Street Church, Boston, USA, 1819–45. He had visited Manchester during his tour of Europe and Palestine in 1835.

2 Probably *Airs of Palestine and Other Poems* (1840). Pierpont also published *Anti-Slavery Poems* in 1843.

3 From 1838 Pierpont's anti-slavery and temperance activities had brought him into conflict with some of his congregation.

4 WG's *Temperance Rhymes* (1839) were praised by Wordsworth: 'I have read your Temperance Rhymes with much pleasure and cannot but think that they must do good' (Uglow, p. 114). William Howitt (1792–1879) and his wife Mary, née Botham (1799–1888), were prominent radical thinkers and popularisers. He had just included, anonymously, ECG's short piece 'Clopton House' in his *Visits to Remarkable Places* (1840). See *EY*, p. 134.

5 Unlike Robberds* and local Unitarians, WG did not appear at the 1841 Manchester conference of ministers in support of the Anti-Corn Law League (*Portrait*, p. 30).

6 Bessie Holland (1796–1886) had married Franklin Howorth (1804–82), widowed Unitarian minister of Bury, on 24 September 1835.

7 The Gaskells were invited to stay with the widowed Friederike von Pickford, née Schunck. She had married on 22 June 1802 John Middleton Pickford (d. 1830), who had a great villa (now destroyed) built to the east of the Karlstor. The Howitts were renting the first floor. See *Letters*, pp. 42–3, Marquardt, I. 36, II.333; *Howitt Autobiography*, I. 293; Peter Skrine, 'Elizabeth Gaskell and Her German Stories', *GSJ* 12 (1998), pp. 1–4.

8 Marianne (MA), born 12 September 1834, and Margaret Emily (ME or Meta), born 5 February 1837.

9 Isambard Kingdom Brunel's *Great Western*, launched in 1837, took only 15 days to reach New York in 1838, initiating regular steamship services between Britain and America.

10 Manchester College had its origins in Manchester Academy. Re-established at York in 1803, it educated many Unitarian clergyman like William Gaskell, 1825–8. It had just moved back to Manchester in 1840.

11 John James Tayler (1797–1869) Unitarian minister at Mosley Street chapel from 1821, later Upper Brook Street Chapel, Manchester; Professor in Manchester College from 1840 and Principal on its removal to London in 1853.

12 His second son John Robberds (1814–92) was minister at Yeovil 1838–40, and then of the Ancient Chapel of Toxteth Park, Liverpool, 1840–66. He married the eldest daughter of the Reverend William Blake of Crewkerne, Somerset, in 1841.

13 See p. 23 above.

14 John Relly Beard (1800–76), Unitarian minister whose congregation at Strangeways, Manchester, had supported him against a majority of the Trustees, even when they appointed a new minister. A prolific author, propagandist and literary collaborator of WG, he was awarded a doctorate by the University of Giessen in 1838 for services to religious literature. He married Mary Barnes (1802–87) of Portsmouth in 1826.

MISS BARBARA FERGUSSON[1]

[Knutsford]
Friday [?6 June 1845]

My dearest Daddy,[2]

I enclose you Sam's[3] letter, (only received this morning,) which after you have read you may give to Mr Gaskell. It is very decided & comfortable, & I have written forthwith to Martha, engaging the rooms (bad-smelling & all, we must air it well) for July 3rd. Mrs Evans[4] *distance* is more than I expected but nice little woman for making the abatement in her charge which nearly counterbalances – and her moderate charge for *meals* &c will quite make the difference I expect. So much for our own affairs.

I was very sure you wd over-sleep yourselves, wanting the alarum of *my* two children.[5] They are both well & flourishing, and nothing has occurred worthy of note since I wrote to *your* two children yesterday, but that my new green gown is spoilt – owing to hot milk being poured, *not* by me, into a glass which cracked & flew up & down, & the milk came splash into my lap – very provoking indeed and as people say many shillings [out] of {of} my pocket. What is Ursa Major about – and at any rate why does not Charlie tell you that *nothing* is doing – it is a comfort even to hear that; it is less suspense than hearing nothing. Don't be mine 'very sincerely,' again there's a good girl.

Florence is sleeping with Hearn[6] but Hearn says she sleeps so much worse than she did when I was at Lancaster she can't account for it. To be sure we have had such windy nights. She went yesterday to Mrs Green's,[7] and saw a little puppy-dog there that barked at her, & she has dreamt about it, and been frightened all night. But she is very well, very hungry, very merry, and very independent. Hearn & I between us, made some terrible forgets in our packing up, no night gown, no night cap, no dressing gown, no tooth-brush; the last bought, the first I borrowed. The dress-maker says my gown is gone, nothing can be done but dying it. What else have I got to say? I try to think of something that will interest you, but I can't.

Will you ask Margaret to make out a washing bill & send the clothes to the wash – and *if* the new washerwoman sent by Miss Marsland[8] calls on Saturday afternoon, to show her one of our washing bills, as explanatory of what clothes we send out, and say I am particular about having the clothes sent home \ *all* / on Saturday *morning not torn,* and *of a good colour,* and if she will engage to wash for us, to say that at the end of July I should like to begin with her (no use before we go away.) We shall certainly be at home about 10 on Monday morning and I do hope you won't have much trouble or annoyance in the mean while. –

I suspect Dr Kitto's book on deafness[9] (Knight's 1s. volume you know) has never gone back to Mrs Lamport.[10] I know I meant to take it but I think I forgot. And Mr Gaskell has a sermon of Mr Cameron's that ought to be returned to Mrs Lamport. Wd you be so kind as to see after them. I am going to bring you some Knutsford humbugs in fulfilment of my promise to bring you some *goody*. I hope you have no more tic – do try the ointment if you have. Goodbye, dear – Ever your very affect friend

E C Gaskell

My dearest love to my girls. Remind MA to send love to Aunt Ab.[11] I thought & so did Aunt Ab their notes were *very* nicely written

Address Miss Fergusson / Revd William Gaskell's/ Upper Rumford Street /Oxford Road / Manchester

Stamp (defaced); postmarks (mostly illegible) <KNU>TSFORD / 6 [?]JU / 1845

The Gaskell Society

1 The Christian name of ECG's young governess, Barbara Fergusson*, is derived from this group of letters, accidentally discovered at a very late stage in our editing. However, they illuminate ECG's description of her as a 'dear household friend' (p. 34 below), who evidently played an important part in the Gaskell's family life. In 1857 ECG wrote that her 'dearest friends, all throughout [her] life, have been governesses, either past, present or future' (see *EY*, p. 171).

2 A pet name for Miss Fergusson*, also used in Letter 16a, and in Letter 17, redated [?Early March 1847] (*Letters*, pp. 48, 824). Cf. the use of 'wife' and 'husband' between Catherine Winkworth* and her sister Susanna* (*L & M*, I. 435). Margaret was ECG's nursemaid. See *Letters*, pp. 823–4, for ECG's domestic regimen about this time.

3 Either Uncle Samuel Holland (1768–1851) or his son Samuel (1803–92), ECG's cousin, of Plas yn Penrhyn, near Porthmadog, North Wales.

4 Possibly ECG's summer landlady in Ffestiniog, about 7 miles from Plas yn Penrhyn.

5 ECG refers to her daughter Florence, born 7 October 1842, and William ('Willie'), born 23 October 1844, christened 23 January 1845 at Cross Street chapel. Marianne and Meta were at home in Upper Rumford Street.

6 Ann Hearn, servant and friend of the Gaskells for over fifty years (Uglow, p. 150).

7 Mary*, née Brandreth (c. 1803–71), wife of the Reverend Henry Green*, Unitarian minister of Knutsford.

8 ECG was friends with the Miss Marslands from 1838 (*Letters*, pp. 18, 25). Henry and Samuel Marsland were members of Cross Street chapel's congregation.

9 Dr John Kitto (1804–54), author of *The Lost Senses,* published in two parts in *Knight's Weekly Volume* in 1845 (Series 1, 'Deafness'; Series 2, 'Blindness'). Kitto was himself totally deaf.

10 A Mrs Charles Lamport is mentioned in 1847 (p. 35 below).

11 Aunt Abigail Holland (1773–1848), sister of ECG's mother.

MISS BARBARA FERGUSSON*

[Upper Rumford Street
Manchester]
[c. 17 January 1846][1]

< ... > humour, for I think these frights about one's children make one more inclined than ever to make their childhood happy if possible. Last night if I had had a creature to send to the P. office I shd have written to you, but Hearn was engaged with F. & all Mr G's books down to be dusted, & all the carpets in the house up. Today I was right glad I did not frighten you; & tomorrow I dare sa<y> all will be right & well. Miss Mitchell[2] is still at Knutsford, – oh dear! I feel yet sick with the fright of yesterday; and I am so thankful I did not go to Warrington. –

The children write very good accounts of themselves & all there – & Wm says Meta's appetite is glorious, & her strength increasing.[3] In greatest haste but with dear love

Yours very affecly
E C Gaskell

Address Miss Fergusson / J. A. Turner's Esqre / Cross Street /Manchester
?Stamp removed; postmarks GREEN-HEYS and MANCHESTER / JA 17 / 1846 /A
Seal [?]sheaf of corn.

The Gaskell Society (incomplete)

1 ECG's son 'Willie' had died before this date, on 10 August 1845. He is said to have caught scarlet fever from his sister Marianne at rooms in Ffestiniog. They were both taken to Porthmadog, where only MA recovered (*EY*, pp. 324–5).
2 In the mid–1840s this 'very cultivated lady' provided lodgings for Manchester College students at 93 Lloyd Street (H. McClachlan, *Records of a Family 1800–1933*, 1935, pp. 119–20). She also taught the Gaskell daughters till 1852 (*Letters*, p. 217).
3 WG had perhaps taken MA and ME to his home town of Warrington. Willie had been buried in 'the dull, dreary chapel-yard' of Sankey Street Unitarian Street chapel there (*Letters*, p. 57). Julia Bradford Gaskell was not yet born.
4 Note that there is no separate envelope. It is not known why Miss Fergusson* was at this address. See p. 36 n. 3 below.

MISS BARBARA FERGUSSON*

[?The Greens', Knutsford][1]
Sunday [c. 23 February 1846]

My dear Daddy,

You have been very good in writing to me twice; and pray thank MA & Meta for their letters. I will try and answer them tomorrow. MA's had much more news in it than usual. I am sorry to say Aunt Ab *has* got both housemaid & cook; the former a young woman who has gone into service for the first time under much such circumstances as the Miss Blackmores; and the latter an awful 'treasure' of a servant; such a treasure for faithfulness, good cooking &c that she may be as cross as she likes, and do what she likes and Aunt Ab daren't say a word. Aunt Ab is pretty well; but Uncle Holland is *very* poorly; and his staff Mary[2] is so ill she is ordered to be from home for some time.

Louisa Long's legs are larger than Marianne's. Harriet Long begs Florence may be told they have got a new baby; a real live baby; to be called Fanny.[3] Do you remember Mr Gleeson the Irish assistant here? and the very disagreeable reason there was for his leaving? Well he has settled at Knutsford , and plagues Mr Deane[4] every possible way. I don't think I named to anyone that I called on Sally Felton[5] on her birthday 'Valentines day', and found her overpowered with valentines, and sitting in state with spunge biscuits to receive callers. Pity Willm Turn did not call then on the old lady. I never saw such a place for cleanliness!

Emily Green[6] asked so nicely after you. She is *so* pretty in an evening having quite a brilliant colour, and both she and Annie & Ellen are so beautifully dressed – they three seem all very nice, but Isabella is a little abomination as I can tell you when I see you. *Here* Emily is charming in temper manners and household ways. But [double stress] *very* dull over her lessons Susan[7] says. Maggie is just as quick, but a little self-conscious body. Under my nose is a large nosegay of sweet violets, wall flower, snowdrops, anenomes[*sic*; alteration] &c.

I am going to drink tea with Aunt Ab tonight whose Sundays are generally very lonely.[8] I have begun a piece of worsted work, only think of that! It is a very pretty pattern and will be easy for the children to finish if I do not. Anne Buckley is in service in Manchester; has been there about six weeks. Susan is in some distress about her servants the nurse being very ill, the cook obliged to go home to her sister who is dying. I have copied for you dearest Miss Fergusson, the lines enclosed – they are all from Barry Cornwall's poems,[9] which they have here, – all are new to me *but* the P<ra>yer in sickness which was often in my mind that most mournful week of watching.[10] I think I then named the verse with '*striving not to weep*', they come so home to the sore spot in my heart, and I am sure you will like them. Read them carefully and when you are not in a hurry; and don't they all seem suited to him. Goodbye – ever your very affect friend

E C Gaskell

Address Miss Fergusson / Revd W. Gaskell's / Upper Rumford St / Oxford Road / Manchester

Stamp removed; seal; postmark MANCHESTER /FE 23 / 1846 / A

The Gaskell Society

1 Cf. *Letters*, p. 17, where ECG was staying with the Greens in July 1838.

2 Aunt Abigail's brother, Peter Holland of Church House, surgeon, and his daughter Mary.
3 'I saw a good deal of Mrs John Long whom I like, – and something of Mrs Henry Long ... ' at Knutsford (*Letters,* p. 17).
4 Dr Richard Timothy Deane (d. 16 January 1851, aged 46) of Princess Street, Knutsford, surgeon and partner of Peter Holland. He would seem to have, typically, taken medical apprentices. See *EY,* pp. 126, 145, 166.
5 A minor celebrity in Knutsford, seller of pies and pastries (*EY,* pp. 130, 293).
6 Henry and Mary Green* had five surviving children: Emily (b. 10 Aug. 1828), John Philip (b. 2 Jan. 1830), Ann Louisa (b. 26 Aug. 1833), Mary Ellen (b. 28 Jan. 1835) and Isabella (b. 13 Jan. 1841). Annie, Ellen and Emily often figure in ECG's letters, Isabella only rarely.
7 Probably Susan* (1811–89), daughter of Peter Holland. Dr Deane, then a widower with three children, married her on 10 April 1844. Surviving children of his first marriage were Emily, (b. c. 1836), Arthur, (b. 1837), Margaret (b. 1838).
8 Aunt Hannah Lumb had died on 1 May 1837. It looks as if ECG was not staying at her childhood home, Heath(side), with Aunt Abigail.
9 Barry Cornwall was the pseudonym of Bryan Waller Procter (1787–1874). His 'A Prayer in Sickness' was reprinted in his *English Songs and Other Small Poems* (1846), where ECG would probably have seen it. It begins, 'Send down thy winged angel, God! / Amongst this night so wild; / And bid him come where we now watch / And breathe upon our child!'
10 For Willie's death see p. 29 n. 1 above. 'To turn her thoughts by her husband's advice she began to write' *Mary Barton* (*EY,* pp. 457), publ. late 1848. After its success ECG was lionised in London, finding herself 'intoxicated with sparkling conversation heard tonight at Mrs Procter's' (*Letters,* p. 77).

MISS BARBARA FERGUSSON*

[Southport][1]
Wednesday
[? Summer ?1846]

My dear Miss Fergusson,

Just a line to ask you how you think Mr Gaskell *really* is; he sends me word of his fainting on Sunday night which makes me very uncomfortable, and I shall certainly think it right to return unless I hear from you a better account. So do write please directly.

And will you tell Anne that I wish she would *particularly* attend to Mr Gaskell; to tempting him with the food he likes best, and *change* of diet; to *always* taking him up some supper. *Milk* I think he likes best for a constancy; and not too much bread in it; but *always* to take something up. I wish you wd make Marianne attend to taking him an egg beaten up with a little warm milk & sugar, every morning when he has not pupils[2] before she goes out; & will you send her ¼ of an hour or so before to ask Anne to get it ready – & will you tell Anne always to send something either meat or eggs in to tea, 'specially on Sunday; and to get kidneys sweet-breads & such tit bits – and fowls by way of variety, and devil the legs &c – She only wants reminding I am sure to attend to all these things; so will you read her aloud what I have said, & not think me very troublesome in making you the medium. I wish he wd just see Mr Partington[3] if only once; it would be such a satisfaction to me, and I wish he wd get up earlier so as not to have to hurry over his breakfast.

I shall be very uncomfortable till I hear; and would much rather come home. If Hannah has (as I told her) taken the sofa out of his study, ask her please to take it back again; that he may have the oppy of lying down – We are all quite well, only I'm lame. Thank MA for her gift to Florence of the pretty little sheet of paper. F was much pleased. Excuse this dull selfish note, and ever believe me

Your affect friend,
E C Gaskell –

Envelope Miss Fergusson / Revd W. Gaskell's / Upr Rumford Street / Oxford Road / Manchester[4]

Stamp; seal; postmarks SOUTH <PORT> *and* [?]584

The Gaskell Society

1 On the sandy coast of Liverpool bay, north-west of Manchester. ECG used to go to such resorts (e. g. Crosby in July 1837) when feeling ill after the births of her children (*Private Voices,* p. 63).
2 By late 1840 Agnes and Eliza Paterson* were being given lessons; in the following year WG was teaching Susanna*, Emily* and Selina Winkworth, daughters of Henry Winkworth (d. 1869), silk manufacturer, and his wife, née Dickinson (d. 1841), of The Polygon, Ardwick. Gaskell made Catherine Winkworth* translate German poetry (*L & M,* I. 36, 44, 65, 73, 454).
3 James E. Partington, surgeon, 78 Oxford Road, Manchester (*Letters,* pp. 13, 45).
4 The Gaskell Society has a note on mourning paper, not in ECG's hand: sent from 94 Bloomsbury, Manchester, 17th October, and addressed to Miss Ferguson[sic] / Revd William Gaskell / Rumford street / upper Brook Street; stamp removed; postmarked 17 October 1846. It reads: 'Robina Dunlop died here this morning at half past Eight oClock.'

WILLIAM BEAMONT[1]

Ashfield,[2]
Tuesday Morning
[c. 17 June 1846]

My dear Sir,

I have just received an answer to my enquiries; and I will copy for you that part of my cousin's letter[3], which refers to the subject about which you are interested.

'It was Harry', (Dr. Holland's eldest son) 'not Frank who was with Mr Raule,[4] and he liked him so much that he asked to go again during another vacation. He is a very good mathematician and an elegant scholar. He is a Puseyite, though of course neither he \ himself / nor Harry call it so. He is an excellent man, and does much good in the way of schools &c in his parish (Cheadle *in Staffordshire.*) But I rather think he has quite given up taking pupils. He only took them that he might have more means to aid in church adornments, alms-giving, schools, and other good deeds &c &c. He is unmarried, and keeps a houseful of curates. It was a personal favour to Harry to take him again, for a short time.

Frank is with Mr Alford[5] (the poet,) at Wymondswolde, Leicestershire. He too is Puseyite, or at least very high Church. Not quite so good a mathematician as Mr Raule, I imagine, but Frank likes him very much, and is going to travel abroad with him. I know nothing *personally* of either of these two gentlemen, but Mr Alford was highly recommended to me by Judge Coltman and Miss Duckworth.[6]

I am afraid that Mr Raule's unwillingness to receive pupils[7] will not be very welcome information to you.

With very kind regards to Mrs Beamont, believe me to remain,

Yours very truly,
E. C. Gaskell

Endorsement June 17 /1846 /E. C. Gaskell

Warrington Public Library

1 William Beamont (1797–1889), of Bewsey Street Warrington, solicitor, antiquary and travel-writer; married Ann (d. 1859), daughter of John Gaskell of Warrington.

2 Ashfield, Thelwall Lane, near Warrington, was the home of Charles Broadbent, whose nearby tannery was worked by a Roger Gaskell (G. A. Carter, *Latchford*, Warrington 1989, p 35).

3 (Sir) Henry Holland's sons were Henry Thurstan (1825–1914), created Viscount Knutsford 1895, and Francis James (1828–1907), later Canon of Canterbury.

4 Richard Rawle[sic] (1812–1889), Rector of Cheadle, Staffs; he later took up a church appointment in the West Indies.

5 Henry Alford (1810–71), Vicar of Wymeswold 1835–53, hymnodist, poet and prolific author of theological works. His edition of the Greek Testament was cited repeatedly in Victorian religious controversies.

6 Thomas Coltman (1781–1849). Barrister 1808 on Northern Circuit, KC 1837, Judge in Court of Common Pleas and knighthood 1832. Died of Asiatic cholera at his home in Hyde Park Gardens, leaving four children by his wife Anna, née Duckworth.

7 Beamont's son (see p. 72 below) was at Eton in 1846.

Letters 17 and 17a to MA and ME [?from near Rivington, Lancashire] redated [?Early March 1847][1]

1 Julia Bradford Gaskell was baptised 17 March 1847.

FANNY HOLLAND[1]

Upper Rumford Street,
Tuesday [9 March 1847]

My dearest Fanny,

I am always so glad to have a letter from you; and just now your sympathy about *both* my feelings for Miss Fergusson was[altered word] so acceptable; as so few people can understand how *deeply* I, personally, regret her loss, and yet how desirable I feel it to be on the children's account. You know most exactly the state of the case with regard to them. I disapprove and see more and more the bad effects of her mode of treatment; and yet I, my own self, scarcely dare to look forwards to the time when she will no longer be our inmate, and my dear household friend, and sometimes I can not keep down the feeling which I yet know to be morbid, that it is ungrateful to ever part with one who was *so tender* to my poor darling boy,[2] and that makes me most miserable. However I do try to look stedfastly[sic] to the *right* for my children; and I am comforted by Miss F's *own* right understanding of my different feelings, and own agreement of judgment with mine, as to her not managing the girls well.

She is going *very* soon; on the 20th of this month, – next Friday week. Her plans are (as far as they are decided,) these – She goes from here to Pendlebury; thence as soon as the weather is at all spring-like to Lytham with Kitty Turner (- Mrs T-s daughter, aged about 16) who is not strong. There they remain for a month or six weeks, and then Miss F goes to see her friends in Scotland for another six weeks or 2 months; and then (if Kitty Turner is well enough) Miss F goes abroad with the Turners[3] for some months on the Continent, either to school in Paris, or travelling; not yet settled. *Then* on her return she comes to pay us a visit until {there's} her plans are settled for the future.

Meanwhile I am going to try teaching the girls with the aid of masters at home.[4] I will try & tell you some of my arrangements, altho' I am leaving many ideas to be developed by time. (I want them very much to learn to act from inner sense, rather than from outward force of either scolding or reminding) Mondays and Thursdays they will have an hour's french lesson here from Mme Frielot; a very good teacher who sets a good deal to be done in her absence; but is so kind & spirited that all her pupils are fond of her. On Monday this lesson will be from ¼ to one to ¼ to 2, on Thursday ¼ to 2 to ¼ to 3. Thursday morning from {½ past} 9 to 10 their papa will teach them, and one other hour in the week, the time for which is not yet fixed. Wednesday from 11 to 1 they have dancing. On Tuesday & Friday evening a Miss Hooley (one of the Knutsford Hooleys, now teacher in Mr Jones' school) comes at ½ p 7 for an hour to teach writing and arithmetic – this, in order to set me at liberty for visiting those two evenings. Emily Winkworth[5] has offered *for the present* to teach Marianne music, & gives her lesson at 10 o'clock on Fridays; and we have engaged Rosa Mitchell to give Meta two ½ hour music lessons in the week. Add to which, most probably they will both go to the School of Design on Tuesdays & Thursdays from 11 to 1 (to be there,) and you have drawing, dancing, music, French, writing and arithmetic fixed & arranged for, besides the probable lessons in History & Natural History from their Papa. My part will be reduced to general superintendence & help-giving in the preparation of their lessons; we shall work together, & read some book aloud at nights. I shall give them dictation & grammar lessons, walk out with them (to be regular in *this* will be one great difficulty,) and make myself as much as possible their companion and friend.

My writing time today is rapidly drawing to a close, but I have 2 especial things to say. One is I want you dear Fanny to come & stay with us. I *want* you; I don't know if I can offer you any inducements, but you wd be such a comfort & help to me – just when I shall be feeling the blank of Miss F's absence, and when I shall want advice about plans &c for the girls. I should be *particularly* glad if you could come, & I would do all I could to make it a pleasant visit; I see it would depend a good deal upon Aunt Sam's health[6] but if she continues better as I hope and trust she is doing, I shall look forward to your coming for a *stationary* visit very soon; as soon as you can. – Secondly about your Elizth. I know Mrs Chas Lamport's place is filled up about which she wrote to Hearn and I feel almost certain the other is, as the advertisement was an old one, and *Monday* morning is often too late to apply for a Saty advertisement. Both Hearn & I are on the look out; and if Eliz would like to come to Manchester and be on the spot, I should be very glad if she would come here, & share Hearn's bed;[7] – in a fortnight's time I have no doubt some of us would hear of a place. Will you name this to her –

I saw Mr Shaen last night at the Salis Schwabe's (Mr Cobden's travelling companion through Spain.)[8] He is now engaged in Mr Leisler's warehouse, and is to be American traveller for that house. He sails for Boston the 4th of next month. I correspond pretty closely with my friend Annie Shaen.[9] Baby is to be christened next Wednesday week, (just before Miss F goes,) Julia Bradford Gaskell is the little lady's name.[10] She is a very big, healthy, merry, plain child[.] Florence is very thin & not very strong owing to her growing so fast we think. Marianne is growing too a good deal; Meta is remarkably well –

I don't think there is much news a-float, or if there is I don't hear much of it; I feel so absorbed in the prospect of Miss F's departure and at times I feel it hard work to keep up Do you know if Mrs Hughes[11] ever got a work-box I sent (through Lizzy when she came over to see her mother,)[12] to Jane-Anne Hughes. Give my love to Mrs Hughes. We all mean to write to her oftener than we do. Wm is engaged morning noon & night; what a curious adventure of Mr Rowland Wms! Tell me about

Sophy Greave's engagement – I never heard a word of it.[13] I *must* end now – *do* come if you possibly can. Give my kindest love to dear Anne, & tell her I rely on her coming for a nice long visit, next time she comes to England.

My dear love too to Aunt Sam & my Uncle.[14] I don't forget his coming to Festiniog, and noticing my lost darling so much that day. All those awful days are stamped in my heart, and I don't believe even Heaven itself can obliterate the memory of that agony, – and I am haunted by the thought of the person who knew him most, & loved him most at last, going to leave our house which ought to be her home – and our doing. He died in her arms too. I dare not tell her how much I feel it, & yet I believe it is right. Do come & help me – give my love to Sam –

Yours very affecly
E C Gaskell.

Brotherton Collection, Leeds University

1 See p. 12 n. 13 above. In ECG's early life she was close to her Liverpool first cousins, Anne, Fanny and Kate, though only letters to Fanny have been found.
2 For Willie's death, see p. 29 n. 1 above.
3 James Aspinall Turner (1797–1867) m. Sarah Blackmore (1796–1871); Sarah Catherine Turner (1830–78). Their home was at Pendlebury, which Miss Fergusson* had just visited (*Letters*, p. 826). J. Fergusson to Miss Fergusson, Kirriemuir [north of Dundee, near Glamis Castle], 14 June 1847, is addressed c/o J. A. Turner Esquire / Cross Street / Manchester, but mentions Pend<lebury> also. MS, The Gaskell Society.
4 Elaborate education of girls at home was traditional. See Vickery, p. 343 n. 86.
5 Emily Shaen*, née Winkworth (1822–87), who was to marry William Shaen* (1822–87) on 2 September 1851 (*Letters*, p. 159), WG performing the ceremony at Dean Row Chapel, near Wilmslow, Cheshire (*L & M*, I. 295). She was one of ECG's greatest friends.
6 Aunt Catherine Holland, who died on 1 September 1847, aged 76, at Caernarfon.
7 Hearn could evidently liberate ECG from the most irksome aspects of servant management.
8 On 26 September 1846 Salis Schwabe* (1800–53), of Crumpsall House, a calico printer like Richard Cobden*, and his wife Julie (a cousin) had joined the Cobdens for a tour of Spain. Julie Schwabe* (1819–96) wrote *Reminiscences of Richard Cobden* (1895).
9 The earliest known letter to Anne Shaen, sister of William*, is probably to be dated 24 April 1848. She had visited the Gaskells in November 1847 (*Letters*, pp. 50, 56).
10 Julia Bradford Gaskell was born on 3 September 1846 and christened on Wednesday, 17 March 1847 at Cross Street chapel. See J. A. V. Chapple, 'The Bradfords of Seedley', *GSN* 17 (1994), pp. 7- 8.
11 Mrs Jane Hughes (aged 30, 1851 Census), née Thomas, of the Penmorfa inn, Bwlch-y-Fedwen, married a master-mariner, William Hughes (d. 1858). She had been especially kind to ECG (*Letters*, p. 826) when Willie Gaskell died as a baby of nine months, probably at her house, Belle Vue, Marine Terrace, Porthmadog. Her two eldest daughters in 1845 were Jane-Anne and

Margaret; Fanny Holland had a small house nearby. See Dewi Williams, 'The Death of Willy Gaskell', *GSJ* 13 (1999), pp. 108–9.

12 ECG's sister-in-law Eliza Gaskell (1812–92) had married Charles Holland (1799–1870), son of ECG's aunt Catherine Holland and brother of cousin Fanny.

13 Cousin Kate Holland (1804–86) had married Richard Greaves (d. 1870) in April 1838; Sophy was his sister. Rowland Williams might be the surgeon of Tremadog. See *EY*, pp. 322–5.

14 Uncle Samuel and aunt Catherine Holland of Plas yn Penrhyn. See p. 40 n. 3 below.

MISS BARBARA FERGUSSON*

[Manchester]
Thursday [9 September 1847]

My dearest Miss Fergusson,

I was so glad of your note; it was so exactly the sympathy I wanted. And you will think I did *not* sympathize with you about your brother;[1] but I did, and having heard Miss Shaen[2] name that one of her cousins had had fits sounding *very like* Johnny's, and had been entirely cured by a persevering application of some remedies I asked her to write for the prescription [-] 'Oh dear Mrs Gaskell I do wish I had never told you anything about it. Please don't trouble yourself about me. I had much rather you would not. I will never name anything about myself again &c &c.' Well now that's said, & deserves just such a scolding as I have given you many a time in times past, I will again please the pigs,[3] some day.

This is the physician's letter 'Each case of epilepsy should be treated on it's own merits, (you see even epilepsy has *merits*, though you & I can't find out what they are.) it is therefore impossible to prescribe for a case unseen. The enclosed prescription might be of service, and you can send it with direction to have the effect observed by a medical man. It should be continued some months.'

You will like to know about Anne. I don't know where I left off in my story – did I tell you we asked Mr Curtis[4] to go & rummage up the man & tell him her state, and *ask* not *urge* him to marry her ; for she had told us she had not seen him for months & that her[sic] knew nothing of her condition, – told it again & again and once most solemnly – Well! Mr C. went. The man of course refused to marry her, but worst of all it came out he knew all about her state – when she expected to be confined , – she had been at his lodging only the Sunday previous, although she told me she had no idea where he was, & thought he had left Manchester – and all this when I was so full of sorrowful pity for her, – it makes one feel so angry to be so deceived, & so uncertain as to where the deceit begins or ends that I was nearly throwing the case up in despair, but I did not –

I wrote to her mother to come over which she has done unknowing of the intelligence which awaited her, & which I told her, – selfish woman – for she won't let Anne be confined there, – nor take any charge or care of the child, 'for babies makes her nervous', and seems to think her visit to Manchester a *ploy*, & that she'll see all that can be seen; and I've written to Mr Deane[5] to try & get Anne a wet nurse's place *out* of Manchester, & away from the man, – & there the matter stands. I think as the man is here, & as Anne shows how much she can deceive that she ought not to come back \ both for Hannah's sake & her own / – so I have all but decided to take a god-send of a cook, who has lived nine years with Mr Wallace & Miss Dakin,[6] & most highly valued by them, but whom Bath does not suit. So thats *that.*

I am very sorry for Anne, notwithstanding all, she hides herself so from observation & looks so broken & ashamed. My dear Aunt Sam is dead – died last Wednesday week at Caernarvon (do you remember our night there), in lodgings – they were trying to get her to Liscard[7] for change of air – All seems sorrowful just now in many ways – our darling Baby is ill – has thrown up *every thing* she has taken \ even *water* / since Tuesday night – Mr Partington says she is a little better this morning or else Wm would not have gone to Southport where he, MA, & Meta went an hour or two ago – but she cannot sit up – is very weak. Her < ... >

Mourning paper and Envelope[8] Miss Fergussn / Miss Fergusson / J. A. Turner's Esqr / Cross Street / Manchester

Endorsed [?]assailant

Seal; stamp (cut away); postmarks MANCH<ESTER> *and* MANCHESTER / S<EP> 9 / 18<4>7 / C

The Gaskell Society (incomplete)

1 Presumably the J. Fergusson (p. 36 n. 3 above), who wrote from Kirriemuir, where he seems to have been under the care of Dr Robb, Mrs Robb and Mr Lucas.

2 Perhaps Anne Shaen (p. 35 above).

3 Proverbial: please the fates. *NED* 10a states that suggested derivations (e.g. pixies) lack historical authority.

4 Perhaps John Ogle Curtis (1802–57), for twenty-one years Master of the Cross Street chapel schools, Manchester.

5 Richard T. Deane, surgeon of Knutford.

6 Hugh Wallace, attorney, and Mary Ann Dakin, both of Princess Street, Knutsford.

7 Catherine Holland died on Wednesday, 1 September 1847. Her son Charles had bought the estate of Liscard Vale, Cheshire, in 1844.

8 A detached envelope has survived without an associated letter. It is addressed in ECG's hand to Miss Fergusson, / J. A. Turner's Esqr / Pendlebury. The stamp has been removed; postmarks PENDLEBURY *and* MANCHESTER / NO 2 / 1847 /I; seal, a sheaf of corn. Also, ME to Miss Fergusson, c. 23 April 1848, and 14 July 1849 (texts in Miscellanea, pp. 293–4 below).

EDWARD CHAPMAN[1]

May 26 [1848]

Dear Sir,

I am at present staying in the country, whither my husband (the *revd* W G –) brought me the note he had received from you. I was delighted with it; it is such a relief to find I shall not have to dilute my story so much as I feared.[2] It would be like adding water to an already drained tea-pot. Will you be so good as to send me sometime before very long the M. S. of the *last chapter*, which is a very short one? It contains a summary of events I must amplify, and yet there are one or two things in it which I have forgotten, yet should not like to omit. If you have no objection I should on reflection prefer *no name* being given as that of the author.[3] I do not like assuming a name, although my desire for secrecy is as strong as ever.

Yours very truly
E. C. Gaskell

New York Public Library, Berg Collection

1 Edward Chapman (1804–80), who with William Hall (d. 1847) founded the innovative publishing firm of Chapman and Hall at 186 The Strand in 1830 (193 Piccadilly from 1850). Chapman was responsible for negotiations with ECG for *Mary Barton*.

2 ECG told a friend that the tale 'was originally complete without the part which intervenes between John Barton's death and Esther's', and said that she 'would rather relinquish some of the payment than interpolate anything' (*Letters*, p. 75). Cp. the critical analysis of this statement by Sharps, p. 553 n. 9.

3 On 19 October 1848 ECG proposed 'Stephen Berwick' as a pseudonym (*Letters*, p. 59), but the suggestion came too late and it was published anonymously (Smith, p. 3).

EDWARD CHAPMAN

Saturday Evening [?late June 1848]
121, Upper Rumfor<d St>
Mancheste<r>

Dear Sir,

We are going to travel on the *26th*, of this month, and I should be very glad to have my part[sic] towards the completion of my book <.> Any letters might be forwarded it is true, only I would so much rather get {it} \ the completion / off my mind before going northwards,[1]

I remain dear Sir
Yours very truly
E. C. Gaskell.

Mrs Lucy Magruder

1 On Monday 10 July 1848 ECG, writing from Gale[sic] Cottage, [Keswick in the Lake District], agreed to write an explanatory preface for Chapman (*Letters*, p. 58). By early October ECG was in Southport. She looked 'very thin and not at all well', but retailed 'nice long stories, and the very fact-ual style of conversation that Kate [Winkworth* was] so fond of' (*L & M*, I. 138, 155, 157–8).

MISS BARBARA FERGUSSON*

[Plas yn Penrhyn]
[c. 29 October 1848]

< ... > We shall go home *either* next Friday or next Monday but one, (tomorrow week.) Do you know 'my book' is out, and (I believe) praised from what the publisher writes me word in the Athenaeum[1] and Jerrold's newspaper.[2] Of course here I hardly hear anything of that kind; nor do I care. Emily W. \ Winkworth / is here [-] my cousins asked her to come as she has not been well; so she came last Thursday, and they are doing their best to make it pleasant to her.[3]

My cousins say they saw Mr & Mrs Turner on the road a few weeks ago; and wish they could have stopped here. Capn Hughes[4] has got a new vessel called <t>he Ariel; and Mrs Hughes wants MA <&> me to go & look over it & drink tea there. We shall go as it will give her pleasure. And now I must end. I *wish* you would write, but I don't expect it you naughty young lady. I have got a recipe for tic, which they say is never failing. Did you ever get my bill from Mr Rob for the ointment?[5] Ever your affect & most grateful

E. C. Gaskell

Address Miss Fergusson / care of / J. A. Turner's Esqre / Cross Street / Manchester.
Seal; postmarks CARNARVON / OC 29 / 1848 / B; MANCHESTER / OC 31 / 1848 / A *etc., and script stamp:* Too Late.

The Gaskell Society (incomplete)

1 *Mary Barton* was reviewed by [H. F. Chorley] in the *Athenaeum* for 21 October 1849: 'we have met with few pictures of life among the working classes at once so forcible and so fair'. ECG was to meet him in May 1849. He gave her 'a great dose of literary advice', which she found 'really valuable', Emily Winkworth told her sister. See *Letters*, p. 77; *L & M*, I. 179.
2 *Douglas Jerrold's Weekly*, first issued 18 July 1846.
3 With a ball and plenty of talk (*L & M*, I. 164–5). ECG reported that Uncle Sam Holland was 'charmed with Emily and they carry on a regular flirtation. After dinner, slip-slop sleepy talk; a little music; a good deal of lounging ...' (*Letters*, p. 61).
4 Captain William Hughes.
5 See p. 38 n. 1 above.

~

Letter 614 to George Hope dated from 121 Upper Rumford Street, 13 February [1849]

~

EDWARD CHAPMAN

121 Upper Rumford Street
Wednesday, April 11 [1849][1]

May I ask you, (if from any reason you are not able to return your letter about MB. to me by tomorrow's post,) to send it addressed to me, 11 Panton Square Haymarket London – ?

Elizabeth Gaskell

Mrs Lucy Macgruder

1 This letter supports the view that ECG could not have been at a Dickens dinner in London on 31 March 1849, and probably went up to her 'little, dusty, noisy lodgings' in mid-April. See Uglow, pp. 219, 642 n. 11.

?EDWARD CHAPMAN

11 Panton Sq.
Wednesday [?18 April 1849][1]

Dear Sir,

I am afraid you will be tired of my thanks before I am tired of your kindness; nevertheless I must thank you for all the trouble you are taking. You are very good; and by dint of hard study I think I understand, and know how to apply all his orders.[2] I heard last night that Jenny Lind[3] is not going to sing; so I have made Mr Forster's order do duty for an autograph.[4] I suppose I might?

Mr Ewart[5] has offered to take us over the 'houses of parliament', which I suppose includes the House of Lords. I return you the 'Science' as it is for Friday Evening, for which you provided us with orders for the French Play,[6] but thank you nonetheless very much for the Royal Institution order.[7] I wonder if you have a copy of the last Edin. if you would send it to me – I have not seen it yet, but Mr *Sam* Greg[8] \ brother to *Wm* Greg the writer[9] / has written to me, calling it 'harsh strictures', &c, so I should like to make a wry face, and swallow the unpalatable medicine with a gulp From a *friend* I think it sounds pretty severe.

Yours very truly
E C Gaskell

Pierpont Morgan Library (Gordon Ray Collection)

1 See *Letters,* pp. 76–8, 827–29, and *L & M,* I. 175–88, for details of places and people ECG visited in London, though precise dates are problematic. Emily Winkworth* writes that the 'regular whirl of interest and excitement as she is in would turn my brain' (L&M, I.176).
2 An 'order' is a free or reduced-price pass for admission to a place not normally open to the public, such as a theatre, museum, park, etc.
3 Famous Swedish singer (1820–87). Her London début was in 1847, and she also sang in Manchester, staying with the Salis Schwabes* in December 1848 (*Letters,* p. 62). Her last stage performance in England was 10 May 1849, after which she left for the USA.
4 'Autograph' means sample of handwriting. John Forster* (1812–76), man of letters, business and literary adviser. He wrote to ECG on 3 May 1849 offering to call on her at Panton Square (MS, Princeton UL).
5 William Ewart* (1798–1869), of Broadlees, Devizes; MP for Dumfries, and previously for Liverpool and for Wigan. A supporter of Free Trade, he became a close friend of the Gaskell family.
6 At St James's theatre was playing a lengthy, popular season of *opéras comiques,* i. e. spoken dialogue interspersed with songs and music. The *Times* reports that a distinguished audience, which included the Queen and Prince Albert, attended the first London performance in French of Daniel Auber and Augustin Scribe's *Fra Diavolo* on Friday, 20 April 1849. We are grateful to Professor Donald Roy for this information. Cf. *Letters,* p. 298.
7 Probably not to hear Michael Faraday, who lectured in the Royal Institution on Friday 30 March and Friday 1 June in 1849.
8 Samuel Greg (1804–76) had tried to establish a model factory colony at Bollington in Cheshire, but by 1847 had incurred massive debts, causing him great personal distress (*Letters,* p. 120, and below, p. 47). The Gregs were family friends ECG had known since childhood (*EY,* pp. 139–42, 146–7).
9 William Rathbone Greg (1809–81), writer and advocate of Free Trade, published a critical review of *Mary Barton* in the *Edinburgh Review* of April 1849. This was one of the great intellectual quarterlies of the century, begun in 1802 by Francis Jeffrey and Sydney Smith, to which ECG's father had contributed learned articles (*EY,* p. 70).

?THOMAS CARLYLE[1]

11 Panton Square.
[?April 1849]

My dear Sir,

I am very much obliged to you for your kind present of your books. That 'with the terrible name', attracts instead of frightening me; but while in the whirl and bustle of London I must deny myself the pleasure of reading it, and reserve it for some quiet time at home, when I shall recall with {the} pleasure the evening I passed with one, (whose name I had so long looked upon with respect and interest,) at Mr Fox's.[2]

Believe me Sir, I value your expressions of approbation; and I remain ever

Yours faithfully
E. C. Gaskell

Princeton University Library

1 Possibly Thomas Carlyle (1795–1881), who had written to ECG praising *Mary Barton*; his book could be *Sartor Resartus* (1833–4). When ECG called on the Carlyles in late April 1849, he stayed in his garden 'walking backwards and forwards in a dirty Scotch plaid smoking'; she eventually met him in May lolling and fidgeting and 'spouting for a good hour'. See*L & M,* I. 176, 183.

2 William J. Fox (1786–1864), Unitarian minister and radical orator, by 1847 MP for Oldham. He lived at Charlotte Street, Bedford Square, from February 1844.

Letter 620 to Mrs Jane Loudon from [London] dated [?early May ?1849]

WILLIAM WHEWELL[1]

27, Woburn Square.
May 12th [1849]

Dear Sir,

I can hardly tell you how much honoured I feel by your present;[2] which I have just received, and for which I am most truly obliged to you. It was *very* kind in you to think of sending it to me; and I shall highly va-[lue] the note which accompanied it. I do not read German, and was unaware of the coincidence to which you allude, to which I shall turn with great interest. I believe there is a similar coincidence[3] in one of Geo. Sand's works, 'Mauprat', of which I was also ignorant until it was pointed out to me.

Believe me to remain, dear Sir,

Yours with deep respect
E. C. Gaskell.

Trinity College, Cambridge

1 William Whewell (1794–1866), scientist, historian and philosopher; Master of Trinity College, Cambridge 1841–56. ECG's relations in Lancaster knew him as a brilliant young man and 'fluent chatterer'. When the wit Sidney Smith was told that his forte was science, he riposted, 'Yes, and his foible is omni-science' (*EY,* p. 168).

2 See *Letters,* p. 828; and Waller, p. 63, for WW to ECG, 12 May 1849, sending a book he had edited and part-authored, *English Hexameter Translations* (1847). He met ECG at one of R. Monckton Milnes's* breakfasts this month (*L & M,* I. 188).

3 The likeness between a declaration of love forced by despair in *Mary Barton* and one in the last book of Goethe's rural epic *Hermann and Dorothea.*

MRS OGDEN[1]

27 Woburn Square
May 15, 1849

My dear Mrs Ogden,

I am quite glad to have given you so much pleasure, as to make you care for my writing.

Yours very truly,
E. C. Gaskell

New York Public Library, Carl and Lily Pforzheimer Collection of Shelley & His Circle (Note kindly transcribed by Ruth Meyerson.)

1 Not identified.

ELIZA FOX[1]

121 Upper Rumford Street[2]
Manchester
29 May 1849

My dear Eliza,

Have you read Southey's Memoirs?[3] But of course you have, happy creature – and do you know Dr Epps[4] – I think you do – ask him to tell you who wrote Jane Eyre and Shirley[5], – < ... >

remain yours ever affectionately
E. C Gaskell.

Do tell me who wrote Jane Eyre

Brotherton Collection, Leeds, and Harvard University

1 ECG's unconventional friend, Eliza* (1823–1903), daughter of W. J. Fox. See E. F. Bridell Fox, 'Memories', *The Girl's Own Paper,* 19 July 1890, 660; Brenda Colloms, ' "Tottie" Fox, Her Life and Background', *GSJ* 5 (1991), pp. 16–26.
2 From 'remain' to 'Eyre' is a MS fragment at Harvard (47H – 259). The rest is taken from a part of the typescript of Letter 55 (*Letters,* p. 90), supplemented by Sharps, p. xix, who supplies the new date. Jeanette Eve, 'A Misdated Gaskell Letter and the Background Story to *Ruth*', *N & Q* 34 (1987), pp. 36–39, has clearly shown that the typescript source of Letter 55 silently includes portions from more than one letter.
3 *Life and Correspondence of the Late Robert Southey,* ed. C. C. Southey, 6 vols, 1849–50.
4 London physician consulted about Emily Brontë's final illness in 1848, when 'galloping consumption ... merited its name'. See Barker, pp. 572, 577, 614–15.
5 *Shirley* was published, anonymously like *Jane Eyre,* on 26 October 1849.

~

Letter 635 (undated) to [W. C. Bennett] now dated [?August 1849]

~

W. C. BENNETT[1]

121, Upper Rumford Street
Oct. 12 [1849].

Dear Sir,

I return you many true and hearty thanks for the kind present of the sheets of your poems, you were so good as to send me a few days ago. I have had great pleasure in renewing my acquaintance with some old friends, and becoming acquainted with many new ones. Baby May, & Baby Kate, and your Epitaphs on Infants are my great favourites.

Yours very truly
E. C. Gaskell

Envelope W. C. Bennett Esq. / Greenwich.
Stamp removed, postmarks MANCHESTER / OC 12 / 1849 / L *plus another.*

Mrs Lucy Magruder

1 William Cox Bennett (1820–95) was a prolific and popular poet, specialising in domestic themes and 'baby' poems, as in *Poems* (1850), perhaps the 'sheets' mentioned here. 'His works show a clear eye for the beauty that surrounds common life and a sympathetic heart for those who often miss it in the stress of toil or suffering' (A. H. Miles, *Poets and Poetry of the Century,* vol 5). In March 1851 ECG thanked him for his 'lately published vol' of poems (*Letters,* p. 146).

AGNES PATERSON[1]

[?c. October ?1849]

My dear Agnes,

I meant to have come to call on you this morning. (I was so sorry to miss you on Monday;) but I am so much tired with necessary work that I cannot walk so far. Will you lend me the Ladies Companions?[2] to say nothing of any stray Athenaeums[3] since August last? My kind regards to Miss Satterfield, and love to Leislers[4]

Yours affecly
E C Gaskell

Address Miss Pattersons[*sic*; mourning paper].

Mrs Susan Kearney

1 Agnes (b. Rotterdam, 1822–89) and Eliza (d. 1856) Paterson*. Orphaned when young, they lived with their uncle Joshua Satterfield and his spinster sister Harriet, and were known to the Winkworths by December 1839 (*L & M,* I. 28). 21 August 1849 seems to mark a renewal of contact (*Letters,* p. 83).

2 ECG refused to write for *The Ladies' Companion and Monthly Magazine* in October 1849, when its was edited by Mrs Jane Loudon (Sharps, p. 113, n. 1). Henry Chorley (1808–72), 'then leading a somewhat luxurious, literary,

bachelor life in the West End', took over about May 1850 (*Howitt Autobiography*, II. 57), and published, anonymously, ECG's 'Mr. Harrison's Confessions', February–April 1851.

3 The *Athenaeum: Journal of Literature, Science and the Arts* was a highly influential reviewing weekly, especially of fiction. See Angus Easson, 'Elizabeth Gaskell and the *Athenaeum*', *Modern Language Review* 85 (1990), pp. 829–32.

4 John Leisler, merchant, and his family lived in Victoria Park, Manchester, a fashionable residential estate with fences and toll-gates.

AGNES PATERSON*

[?c. October ?1849]

My dear Agnes,

Will you excuse this shabby piece of paper? But I write in a great hurry, to express my thanks to you, & dear Eliza, for your crochetting kindness to the little ones. I am very much obliged to you indeed; (and a little bit ashamed of imposing upon you as well.) Have you any Athenaeums for a poor starved[altered word] creature? Mrs Hervey[1] promised to send them and has never sent one. I saw the 2nd-week-in-September one.

Yours affecly
E C Gaskell.

Address Miss Paterson / South End.

Mrs Susan Kearney

1 Perhaps Mrs Hervey of Lea Hall, Wimboldesley, Cheshire, whom EGC had recently visited (*Letters*, p. 159).

Letter 21 to MA and ME [from the Samuel Gregs, Bollington]
redated [6 November 1849]

AGNES AND ELIZA PATERSON*

Plymouth Grove,
Thursday. [?late 1849]

My dear Agnes & Eliza,

Will you come to tea *tonight* at 7 o'clock to meet a Dr Springer[1] a German of 'great attainments', and a tremendous beard? A verbal answer will do. And *would* you send me any Ladies Companions by Frank[2]?

Yours very affecly
E C Gaskell.

My poor bearded gentleman wants to see works &c. – I have got a note for Bellhouse's[3] & Sharp & Roberts.[4] *Could* Mr Satterfield[5] kindly give him any more against this even[in]g.

Address Miss Patterson[*sic*] / South End.

Mrs Susan Kearney

1 Possibly Dr Anton (Heinrich) Springer (1825–91), an art historian who in 1849 undertook a study-journey in the Netherlands, France and England. He later became a Professor at Strasburg and at Leipzig.
2 Frank was the Gaskells' servant.
3 Wainright Bel(l)house, who lived at 48 Plymouth Grove, was a cotton-spinner. A Joshua Bellhouse married Eliza Satterfield in 1839. Bellhouse, Edward Taylor & Co. were iron founders, engineers, millwrights, etc. of Hunt Street, Brook Street (1851 directory).
4 Sharp & Roberts, Bridgewater Foundry: 'good to see in the Railway-Engine line' (*Letters,* p. 730). 'The advent of the railway-system gave them an opportunity of which they took the fullest advantage' (Swindells, *Manchester Streets and Manchester Men,* 2nd series, 1907, p. 243).
5 Satterfields (Lamb & Morris) drapers, 11 & 13 St Ann's Square, Manchester, a long-established firm.

~

Letter 55 to Eliza Fox* (Macready part) redated [3–24 February 1850]
Letter 114 to MA from [the Samuel Gregs], Bollington, redated Saturday [?11 May ?1850]

~

MRS AMELIA STRUTT[1]

121, Upper Rumford Street
Manchester
Saturday [?18 May ?1850][2]

My dear Mrs Strutt,

I am to have the final answers from Mr Edwards this evening; so I shall begin my note to you this morning; as I do not want it to be quite and solely on business. It is a week today since we both left Capesthorne,[3] and I have but little hope that you felt as sorrowful as I did when you went away and I thought how very unlikely it was that I should ever see you again. I have been quite pleased since I came home to find out a sort of cobweb link between us, only to be seen by very willing eyes; but my husband says he thinks your sister married an old friend of his, a Mr James, a barrister.[4] I have often and often heard my husband talk of this Mr James, with whom he was at Glasgow; and who was of Welsh descent. Will it fit? I hope it will.

I went to pay another visit before coming home, to another admirer of yours, who also met you at Capesthorne, years ago:[5] Mr Sam

Greg. He is now a great invalid of the most melancholy kind, for his illness is on his spirits; and it amused and interested me to find how in his sad solitary life he cheered himself by planning to emigrate to New Zealand, and surrounding himself with pictures of the country and the inhabitants.[6]

I came home on Wednesday, and had a charming welcome from my children, two of whom had joined me at {Capesthorne} \ Bollington /; but the eldest girl had worked me a cushion for the drawing-room, as a surprize, and the little one[7] (Baby as we call her,) took fast hold of my {hold} gown, and stuck fast to me wherever I went. I found a famous autograph also awaiting me; being no less than Thackeray's preface to Rebecca and Rowena,[8] corrected up and down by himself, and the funniest little pen and ink vignette at the end, which I can't look at without laughing. It is rather a shame in me to be so ungrateful as to abuse Manchester and its smoky skies, but I have been longing for the moon-light Capesthorne nights, even at the expense of being tempted out by a traitress who laughed at me afterwards. Now I shall put this note bye[sic], and add a business-piece this evening. If you have a musical Schoolmaster, I will send you one or two pretty \ musical / things for your school.

Mr Curtis[9] called last night. Mr Edwards declines leaving Manchester, and for reasons which make me feel that he would not have done for you. One is that he is near relations here; another that he prefers *book*-keeping to *school*-keeping; which at once shows him unfit for the latter whatever his mere knowledge may be. Mr Curtis names another man of whose *moral* character, and fondness for teaching, and love for children he could speak highly; (he}\ the young man /is now keeping a school in Manchester; but Mr Curtis believes that he had never received regular instruction at a training school; Mr Moule,[10] our Inspector had however examined him, and allowed him to have pupil teachers apprenticed to him. His wife was also a school-mistress. Mr Curtis spoke highly of all *moral* qualifications. Mr Gaskell then wrote to the President of the Lyceum school[11] and received the answer I enclose.

I am anxious to despatch this note to you without delay. If I can do anything more pray make me of use. I remain dear Mrs Strutt,

Yours most truly
E. C. Gaskell.

Brotherton Collection, Leeds University

1 Amelia Harriet Strutt, née Otter (1817–90), wife of Edward Strutt (1801–88), Manchester College, York; Trinity College Cambridge BA 1823, MP for Nottingham 1852–6, Chancellor of the Duchy of Lancaster 1852–4, later 1st Baron Belper 1856. He was an authority on free trade, education and law reform.

2 Dated from Capesthorne reference in Letter 72 of 14 May [1850] (*Letters*, p. 116).

3 Capesthorne Hall, near Alderley Edge, Cheshire, was the home of ECG's friend, Mrs Caroline Anne Davenport*, née Hurt (d. 1897) and Edward Davies Davenport (d. 1847). She married Edward John Lyttleton (1791–1863), 1st Baron Hatherton, in 1852. See *Letters*, pp. 116, 178 (Letter 114 now redated [?11 May ?1850]). Sharps, p. 282.

4 Amelia Strutt's sister Maria Otter (d. 1891) married William Milbourne James (1807–81), who was educated in Glasgow and called to the Bar in 1831. His distinguished legal career culminated in his appointment, in 1870, as a Lord Justice of Appeal and a Privy Councillor.

5 MS copy extracts from Mrs Davenport's* lost Diary (September-November 1841) in John Rylands UL, Manchester, involve Mrs and Mrs Strutt, Miss Otter (later Mrs William James), and James Kay (later Kay-Shuttleworth) in educational matters, at a time when Samuel Greg came over from Bollington.

6 Letter 114 of [?11 May ?1850] gives the same information. Also, Letter 21, describing an earlier visit to the S. Gregs, is now redated [6 November 1849].

7 ECG here refers to Meta and Florence Gaskell, with her at Bollington. Marianne and Julia Bradford Gaskell, b. 3 September 1846, were at home.

8 W. M. Thackeray (1811–63). His heavily corrected holograph MS of three small pages is now in John Rylands UL, Manchester (ELM 728). It is headed: 'Mr M. A. Titmarsh's New Romaunt of the days of Chivalry', and begins, 'Messrs Chapman and Hall have the pleasure to announce for Xmas [1849] the publication of a highly chivalrous legend by the above author, entitled / Rebecca and Rowena / or / Romance upon Romance'. It concludes, 'Receive it kindly, you gentle novel readers who love poetical justice, and you honest children of large and small growth who still have a relish for a little play & nonsense, and the harmless jingle of the cap and bells / M. A. Titmarsh / Kensington December 15'. At the foot of the third page is a pen drawing of the jester, with cap and bells, sittingup in bed.

9 John Ogle Curtis. WG delivered his funeral address.

10 Probably ECG's friend (*Letters*, p. 148).

11 Love's *Manchester as it is* (1839) lists such schools in Ancoats and Chorlton on Medlock. The Lyceums were for the respectable working-class, with libraries and news-rooms, but also incorporating formal classes – 'for children and adults in the essential branches of education' in the case of Ancoats.

OCTAVIAN BLEWITT[1]

121, Upper Rumford Street
Manchester.
June 3 [1850].

Sir,

I should feel greatly obliged if you would have the goodness to bring under the consideration of the Managers of the Literary Fund the case of a poor authoress, whom I recently discovered living in very humble circumstances at Knutsford, in Cheshire, and who appears to me well deserving of assistance. Her name is Davenport;[2] and about 20 years ago she published a number of novels, which seem to me not without merit, and may in many instances, (as I happen to know they have done in some,) have afforded innocent amusement in hours when works of higher pretension, requiring greater exertion of mind, might have failed to do it.

For sufficient reasons, she has for many years lived apart from her husband, who, I am informed, has received several grants from the Literary Fund; but in none of these has she at all participated. Her sole dependence, a very precarious one, is on a small shop, the rent of which is 8£ a year, and on an annuity of 10£ payable during the pleasure of a relation.[3] Out of her very small earnings she has to support two widowed daughters besides herself, and, as she is now advanced in years, the struggle to do this is becoming daily more difficult. Her character is in every respect excellent, and from the pains which I have taken to ascertain her real condition, I feel assured that if you can procure her a grant from the Fund it will be conferred on a well-deserving person, and materially add to the comfort of her old age, which during the past winter has been very insufficiently supplied with either food or firing.

I remain, Sir,
Yours obediently,
Elizth C. Gaskell.

Octavian Blewitt Esq

British Library, Royal Literary Fund (case file 1247)

1 Octavian Blewitt (1810–84), Secretary to the Royal Literary Fund 1839–84; travel-writer and contributor to Victorian periodicals. The Fund had been set up in 1790 for the relief of needy authors, the first royal patron being the Prince Regent.

2 Selina Davenport published a number of novels, 1813–34. The deserted wife of Richard Davenport (case file 236), she went under the name of Mrs Granville in Knutsford (*Letters*, pp. 182, 265–6). ECG made a formal application in her name on 10 May 1850, supported by her cousin Mary Holland and the Vicar of Bowdon. £30 was granted on this occasion. ECG's step-mother, the widowed Mrs Catherine Stevenson, had been granted £40 in April 1829; she had claimed to be 'perfectly destitute' in January 1833. See *GSN* 23 (1997), pp 10–12, and Nigel Cross, *The Common Writer*, Cambridge 1985.

3 The owner of Otterden Place, Kent (*Letters*, p. 265).

Letter 88 to [?J. R. Beard] from 121 Upper Rumford Street redated [? June 1849 or 1850]

MARTIN SCHUNCK[1]

121, Upper Rumford Street
Manchester,
Tuesday, June 12 [1849 or 1850][2]

My dear Sir,

I am sure you will excuse my troubling you with this note. The time is drawing very near to the commencement of Mr Gaskell's holidays and I am particularly anxious that he should have the *complete* change of a journey to *some* part of the Continent. He has had much harassing business to transact lately, as well as the usual round of duties; and he is appearing to me to require a complete and exhilirating[sic] change both for health and spirits.[3] He did once hope to have joined you in some continental trip; but now he seems quite ignorant as to whether you will leave Frankfurt or not this summer; and indeed we hear such different reports of the state of the Continent and Germany in particular that I do not know how far, or *where*[double underline] any town would be desirable. In this dilemma I write to you, my dear Sir, trusting to your kindness to write a few lines to Mr Gaskell (who does not know I am troubling you,) telling him how far you really think of going to Switzerland; or if that plan should have fallen through, where you think a \ pleasant / journey might be taken with safety. *Here* as I said before all sorts of contradictory reports are in circulation, and one does not know what to believe. I saw Mr and Mrs Hannah Tayler[4], last night; they are very well, and so are our friends Miss Marslands. Mrs Robberds too is much better for her visit to Lytham. With kindest love to Mrs Schunck and Juliet, & compliments to Mr Gallenga,[5]

Believe me to remain, dear Sir,
Yours very truly
E. C. Gaskell

Address Martin Schunck Esq.

Huntington University Library, Irvine Collection

1 Martin Schunck* (1789–1872), merchant. See Marquardt, II. 43 n. 102.
2 Either day or date wrong if 1850.
3 Compare *Letters,* p. 141. Letter 88 perhaps of 1849 if it refers to WG's continental journey of 1839 (see p. 25 above).
4 Hannah Tayler was his daughter (cf. *Letters,* p. 204), probably standing in for Mrs Tayler, who suffered from epilepsy.
5 Antonio C. N. Gallenga (1810–95), author, revolutionary and Italian refugee who came to England in 1839, and married Juliet Schunck (1826–55) on 12 July 1847 (*L & M,* I. 124; Marquardt, II. 445 n.328, 475 n.380).

JOHN W. PARKER[1]

[12 January 1851]

I have received 'The professor's wife'[2] this morning, and I long to thank somebody for it, and I do not know whom. Does 'From the Author', mean from Auerbach himself? That would be an honour; but I fancy it only means from the translator; in which case the kind thought would still be most deserving of gratitude. May not I know who it is? Is it Mr Conington?[3] or whom? I do not know at all what is the right form for thanking in such cases, but I wish to say something more than a dry acknowledgement of the receipt of a book of which I have heard much, and from which I anticipate a great deal of pleasure. I want to thank for the kindness which makes the book doubly valuable. So please tell me who has thought of sending it to me? and excuse the informality of this note.

Yours respectfully
E. C. Gaskell

(My address is

Crix[4] near
Chelmsford.)
John W. Parker Esq
West Strand

Trinity College, Cambridge

1 John W. Parker (1792–1870), publisher of 445 Strand, London, from 1832. His business was sold to Longman in 1863.
2 William Whewell had translated a Black Forest village tale of 1848, *Die Frau Professorin* by Berthold Auerbach (1812–82), under the title of *The Professor's Wife, From the German* [*Dorfgeschichten*], J. W. Parker, 1851.
3 John Conington (1825–69), Oxford Professor of Latin.
4 Home of a wealthy Unitarian family, the Samuel Shaens, some of whom are described in *Letters*, pp. 50–1. Mrs Shaen seemed '*the* genius of the family; says all the wittiest things; shews by her way of quoting French, Italian, &c., that bringing up nine children has not obliterated her cultivation, and for her day she must have been a very highly-educated woman' (*L & M*, I. 144).

WILLIAM WHEWELL

Crix, near Chelmsford.
Janry 13th [1851].

Dear Sir,

I have several reasons for well remembering the pleasure I had in meeting you at Mr Milnes,[1] and am only too proud to think that you have not forgotten me. I suppose it may be possible to be overwhelmed with complimentary correspondents, but in the case of the letter which I received from you this morning,[2] I can only say that the expression of your approbation has gratified me more than any other circumstance arising out of the publication of the 'Moorland Cottage'.[3] I am very much obliged to you for taking the trouble to write, and tell me that you liked it. It is an encouragement of which I feel the honour.

I duly received 'The professor's wife' yesterday morning, and I was delighted at the acquisition of a book I had been much wishing to see; and even more at the kind thought of me, which some one must have entertained. You may believe me Sir, the pleasure arising from the idea of such anonymous kindness, has not been diminished by your note of this morning. I am deep in the interest of the natural, exquisite little story, and heartily thank the translator, who has given me the power of reading it in strong simple English. I had heard of Mr Satterthwaite's death in his lonely old age.[4] He was very ill when I was at Lan[5] caster this autumn. We followed you and Mrs Whewell as guests at Mr Mackreth's of Halton[6] ... I wrote the Moorland Cottage at Silverdale,[7] and I tried to convey the impressions made upon me by that wild moorland Scenery, with the Lake, and the Yorkshire hills girding it round < ... >

and believe me dear Sir

Yours very truly
E. Gaskell

Trinity College, Cambridge (incomplete)

1 Richard Monckton Milnes* (1809–85), later 1st Baron Houghton. For this meeting in London, when 'he began to talk about Silverdale & all our dear old places in the North', see *Letters*, p. 827–8.
2 In WW to ECG, 12 January 1851 (MS, Princeton UL), he thanks her for her 'very touching story' and jokes that she might be 'ambushed' by complimentary correspondents.
3 *The Moorland Cottage* was first published as a Christmas Book in December 1850.
4 Benjamin Satterthwaite, wine merchant and one of Whewell's oldest friends. See *EY*, pp. 206–7 [n. 37: read PUL for TCC].
5 The Trinity College MS ends here. The remainder was in an album sold at Sotheby's, 11 July 1996, lot 190 (part only transcribed).
6 Probably the Reverend Dr Thomas Mackreth (d. 1870), Rector of Halton, N. E. of Lancaster. We are grateful to Lancaster Public Library for this information.
7 A favourite country spot by Morecambe Bay (*Letters*, p. 119). The Gaskells first went there in 1843 (MA to C. E. Norton, Silverdale, 5 July [1858], Harvard bMS Am1088 13494). Cf. *L & M*, I. 69.

?ROBERT CHAMBERS[1]

[Crix]
[?January ?1851]

May I ask you a question without being considered obtrusive[?] My husband had the pleasure of meeting Miss Fanny Lewald[2] at your house, at the time of the meeting of the British Association in Edinburgh[3]. We hear that she is writing a series of papers descriptive of England and English society[4] in some German newspaper. Would you be so good as to give the name of the paper in which she writes?

Yours respectfully
E. C. Gaskell

My address is

Mrs Gaskell
S. Shaen's Esq
Crix near
Chelmsford Essex.

National Library of Scotland

1 Robert Chambers (1802–71), Edinburgh publisher and author of the sensational *The Vestiges of Creation* (1844). He established, with his brother William (1800–83), a famous publishing firm devoted to the publication of cheap and useful literature. A notable example was *Chamber's Encyclopaedia,* published in 10 Vols 1859–68.
2 Fanny Lewald (1811–89), novelist and travel writer. Lewald was in Edinburgh during the first two weeks of August 1850. She saw, but did not meet, ECG in Manchester in early September. See Peter Skrine, 'Fanny Lewald and Mrs Gaskell', *GSJ* 4 (1990), pp. 53–4.
3 Sketches published as *England und Schottland,* 2 vols, Brunswick, 1851–52.

~

Letter 100 to ?MA from [London] redated [9 February 1851]
Letter 115 to George Richmond from Plymouth Grove, Manchester, redated 24 February [1851]

~

JOHN M. F. LUDLOW[1]

Plymouth Grove
Manchester
March 18 [1851].

My dear Sir,

I think I shall return you your excuse of laziness as an apology for what I really am very much ashamed of, namely not acknowledging the receipt of your lecture[2] sooner. But every day has been brimming over with something to do lately, so I dare say my reason of laziness is no truer than yours, but that the fact is we have both been very busy with things that *must* be done. I like your lecture very much on a once reading; but I mean to read it again to try and understand the monopoly and competition part. I like exceedingly the distinction you draw between communism and socialism,[3] and the part where you say that enjoyments should be in common, affections and duties should belong to the individual. I am very glad if anything I said made you moderate any harsh expressions towards Mr Greg. I am sure if we only knew people better we should cease to be sarcastic or harsh in speaking of them; and besides harshness and sarcasm are neither good for ourselves, nor productive of right feelings in those against whom they are used; and {to}\ with / the indifferent, they almost always make such people take the part of the oppressed and harshly spoken-of. I do not think you would ever *like* Mr Greg; but I think you would respect him even though he were mistaken; and I am sure you would be sorry for a life which has been a series of disappointments.[4] Thank you once more for your book, & believe me yours very truly

E. C. Gaskell

Cambridge University Library, Add 7348/10/115

1 John M. F. Ludlow* (1821–1911).
2 The reference may be to one of the *Tracts on Christian Socialism* (later *Tracts by Christian Socialists*), published during 1850 and 1851 for the Society for Promoting Working Men's Associations.
3 Cf. *Letters*, p. 108: 'One of my mes is, I do believe, a true Christian – (only people call her socialist and communist) ...' For a contemporary definition, *NED* cites Ebenezer Elliott, 1849: 'What is a communist? One who hath yearnings, For equal division of unequal earnings.'
4 This would seem to be Samuel Greg.

MRS SUSANNA SCHUNCK*

Plymouth Grove
Wednesday
[2 April 1851]

My dear Mrs Schunck,

Will you and Mr Schunck give us the great pleasure of your company to tea on Friday Evening next? Dr Wm Carpenter[1] will be staying with us, and we hope to see one or two other friends. We should be particularly glad if you could induce Miss Brooke and Dr Schunck[2] to accompany you.

Yours very truly
E. C. Gaskell

Huntington University Library, Irvine Collection

1 Dr William Carpenter (1813–85), naturalist, zoologist and marine biologist, was staying with the Gaskells to lecture in the Royal Institution (*Letters*, p. 146).
2 On [7 April 1851] ECG mentioned 'the two Miss Brookes, one of whom is to be Mrs Edward Schunck' (*Letters*, p. 148). Judith Howard Brooke married (Henry) Edward Schunck (1820–93), son of Martin*.

~

Letter 96 to MA, from [Manchester], redated [?13 May 1851]

~

MARIANNE GASKELL[1]

[?13 May 1851]

< ... > (it is the cheapest and best by far in the long run,) & then take care of them. We all want *very* much to know when the holidays begin. Have you *no* idea? and suppose, for variety's sake, you put in a

few stops into your next letter.[2] Old Wm[3] is rather bitter today. The little ones and he are going to have a *boiled* sole for dinner. And now goodbye, old child, & believe me your very affecte

Mammy E C G.

Brotherton Collection, Leeds University (R. T. Dabbs deposit).

1 Letter 97b, from MS. Perhaps part of Letter 96.
2 Cp. WG to ECG (the only letter known between them), 25 July 1860, *GSN* 14 (1992), p. 10.
3 Perhaps the Gaskells' gardener, described p. 56 below.

?LADY KAY-SHUTTLEWORTH[1]

Plymouth Grove.
Tuesday [?24 June 1851]

My dear Lady,

I have been making enquiries about singing-pupils; but it is a bad time of the year, so many people are absent from Manchester; and perhaps this may be the reason why I meet with so little encouragement for your friend. One thing appears clear at any rate; that she will have no chance of ascertaining what chance she would have in settling here, if she came in the Midsummer holidays; or indeed any time between June and October. All masters, and schools lay their account to have very few pupils at that time, for so many families are at the sea. Some masters do not even profess to give lessons at that time, because they say it is not worth while to open classes, when the attendance is so very irregular and unsatisfactory. If Miss Wilkinson will wait till the close of the autumn I will try and find out what probability there would then be of her obtaining pupils, and do all that I can towards furthering her plans, should she determine on coming here. Mr Gaskell desires me to say how glad he shall always be to do anything in his power for you. We are very glad to hear that Mrs Holmes has met with a teacher.

Is Mrs Davenport with you? If she is I have a request which I should like to make to her, if the granting it will not be against her rules; we have a gardener, for whom we [have] a great respect, as he does a great deal of good amongst the poor &c; I find that he has a great wish to see the gardens at Capesthorne;[2] and I should be glad to know if this is ever permitted. He is a very simple, quaint Shropshire man, not very clever in his business, but singularly good and generous as far as he is able; giving time and strength as well as what little money he can spare.

Miss Brontë is I hope coming to us for a day or two, on her way from London on Friday or Saturday.[3] She sounds as if she were far from well to judge from expressions in her note, which I < ... >

Annotation Incomplete. The editor of CB's correspondence, Margaret Smith, cannot supply a location for the missing portion.

Princeton University Library

1 Lady Janet Kay-Shuttleworth* (1817–72), of Gawthorpe Hall near Padiham, Lancashire. ECG corresponded with her fairly often from 1850 to 1855.
2 In 1850 ECG preferred gardens with 'scarcely any grass ... laid out in terraces with narrow gravel walks, and beds of flowers beside them' (*L & M*, I. 235).
3 ECG had met Charlotte Brontë at Briery Close in August 1850. CB made her first visit to ECG from London at the end of June 1851, when 'the weather was so intensely hot, and she herself so much fatigued with her London sight-seeing, that we did little but sit in-doors with open windows, and talk.' See *Letters*, p. 123; *CBL*, II, ch. 9.

MRS MARIA JAMES[1]

Plymouth Grove
Manchester
Sept 1st [1851]

My dear Mrs James,

I was so very glad to receive your letter, and to hear that in spite of all alarms, everything was going on well, and hopefully. In the meantime your Petersham life sounds very pretty; with the little lady trotting about on the grass: does not it always remind you of the hymn of Mrs Barbaulds 'If you fall, little lamb, you will not be hurt. God has spread under you a carpet of soft grass.'[2] Perhaps these Prose hymns are rather a *dissenting* book, and may never have fallen in your way; and I don't like all of them, but my eldest girl used to quote that hymn to her second sister when she could just walk, so I think the pleasant remembrance of those days has fixed it in my mind. It *was* a great pity we could not see more of you and Mr James. And I wanted to have seen the baby again; babies at that age do so stride out of their identity.

We did a very unusual thing I fancy; we left London on the day that we planned; the Saturday following the Sunday on which we saw you. Then we again left Manchester, and went to a little Cumberland village called *Holborn-Hill*. As unlike the other Holborn Hill as it could well be! Much more like the village at the Baron of Bradwardine's gate named in Waverley[3] ; for it was built on the side of a hill, of cold grey stone houses, with certain appendages in the way of dirty ponds, which I remember Scott gives as characteristic of a Scotch village. Here we were very happy and quiet for a fortnight; when the desire to be among the purple Lake Hills that we saw at a distance, became too strong to be resisted, and we set off for a well-known farmhouse at Skelwith,[4] – near Ambleside; and the<re> we passed our remaining fortnight of absence from home. We have several dear friends in that pretty valley; and, although Mr Wordsworth's, and Mr Quillinan's deaths, each in their separate ways, make a great blank in the society there, yet the people who remain are in harmony with the place, and I don't know a neighbourhood where there is so much really enjoyable society.[5] Miss Martineau's book[6] is a small apple of discord; that is to say some of her old friends feel such a repugnance to it that they have declined meeting her except on 'questions of humanity'; but she was not at home when we were there, so there was no disturbance on her account among the set of friends.

We came home about a fortnight ago, and I have been very busy since, working up accumulated duties and sending my eldest girl back again to school. Now we are falling into the stationary routine, which comes quite like a rest, after the length of time we have wakened up every morning to feel it an open question 'What shall we do today?' It is settled *for* us now; and that is very peaceful. I am *not* writing anything. I am sorry for it, if it would have come in well for your amusement in your quiet time; did you ever read 'Santo Sebastiano or the Young Protector'[7] in 5 volumes? It *is* so funny and so ridiculous, that it carries one on through all that quantity of reading. I do not mean that it is *meant* to be funny, for it is rather highflown, and very sentimental; but the heroine speaks broken English all throughout, and faints so often &c &c, and yet there is a degree of interest in the story to carry one along. It is a very old novel, written by one of Geo. 3rd's daug<hters> I forget which; and I knew a very clever, sensible lady who read it ov<er> and over again in each of her 14 confinements. They say Thackeray is coming to lecture here;[8] do you know if it is true? If he does come, I am afraid he is coming to the Royal Institution where we shall not hear him.[9] Perhaps you will allow me to write again soon.

Yours ever very truly
E C Gaskell

Pennsylvania State University Libraries
Printed by Andrea Lewis, *English Language Notes* 30 (1992–93), pp 53–8.

1 Maria James (née Otter). See p. 49 n. 4 above.
2 Anna Letitia Barbauld, née Aikin (1743–1825), a friend of the Turner* family (*EY*, pp. 89–90, 352). ECG slightly misquotes from Hymn II of her *Hymns in Prose for Children* (1781), which had many editions. 'The peculiar design of this publication is to impress devotional feelings as early as possible on the infant mind' (Preface).
3 Victorian maps show Holborn Hill near Millom in Cumberland, far from London's Holborn. Chapter 8 of Walter Scott's *Waverley* (1814) has no dirty pond.
4 Mill Brow farm, where ECG had stayed in summer 1849; she met Wordsworth, Edward Quillinan, J. A. Froude, Max Müller and a Mr Morier there. See Sharps, pp. 88–9; Waller, pp. 34, 59–61.
5 E. g., Harriet Martineau*, Mrs Fletcher*, Mrs Arnold*, the Davys and the Richardsons (*Portrait*, pp. 95–6).

6 *Letters on the Laws of Man's Social Nature and Development* (1851), based on the ideas of Henry Atkinson (1781–1829). ECG's friend Catherine Winkworth* thought it sad that 'she should have gone so wrong'; Susanna* believed that 'mesmerism has really a little touched her brain' (*L & M*, I. 276).
7 *Santo Sebastiano, or, The Young Protector,* published anonymously in 5 vols, 1806, was by Catherine Cuthbertson, author of sentimental and gothic romances. No connection with a daughter of George III has been traced.
8 His 'English Humorists of the Eighteenth Century' was given in Manchester in September and October 1851.
9 The Royal Institution, erected in Mosley Street in 1823, was Manchester's finest centre for exhibitions and lectures. Andrea Lewis suggests that the Gaskells had not paid the substantial membership fee. See *Letters*, p. 203.

AGNES SANDARS (née PATERSON*)[1]

Plymouth Grove.
Octr 12th [?1851]

My dear Agnes,

Mr Gaskell, I find, is at liberty on Friday next, and I know \ so well / how much pleased he would be by an invitation from you, that I am writing, as may seem rather strange, to remind you of the wish you expressed to have him to stay with you.[2] I know there is nothing he would like better; but he would not believe in the least that you would care to have him if *I* said so only.

Ever yours very affly
E. C. Gaskell.

Mrs Susan Kearney

1 Agnes Paterson* had married Charles Sandars (1813–77) on on 22 April 1851 (Family Bible; *Letters*, p. 151 n. 1).
2 She seems to have gone to live at Edgewick (*L & M* , I. 330), near Coventry and Leamington (*Letters*, pp. 152, 209).

AGNES SANDARS (née PATERSON*)

Tuesday.
[?December ?1851][1]

My dear Agnes,

I am afraid we can't stay with you in going *up;* much as we should like it, & much as my dear husband is gratified by your wish to have him; wishes of this sort always coming as a matter of surprize to his sense of humility. We go up on Friday next, by a slow cheap train. Wm returns on Saturday the 5, leaving Emily[altered word][2] on the Friday to go to the Tagarts[3] at Hampstead, & see Marianne. I stay longer; how long I don't exactly know; – I have an idea that if I am asked I *may* stay to bring MA down on the 23rd[2 an alteration]; but so much will depend on 'futurity' that I don't know.

But I should exceedingly like to spend a quiet day or two with you, dear Agnes, and thank you much for asking me. *Supposing* MA should be with me, you see we \ she and I / should only occupy one of your spare rooms, – but perhaps in case I staid until the 23, it might not suit you for me to come?

Any how I know you would tell me truly if any thing occurred to make it inconvenient. I should so like to see you in your own house, my dear lassie. And we have long wanted you to come to *us*, your next visit to Manchester, & Mr Sandars to come when he could, – but that we will talk over when we *meet* – which is very pleasant to think of.

Wm is quite grudging not being able to go *this* time. He sends his best love; and so do my three girls. I wish you could hear Meta give her drawing-*lecture*. It is such fun. Our kind regards to Mr Sandars.

Yours very affecly
E. C. Gaskell

Mrs Susan Kearney

1 MA is perhaps still at school in Hampstead. See *Letters*, p. 173.
2 Probably Emily*, wife of William Shaen*, of 8 Bedford Row, a large, gloomy house with ground floor used as offices by the Law Association (*L & M*, I. 292).
3 Edward Tagart (1804–58), Unitarian minister of Little Portland Street chapel. He married a prosperous widow, Mrs Thomas Martineau (née Bourn); their daughters were Helen and Emily. They moved to a grand home in Hampstead in 1851, but ECG did not approve of the 'rude quarrelsome tone' there in February 1851 (*Letters*, p. 145).

ANON

Plymouth Grove.
Decr 30 [?1851]

Dear Sir,

I have received the enclosed letter from Mr Travers, whose name is perhaps known to you, as a clergyman who seceded from the Church of England; and was afterwards for a year an assistant to Mr Fox at Finsbury Place.[1] Since then Mr Dukinfield Darbishire was advised by Mr Frank Newman[2] to engage him as tutor to his children;[3] but he was afraid of Mr Travers' want of positive opinions on the subject of religion; and I fear since that \ time / that poor Mr Travers has had a great struggle to *live*; he has a very pretty young wife (married at seventeen against her relations wishes, who have utterly cast them off in consequence of Mr Traver's change of opinion,) and three or four very lovely children.

I know little more of him than his looks; he appears thoughtful, refined, and almost femininely[?] gentle; and as if he suffered acutely from the position in which he has been placed by his conscientiousness. Mr Gaskell fears much that this lecturing plan would not answer; but knowing that although Mr Travers conceals the fact, it is an attempt to find bread, I want you to be so very kind, as to give the proposal a little consideration, and to tell me if you think there would be any chance of its succeeding. I am sure you will excuse the apparent intrusion of this note; I did not know any one else so well qualified as you to give an opinion.

Yours truly
E. C. Gaskell.

Haworth Parsonage Museum

1 In 1849 the Rev. Newenham Travers was engaged as assistant minister at South Place, Finsbury, but by 1851 someone else was in post (R. & E. Garnett, *Life of W. J. Fox* (1910), p 295). Cf. *Letters*, p. 353, where ECG says she knows a clergyman with 'a character just like' her Mr Hale in *North and South* (1854–5).

2 Francis W. Newman (1805–97), Professor at Manchester New College 1840–46, and at University College London 1846–69, author of *The Soul* (1849) and *Phases of Faith* (1850). See esp. *Letters*, pp. 87–9; *L & M*, II. 391–2; Angus Easson, *Elizabeth Gaskell*, London, Boston and Henley 1979, pp.13–15.

3 James Anthony Froude (1818–94) had recently been a tutor in the Darbishire family (*Letters*, p. 83). Author of *The Nemesis of Faith* (1849), a story of disbelief and passion, he later became the biographer of Carlyle and a major historian. Froude and his wife Charlotte Grenfell have also been suggested models for characters in *North and South* (Sharps, p. 220 n. 93). See also Angus Easson, 'Mr Hale's Doubts in *North and South*', *RES* 31 (1980), pp. 30–40.

AGNES SANDARS (née PATERSON*)

Plymouth Grove
Wednesday
[11 February 1852]

My dearest Agnes,

I think you will perhaps like to hear something of my doings lately; of my visit to Capesthorne in the first place, and of the Amateur Play in the second. You know Mrs Davenport[1] was going to be married on the 11th of Feb, so she wrote to ask me to come and see her a long time ago, & renewed the invitation when she knew the girls were gone. So I went. I joined her at Macclesfield as she was coming home from Staffordshire, and we drove together to Capesthorne (5 miles,) and on the way she surprized me by praising the President,[2] and believing from all her private information from Paris, that he was going to try to be the

Napoleon *of Peace* (whatever that means.)

At Capesthorne I found her uncle, Mr Charles Hurt, her cousin Miss Emma Wolley (*such* a nice girl do you know her? daughter of a clergyman near Nottingham, her father's name was Hurt.) Mr Osborne the Principal of Rossall School and a very clever agreeable ugly man, and Mr Weigall a clergyman at Macclesfield. It was very pleasant *that* day, but the next our two nice clergymen left, and a *very* [double stress] stupid Mr and Mrs Blore[3] came. He is an architect, who has made his fortune, and his wife has been a beauty. Her daughter is married to a Mr [?]Careton a minor Canon of Westminster. Her dresses and jewels were something to wonder at, & as we could not find out anything to talk to her about, Mrs Davenport brought down all *her* wedding finery for public amusement.

A set of diamonds and opals, and a set of diamonds & emeralds – (the first far the most beautiful & far the most expensive too,) a green velvet cloak down to her heels lined & trimmed with miniver 6 Indian shawls of various kinds, the lowest priced one 90 guineas – one a soft green exquisitely embroidered in pale lilac & gold another a crimson or Indian red ditto in white & gold, another a blue scarf, ends in gold – *oh dear*! they were so soft and delicate and went into such beautiful folds. Her gowns (only 7) were in London, – a white moiré antique a maize coloured do trimmed with black lace & coral-branch 'fittings', a blue silk with white lace, a green velvet, a black cloth (the only one with a waistcoat whh her dress maker told her was only to be worn with a *cloth* dress, &[?] rather going out in that) a dark blue silk, & a mouse coloured ditto. Her \ everyday / petticoats were all made without bodies, set into a round band [small sketch] with *pretty* jacket bodies with little skirts [small sketch] loose; trimmed all round with Valenciennes and with *high-bodied* jackets with *long* sleeves for high bodied gowns. They looked so pretty. Then her tip-top best were with embroidered stomachers. Everything else was as pretty as could be, only nothing else so very new and fancy[?]. Mrs Blore was in ecstasies at every separate piece of finery, & put on rings till she could not bend her knuckles to try & come up to Mrs Davenport's grandeur. She left on the Monday, & good go with her! *I* hope I shall never see her again. Such a testing of everything by money I never heard in my life. If she heard of[altered word] a man being successful, she asked directly what income he had, & neither Mrs Davenport nor I could knock any other idea into her head.

Then on the Monday your friend Mr Nathan Hubbersty,[4] and Mr Alfred Arkwright came; I liked the latter much. I did not like the former, & could not imagine how any sister of Mrs Davenport's could have married him. On Tuesday I went, with much regret to the Sam Gregs. *He* was ill, and they thought my coming might cheer him up, and do him good. When I came home on the Friday – (somewhere about Febry 5th) I found a note from Mrs Davenport, begging me to come back on the Saturday & stay with her over the Monday, when the tenants were to give her their presents; she had expected Lord H to be with her, but now she found he could not. So I went. I expected her to meet me at Chelford but she was not there & I took a fly. On the way I met another fly, and out jumped a nice-looking elderlyish gentleman, & introduced himself to me as Lord H. He had come down from London by the express train to see Mrs D unexpectedly as she had said she [was] not quite well, staid 3 hours at Capesthorne, & was going back by the evening express.

Sunday was a very nice day at Capesthorne. The S[unday] School come into the beautiful conservatory[5] to be taught, and are clean wholesome country-looking children in the midst of camellias, & [?]sweet-scented geraniums &c &c – the chapel through the conservatory – the pew a parlour with low luxurious sofas, a fire place &c, – how easy it seems to be good compared with a long wet[?] tramp down to a close school-room, full of half-washed children, – that's very wicked is it not? Then in the evening after dinner the children & choir sing chants in this same beautiful conservatory (almost as large as that at Chatsworth, & we opened the library door, \ which went into the conservatory / & heard them singing in a green bower[.]

Then on Monday came all the present giving [-] a present for every servant – for nearly all the out of doors servants too, for the school children[.] We arranged all: desks for the men-servants, nicely fitted up, – gowns for the younger, fur-cloaks for the older women servants – ladies' companions for the school-girls, double-bladed knives for the boys: & towards 12[altered to 2] o'clock came a poor idiot to whom Mrs D had been very kind. 'Silly Billy' dancing along the park dressed in a gay horse-cloth, and preceding a band then came 200 school-children, – then women, then men upwards of 500 in all. Mrs Davenport put on her beautiful cloak and went and stood in the raised & covered terrace in front of the house, while they formed a semicircle round her. Then an[altered word] old farmer came forwards, crying & trembling with a little speech of farewell & a bracelet (value 60 guineas) the farmers had bought for her, – & she made a little speech, & then *she* cried – then came forwards the labourers who had bought a clock for her dressing-room but she could not answer them for crying – then her house-servants – a church service all in purple & gold; then the school children a silver vase for flowers; then they all came to wish her goodbye; but as we saw they each had their separate private thanks to[altered word]render for some little kindness done to them; it was proposed they should raise a cheer that she might not be utterly worn out; & the band played Should auld acquaintance &c, – and then the crowd went to have refreshment. All that day we were helping Mrs Davenport, & the next morning she & I & Mr Crackenthorpe (her co-executor) went to Chelford; and now I shall leave Lord Hatherton to finish out the story;

you'll find a letter from him, among those I send which I thought you might like to see. I can't read Meta's all over again, but I am sure I may trust to your & Eliza's discretion *if Meta is imprudent*; and I should like to have all the letters back again sometime.

Yes! we went to see the Amateurs;[6] we asked Mr Forster & Dickens to stay here, but they could not. Mr F came up however to call, & told us they expected to gain 1000£ by these 3 nights (2 at Liverpool, where he was not going to act.) He said the play was *very* heavy, and so it was. He gave me a private admission for any friends, so I took the Winkworths & we escaped the crowd. We sat right under the very much raised stage, on the front row, & I think I got Braidized[7] for I had *such* a headache with looking up The play is very very long too – 3 hours & a half, & they omitted 1 scene. And very[altered word] stupid indeed. The farce was capital. Dickens was *so* good, & Mark Lemon, – D Jerrold[8] was not there and Mr Forster was sadly too long over his very moral sentences in the play.

We hope to see you here dear Agnes before long. I must beg your pardon for my writing. I have *so much* to do just now I can hardly get through it. My kind love to Eliza. Wms remembrances to both of you.

Yours very affely
ECG.

Our remembrances to Mr Saundars[*sic*].

Mrs Susan Kearney
Printed in *GSN* 10 (1990), pp. 4–9.

1 Mrs Davenport* married Lord Hatherton on Thursday, 11 February 1852.
2 Louis Napoleon, who had assumed power in a coup d'état in October 1851.
3 Mr Weigall is described below (p. 165). Edward Blore (1787–1879), architect to Queen Victoria, was employed by Edward Davenport in the 1840s to remodel and enlarge Capesthorne Hall.
4 Nathan Hubbersty (1803–81), headmaster of Wirksworth grammar school 1832–51, called 'Mr *Hubble-Bubble*' by Charles Darwin's sisters.
5 The conservatory was by Joseph Paxton c. 1845, predating the one at Chatsworth.
6 Dickens's amateur players gave a single performance at the Free Trade Hall in Manchester on 11 February 1852: Bulwer-Lytton's melodrama *Not So Bad as We Seem* and Mark Lemon's farce *Mr Nightingale's Diary*.
7 Dr James Braid of Manchester first coined the term 'neuro-hypnotism' in 1842; it was shortened to 'hypnotism' in the following year, though 'Braidized' continued in use.
8 Mark Lemon (1809–70) and Douglas Jerrold (1803–57) had very similar careers in acting, writing and journalism. Jerrold was a playwright, and Lemon a founding editor of *Punch* (1841), to which Jerrold contributed. Both performed for Dickens; on this occasion Jerrold defected from the company (*CD Letters*, VI. 601).

ELIZABETH FLETCHER[1]

Plymouth Grove, Manchester.
February 17 [1852]

My dear Mrs Fletcher,

The accompanying memorial will show you what has been done in accordance with your advice; but I am afraid Government have little to spare; they talk of a pension of 50£ only, which is very well as a recognition of his merits,[2] but it will be but little for him to live upon, – he his wife two children and two \ fatherless / grandchildren, with his generous dispositions. There is to be some public meeting in London; where I do not know. I hope it will be announced in some widely spread newspaper. Meanwhile his friends here are collecting subscriptions to be invested in an annuity for him; there was a public meeting held here last week the Mayor in the chair, and 380£ subscribed there and then, but since then but little has come in, and that principally from poor people, *convicts* and prison officers, and although their 'mites' are a beautiful testimony, yet we want the knowledge of this subscription to spread far and wide, and be as 'national' a thing as we can. There are many people who know Mr Wright at Gosport – can you my dear Mrs Fletcher interest any of them? He is very feeble and out of health. *We* are all well, thank God.

Yours very affecly
E. C. Gaskell

Address Mrs Fletcher Sir John Richardson's Haslar
Gosport.

Manchester Central Library
Printed and put in context by Joan Leach, 'Thomas Wright, the Good Samaritan', *GNL* 3 (Spring 1987), p 15.

1 Mrs Elizabeth Fletcher* (1770–1858). She had been involved in philanthropic work in Edinburgh, but now lived at Lancrigg, Grasmere (*Letters*, p. 206).

2 This and following letters concern the efforts by ECG and others to obtain support for Thomas Wright (1789–1875), a working-class 'philanthropist of no ordinary cast of mind, profoundly pious and humble-minded, with the most energetic devotion to the principle of doing good. He devotes every hour he can spare from his employment, that of an overseer of an iron foundry, to visiting the prison, and doing all he can to reclaim convicts from their evil ways. He has been the means, under God's grace, or reclaiming more than four hundred, and is so self-denied that he seldom allows himself more than four hours out of the twenty-four for sleep. He is a hale man at sixty-six years of age' (Mrs Eliza Fletcher, *Autobiography*, ed Mary Richardson, 1875, pp. 293–4).

RICHARD COBDEN[1]

Plymouth Grove.
Feb. 19 [1852]

My dear Sir,

Mrs Schwabe[2] begs me to write a sort of supplement to her letter to you about our dear Mr Wright; but when she tells me all she has said I scarcely fancy I can add anything to it. We are all (Mrs Bagshawe, Mrs Schwabe and I,) rather in dismay at a letter of Mr James Heywood[3] in which he speaks of 'arranging a meeting in London to ask Government for \ a / *50* £ pension.' And we were hoping for 200£, but quite expecting one hundred. I do hope some one will persuade Mr Heywood that the greatest kindness he can do to Mr Wright will not be to propose any sum, but leave it to Government to fix it; for I suppose they cannot give[altered word] *less* than 50£, can they?

You can not think how beautifully Mr Wright bears all this talking about himself; quite simply, and gratefully, and in a very humble and pious manner. It makes one long all the more to put larger means, both of time and money, at the disposal of one, who would use them so well. Besides after this public stir, many, who have given him 5 or 10£ occasionally before, will think themselves exonerated from doing so any more; so if we do not exert ourselves he may be worse off than he is. The worst is that here every one has a separate plan; and these plans clash against each other. I hardly know why Mrs Schwabe wished me to write to you, for I am afraid I am only taking \ up / your time, and I *know* you are as anxious to succeed in this matter as we are. If you think of anything I can do, I shall be most glad to hear of it, otherwise pray do not trouble yourself to acknowledge this letter. *Could* I ask any one to attend this London meeting? I don't think I could, but I would gladly try if you can suggest any one.

I saw Mrs Davenport of Capesthorne just before her marriage.[4] She showed me a great packet of letters of congratulation, and then said 'I think I would have given half of these up for a line or two from Mr Cobden.' Your portrait hangs up among her 'heroes' in her bedroom. I thought that perhaps that you had not heard of her engagement in time enough to write. May I send my kind regards to Mrs Cobden? & will you excuse the purposelessness of this letter? from yours most truly E. C. Gaskell

Annotation 1852

West Sussex Record Office (Cobden Papers 17)

1 Richard Cobden* (1804–65), Manchester manufacturer and MP for Stockport from 1841. His wife was Catherine , née Williams (1815–77), a governess.

2 Erasmus Darwin wrote on 10 May 1855 that Snow Wedgwood went about like Mrs Schwabe*, carrying stamped envelopes so that she could write notes in the intervals of business. See also p. 35 above.

3 James Heywood (1810–97). founding member and first President (1835–40) of the Manchester Athenaeum. From a prominent Liverpool banking family, he was elected MP for North Lancashire in 1847. A member of Cross Street chapel and President of Manchester New College 1853–58.
4 To Lord Hatherton, on 11 February 1852.

Letter 180 to James Crossley from Plymouth Grove, [Manchester], redated February [1852]

OCTAVIAN BLEWITT

Plymouth Grove
Manchester. March 17 [1852]

Sir,

I take the liberty of requesting that you will bring the case of Mrs Davenport a second time[1] under the consideration of the Committee of the Literary Fund, and at the same time kindly give her the benefit of your support. As her claims were admitted on the former application I need hardly trouble you with going over them again, but I may just mention that, by the recent death[2] of her husband, Mr Richard Alfred Davenport, (who, as I believe you are aware, was likewise an author,) those claims have been considerably strengthened. His death, from the manner of it, has been a great shock to the poor old lady, and has in no way made the slightest addition to her scanty income, which amounts to only 10£ a year, and is altogether dependent on the kindness of a friend.

The assistance afforded to her by the Literary Fund, two years ago, enabled her to open a small shop,[3] which together with what the two widowed daughters earned by plain sewing yielded for a long time sufficient for their support; but, of late, owing to changes beyond her control in the little town where she resides, this resource has utterly failed; and to add to her difficulties, trying enough before, both her daughters, at all time feeble, have fallen ill on her hands, and she is reduced to very great straits.

The only course which seems open to her is to turn that portion of her small house, which is now occupied as a shop for the sale of tapes thread bobbins &c, into accomodation[*sic*] for a lodger; which a moderate degree of help from the Literary Fund might enable her to do; and I venture to say, from my knowledge of the circumstances, that a grant could scarcely be more seasonably, or in many respects, more worthily bestowed.

I remain, Sir,
Yours truly
E. C. Gaskell

British Library, Royal Literary Fund (case file 1247)

1 Supported by Lucy Holland, Susan Deane* and, ecumenically, Robert Clowes (Vicar of Knutsford, 3–4 years knowledge). £20 granted. See pp. 49–50 above, and below.

2 Documents note that he was born 18 January 1877, and died 25 January 1852 at Camberwell.

3 Cp. *Cranford,* ch. 15: Miss Matty's success with a shop in the last number of *Household Words,* published on 21 May 1853. 'Knutsford you know is Cranford, only the people here don't at all approve of its being called Cranford' (MA to C. E. Norton, Knutsford, 1 September [1857], Harvard bMS Am1088 3488).

OCTAVIAN BLEWITT

Plymouth Grove.
March 22. [1852]

Sir,

I wrote to you last week on behalf of Mrs Davenport of Knutsford, who wished to apply for relief to the Literary Fund; but since I wrote I have heard a few additional particulars of her case from my cousin Miss Holland[1], which perhaps you will allow me to add to what I mentioned before. One of her widowed daughters, in very despair of obtaining even food enough at home, took a place in a small tradesman's family as servant of all work. She had never been accustomed to hard labour, and was not strong when she went to this place; and now the medical man says she is likely to be an invalid for life. The other daughter remained at home to assist her mother; and these two poor women have tried *many* ways of earning a subsistence; they have had a little shop, taken[alteration] in plain sewing, kept a temperance coffee-house, opened a dance-school &c.

When Mr Davenport died he left behind him rather a valuable collection of coins, papers, books &c; and Miss Holland imagined that perhaps some of these things might come to Mrs Davenport; but on enquiring a will was found in the surgeon's hands leaving every thing to his natural son, not even naming his wife and daughters. But the surgeon stated that this son was well off and might possibly be inclined to assist his father's widow. This however he refuses to do. With an apology for troubling you with this note,

I remain, Sir,
Yours obediently
E. C. Gaskell

British Library, Royal Literary Fund (case file 1247)

1 Mary Holland was the senior.

RICHARD COBDEN*

Plymouth Grove
March 22, [1852]

My dear Sir,

I do not know if any one has told you of our progress with regard to Mr Wright. 2700£ subscribed; and the list still kept open! The poor old man behaves so naturally and beautifully about it all; if he troubled himself at all to think how he *should* behave he could never be so true and simple. But last Thursday he gave his family a great fright by coming home so completely exhausted that it was necessary to undress him, and lift him into bed. He keeps the same long hours at the Foundry, and in addition he has much anxiety in teaching all the new hands who are taken in to supply the place of the turned-out men. However this illness of his, which Mr Turner said arose completely from exhaustion<,> brought out some good; for there had been a little delay and hanging back about the best mode of investing the money collected; Mr Saml Fletcher wishing it to be sunk in an annuity, and Mr Schwabe quite sanctioning Mr Wright's own wishes that it should be placed in the funds or somewhere where his family could benefit by it after his death. But after this fainting fit &c it was evident that there was no time to lose; and Mr S. Fletcher gave up his opinion (are not you glad of it?) and he and Mr Schwabe went on Saturday to give Mr Ormerod notice that Mr Wright was going to leave him; how soon I do not know, but I hope *very* soon. So much for the subscription!

Now may I take up a little of your time in telling you about the pension? Do you remember an old lady, a Mrs Fletcher to whom Mrs Schwabe introduced you two or three years ago in London? She was staying with us and was introduced to Mr Wright last autumn. She has been much interested all along in the affair; and as she is now staying with her son-in-law Sir John Richardson at Haslar.[1] The clergyman of the parish is, it seems, a brother of the new Home Secretary; and Mrs Fletcher interested this *revd* Mr Walpole about Mr Wright so much that he wrote her word that he had spoken to his brother about it, and that although he could make no promises yet that the memorial, if re-signed by the magistrates, and addressed to Lord Derby, should have Mr Secretary Walpole's best attention & help.[2] Mrs Fletcher enclosed this note to me; and I sent it to the Secretaries about a fortnight ago. But owing to Mr Bagshawe's illness, – Mr Hulton's indifference, and Mr Railton & Mr Megson's considering themselves as concerned in the private Subscription only, it seems that nothing has been done; (at least had not, on Friday.) On Friday I received another letter from my dear warm-hearted Mrs Fletcher, enclosing a letter from Mr Hornby of Winwick, who had sent the memorial & all the papers concerning Mr Wright which I had sent him \ at Mrs Fletcher's desire /, to his nephew

Lord Derby; who, he says, is *quite* willing to give the matter his best consideration, (I don't know how much that means in diplomatic parlance) if brought before him in the proper formal manner; he (Ld Derby) has read the memorial with 'great interest'; and Mr Hornby suggests that the application should be formally made *before* the Easter holidays, – and says something about the Chancellor of the Duchy of Lancaster being the \ most / proper person to present it formally.[3] Mr Heywood at any rate seems very indifferent about the whole affair; and with these sort of messages from Mr Walpole and Lord Derby, will it not be a pity (even allowing for a great deal of diplomatic talk) not to try the chance of getting a pension.

I went over to see Mrs Schwabe about these letters, when I found no person seemed taking the business up; it was Friday {Eveng} Afternoon, & Mr Schwabe was in Wales, coming home that eveng – and I left the letters there for her to show to him; and I called on Mr Megson & Mr Railton to ask them to do what they could to get the Memorial re-signed; and I am sure Mr Schwabe would do *something* energetically, only Mrs Schwabe says he is very languid and unwell. But you said, and Mr Hornby partly confirms you, that it should be presented by someone favourable to this ministry. – now I know so little about either parties or men, but it comes into my head that Mr Monckton Milnes would feel interest in such a case (I know he would in *some* of his moods,) and that he was perhaps a Derbyite? – I am afraid I have taken up too much of yr time, and yet I have a little more to say, and a favour to ask of you.

Some friends of mine are much interested in the distressing case of a M. Avrill formerly a member of the House of Assembly, but now suddenly banished from France, & even sent at request of the French government out of Switzerland.[4] He was a Professor in one of the Departments; and does not know English or could perhaps teach. He has one son a boy of 15, and a wife, a Swiss lady, who has been brought up as a designer for Swiss & French muslins; she believes she could support her family if she could obtain employment, and has applied through these friends to me, to know if any house in Manchester would be likely to take her designs, – which she has sent to some firm in London, who have copied them and returned them to her; so now she does not like to let them out of her hands again.[5] I thought you would perhaps allow her to call on you, and that you could judge if her designs *are* what wd be used in Manchester; but I have said nothing about this plan of mine to *her*, so that it will be no disappointment if you should be too much engaged to allow her to call on you for this purpose.

They live near Soho Sq. I do not know the exact address, but it shall be put in this letter; and *if* you should feel it right to spare this time to her, perhaps you would kindly write and tell her *when* she might call on you, and ask her to bring her designs. I wrote to Lady Hatherton, and gave her your message. I must apologise for the length of this note. I have really tried to make it short. Will you be so kind as to give my best remembrances to Mrs Cobden, & believe me to be,

Yours respectfully and truly
E. C. Gaskell

There is no occasion for an answer of any kind. Mme Avrill does not expect to hear from you; and I shall fully understand your being too busy to see her. And the first part is only to put you fully au fait as to Mr Wright's affairs.

Mme Avril[*sic*]
27 Gerard Street,
Soho Square.

West Sussex Record Office (Cobden Papers 17)

1 See p. 58 n.5 above.
2 A new government was formed by the 14th Earl of Derby (formerly Lord Stanley) in February 1852, with Spencer H. Walpole as Home Secretary.
3 In 1845 Charles Henry Somerset, Lord Granville, assumed this office.
4 Louis Napoleon's coup d'état in December 1851 was followed by arrests, transportations and expulsions from France.
5 ECG tried to place Mme Avril(l)'s designs with the Schwabe calico printing business, but unsuccessfully (*Letters*, pp. 185, 850).

ANON

Plymouth Grove
March 22 [?1852].

Sir,

I am sorry to say I do not approve of the plan of making any fresh appeal on behalf of Mr Wright just now, because I am almost sure such a step would be very injudicious. There was some difficulty (as I personally experienced), in procuring the small sum necessary a few months ago, in order to replace what had been absolutely necessary for Mr Wright's \ expences / during the year. I heard repeated complaints, and many remarks which made me regret the necessity for what was then being done. And I am quite sure that any appeal to the Ladies of Manchester in any public way will call out, – not any ill feeling to our dear Mr Wright, – but many thoughtless sayings which if repeated, will not only hurt him, but injure his influence. Already he feels the want of those donations which people formerly bestowed upon him for the furtherance of his benevolent objects. Many seem to think they have done enough in subscribing in the first instance to the fund, and now, no longer give him what his generous hand so often needs. I am not expressing my own opinion alone, but those of several who love and honour our friend. It seems to me that a far more real, though less ostentatious kindness on the part of the ladies of Manchester wd be to furnish him with some of the money which he needs (or which his friends feel that he needs and ought to have, rather than spend his own income,) for his works of charity. I am, Sir,

Yours truly
E C Gaskell

Mrs Lucy Magruder
Letter 147a to MA from [8 Bedford Row] redated[?5 June 1852]

WILLIAM JOHN BEAMONT[1]

Lesketh How[2]
Ambleside
Thursday [October 1852]

My dear Sir,

Please I want to make use of the penny-post to ask you a question, and I would not trouble you with \ writing more / more[*sic*] than a 'Yes' or 'No' just as you would \ answer me / in conversation. Is that friend who accompanied you Mr West-*lake*, or Mr West*cott*; and if he be Mr Westcott is he Mr Brooke Foss Westcott? I am just plunged into a book which I found interesting my friends here. Elements of the Gospel Harmony.[3] With kind regards to Mr and Mrs Beamont, believe me, dear Sir

Yours very truly
E. C. Gaskell

I suppose you have left Cambridge – or else I have a young friend just entered at Trinity to whom I {lik} should like to give a letter of introduction to be presented to you. He is a Rugby boy & hopes in process of time to take orders. His name is Archibald Davy.[4]

Warrington Central Library

1 William Beamont's son, William John (1828–68), educated at Eton and Cambridge. He became Vicar of St Michael's Cambridge in 1858, but died of an illness contracted when travelling in the Middle East.

2 Home of Dr John and Mrs Davy* (née Margaret, daughter of Mrs Elizabeth Fletcher*), where on 24 July 1849 Wordsworth had written in her autograph book.

3 See *Letters*, pp. 203–4, where ECG met Beamont with 'a Mr [John] Westlake [1828–1913] ... both Fellows of Trinity'. Brooke Foss Westcott (1829–1901), who later became Bishop of Durham, was then a Master at Harrow. *The Elements of the Gospel Harmony* (1851) was one of his earliest theological works.

4 A son of Margaret Davy, at Rugby from 1846, Trinity B. A. 1856; vicar of several Cheshire parishes (d. 1890).

LADY BELL[1]

Plymouth Grove,
Manchester
Monday, Novr 29 [1852].

My dear Lady Bell,

Is the situation of a governess which you mentioned to me still at liberty? I mean for Lady Mounteagle's nieces. I forget the exact name, but somewhere in Kent. Because if it is, I think I know of a lady who may suit. She is a Miss Charlotte Winkworth (cousin to Susanna Winkworth, the Editor of the English Life of Niebuhr, whom I think you met at our house:)[2] Miss Charlotte Winkworth is 25 years of age; has learnt German during several years residence in Dresden, where she also leant music very thoroughly, scientifically as well as practically; French she knows, having resided 6 or 8 months in Paris; so it is 'full fair & fetisly, *not* after the school of Stratfor<d->atte-le-Bowe'; drawing she can teach without a master, indeed she has thought of becoming exclusively a drawing-mistress, and her cousins, who are most desirous to speak of her truthfully and not poetically, speak most highly of her general intellectual attainments, temper and (last not least) strong religious principles. She is Church of England <of> course. They tell me she is *not* <p>repossessing in manner; 'not ladylike, yet not at all vulgar; very straightforward, and to the point.' She has '*finished*' the daughter if Mr Bacon, Q. C.; and Mrs Bacon would gladly answer any questions; having a very high opinion of her; and having urged her to ask 100£ < ... >

Pierpont Morgan Library (Gordon Ray Collection)

1 Perhaps the wife of Sir Charles Bell, née Maria Shaw, of Edinburgh. See *CD Letters*, VII. 439 n.

2 Charlotte was the daughter of Thomas and Eliza Winkworth, who went to Germany with her sisters Fanny and Jessie in 1843, accompanied by Susanna Winkworth*. In May 1850 she was so happy in her situation at Walmer that she had 'no idea of leaving it'; in September 1853 she was seriously ill at Boulogne (*L & M*, I. 68 n., 221, 408).

MARY GREEN[1]

Private – Saturday
[?20 November 1852][2]

My dear Mary,

I should not *think* from the terms of Mr Gunton's note that there was the slightest chance of his relenting, or rather of his being *able* to relent, for I give him credit for wishing to come;[3] however I will try, and see what I can do. Meta has taken Emily's box to Miss Elliston's; I am sure she must be wanting it this cold weather. How gay you sound!

Tell Annie & Ellen[4] Meta tells me Mary Ewart[5] who, they know is *her* great musical authority admires Miss Neissent's[?] singing very much. I met her once at the Howitt's, & I did not particularly like *her*.

Meta is in a great state about Esmond – . I don't know if Annie & Ellen are equally greedy about it. Not that we have any of us seen it, or are likely to see it this long time, but Meta is Thackeray-crazy just now. Mr Scott (to whom Thackeray gave it,) likes it very much indeed, I believe.[6] Ruth '*has* yet to be written', which is an expression I used only this morng to Wm before your letter came. I mean it is far from completion and I feel uncertain if it ever will be done, – I have written a good deal of it – \ it is not ended even in that way. / amt[?]

I am so far from satisfied with it myself, that I don't know how much to rewrite, or what to do about it; & was as much startled as you could be by the advertisement. However it will not hurry me, & *until I have thought it out fully* I shall *not* write it, & if I never think it out it will never be either written or (*consequently*) published. And I am very very busy even for the *mechanical* writing, – much so for the thought required. However it may all come in a minute, & it may never come; so you may fancy that in this state seeing the advertisement, or rather hearing of it \ I have not *seen* it / is an annoyance. And if & when it does come I give you warning I doubt if it is a book that you will like to have in your family. This is *forced* from me, and all by Chapman's impatience.[7] I don't want *to be* talked to about it, & I don't want it talked about. It only disturbs me utterly; and I expect I shall have grief & annoyance enough to go through about it, & lack all the strength I can muster to do {wel[?]} right. However it is not yet written & may never be.

{Tell} I would rather have all this considered private please dear Mary; except that *dis*courage any putting it down on the part of my friends please. – I had hoped to have come over to Knutsford before this subject of pain to me was broached. Now I shall not come, because morbid or not morbid I can't bear to be talked to about it. So don't let us say any more. If I decide on *never* finishing it I will tell you all about it, – if not, you will know soon enough.

We (Meta & I) have enjoyed ourselves heartily at the Lakes, only I was very ill one week, partly with worry about this book, – & thought I was going to have the typhus fever. I had such deadly headaches, & faintness, but I got better after the Earthquake.[8] Our visit was very quiet in every way, but very happy. Just the thing I want sometimes, – one day like another, & no press & accumulation of business coming down suddenly upon one till one yearns for a rest, which is not, & never can be here on earth. I am ashamed to contrast my occasional thorough weariness, with Wm's quiet cheerful perseverance in the daily & weekly hard work he has to go through. Mr Robberds is gone too

Yours affectly
E Gaskell

Interrupted

Dr R. Jamison

1 Mary Green*, née Brandreth (c. 1803–71), wife of Henry Green (1801–73), the scholarly Unitarian minister of Brook Street Chapel, Knutsford, 1827–72. She was one of ECG's most intimate and trusted correspondents, whose letters were first described by Mrs Joan Leach, in '*Ruth*: A subject of Pain', *GSN* 8 (1989), pp. 12–16.
2 Cp. *Letters,* p. 210. Meta saw the Ewarts*, and ECG the Scotts, on Saturday 13 November.
3 Manchester music teacher for ECG's daughters.
4 Mary Green's daughters.
5 Friend of ECG who had guessed her authorship of *Mary Barton* (1848). See *Letters,* p. 67.
6 Thackeray gave *The History of Henry Esmond* (3 vols, 1852) to Alexander J. Scott (1805–66), first Principal of Owens College, Manchester. Scott had married Ann Ker (d. 1888) in 1830.
7 In October 1852 Chapman told her that John Forster* (his literary adviser) 'had given him the MS. of Ruth and that the first 2 vols. *were printed*; all complete news to me!' (*Letters,* p. 205).
8 ECG refers to 'the day of the Earth-quake' in a letter to Marianne, [15 November 1852]. See *Letters,* p. 210 and n.

MARY GREEN*

[c. 25 December ?1852][1]

My Dearest Mary,

I do so wish I could come over to Knutsford. I have hoped & tried, – for after that book of mine[2] is published (this week I think) I don't feel as if I ever could. And yet yr letter today makes me wish more than ever. I shd so like to 'compare notes' and talk things over with you. Yet every day brings even more than it's full work; and – we have many visitors coming this Xmas, and an inefficient servant. (I must have another *waiter*, good serving cleanliness & *thoughtful* head wanted.)

A Austin[3] is here; stays till the 11. MA comes home tomorrow or Tuesday[?]; Miss Banks (Mrs Lalor's sister) and Eveleen Lalor come next Monday; Harriet Schwabe, & Miss Martineau sometime after new year's day.[4] And we have many evening engagements, & all Meta's clothes to see after. I can *quite enter* into your feeling about living in Knutsford being a trial to your girls; it is a trial which they will doubtless get over; But just at present I could see that they, (Ellen in particular) were feeling it much, & I did not wonder. Our girls will have a trial different in fact, but I fear more enduring in its consequences, – I mean the constant interruption & dissipation in whh we live, – (you understand how I use the word dissipation. I mean there is always so much to break in upon our leisure & time, and such a want of rest in the house. And *here* too we have a *vast* quantity of poor gossiping talk *out* of our own immediate circle; and the young people are frivolous & worldly. When I come back from the people round Ambleside, Arnolds[5] & Davys &c, I am always so much struck with the want of spiritual mindedness, – so I must call it for lack of a better word. But I believe the truth is we must conquer our circumstances, not seek to change them; at least not too much.

John Philip[6] will be a great gain to you all; only for his sake I hope his stay at Knutsford & in that occupation will be but temporary. If I can I shall joyfully accept yr & Susan Deane's invite for the girls this Xmas holidays; only Meta goes on the 20 [January] (not a month,) and we have many visitors coming before then. I write any how, my thumb being absolutely *swollen* with writing. I will bear you in mind about more boys; and in the right way too, so don't let your delicacy be alarmed and afraid of 'dear Mrs Gaskell's injudiciousness'. (I invent the words, I never heard of any one using them – Oh! I go heartily on Mr Martineau's side;[7] and I cannot bear Mr Kell's letters,[8] & don't think he is right either.

Do you care to know the names of writers in the Christmas extra No. of H Words?[9] Dickens the *two* first. 'Somebody's Story' by a poor young man in London named Thomas. Host's Story a Mr Edmund Ollier. Nurse's Story mine, (I hope it frightens you – Selina[10] just come in –

Yours very affecly
ECG.

Dr R. Jamison

1 See Letter 147, *Letters*, pp. 219–20. (Note new dates of Letters 147a and 147b: [?5 June 1852] and [?22 September ?1854].)
2 Probably *Ruth*, published 10 January 1853 (Smith, p. 58). ECG 'always talks of her personages as if they were real people', Catherine Winkworth* wrote on 9 February 1853 (*L & M*, I. 383).
3 Annie Austin, daughter of Alfred Austin (1805–84), became Mrs H. C. Fleeming Jenkin by 7 March 1859 (*Portrait*, pp. 159–60).
4 Mrs Lalor's school, with about twelve pupils and four women-servants, was at Holly Hill, Hampstead; Miss Banks was Marianne's 'schoolmistress & dearly loved friend' (*Letters*, pp. 238, 803). Miss Martineau was Harriet's* younger sister Rachel (1800–78); Meta was to begin at her Liverpool school on 20 or 27 January.
5 ECG used to stay with the family of Mrs Mary Arnold* at Fox How, near Ambleside, built for them in 1834.
6 Mrs Green's son.
7 See p. 58 above. Harriet Martineau's brother James had scathingly but anonymously repudiated her anti-theological views in the Unitarian *Prospective Review* 7 (1851), p. xxvi.
8 The Reverend Edmund Kell (1799–1874), Unitarian clergyman at Southampton 1853–74 and controversialist. ECG would probably have had misgivings about his *Earnest Appeal to Unitarian Christians on the Duty of Supporting their Own Religious Institutions* (1848), but he produced many pamphlets and sermons.

9 This extra number of *Household Words* was a chain of ten stories, each attributed to a different narrator. Dickens's 'The Poor Relation's Story' and 'The Child's Story' began the sequence; they were followed by W. M. Thomas's 'Somebody's Story' and ECG's 'The Old Nurse's Story'. Cf. CD to ECG, 17 December 1852 (*CD Letters,* VI. 822–23).

10 Probably Selina Winkworth.

EDWARD CHAPMAN

Monday [?27 December 1852]

Oh! you tiresome Mr Chapman – to go and send me Ruth which I *have* read, and not Francis Croft[1] which I have *not* read; and it's a rainy day, and I want a new book! you don't deserve the amusement of reading the accompanying letter, but you may have it nevertheless if you will only return it safely.

Yours most truly
E C Gaskell

Fales Library, New York University

1 See *Letters,* p. 854. *The Fortunes of Francis Croft* (1852), by Bayle Saint-John. A novel of incident, involving crime, sexual and other adventure, and the intermixture of social classes. 'Many ... scenes argue power and reflection and though they are often of a hard and objectless kind, the writer seems to have some moral or critical objects in view' (*Spectator,* 7 May 1853).

MARY GREEN*

Wednesday
[?early January ?1853]

My dear Mary,

I am writing without Emily's knowledge to beg that you will allow her to stay a little longer. The reason I did not ask her for longer at first was because we have one or two friends who have promised to let me know when they can come and stay with us, but I have arranged with all those that they should choose their own time, only give us a week's notice; so that we have a week clear before us at any rate; and in that week i.e. on Friday there is a very pleasant invitation to meet the Deanes[1] at the Railton's, & *the* last 'open (Monday) evening' at Mr Tayler's,[2] which is sure to be good. So pray don't expect her, & write & tell her so, will you, dear Mary, for I am sure this change is doing her good, & one and all are so glad to have her here; her sweet thoughtful unselfish nature does us all good to see, & to be near: and I think she enjoys herself even when we are quite quiet.

She is looking better, every one says; more colour in her face, and not so very pale as she was at first. I was a little afraid she fancied *she* had prevented my going to Lady Hatherton's, & I could not explain to her why I did not go; which was because Marianne is engaged to go with us to Dr Bell's[3] on Thursday night; and I ascertained that Mr & Mrs Joe Ewart[4] would be there, and as none of the parties had met before since two years ago, I thought that the disagreeable encounter would be helped over by my being there.

I write in a great hurry. I always have to do almost.

Ever yours very affecly
E C Gaskell

Dr R. Jamison

1 See next letter.
2 The decision to move Manchester New College to London was taken in December 1852. The Taylers were removing to London in September 1853 (*L & M*, I. 400).
3 Dr Charles W. Bell. See *Letters*, p. 363, for the three Miss Bells and their brother.
4 See ECG to MA, [25 September 1852] (*Letters*, p. 201) for the forthcoming marriage, 'sometime this winter', of J. Ewart to a Miss Molineaux of Lewes.

ELIZA PATERSON*

Plymouth Grove
Monday morng
[3 January 1853]

My dear Eliza,

We are making an *attempt* at a *small* dance on the 4th (Tuesday) for A Austin's sake, & also because the children (17 – & 15) of my dear friends Mr & Mrs Deane of Knutsford[1] will be {there} then at the Railtons, V. Park.

Will you come and *help*? You will be *very* kind if you will. We have some proper grown-ups besides but most will be from 17 to 20 years old. Moreover I want to make the smallest preparations consistent with hospitality; not from absolute shabbiness, but because I have rather an inefficient staff of servants, and shall have the house full of friends staying here.

Do people get a cook to cook the supper? (In the school room, for about 30 people, standing about not sitting,) and what do cooks charge? – and who is a nice one? And again can you send me a carte of your supper the other night, and tell me how many you were altogether? I am just off to Knutsford, Flossy with me; come home tomorrow afternoon, and shall be glad of any wisdom you can impart.

Yours very affecly
E C Gaskell

1 Emily (b. c. 1836), Arthur (b. 7 June 1837), and Margaret (b. 25 June 1838) were children of Dr Richard Deane's first marriage, which is presumably why ECG mentions him, though he had died in 1851.

ELIZA PATERSON*

Sunday [?c. 16 January ?1853]

My dearest Eliza,

I *am* so glad; so very *very* glad. Dear Agnes! how happy it makes my heart to think of her. God bless her & her child![1] How famously she must have got on! Meta scampered after Mr Satterfield on coming home from chapel, & he had tears in his eyes about it – I am rejoiced you missed the anxiety & came in for the rejoicing. Write again, there's a darling in the course of this week. I need the comfort & *great* pleasure of thinking of you two girls, & your faithful love for me through 'good report & evil report'. William is just as glad as I am, & the children are full of the whole affair. Agnes will get strong before 'hatching time' comes; that 'anxious period of the year' as Mrs Wilmot[2] calls it. No time for more, but dear love to you both, & congratulations to Mr Sandars.

Yours most truly affectionate
E C Gaskell

Mrs Susan Kearney

1 Agnes Sandars's first surviving child, John, was born on 15 January 1853.
2 ECG had been staying with Emma, née Darwin (1812–98), wife of Edward Woollett Wilmot (1808–64), at Hulme Walfield near Congleton, Cheshire, in December 1852 (*Letters,* pp. 216, 816).

Letter 647 (undated) to ?Wilmots now dated [?early 1853]

MARY GREEN*

[c. 25 January 1853]

My dearest Mary,

Your letter was such a relief (first) & pleasure afterwards. I had fancied from what Miss Mitchell had said of what Mr Green had said that both you & he wd be shocked. – I could not wonder, for I am sure I should have been repelled by hearing that a 'tale of seduction' was chosen as a subject for fiction, – *that* was the opinion I dreaded; – I felt *almost* sure that if people would only read what I had to say they would not be disgusted, – but I feared & still think it probable that many may refuse to read any book of that kind – (I am writing in such a hurry I can't stop to make myself clear,) but yet I did feel as if I had some thing to say about it that I *must* say, and you know I can tell stories better than any other way of expressing myself.[1]

This is all a muddle, but I am trying in my heart to arrange how I can do my duty (i.e. stop at home this eveng for a class of Sunday School girls) & have my pleasure (i.e. go and dine at the Schwabes with the Scotts, Mrs Fanny Kemble[2] –) & I find I 'cannot serve two masters', but must just stop at home – and now that's decided – I've written to Mrs S. – so now I can make myself distinct to you, about the Music Master, – I cannot hear of him in any quarter – the Schwabes, intimate & musical friends of the Hallé's, have never heard of such a project; Darbishires ditto &c – I have not yet fairly gone to Mme Hallé[3] because the Hs have been in great distress about Mr de Mery's death,[4] – but in a day or two I will quite finally ascertain. Meta goes to Miss Ms on the 27th. If you liked ever to have MA by herself \ without Meta / I could & should be glad for her to have the change (after teaching from Friday afternoon to Monday morng

Yours very aff
ECG

Dr R. Jamison

1 See Uglow, p. 338, and *CH Gaskell,* pp. 208 et seq., for expressions of disapproval of *Ruth,* though generally responses were favourable. In October Charles Darwin, turned 'quite an abandoned novel-reader', began *Ruth* and found it 'quite charming' (*CD Corresp.,* V. 161).

2 Frances Anne Kemble (1809–93), American actress, 'extra quiet ... not allowed to correspond with her two children till they are of age' (Susanna to Emily Winkworth*, 25 January 1853. *L & M,* I. 379).

3 Charles Hallé (1819–95), German immigrant in 1848, whose orchestra soon became a Manchester institution. He had married Desirée Smith de Rilieu (d. 1866) in 1841.

4 De Mérey, a Hungarian noble, and his wife were friends of the revolutionary leader, Lajos Kossuth, exiled with him in 1849. De Mérey 'died of virulent typhus' in 1853, leaving four children in poverty (*L & M,* I. 333, 379). ECG helped place his wife's 'Wild-Flower of the Danube' in *Household Words* for 5 June 1852.

WILLIAM BEAMONT

Plymouth Grove
Manchester
February 2 [1853]

My dear Sir,

I was exceedingly interested by what you told me, on Saturday night last, relative to the letters which have been lately discovered at Lyme Hall;[1] and I named some of the circumstances to a friend of mine, Mr Forster, author of the 'Lives of the Statesmen of the Commonwealth'.[2] He is now engaged upon a new 8vo edition of the book for the Messrs Longman, – who would of course join in any guarantee for the

safety of any papers entrusted to him. And he is most anxious to have permission to inspect, and take extracts from such of the MSS discovered lately in Mr Legh's possession, that may relate to the period between James 1st and the Restoration. Or if it is objected to {that}\ trust / the papers into any but the owner's keeping, could you tell me if facilities < >
without difficulty to yourself, and without the danger of being involved in any unintentional impertinence on my part. Name this request to Mr Legh [,&] you would, I know, confer a great favour on Mr Forster, an < ... > [Signature cut off last leaf]

Endorsed Feb 18 /1853

Warrington Central Library

1 The letters are those referred to in W. Beamont's *A History of the House of Lyme* (Warrington 1876), pp 150–1, 154.
2 Forster's* work was a series of biographies of seventeenth-century figures, first published under this title in 5 vols, 1840.

ELIZA FOX*

P Grove
Monday [pre–14 February 1853]

My dearest Tottie,

I *have* been *so* ill; I do believe it has been a 'Ruth' fever. \ The beginning of / last week my own private opinion was that I shd never get better I was so utterly weak after it, but I have perked up, & this cold weather braces me. I suppose you abominate it. I shd never have left yr last letter unanswered so long if it was not for that – but oh! I was so poorly! I cd not get over the hard things people said of Ruth. I mean I was just in that feverish way when I cd not put them out of my head by thinking of anything else but dreampt about them & all that. I think I must be an improper woman without knowing it, I do so manage to shock people. Now should you have burnt the 1st vol of Ruth as so *very* bad, even if you had been a very anxious father of a family? Yet *two* men have; and a third has forbidden his wife to read it; they sit next us in Chapel & you can't think how 'improper' I feel under their eyes. However some people like it. Mr S. D Darbishire for one. However I won't bother you or myself any more about it.

I don't like the notion of Brighton, dear, because it's so far away nobody knows where, at least *I* don't, and I can't fancy you there at all. It may be the best place for all that, and I fancy the Mallesons are nice people, & it's as well to go when you have ready-made friends: but is it not awfully dear as a place to live in; & yet people never take that into account in the school-bills.[1] Wm says railways have equalized prices.

I have been interrupted a dozen times, & now must try & write up my letter *any* way. I want a letter from you or else I should not have written for I have little enough to say. We have capital accounts from Meta, & Marianne *does* famously with the children; especially as her only two dances as yet have come on a *Friday* allowing her a good long sleep on Saty morning when the children have no lessons. Florence has music lessons from Mr Gunton, but MA hears her practice. Today is the day for a little brood of chickens to be hatched; one has already popt out. We are very proud of our early brood, tell George. They are capital *Spanish* eggs as we had no CCs[2] ready, as they have only just begun to lay, and that very sparingly on account of the cold. We had 128 eggs in Janry but shan't have so many this month. Mrs Schwabe has been here today; not that she has told me any news. We are to dine there to meet the Relskys[?] (hang 'em! on account of Mme Von Beck) on Wednesday; & there was a dance on [altered to] Thursday but there is some death in the Schwabe family which prevents *dancing*, but not *eating*. Marianne does not see the difference, or why if people can dine they mayn't dance.

This is a most stupid letter, but we are expecting Helen & Emily Tagart every minute by some train or other, & that prevents one's writing on any *large* subject for fear of interruption. Besides all I write for is to get a letter from you. Mr Robberds comes home tomorrow; he has been away 3 months, so Wm has had enough of it, has not he. – Send me some London news, – the world here is very flat, & my heart is very flat. Goodbye my own dear Tottie

Yours ever very affect.
E C Gaskell

Pierpont Morgan Library (Gordon Ray Collection)
Letter 150, formerly printed from a defective typescript copy, like almost all to Eliza Fox*, now from MS.

1 Eliza Fox was thinking of starting a school in late 1852 (*Letters*, p. 224).
2 Probably Cochin-China birds, the largest breed available in 1853 (*Enc. Brit.*, *cit. NED*). See also *Letters*, pp. 816 (a reference to 'prize black Spanish' birds), 301 (for Dorkings), and *CD Corresp.* V. 293, 415.

GERALDINE JEWSBURY*

[c. 14 February 1853]

My dear Geraldine,

I have not been out for a week or more; – but have just sent to ask about Ma Y, & shall put in Mrs Owen's answer as a PS; only please the Athenæum did not come, (I crave for it in my shut-up-in-the-house-with-influenza-state) & Villette, 3 vol, did go some days ago to Southport.[2] Did you really send the one, & have you received the other? The two Tagarts are here; Helen going to be married to a Mr Harvey at

Liverpool &c &c.[3] I do hope your cold is better – I am so stupid with mine, & so weak.

Ma Yendan[?] is at Mrs Owen's; has been since Wednesday, – has a pretty figure & 'looks very ill – sallow Ma'am' – no time for more –

Send the Athenæum I beg –
Yours ever affly
E C Gaskell

Annotation [c. Feb. 1853].

Duke University Library

1 Geraldine Endsor Jewsbury (1812–80), unorthodox Manchester novelist. Her first novel *Zoë* (1845) achieved notoriety for its treatment of female passion; it was followed by *The Half-Sisters* (1848) on the theme of the woman artist, an industrial novel, *Marian Withers* (1851), and by further novels on feminist and social issues. She was a major reviewer of fiction for the *Athenaeum*.
2 Charlotte Brontë's *Villette* (1853) had been sent to Southport, where Geraldine Jewsbury was then living.
3 See*L & M,* I. 384 (letter of 14 February 1853). Enoch Harvey was a Liverpool solicitor, a relation of WG (*Letters,* p. 224).

MRS MARY RICH[1]

Plymouth Grove,
Manchester
March 10 [1853].

My dear Mrs Rich,

I have just so many things to say to you, that I don't know where to begin. I have been like blotting-paper for a long time, soaking-in all your letters, but apparently retaining no impression. First of all about the chimney-sweeps. I have spoken about it everywhere, and so has Mr Gaskell, and we have threatened to turn{ed} informants, and receive the sum of 10£ on every such conviction.[2] It is one of those cruelties which people's consciences seem dead to, and it is very difficult to attack them in any way save through their pockets. Then Mr Spottiswoode[3] *sent* me your note, but had not time to call; which we \ were / very sorry for, as all who saw him (Schwabes, Scotts[4] &c) seemed to like him much. Lastly Miss Gillies; whom I did see; but only the day before she was leaving Manchester; however she is returning here in April, when I hope we may have some opp[ortunit]y of becoming further acquainted with her.

I have often heard of you through the dear Scotts. Sometimes we go two or three months without seeing anything of them; and then we plunge into intercourse and see each other pretty frequently for a week or a fortnight; and that has been the case lately; partly owing to Mme Pulsky, and the Leonard Horners,[5] & Mrs Fanny Kemble being afloat. Through them (the Scotts) I have been very glad indeed to hear of

Snow's continued improvement; although, as yet, this year much have been very trying to her, with it's odd, unnatural changes. I wish she would write to me herself, and tell me how she is, and what she is doing; I should give a letter from her a great greeting, and consider it as a sort of pledge that sometime or other she would pay the long-projected visit.[6]

Meta has gone to school at Miss Martineau's, and rather to our surprize began to be happy from the very first. We had prepared her, and ourselves for a good deal of suffering at first from the change from all home habits, to which she was particularly wedded, and of which she is almost a bigotted admirer. Now I must make my letter worth reading by telling you more particulars about some of the people you care for.

We met Mr & Mrs Scott last night in a very crowded room, where we none of us had anything to do, but nod at each other's heads, seen above an indiscriminate multitude of shoulders. He looked well, but weary of his present circumstances, & Mrs Scott said he was anxious to get home to Mrs Fanny Kemble, whose last night it was, and who was all alone at Halliwell Lane. She has been reading the Midsummer Night's dream with Mendelsohn's[*sic*] music,[7] at the Concert Hall, Hallé conducting; and she has been visiting the Scotts meanwhile. I was with Mrs Schwabe & Mr Wright a good while on Tuesday about a poor prisoner, so I can answer for their being well, at least I hope Mr Wright is by this time, just then he looked very pale with anxiety about the man, as it was then represented *in the newspapers* (it was not the truth) that a confession Mr Wright had obtained from him was to be used as evidence against him on his trial; and Mr Wright was very much distressed at the probable lessening of his influence over the prisoners &c. However the end of the day was so good & satisfactory that I trust our dear old friend is looking much better now.

Mr & Mrs Schwabe went to Glyn Garth on Wednesday, but return on Saty, and on Monday Mrs Schwabe & I are going on a New Bailey[8] expedition, and then I take my children up to early dinner at Crumpsall.[9] Mr Gaskell will be in Northumberland. They plan now that Harriet shall go for a year or two to Germany at Midsummer. Edward is doing satisfactorily at the preparatory school at Rugby. Where are the Prices now? Rugby reminded me of them. Ah! Mrs Rich! I am in such scrapes about Ruth; which is apropos of the Prices which was apropos of Rugby; so don't think I rush off without *some* connexion in my own mind. But Mrs Arnold would tell me about the Prices, only I hear of her disapprobation of Ruth, and dare not write to her.[10] I can't think how it is, that I who am such an arrant coward, *must* always go headlong into people's black books; and *good* people's too. Well! if I have but got the smallest edge of the wedge in, any how, I will be thankful to God.

What are you all doing? I do so want to hear something direct of you, & my dear Mrs Wedgwood. I nearly forgot to tell you that I have been ill, & a prisoner for five weeks with the Influenza. My kind love to

42 Chester Terrace, especially to Mrs Wedgwood. Mr Gaskell desires his kindest regards to you & her and Mr Wedgwood. My dear love to Snow

Yours dear Mrs Rich
very affectionately
E C Gaskell

Keele University Library (Wedgwood MS E58–32354)

1 Mary Rich*, née Mackintosh (1789–1876), 'full of information and of wit'. She had been staying with ECG in November 1852 (*L & M*, I. 368).
2 Under legislation of 1840, informers were paid half the fine of anyone convicted through their evidence of employing under-aged labour. In 1853 Lord Shaftesbury proposed an amendment to strengthen the Chimney Sweepers Regulation Act of 1834, but was unsuccessful.
3 One of the King's Printers (see esp. *Letters*, p. 237).
4 Alexander J. Scott and his wife. Their Manchester address was Cheetham Hill.
5 Leonard Horner (1785–1864), factory inspector and educationist.
6 'Snow' Wedgwood had suffered an attack of rheumatic fever at the Scotts. She commented upon Mrs Scott's 'irrepressible sociability'. See also J. A. V. Chapple, 'An Author's Life: Elizabeth Gaskell and the Wedgwood Family', *BST* 17 (1979), pp. 287–92.
7 Mendelssohn's overture to *A Midsummer Night's Dream* was first performed in 1829 and the incidental music in 1843.
8 A Manchester prison sited at Salford. Built in 1787, 'the New Bailey prison is one of the best conducted prisons in England; and the order and cleanliness which prevail are no doubt highly conducive to the healthy state of the prison' (B. Love, *Manchester as it is*, 1889, p. 164).
9 The Salis Schwabes* had Glyn Garth on the Menai Strait, 'a splendid place, – far more striking inside than Crumpsall' House on Cheetham Hill (*Letters*, p. 238), where they entertained famous visiting performers. See Uglow, p. 161.
10 Bonamy Price (1807–88), schoolmaster at Rugby under Thomas Arnold 1832–50 and then Professor of Political Economy at Oxford 1868–88.

MISS ?MAGGIE BELL[1]

[22–24 April 1853]

My dear Miss Bell,

Thank you exceedingly for your kindness, but I find that Miss Bronté[sic] would rather enjoy going to the Amateur Performance;[2] at least such is her feeling in the quiet repose of today. I think it is most likely that the 'songs and sketches' will be a strong temptation for us to call on you on Monday or Tuesday (probably the latter,) but if you will allow me (after our sympathetic dislike of early callers,) to come, for that once only, before twelve & after ½ past eleven on either day, I shall be very much obliged to you. Marianne will be only too glad to come for the practising at some not very distant future time. With very kind regards, I am ever

Yours most truly
E C Gaskell.

Princeton University Library

1 Maggie Bell had asked ECG to look at her MS novel in January 1850 – 'she is a nice person, and I know I once wanted help sorely, or else I am *so* busy ... ' (*Letters*, p. 101). See also MB to ECG, Aberdeen, 8 May 1850 (MS, Princeton UL).
2 CB came to ECG on 22 April for a week. The Manchester Shakespearian Society staged *Twelfth Night* in the Theatre Royal in aid of Manchester Free Library on Monday 25 April 1853. See Barker, pp. 726–8.

MRS ANN COLTMAN*

Plymouth Grove
Manchester
May 2 [1853].

My dear Mrs Coltman[1],

I received your most kind letter, and was truly glad to hear that you approved of 'Ruth'. Indeed I have reason to be very well satisfied with the reception she has obtained, especially as I was trenching on rather delicate ground. You may fancy then that I was very glad indeed to have the assurance of approbation from one, whom I knew of old, to dislike any thing forward or immodest or unwomanly.

I will bear dear Mrs Charles Frye's wish in mind. It sounds as if it would be a most charming house for any little Indian, or orphan girl, and you may rely upon it I will not forget her if any opportunity comes in my way. My eldest girl has left school, and is a 'come-out' young lady, & governess to her two little sisters. My second is at school still at Miss Martineau's, at Liverpool, and my two little ones at home.

I often want to hear something of Miss Jane. I have called once or twice at Dr Parkes', but never when she has been in London.[2] Mr Gaskell desires his kindest remembrances to you, & with my kind regards to Mr Coltman, believe me to remain my dear 'Miss Anne',

Yours truly & affectionately E. C. Gaskell

Pierpont Morgan Library (Gordon Ray Collection)

1 Ann Coltman*, née Byerley(d. December 1865, aged 76), one of ECG's teachers at Barford and Avonbank, Stratford-upon-Avon.
2 After the death of Maria Byerley on 2 April 1843, Jane stayed at Greville Place, Kilburn Priory, with Dr Edmund A. Parkes, a relation who was to be with Florence Nightingale* in the Crimea. Jane seems to have gone on a round of visits before her death in 1868, aged 75.

JOHN FORSTER*

Plymouth Grove,
May 3 [1853].

My dear Mr Forster,

I was going to write to you today. I should have written sooner, but for a reason, which I will tell you bye and bye. First however I want to thank you for your story. What relation was Mrs Dawson [?Dawes] to Mrs Fitzherbert, – or any?[1] Mr Gaskell has seized upon your letter, and locked it up, and considers it his property, – and the story too, – am I not generous to give it up, and allow him the use of it? I did not know what 'Friends in Need' was, at first; you know the HW people always make titles for me.[2] Oh dear! I suppose I must come to the fact about publishing Cranford. About that unlucky letter I wrote to Mr Chapman, & part of which he repeated to you so falsely, – well! When I received your first letter, I wrote to him very indignantly, not to say angrily; I don't remember the exact words, but I know it was something to the effect that I would have nothing more to do with him; and of course no communication whatever has passed between us since.[3]

Now I would rather go on with him, for many reasons; but there is the one great reason of his falsehood in this instance; and also that after what I said it is very 'awkward' to be the first to make advances. For this reason I did not write at once, as I should have done, to thank you for your advice and offers of help. I seldom see the Household Words, and I do not even remember if I have written six or seven Cranford papers, – (they have one, the final number, still unprinted,) and I do not know how large a vol it would make, nor in the very least do I know how much would be a fair price for it. All that I must leave to you, kind friend as you are. And whatever you think right I will do, – only for the reason named above I would rather any one else had it than Mr Chapman.

You never say what you thought of the Railway Library[4] suggestion? Mr Gaskell is so excessively against any change of any kind that I have not liked to reply to a kind of message I had through Miss Brontë; and that reminds me of her warm message back to you. I gave yours to her, – and she said 'Tell Mr Forster, he is not so easily forgotten, as he seems to imagine, – I thank him for his remembrances & send him mine.' She staid with us a week; from Thursday to Thursday. She did not care for Manchester sights, which was a great relief; I like her more & < ... >

Huntington University Library, HM 52614
MS first half of Letter 155 (*Letters*, pp. 230–1), printed by Dorothy W. Collin, 'The Composition and Publication of Elizabeth Gaskell's *Cranford*', *BJRUL* 69 (1986), pp 94–5.

1 Collin suggests reading 'Mrs Dawson [?]Dawes'.
2 'Friends in Need at Cranford' was the title given to the penultimate instalment of *Cranford* in *Household Words* for 7 May 1853.

3 In her analysis, Collin gives a detailed account of *Cranford*'s publication and the disagreements with Chapman.

4 Routledge published a Railway Library, but *Cranford* appeared during 1855 in Chapman & Hall's 'Select Library of Fiction', a similar series of cheap reprints.

~

Letter 149 to [Catherine Winkworth*] redated [c. May 1853]

~

?LEOPOLD RANKE[1]

[? June ?1853]

Since we heard yesterday that Professor Ranke was engaged on a new work[2] it has struck me that it might be a mutual accomodation, (while at the same time my friend would esteem it a great honour,) if Miss Winkworth, the translator and editor of the Life of Niebuhr,[3] were to undertake the translation of Professor Ranke's forthcoming work. I am aware that this honourable task has hitherto been most ably fulfilled by Mrs Austin;[4] but, unless I am misinformed, her present state of health must incapacitate her from engaging in any literary work. To any one acquainted with the progress of English literature during the past year I suppose I need hardly go into details respecting the most favourable manner in which the Life of Niebuhr has been received both by the public & by the reviews; most of the latter have concurred in praising the admirable English style of the translation: but perhaps I may add, from intimate personal knowledge that Miss Winkworth's general acquirements and amount of learning are such as are rarely possessed by a woman.

She has received part of her education in Germany, and since then has had the advantage of spending the greater part of a year in the family of Professor Brandis at Bonn. She is at this present time visiting the Chevalier Bunsen, at the Embassy, Carlton Terrace; she leaves his house on Tuesday; & goes for a few days to 8, Bedford Row, London, before returning to Manchester. Her sister has partaken of the same advantages, and is also an excellent German scholar; her racy & idiomatic English has been of great assistance to Miss Winkworth in writing the Life of Niebuhr.[5] Elizabeth Gaskell.

Staatsbibliothek zu Berlin, Preußicher Kulturbesitz: Nachlaß Ranke Erg.

1 Definitely in ECG's hand, this might be a draft of a letter to a publisher, who perhaps forwarded it to the highly influential historian, Leopold von Ranke (1795–1886). We wish to acknowledge the valuable assistance of Professors Peter Skrine and Frank Shaw.

2 Probably *Französische Geschichte, vornehmlich im 16. Und 17. Jahrhundert*, Stuttgart, 5 vols 1852–61.

3 The *Life and Letters of Barthold Niebuhr* was printed by 29 December 1851 (*Letters*,

p. 190 n.) and sold rapidly. Susanna Winkworth* was asked to prepare a 2nd edition for autumn 1852, and to include a further volume of Niebuhr's minor writings.

4 Sarah Austin, née Taylor (1793–1867), wife of John Austin (1790–1859). She had translated from both French and German, including a *Life of Carsten Niebuhr* (1833), Ranke's *Ecclesiastical and Political History of the Popes* (1840) and *History of the Reformation in Germany* (1845, etc.). The Prussian ambassador (see next note) had recently previously written to ECG on the assumption that Mrs Austin would translate Niebuhr ([Bunsen] to ECG, Totteridge Park, 16 July [1849]: MS, Princeton UL, AM 21900, incomplete). See also *L & M*, I. 169–70, 184–5; Waller, pp. 59–60; Susanne Stark, 'Women and Translation in the Nineteenth Century', *New Comparison* 15 (1993), pp. 34, 37–42.

5 Susanna Winkworth* was visiting Baron C. K. J. von Bunsen (1791–1860) and his wife Frances, née Waddington (1791–1876), in London in May and June 1853, leaving on 24 June; she also introduced her sister Catherine* as a translator at this time (*L & M*, I. 375–6).

?MRS CHARLOTTE HOLLAND[1]

47 Wimpole St.[2]
Saturday Morning.
[4 June 1853]

My dear Madam,

I am sorry to say I do not think there is much chance of my being able to avail myself of your kind invitation for Monday evening. Mrs Frederick Maurice[3] has asked me to fix an evening on which I could go to them; & I have written to offer myself for either this, or Monday evening, and if she fixes on tonight, there is some kind proposal for our going to see Rachel[4] on Monday. My husband, I am sorry to say, was obliged to leave town last week; and I have been detained from day to day by unexpected business. Now however, it seems decided that on Thursday next I shall leave London; if I can, before that time, call again in Portland Place, will you allow me to do so?

Yours very truly
E. C. Gaskell

Envelope Mrs Holland / Portland Place
Stamp; postmark Ju. 4 53 [a Saturday]

Mitchell Library, New South Wales (Autographs of Sir Henry Parkes)
Printed by R. J. Dingley, 'Mrs Gaskell: An Unpublished Letter', *N & Q*, 35 (1988), p. 320.

1 Possibly Charlotte Dorothy, née Gifford (c. 1818–97), wife of George Henry (1816–91), son of Swinton Colthurst Holland. See *Letters*, p. 557.

2 ECG was staying with Mrs Maria James at this address.

3 Frederick D. Maurice (1805–72), Christian Socialist greatly admired by ECG; he married Anna Barton in 1837.

4 Elisa Félix (1820–58), French actress, famous for passionate performances. In early June she was acting in *Phèdre* (*L & M*, I. 398).

JOHN M. F. LUDLOW*

39 Hyde Park Square[1]
Tuesday morng
[?7 June 1853]

My dear Sir,

I never knew positively till yesterday who wrote that North British article;[2] I always fancied that it must be yours, but I never felt sure till the moment when you spoke of yourself as 'a critic', & then, of course, I knew all directly. When I first received it, I did so want to write to the author of it; but I was rather afraid of doing so, lest, if he were a perfect stranger, it might be impertinent. But now I should be glad if I might tell you how *very* much I liked it; it is not a thing to thank for, because, of course, you only spoke what was the truth to you; but it made me so happy to feel that much of what I had wanted to say, was so fully & completely understood, – indeed brought out more clearly than I could do it, by the writer of that review. I have asked one or two people to read it, who had extremely objected to Ruth, and it has in each instance had the effect, – if not of doing away with their objections to the story – of making them think more freely & seriously on the subject that I wanted to bring before them; particularly on the saving blessing that the child may be. I have no right to take up your time, – for the fact of being reviewed in a spirit after my own heart gives me no claim on my reviewer. Still there are one or two things I shd like to say; but they are so difficult to put into the right words that I am afraid I can not do it.

You have convinced two of my dear friends (Mr & Mrs Bonamy Price) that Ruth ought to have married Mr Bellingham. – I am shaken, – not yet convinced, quite out entirely. Then again, though perfectly agreeing in the sense of what you say about {literature}\ writing / being a bad occupation for unmarried women, I feel a little as if there was a slight tone of contempt in that part of the article < >[3] and besides all this, I should like to tell you a good deal about Miss Brontë, – & her wild sad life, – and her utter want of any companionship[.] I mean literally *companionship*, – for she lives alone, (although in the house with an old blind father); the last of six children, – in ill-health; & after all she is so much better, & more faithful than her books; you should know how the poor & they that have none to help in that great desolate parish speak of her! She puts all her naughtiness into her books; when the suffering that falls so keenly on one of her passionate nature, pierces her too deeply 'sits by her bed & stabs her when she awakes' (to use her own words,) & when others could go to some friend, & claim sympathy & receive strength her only way of relieving herself is by writing out what she feels, & so getting quit of it. I know what you will say, – but she *does* cling to God, as to a father, in her life & in herself – but somehow she only writes at her morbid times. I am going to stay with her on Thursday.[4] I wish I could make her known to you. –

Yours very truly
E. C. Gaskell.

I don't know what possesses me to want to tell you this funny little sentence out of a letter I have this instant received from one of my little girls; I suppose it is because I am alone, & I want some one to enjoy it's drollery with me.

The chickens are quite well; they only want to see you, and then they would be hens.'

I have just arranged with the lady with whom I am, (a Lancashire woman) that she should go with me tomorrow to St Bartholomew's[5] & make Mrs Glover's acquaintance as Mrs[altered word] Booth would be so glad to be of use in going to see her every now & then, – having had a good deal of experience in the same kind of illness, & great sympathy with Mrs Glover's dislike of the publicity – I suppose I may take her! We plan going *from here* about 3, – if I don't hear from you previously either that I had better go alone, or that that time wd be inconvenient[.][6]

Annotation [by Ludlow probably] 1853 (part wanting – probably sent to [?]B. Glover).

Cambridge University Library, Add 7348/10/116

1 Mrs James Booth's? See below and *Letters,* p. 233.
2 A '*delicious* review' of *Ruth* (*Letters,* p. 222, redated c. May 1853) appeared in the May 1853 issue. 'The most marking characteristic of the book, we should say, is its perfect simplicity, truthfulness, its following out, step by step, of nature in all its parts, together with its exquisite purity of feeling in dealing with a subject which so many would shrink from.'
3 J. Miriam Benn suggests, in 'Some unpublished Gaskell Letters', *N & Q* 225 (1980), p 508, that a sheet may not be missing here. Ludlow's* annotation may refer to the end of the letter, which lacks a full stop.
4 ECG was to have stayed with CB on 9 June 1853:, but this visit fell through. See *Letters,* p. 233n.
5 Major London hospital, with medical students in residence from 1842.
6 Here, and in the following letters, ECG expresses her concern for a Mrs Glover of Bury, Lancashire, who is suffering from cancer. See p. 95 below for a summary of the situation.

JOHN M. F. LUDLOW*

7 o'clock Thursday morng
39 Hyde Park S
[?9 June 1853]

My dear Sir,

Instead of being at the mysterious fairy palace (into which the vision of a be-wigged Lord Chancellor[1] intrudes itself oddly,) I have to be prosaic enough to pack up; and as I cannot gather lovely bunches of Banksia roses, I decidedly condemn you as a thief, for taking them. However I see you will be punished, some day when you little expect it. Don't you perceive that (wherever Wimbledon[2] is, – I don't know,) you have got to the palace inhabited by the Beast? The very gardens where Beauty's father, (just like you,) went & gathered the roses for his daughter, fancying himself unseen the while; & some day you will be startled by a deep voice saying 'Ungrateful man, is this the way' &c, – and I should not wonder if the Beast ate you up, as you have no daughter to propitiate him with. That's all sour-grapeism for I would have given a great deal to have seen the place, it sounds so delicious & enchanted.

I was mortified by that review in the Spectator;[3] because although by a process of reasoning I can convince myself that all the articles in a paper are not written by the same person, I always return to the feeling that they are; & {occasionally} I have liked the tone & spirit of some of the literary articles so much – (on Phaethon, & 'my novel' for instance,)[4] that I was afraid it was the same person to whom I had been so utterly unintelligible. Then again I have something to say, if I had time to say it in, about 'girls writing books'. I agree entirely & fully with you \ as to the insincere & unprofitable nature of the employment for them, / – but I thought the little tone of contempt was rather directed against the position of unmarried women in general, – and I am so very much interested – I can't compass all I have got to say into my little space & little time.

That poor woman in the bed to Mrs Glover's left hand – the side your flowers are on – seems such a nice person, & has been trying to comfort Mrs Glover; I think her sympathy & kind words will tend to do away with Mrs Glover's touch of pride, – of which I was aware the first day, but which I thought was rather softened down yesterday. There is a great deal of that pride of respectability among our Lancashire people. – Mrs Booth will go & see Mrs Glover every few days. In greatest haste I remain yours sincerely

E. C. Gaskell.

I know we shd agree about unmarried women writing books, because we are so very close together that it seems as if it were only a different understanding of the same words that separated us [altered word]. I *utterly* condemn, & for the same reasons that you do, girls writing novels;[5] but a *woman*, doing earnest work in the day, may find great solace from restless thoughts in writing such a book as the Life of Niebuhr in solitary evenings.[6] Do you remember the beginning of Victor Cousin's life of Jacqueline Pascal?[7] if not, it is generous in me to refer you to it, as he is on your side – only I think *he* does allow works of history &c &c

Annotation in pencil 1853.

Cambridge University Library, Add 7348/10/117

1 Ludlow* was a barrister of Lincoln's Inn.
2 The Ludlows lived at Wimbledon, Surrey.
3 An anonymous review in the number for 15 January 1853, raising objections to 'the cant of philanthropy [which] is prevalent; not grossly, but in spirit' (*CH Gaskell*, p. 212).
4 *Phaethon, or Loose Thoughts for Loose Thinkers* (1852), by Charles Kingsley, a Socratic dialogue on matters of belief, was reviewed in the *Spectator* for 2 October 1852. *My Novel* (1853), by Psistratus Caxton [E. Bulwer Lytton], was reviewed in the *Spectator* for 19 February 1853, the reviewer calling for 'art' which will deal with 'common life – with that which is the business of a busy struggling world'.
5 In reviewing *Ruth* Ludlow* argued that 'when we look at female writers, we cannot help being struck by the vast superiority of the married, as a class, over the single.' Cf. p. 90 above.
6 ECG appeals to the example of Susanna Winkworth*.
7 A publication of 1853. Victor Cousin (1792–1867) was a French philosopher, whom ECG probably met in Paris, February 1855 (*Letters*, p. 332). She drew upon his 1854 study of Madame de Sablé and other *femmes d'esprit* for her 'Company Manners', *Household Words*, 20 May 1854. See Alain Jumeau on Madame de Sablé and Madame de Sévigné, *GSJ* 13 (1999), pp. 15–24.

JOHN M. F. LUDLOW*

Plymouth Grove
Thursday [?16 June 1853]

My dear Sir,

Please don't be angry at me for writing just one little bit, though you've told me not, and though I'm afraid you may think it 'self-pleasing', & that in fact it is so, – but silence is only comfortable between friends, when there is a full understanding, & so I want just to say why I did not stop to say goodbye. I did at first wish for your companionship down that street, for I was walking, & had missed my way & been rather frightened by a rush of cattle in going to St Bartholomew's; & I wanted besides to ask you more about the risk of the operation than I could do before Mrs Glover, – & to hear whether you thought it right to tell her husband &c. So I rather lingered in that great court in hope you would come out, till I bethought me how I had broken in upon a conversation which either you or she or both might desire to finish, – and that one of you had spoken about your writing a letter to her dictation, which it might be a comfort to her if you did there & then, &, if so I knew you would do it. So I was ashamed of being a coward any longer, & dashed out of the gate and away through that disagreeable street in double quick time! My carriage you could not see for the good reason in the Critic

The Spanish fleet you cannot see
Because it is not yet in sight.[1]

But I was very sorry not to wish you goodbye; *very* sorry indeed, so you must take this as a goodbye. I think we understand each other pretty well, considering our strange little broken bits of intercourse, in which, at any rate, there has been no loss of time in getting to things we really cared about. I like to think of you as a friend; to whom I shall apply (never fear!) if ever I want anything that I think you can help me in. When you go to your country house (Cottenham Park?)[2] you shall have the hens if you like. – And perhaps all this time I am writing so lightly poor Mrs Glover is bearing mortal pain & anxiety, the depth of which must be unknown to any one but God, for Mrs Shaen sends me word the operation is to be today.[3] Mrs Shaen is my dear, dear friend,[4] a person after your own heart 'I guess'. Perhaps someday you & she may find each other out –

Yours very truly
E. C Gaskell

Cambridge University Library, Add 7348/10/118

1 R. B. Sheridan, *The Critic* (1779), II. ii.
2 In 1852 Ludlow* and Thomas Hughes had a house built by a Christian Socialist builders' association on land purchased from Lord Cottenham at Wimbledon. Ludlow lived there with his mother; the two families each had half of the building and met in the library for prayers. Ludlow records an early visit to the house by 'charming lovable Mrs. Gaskell' in which they discussed his review of *Ruth* (*John Ludlow: The Autobiography of a Christian Socialist,* ed. A. D. Murray, 1981, p. 280).
3 The operation was on a Thursday (see also below), so perhaps on 16 June. It proved to be an inadvertent abortion, Ludlow, MS *Autobiography*.
4 Emily Shaen* writes of visiting the 'Hospital [for] a poor woman Lily bequeathed me' in 'June 1853' (*L & M,* I. 399)

MRS ANN SCOTT[1]

Monday morng –
[?20 June 1853][2]

My dear Mrs Scott,

I do so want to see you, & Cheetham Hill is so far away, – and it is such a chance if I find you in! I think I shall try to come tomorrow – and meanwhile I want to know if you & Mr Scott have ever had any experience about *mesmerism*. I have rather a dread of it altogether I *think* because I have a feeling that it *twisted* Miss Martineau's mind;[3] but it may not be that, & it may be a superstitious feeling (& consequently a faithless one) of mine. Now I'll tell you why I want to know your & Mr Scott's opinion.

Do you remember a fortnight ago our meeting at Lincoln's Inn \ Chapel, / & my stopping to speak to Mr Ludlow. The 'upshot' of our talk was that I went to see a poor woman at St Bartholomew's – wife of a very good pious book-seller at Bury; (our Lancashire Bury,) – known to Mr Maurice & Mr Ludlow as a practically good man. His name is Glover. Well! his wife, – aged 33 – has subdued all complaint for seven years, during which they have had to struggle hard, – but all this time {they} \ she / has been suffering from mysterious pains which at last became so bad that a surgical examination was requisite, – (it was a tumour at the mouth of the womb) – & she was taken (by Mr Ludlow's advice) to St Bartholomew's, where last Thursday an operation was performed by Dr West, & from the puncture blood flowed instead of water, showing it had been neglected too long. (I must give you all these details to enable you to judge about employing mesmerism, if you *have* any experience on the subject). Today I receive a letter from Mr Glover, enclosing one from Mr Ludlow, communicating these facts, – saying that as soon as Mrs G. is a little better she will have to be dismissed the hospital as incurable, & that then two courses will be open, – one to try for admission to the Women's Hospital (Soho Square) set apart for such diseases, – over which I went with Mr Ludlow, & in which the \ house & room / arrangements are comfortable *for a hospital* but whh is attended by Dr Protheroe Smith[4] about whose *wilfulness* in operating \ when there was no hope / I heard stories whh amounted to absolute cruelty, – & – Mr Ludlow suggests mesmerism as the other course, – believing \ it efficacious / {that} 'when applied in Christian faith, because it appears to me the fulfilment of our Lord's commands, which I find nothing in scripture to limit in point of time or circumstances, that of "Laying hands on the sick", when we are told "they shall recover," – as far as I can make it out it is simply a transmission of life & strength from one person into another, and which has certainly proved frequently efficacious in uterine diseases – This it has done, I believe, when all local applications of surgery & all endeavours to treat the[altered word] particular disease have failed simply because it alone has power to renew the constitution itself, \ & / so enable it to throw off the evil. Where that is beyond cure I believe mesmerism will still greatly augment the stock of strength to grapple with it, – as well as soothe the pain. May I ask you to consider these views, both in meditation before God, & in conversation with &c I should say at once, that if there is any prejudice against mesmerism in the mind of any party concerned, I would rather that every available mode of ordinary treatment should be first {tried} exhausted.'

So far Mr Ludlow. Poor Mr Glover writes to me to beg for my opinion. He seems utterly felled by the shock of finding the operation unsuccessful, & the disease incurable by ordinary methods, & says his friends must decide for him. I am vexed with myself (Oh, *so* vexed!) because last week when I was at Bury I spoke to Mr Glover, with a careless tone of contempt of mesmerism, – really knowing so little about it as I did; I want to try now to get all the wisdom I can to help me to give the best judgment I can. I hope I've not tired you out with my long story – & will you tell me your opinions. I shall *try* to come tomorrow, – but this afternoon I must go, all uncertain, & confess my ignorance to Mr Glover – & see what can be done to comfort him – and tonight Mrs Shaen comes *here* for a fortnight; with a baby[5] to fill one's heart with delight, – so I may*n't* be able to come – & then will you write? And moreover we want Susy to come here, – we will fetch her in the little pony carriage on *Thursday* morning next, – & then she can go home with you on Friday evening, & you'll be *obliged* to come to reclaim your child.

This is the beginning of a plan I have at heart of making your children & mine *friends*. Meta is only at home till next Monday, – and till Thursday we have not even the weeest scrap of a bed disengaged. Thanks for telling me of the 1st of July. I hope to come – in greatest haste

Yours affectionately
E. C. Gaskell

Wellcome Institute Library (Western Manuscripts MS. 7141)
Printed in full with commentary by Christopher Hilton, 'Elizabeth Gaskell and Mesmerism: An Unpublished Letter', *Medical History* 39 (1995), 219–35.

1 See p. 85 n. 4 above.
2 Hilton argues for 1854. But see *Letters,* pp. 313, 315, which may refer to a separate occasion, when Florence Nightingale's* aid was enlisted to enable Mrs Glover to enter the Invalid Gentlewomen's institution. See also FN to EGC, [October 1854] (Waller, p. 20).
3 Harriet Martineau*, in her *Letters on Mesmerism* (1845), asserted that she had been cured of an uterine tumour by it (Hilton, p. 225). Cf. ECG, *CBL,* II. 200.
4 Protheroe Smith (1809–89), specialist in gynaecology and women's diseases. The Hospital for Diseases of Women, for which he had campaigned, was founded in 1843 in Red Lion Square, Holborn. He was a pioneering surgeon, with the reputation of caring for his patients. See O. Moscucci, *The Science of Women,* Cambridge, 1990, p. 85.
5 Margaret Josephine Shaen, b. 18 August 1852 (*L & M,* I. 324, 360).

JOHN M. F. LUDLOW*

Plymouth Grove
June 25th [1853]

Dear Sir,

My cousin is the vicar of Leighton Buzzard[1] where the Mrs Wagstaff you named as a clair-voyante, lives; and when I named this to Mr Glover he wished me to learn if possible something of her general character &c. I accordingly wrote to Mr Stevenson, saying that we would leave the discussion of mesmerism or clairvoyance[2] on one side, but that I should be glad to know anything he could tell me of her as a parishioner of his, and that I should consider what he said as confidential,

& only to be named to one person. I am sorry (on many accounts) to say that my cousin himself is ill, & has been obliged to leave Leighton within this last fortnight, to try what a little rest at Oxford may do towards re-instating his health. So his wife[3] answers my letter; and on what she says, I place far less reliance, as she is a very different person from[altered from 'to'] him. Still I think that some friend of Mr Glovers ought to see what she says, & take it for what it is worth; I once thought of sending it to Mr Howarth[4], for my 'one person', to whom it might be confided; but I am rather afraid he might read or impart its contents to Mr Glover, & so throw another doubt & anxiety into his mind. So I send it to you, begging you to read and burn it. Mr Glover's letters are to much more decided & clear than he is himself, that I don't think you can tell till you see him in what a state of distressing excitement & indecision he has been {in}. In greatest haste

Yours very truly
E. C. Gaskell.

Annotation in pencil 1853.

Cambridge University Library, Add 7348/10/119

1 Joseph Stevenson (1806–95), Vicar of Leighton Buzzard 1849–62. He had been 'in succession a minister in the Presbyterian Church of Scotland, a sub-commissioner of the public records, a married clergyman in the Church of England, an editor of the Rolls Series, a Roman Catholic priest and, at the end of his long life, a Jesuit' (*EY,* pp. 222–23, 438).

2 Ludlow* himself practised mesmerism, claiming a successful treatment for an apparent tumour when he had been unable to persuade a young woman to attend the Mesmeric Infirmary (Ludlow, *Autobiography,* p. 321).

3 Née Mary Ann Craig (1811–69), married 19 September 1831.

4 So spelt, but perhaps this is ECG's cousin by marriage, the Rev. Franklin Howorth (1804–82) of Bury (*EY,* p. 319).

JOHN M. F. LUDLOW*

[?25 June 1853]

I have opened my letter to say Mr Glover has just left, – he is exceedingly uncertain what to do – has turned all round since yesterday – (but I have turned him back as well as I could, away from Mr Clay,[1] who must be looked at as a last resource I fancy from all I hear). – Meanwhile he plans to go up to London on Saty night, – having previously gained all the information he can; and there to try & gain evidence on which to form a judgment whether the Mesmeric Hospital[2] or that terrible Dr P Smith (I don't say 'terrible' to *him*, because Dr[altered word] Smith's advice may have to be resorted to) would be best. He has received 20£, – the difficulty seems to be leaving the shop even till Wednesday or Thursday, when he hopes to be able to remove his wife to whatever place seems desirable, – your letter is a *most sad* disappointment. I had begun to hope so much. In greatest haste – (will you open & read my letter to Mrs Glover, if necessary or desirable that she shd not see it herself. I may have said unwisely hopeful things. I forget – & this letter must go. – Mr Glover *asked me to write this to* you.

Cambridge University Library, Add 7348/10/120
Perhaps a continuation of 25 June [?1853] letter, but now separate.

1 Charles Clay (1801–93), Manchester gynaecologist, the first in England to remove an ovarian cyst successfully. He also performed 'the first technically successful hysterectomy' (*Some Manchester Doctors,* ed. W. J. Elwood and A. Félicité Tuxford, Manchester 1984, p. 194).
2 The London Mesmeric Infirmary (1849–65), founded by Dr John Elliotson.

J. M. F. LUDLOW*

Plymouth Grove
Friday July 1 [1853]

Dear Mr {Ludlow},

This is bulletin the first – but I dare say you will have another in the course of the day. I saw Mrs Glover about ½ p 12, at the Station; tired, – and most desirous to get home as soon as possible; but after all, not suffering permanently from the journey I think. Mr Glover more like a bird than ever; and she with a substratum (admire my grand word!) of brightness beneath her fatigue, – which wd come out when she had rested at home. They went to the Bury Station almost immediately; & would have ½ an hour's rest there before the train started. She was up at 4 – not to be too late. I am so sorry I am leaving home tomorrow for a month or a few days more;[1] I think possibly however that in a month or so hence, a new face & person coming in upon her life, – which must be monotonous, poor creature – will be of advantage. At present she has the recollection of London excitement & people to cheer her up.

Yours very truly
E. C. Gaskell

In greatest haste to catch the post –

Princeton University Library

1 To visit Wales (Glyn Garth) and France (her plan was Le Havre, Rouen, Caen, Coutances, Mont St Michel). See *Letters,* pp. 237–40; Uglow, pp. 350–51.

BENJAMIN C. BRODIE[1]

Beechwood near
Southampton[2]
July 13 [?1853]

Dear Sir,

I am very much obliged to you for the kind remembrance which prompted you to send me 'The Forsaken Merman.'[3] I like the air very much, though as I don't know a great deal about music my approbation can go but a little way beyond the mere fact of it's giving me, myself, pleasure. And the words of themselves, are music; and haunt one like some old tune. I first read them, sitting by Loughrigg Tarn, but somehow they are associated in my mind with a very different place, – by the sea-shore, – and the little grey church is there, just visible enough from the sands to tempt Margaret away. Thank you once more for sending the song; it is a very pleasant little remembrance of our neighbourhood at dinner at Lady Coltman's.

Yours very truly
E. C. Gaskell

Leicester University Library

1 Either (1) Sir Benjamin Collins Brodie (1783–1862), who became first President of the General Medical Council in 1858; he had attended Salis Schwabe* in his final illness in 1853. Or, more probably, (2) his son of the same name (1817–80), an academic chemist who succeeded his father as baronet in 1862 and became Professor of Chemistry at Oxford in 1865. ECG knew him and his wife, née Philo Thompson, at Cowley House, Oxford (*Letters*, p. 481). 'I believe Mrs Brodie was meant to make an era in decorative art, and instead of that she's gone and married and got five children', wrote Emily Shaen* in 1861 (*L & M*, II. 356).
2 ECG with the William Duckworths (*Letters*, p. 238).
3 Poem by Matthew Arnold, first printed in *The Strayed Reveller and Other Poems* of 1849, still popular. Musical settings all seem to be from a later period.

?JOHN FORSTER*

[post–23 September 1853]

< ... > We turned up a narrow bye lane near the church – past the curate's, the schools, & skirting the pestiferous church yard we arrived at the door into the Parsonage yard.[1] In I went, – half blown back by the wild vehemence of the wind which swept along the narrow gravel walk – round the corner of the house into a small plot of grass, enclosed within a low stone wall, over which the more ambitious grave-stones towered all round. There are two windows on each side the door, & steps up to it. On these steps I encountered a ruddy kind-looking man of no great refinement, – but I had no time to think of him; in at the door

into an exquisitely clean passage, to the left into a square parlour looking out on the grass plot, the tall head-stones beyond, the tower end of the church, the village houses, & the brown distant moors.

Miss Brontë gave me kindest welcome, & the room looked the perfection of warmth, snugness & comfort, crimson predominating in the furniture, whh did well with the bleak cold colours without. Every thing in her department has been new within the last few years; and every thing, furniture, appointments &c is admirable for its consistency < - > all simple, good, sufficient for every possible reasonable want, & of the most delicate & scrupulous cleanliness. She is so neat herself I got quite ashamed of any touches of untidiness – a chair out of its place, – work left on the table were all of them, I could see, annoyances to her habitual sense of order; *not* annoyances to her temper in the least; you understand the difference. There was her likeness by Richmond,[2] given to her father by M[ess]rs Smith & Elder, the \ later / print of Thackeray, & a good likeness of the Duke of Wellington, hanging up < . > My room was above this parlour, & looking on the same view, which was really beautiful in certain lights moon-light especially. Mr Brontë lives almost entirely in the room on the opposite (right hand side) of the front door: behind his room is the kitchen, behind the parlour a store room kind of pantry. Mr Brontë's bedroom is over his sitting room, Miss Brontë's over the kitchen, the servants over the pantry. Where the rest of the household slept when they were all one large family I can't imagine. The wind goes piping & wailing and sobbing round the square unsheltered house in a very strange unearthly way.

We dined – she & I together – Mr Brontë having his dinner sent to him in his sitting room according to his *invariable* custom; (fancy it! only they two left,) and then she told me that the man whom I met on the steps was a Mr Francis Bennoch[3], something Park, Black Heath, who had written the previous day to say he was coming to call on his way from Hull where he had been reading a paper on Currency. His claim for coming to call on Miss Brontë was 'that he was a patron of authors and literature' – I hope he belongs to your Guild[4] –; Miss Brontë sent to the address he gave to say she had rather not see him, but he came all the same, captivated Mr Brontë who would make his daughter come in; & abused us both for 'a couple of proud minxes' when we said we would rather be without individual patronage if it was to subject us to individual impertinence (Oh, please burn this letter as soon as you have read it.) This Mr Bennoch produced a MS dedication of some forthcoming work of Miss Mitford's to himself, as a sort of portable certificate of his merits, & sounded altogether very funny – but still a good natured person evidently, & really doing a good deal of kindness I have no doubt. Mrs Toulmin or Crosland, & Mr Charles Swain of our town, were two authors[5] to whom he hoped to introduce Miss Brontë at some future time.

Mr Brontë came in at tea, an honour to me I believe. Before tea we had had a long, delicious walk, right against the wind on Penistone Moor which stretches directly behind the Parsonage going over the hill in brown & purple sweeps and falling softly down into a little upland valley through which a 'beck' ran; & beyond again was another great waving hill, – and in the dip of that might be seen another yet more distant, & beyond that the said Lancashire came; but the sinuous hills seemed to girdle the world like the great Norse serpent, & for my part I don't know if they don't stretch up to the North Pole.

On the Moors we met no one. – Here and there in the gloom of the distant hollows she pointed out a dark grey dwelling – with Scotch firs growing near them often, – & told me such wild tales of the ungovernable families, who lived or had lived therein that Wuthering Heights[6] even seemed tame comparatively. Such dare-devil people, – men especially, – & women so strong & cruel in some of their feelings & so passionately fond in others. They are a queer people up there. Small landed proprietors – dwelling on one spot since Q. Eliz, – & lately adding marvellously to their incomes by using the water power of the becks in the woollen manufacture which has sprung up during the last 50 years: – uneducated – unrestrained by public opinion – for their equals in position are as bad as themselves, & the poor, besides being densely ignorant, are all dependant on their employers.

Miss Brontë does not what we should call 'visit' with any of them – she goes to see the poor – teaches at the Schools most gently & constantly, – but the richer sort of people despise her for her poverty, – & they would have nothing in common if they did meet. These people build grand houses, & live in the kitchens, own hundreds of thousands of pounds & yet bring up their sons with only just enough learning to qualify them for over-lookers during their father's life-time, & greedy grasping money-hunters after his death. Here & there from the high moorland summit we saw newly built Churches, – which her Irish curates see after – every one of them being literal copies of different curates in the neighbourhood, whose amusement has been ever since to call each other by the names she gave them in Shirley.[7]

In the evening Mr Brontë went to his room & smoked a pipe, – a regular clay – & we sat over the fire & talked, – talked of long ago when that very same room was full of children; & how one by one they had dropped off into the church yard close to the windows. At ½ past 8 we went in to prayers, – soon after nine every one was in bed but we two; – in general there she sits quite alone thinking over the past; for her eyesight prevents her reading or writing by candlelight, & knitting is but very mechanical, & does not keep the thoughts from wandering.

Each day – I was 4 there – was the same in outward arrangement – breakfast at 9, in Mr Brontë's room, – which we left immediately after[.] What he does with himself through the day I cannot imagine! He is a tall, fine-looking old man, with silver *bristles* all over his head; nearly blind; speaking with a strong Scotch accent (he comes from the North of Ireland, raised himself from the rank of a poor farmer's son, – & was rather intimate with Lord Palmerston at Cambridge), a pleasant soothing recollection now, in his shut-out life. There was not a sign of engraving map writing materials &c \ beyond a desk / no books but those contained on two hanging shelves between the windows, – his two pipes & a spittoon, if you know what that is). He was very polite & agreeable to me; paying rather elaborate old-fashioned compliments, but I was sadly afraid of him in my inmost soul; for I caught a glare of his stern eyes over his spectacles at Miss Brontë once or twice which made me know my man;[8] and he talked *at* her sometimes; He is very fearless; has taken the part of the men against the masters, – or vice versa just as he thought fit & right; & is consequently much respected & to be respected.

But he ought never to have married. He did not like children; & they had six in six years; & the consequent pinching & family disorder, – (which can't be helped) and noise &c made him shut himself up & want no companionship – nay be positively annoyed by it. He won't let Miss Brontë accompany him in his walks, although he is so nearly blind; goes out in defiance of her gentle attempts to restrain him, \ speaking / as if she thought him in his second childhood; & comes home moaning & tired; – having lost his way. 'Where is my strength gone?' is his cry then. 'I used to walk 40 miles a day &c.' There are little bits of picturesque affection about him, – for his old dogs for instance, – when very ill some years ago in Manchester, whither he had come to be operated upon for cataract, his wail was 'I shall never feel Keeper's paws on my knees again!' Moreover to account for my fear – rather an admiring fear after all – of Mr Brontë, please to take into account that though I like the beautiful glittering of bright flashing steel I don't fancy fire-arms at all, at all; and Miss Brontë never remembers her father dressing himself in the morning without putting a loaded pistol in his pocket, just as regularly as he puts on his watch. There was this little deadly pistol sitting down to breakfast with us, kneeling down to prayers at night – to say nothing of a loaded gun hanging up on high ready to pop off on the slightest emergency. Mr Brontë has a great fancy for arms of all kinds. He begged Miss Brontë (Oh I can't condense it more than I do, & yet here's my 4th sheet!) to go & see Prince Albert's armoury at Windsor; & when he is unusually out of spirits she tells him over again & again of the different weapons &c there.

But all this time I wander from the course of our day, which is the course of her usual days. Breakfast over, the letters come; not many, sometimes for days none at all. About 12 we went out to walk . At 2 we dined, about 4 we went out again; at 6 we had tea; by nine every one was in bed but ourselves. Monotonous enough in sound, but not a bit in reality. There are some people, whose stock of facts & anecdotes are soon exhausted; but Miss B. is none of these. She has the wild strange facts of her own & her sister's lives, – and beyond & above these she has most original & suggestive thoughts of her own; so that, like the moors, I felt on the last day as if our talk might be extended in any direction without getting to the end of any subject.

There are 2 servants, one, Tabby, aged upwards of 90; sitting in an arm-chair by the kitchen fire, – and Martha the real active serving maiden, who has lived with them 10 years.[9] I asked this last one day to take me into the Church, & show me the Brontë graves; so when Miss Brontë was engaged, we stole out. There is a tablet put up in the communion railing. Maria Brontë, wife of the revd Patrick B died 1821 aged 39. Maria Brontë – May 1825 aged 12 (the original of Helen Burns in Jane Eyre. She & the next sister died of the fever at the Clergy School.) Elizabeth Brontë died June 1825, aged 11. Patrick Branwell Brontë died Sep 24, 1848, aged 30. Emily Jane Brontë died Decr 18. 1848 aged 29 – Anne Brontë, May 28, 1849 aged 27. 'Yes!' said Martha. 'They were all well when Mr Branwell was buried; but Miss Emily broke down the next week. We saw she was ill, but she never would own it, never would have a doctor near her, never would breakfast in bed, – the last morning she got up, – and she dying all the time – the rattle in her throat while she *would* dress herself; & neither Miss Brontë nor I dared offer to help her – She died just before Xmas – you'll see the date there, and we all went to her funeral, Master & Keeper, her dog, walking first side by side, & then Miss Brontë & Miss Anne, & then Tabby & me. Next day Miss Anne took ill just in the same way – & it was 'Oh, if it was but Spring and I could go to the sea, – Oh if it was but Spring' – And at last Spring came and Miss Brontë took her to Scarborough, – they got there on the Saturday & on the Monday she died. She is buried in the old Church at Scarbro'. For as long as I can remember – Tabby says since they were little bairns Miss Brontë & Miss Emily & Miss Anne used to put away their sewing after prayers, & walk all three one after the other round the table in the parlour till near eleven o'clock. Miss Emily walked as long as she could; & when she died Miss Anne & Miss Brontë took it up, – and how my heart aches to hear Miss Brontë walking, walking on alone'. And on enquiring I found that after Miss Brontë had seen me to my room, she did come down every { } night, & begin that slow monotonous incessant walk, in which I am sure I should fancy I heard the steps of the dead following me. She says she could not sleep without it – that she & her sisters talked over the plans & projects of their whole lives at such times. About Mr Branwell Brontë the less said the better, – poor fellow. He never knew Jane Eyre was written although he lived for a year afterwards; but that year was passed in the shadow of the coming death, with the consciousness of his wasted life. But Emily, – poor Emily – the pangs of disappointment as review after review came out about Wuthering Heights were terrible – Miss B said she had no recollection of pleasure or gladness about Jane Eyre, every such feeling was lost in seeing Emily's resolute endurance yet knowing what she felt. < ... >

Brotherton Collection, Leeds
MS (tipped into a volume) of Letter 166: '*to* a Friend', as printed by Elizabeth Haldane, *Mrs. Gaskell and Her Friends,* 1930, pp. 141–8. If a letter ('Oh, please burn this letter... ', ECG writes), it is incomplete; it might almost be an unfinished essay. There is a problematic connection with Letter 167, also incomplete and taken from the MS of ECG's *Life of Charlotte Brontë,* as 'parts of a letter I wrote at the time'.

1 'Come to Haworth as soon as you can: the heath is in bloom now', Charlotte Brontë wrote on 16 September 1853. ECG arrived on Monday, 19 September 1853, to stay for four days (Barker, pp. 738–741).
2 1851, by George Richmond (1809–96). R. Ormond notes that ECG sat for George Richmond in London on 6 February 1851; the bill was paid on 24 February 1851 (redating Letters 100 and 115).
3 Francis Bennoch (1812–90), Scottish merchant and poet, friend of H. A. Bright and Nathaniel Hawthorne. He was instrumental in founding the Guild of Literature and Art in 1850, for the support of impoverished writers.
4 John Forster* describes how Bulwer Lytton and Dickens initiated the Guild of Literature and Art in November 1850 (*Life of Dickens,* II, Book vi, ch. 5).
5 Mrs Newton Crosland, née Camilla Toulmin (1812–95), novelist and miscellaneous writer. Charles Swain (1801–74), poet with 'dark lustrous eyes and intellectual conversation'. He figured in *Manchester Poetry: with an Introductory Essay,* ed. James Wheeler, Christmas 1838, to which WG had contributed two poems, 'Come and Pray' and 'Death and Sleep' (translated from German). See *EY,* p. 412.
6 Emily Brontë's *Wuthering Heights* appeared in December 1847. In *CBL,* II, ch. 2, ECG prints Charlotte's assertion that Emily only knew such families through tragic and terrible stories, 'the secret annals of every rude vicinage'.
7 'Of late years, an abundant shower of curates has fallen upon the north of England' (*Shirley,* ch. 1, opening sentence). Her curates (Mr Donne, Mr Sweeting and Mr Malone) are heavily satirised.
8 ECG was visiting the Parsonage when the relationship between father and daughter 'was at its lowest point ever' (Barker, p. 741).
9 Tabitha Aykroyd (d. 1855 aged 84) and Martha Brown (1828–80), whose narrative and dramatic powers seem to have been as inspiring to ECG as those of Charlotte Brontë.

?A. HALL, VIRTUE & CO.

42 Plymouth Grove
Manchester.
[c. 29 September 1853]

Sir,

I have received your note containing the announcement of Miss Bremer's kind intention of presenting me with a copy of her book.[1] If you can have it sent to {the} \ (Mrs Gaskell, Manchester) / care of Wm

Shaen Esq') *8 Bedford Row* in the course of {a} \ *this* / week, some friends of mind will be passing through from the Continent, & will bring it down for me. I expect that they will call in Bedford Row {about the 14th or 15th of this month} \ on Monday next the twelfth (12th) instant. / Can you ever forward anything to Miss Bremer for me? I do not know her address.

Yours truly
E. C. Gaskell

Mrs Lucy Magruder

1 Frederika Bremer (1801–65) to ECG, Stockholm, 29 September 1853 (Rubenius, p. 40), states that she had ordered her *Homes of the New World* [*Impressions of America*, transl. Mary Howitt, published by A. Hall, Virtue & Co., 3 vols 1853] to be sent. ECG had been in correspondence with Bremer, a Swedish author, from before October 1851, and probably knew her *The Home, or Life in Sweden* (1843: sic) via Mary Howitt's translation of 1846 (Waller, p. 66).

LADY HATHERTON[1]

Dec. 27. 1853

To recur to your note which I received at Knutsford, my Morton Hall[2] was *Morton*, not Moreton, but indeed till receiving the half message from Miss Louisa Stanley I had utterly forgot that there was a Moreton in Cheshire, never having seen it, and not knowing its exact situation to this day. And about the 'poor starving people' the whole story originated in two little graphic sentences from the old Servant (aged 93)[3] at Mr Brontë's at Haworth; I asked her why a certain field was called the Balcōny Field (put a strong & long accent on cōny)[4] and she told me that when she was a girl 'while the Farmers were still about the country & before they had begun to plague the land with their Mills &c' there had been a grand House with Balcōnies in that field, that she remembered seeing Miss — (I forget the name) get into the Carriage with her hair all taken up over a cushion, and in a blue sattin open gown, but Oh! she came to sore want, for her Nephew gambled away the property and then she lent him money, and at last he & she had nowhere to hide their heads but an old tumbledown Cottage (shewn to me) where folk do say she was clemmed to death, and many a one in Haworth remembered him going to Squire (name forgotten again) to offer a bit of old plate for sale to bury his Aunt rather than that the Parish should do it[.] The 'Blue sattin gown' and the 'clemming to death' were a striking contrast, were they not?

And as for Cranford, if any one asks me any questions, I will be as civil as the famous Irish Echo in answering < ... >

Yrs affectionately
E C. Gaskell.

Brotherton Collection, Leeds University

1 'Extract of letter from Mrs Gaskell to Lady Hatherton', pr. in J. A. V. Chapple, 'ECG's *Morton Hall* and *The Poor Clare', BST* 20 (1990), pp. 47–49.
2 'Morton Hall', *Household Words,* 19 and 26 November 1853. Charlotte Brontë 'knew whose it was as well as if [she] had seen the hand' (CB to ECG, [?late December 1853]: MS, Princeton UL).
3 Tabitha Aykroyd, who died aged 84 in 1855, a few weeks before Charlotte Brontë herself.
4 Older pronunciation of balcony.

FANNY MAYNE[1]

[c. 1853]

Dear Madam,

I am sorry to say that we should agree so little in many of our opinions that I should not like to write for you, as it would be sure only to end in disappointment on both sides. If I had not seen how differently we feel over many points I would have written for you long ago; as I do not want money to induce me to write[.]

I respect you exceedingly for the effort you are making, although I do not think it will stem the evil you are so truly aware of, viz the corrupting nature of the {Ch } \ Salisbury Square[2] / literature. I happen to know a good deal of the *actual* working of this literature in this town, & the classes who take in such books as you refer to, would no more think of looking at the True Briton or any other periodical of that description as a substitute for their favourite style of reading than they would of going to a Sunday School, instead of to a dog-fight.

The body of men against whom the Quarterly Reviewer vented his spite[3] have got hold of the true way of working on the great masses of the people. I allude to the Christian Socialists; I do not know how far their œconomical principles may be right or wrong, but this I know, that Mr Maurice in London is weaning numbers of the coarsest, most sensual, most class-hating of the working people to a higher sense of Life, as sacred to God; and Mr Kingsley in many of his less violent writings (such as some papers in the politics for the people)[4] has shown that his sense of their wants is true and wise as far as relates to literature. Before any one engages, with the *slightest* hope of really being read by the great multitudes in our towns, in writing for the people, I would have them read & study & digest certain papers of Mr Kingsley's in Fraser's Magazine for 1849, in which he tells how such literature as Lloyd's should be met and combatted.[5]

I think before this you must have felt thankful that, whether for money or not, you have not me for a coadjutor – I could go on with many other things in which I think your plan unwise, – but I have no doubt I have said enough. If it were not so, and I did write for you I should always choose my own subject and my own way of treating it, as I have been accustomed to write after the ideas of anyone else[sic]. I appreciated your motive so much when I first heard of your plan that I fully intended to give as much help as I could 'without fixing my price', but when I saw the True Briton I felt that *here* at any rate it would be utterly powerless for good, and that much would do harm in a set of people where R. Catholics & protestants are so closely mixed together.[6]

You must excuse this long letter; which I dare say has shocked you; but ask any one, who has *absolutely mixed freely* with the seething population of our large towns – not our agricultural villages where the clergy have great influence for good, & great power of direction, and see if they don't confirm the truth of much that I have said.

I have been looking at your note again. I like the plan of your story,[7] and I do not doubt that it will be read by those *already accustomed* to reading good & moral books; I like what you say about not setting class against class. – & above all having *nothing to do with politics*. But all this is already done by existing periodicals, – why set up a machinery afresh? And this will do *nothing* to combat Lloyd's books. I have said the same to Dickens about his Household Words, – and to the Editor of Chambers.[8] Theirs are read largely by the respectable, – *but never come near*, or touch the vicious the low-minded. They will require a different kind of thing.

Your obedient servant
E. C. Gaskell.

Eton College Library

1 Fanny Mayne was an Evangelical journalist and editor who founded the *True Briton* (1st and 2nd series, 1851–54), a penny periodical, to counter the effects of popular sensationalist literature. See Margaret Dalziel, *Popular Fiction 100 Years Ago* (1957); Sheila Smith, *The Other Nation* (1980).
2 The common term for the kind of literature opposed by Mayne.
3 Several works received a hostile reception in the *Quarterly Review* for September 1851, under the heading 'Revolutionary Literature'. The anonymous reviewer (J. W. Croker) began by calling them 'a clique of educated and clever but wayward-minded men' (p. 524). For ECG's relations with Christian Socialists like F. D. Maurice and Charles Kingsley, see *Letters,* pp. 104–5; Anna Unsworth, *Elizabeth Gaskell: An Independent Woman,* 1996, ch. 8.
4 *Politics for the People,* May–July 1848, a penny weekly.
5 Edward Lloyd (1815–90), publisher, to the wood engraver of his illustrations: 'The eyes ... must be larger, and there must be more blood, much more blood!' (qu. Dalziel, p. 20).
6 Mayne's attack on 'penny dreadfuls' was 'perfectly consistent with the tenets of strict evangelicalism' (Dalziel, pp. 51–3).
7 Mayne's own novel, *Jane Rutherford; or, the Miner's Strike* , 'By a Friend of the People', appeared weekly in the *True Briton,* 9 June – 20 October 1853. She supported the 'true rights of property', portraying a benevolent coal-owner and parodying trades union activism. See Ivan Melada, *The Captain of Industry in English Fiction 1821–1871,* Albuquerque 1970, pp. 142–44, and Joseph

Kestner, *Protest and Reform: The British Social Novel by Women 1827–1867*, 1985, pp. 177–82. Kestner suspects a criticism of the sexual morality of *Ruth*.

8 *Chamber's Edinburgh Journal*, founded in 1832 by the publishers Robert and William Chambers.

HENRY A. BRIGHT[1]

Plymouth Grove
March 14. [1854]

My dear Sir,

Yes! I plead guilty; I am ashamed. Am I forgiven? I received Longfellow, Priestley &c[2] just before I went to Paris, meant to acknowledge them from thence; became too busy; told Mr Chas Melly, who is a traitor not to remember he was especially charged to thank you for them. I should beg you to scold him but he has been so good as to lend us a much-wanted book, so I can't find in my heart to do so.

I don't much care for statesmen and have a handsome quantity of unknown peers at your disposal. (I have Sir Robt Peel, Lord John Russell &c \ in the statesman line whh I do*n't* mean to give you /.) Would you like a royal William Frederick? And I don't very much mind for Everett; (don't think me saucy,) only I like having people I really *do* care for; I myself personally, either in the way of like or dislike, – and not people I am perfectly indifferent to. I should \ rather / like Washington Irving. How would your old Puritan blood have been stirred with glorious circulation, not to say ignominious envy of their possessor, if you had seen, as I did not three weeks ago Lord Nugent's grand autograph book, – *letters* from (Q. Eliz, Burleigh, Raleigh, Bacon &c.) Oliver Cromwell, Falkland[,] Hampden (just like some of Shakespeares for the exquisite & somewhat formal grace of their style, touching upon euphuism.) Beville Grenville, Sir John Elliot, Sir Harry Vane &c &c &c – real identical yellow ragged *letters* that they had touched with the hands, (right royal hands,) now mouldered away.

I have sent Mr Aspland yr Priestley.[3] Do you care for Mérimée?[4] Mr Charles Melly did not know who he was, so I would not give him one for you, but I have two. De Quincey I shall obtain for you some time. When I have a little morsel of leisure I will look over my letters, & send you word what duplicates I have \ *and* what I want /.

Ever your's very truly,
E. C Gaskell.

'Haste! Haste! Post Haste!'

Trinity College, Cambridge

1 Henry Arthur Bright* (1830–84), partner in father's shipping firm, litterateur, Liverpool Unitarian and a favourite of ECG.

2 i. e., autographs.

3 Joseph Priestley (1733–1804) had been a leading Unitarian minister, succeeded by Robert Aspland at the Gravel Pit chapel, Hackney. His son R. B. Aspland was a friend of ECG before her marriage (*EY*, pp. 108, 413).

4 Prosper Mérimée (1803–70), author and politician in the Madame Mohl* circle in the rue du Bac, who wrote to her about ECG in 1852 (MS, John Rylands UL, Manchester, ELM 734–36, vol. 3). See esp. Philip Yarrow, 'Mrs Gaskell and France' *GSJ* 7 (1993), pp. 22, 24 and n. 24; also Sharps, p. 200 n. 9.

OCTAVIAN BLEWITT

Plymouth Grove
Manchester, – April 26th [1854][1]

Mrs Gaskell presents her compliments to Mr Blewitt, and begs to inform him that she has known Mrs Selina Davenport of Knutsford for some years, during which time she has made many efforts to support herself by needlework, keeping a small shop &c, – which have failed, owing to her great age, and infirmity.

Her character has always been very good, as the clergymen of the different parishes in which she has lived, testify. And any grant which the Literary Fund may be inclined to make will be conferred on a deserving old lady, to the best of Mrs Gaskell's belief.

British Library, Royal Literary Fund (case file 1247)

1 See pp. 49–50, 67–8 above. Year date from position in file. Robert Clowes, Miss L. Holland, J. Kingsley Curate supported this claim. £15 was granted. (In 1853, no grant made after an application by Knutsford tradesmen, Miss Holland having refused to sign. In 1855, Robert Clowes, Lucy Holland and Charles A. Merriman supported, result: 'order of the day'. In 1856, Robert Clowes, Charles Mitchell (chaplain, Knutsford House of Correction) and Joseph Swinburne supported: £10 granted. Emily Leycester of Toft Hall and Lucy Holland were providing eight shillings a week.)

~

Letter 165 to MA from [Manchester] redated Friday, [?12 May 1854]

~

MARY GREEN*

Wednesday morng
[?17 May 1854]

My dear Mary,

I am ashamed to think how long your kind letter has remained unanswered; but it shan't go on an hour longer, unless some of the many unforeseen interruptions of my life break in. I have been in a great fright this last fortnight about scarlet fever. It broke out about 3 weeks ago (but

I only heard of it next Friday fortnight,) all around us; within 50 yards in one case; and two nurseries were swept bare by the terrible scourge within 300 yards.[1] The first thought was that little Maggie Shaen, who was coming to us with her Mama, must not be brought into the infected air; & the next was for my own children. Our doctor said they must go from home, & where to send them to, was the question? One heard of Scarlet fever every where. However I wrote to Pearson Langshawe[2] who kindly went over to Poulton, found that there was no (known) case of S. F there, & secured lodgings, 5, New Terrace wherever that is. Then we packed Hearn & the children off, clothes-less, for all their clothes were at the wash. However last Thursday Marianne followed, with a stock of clothes, lesson-books &c; and we have hitherto had capital accounts every day. So much for that.

Then Wm, who pretended to be last week at Bowden, but really *was* here almost every day went to Dumbleton[3] on Monday; & Meta you know is in London. So I am white washing, scouring, chimney-sweeping &c to my heart's content at home. The great thing is that I miss dear Emily Shaen's visit: a visit I look forward to as one of *the* greatest pleasures of the year, from one year to another. She has never had the S. F. & though she has no fear, her father & husband forbid her coming. Today she is in Dundas Place,[4] & I shall get a glimpse of her; that's all. I am *so* sorry. So you see instead of keeping to our plan of not leaving home this summer we are all dispersed. Busy work for letter writing to the different members!

I look forward to the Knutsford strawberries I can assure you, & shall only be too glad as far as I am concerned to come to you. *But* we are expecting friends from Paris[5] in either June or July; and I dare not promise so long beforehand as there are many floating engagements. Marianne shall come sometime, tell Ellen; but she has been so much from home, & the children have had so many holidays that she must be rather stationary the rest of this year. All however seems more unsettled as to our plans than I ever knew it before. We don't know what the 'Chapel' means to do. We *hear* that it is likely to be sold to the Town-Hall[6] and Mr Gaskell says I must not be too impatient & ask questions about anything for that 'it is considered impertinent in a minister's wife'. Oh! I *should* like to see gardens & country in July, if it goes on as dusty as it is today. But I must wind up my note, as it is Mary's[7] last day. Give my kind love to the girls.

Yours affecly
E C Gaskell

Dr R. Jamison

1 Cf. ECG's phrase, 'desolate nursery swept bare', in 1850 (*Letters*, p. 102; *EY*, p. 126).

2 Mrs Joan Leach identifies as James Pearson Langshaw (1814–96), who m. Emily Sharpe (b. 1812), niece by marriage of Peter Holland (*EY*, pp. 117, 152).

3 Bowden was in the Cheshire countryside, south of Manchester (see *Letters*, p. 155). Dumbleton was the splendid estate of cousin Edward, son of Swinton Colthurst Holland, in Gloucestershire (*EY*, pp. 181–2)..
4 Stephen Winkworth was at Dundas Place (Nelson Street) from May 1850; his sister Susanna* left at the time of his marriage in 1856.
5 Perhaps the Mohls* or French friends, apparently coming with a kitten called Cranford (*Letters*, pp. 284, 293). Julius Mohl's Persian cat, 'in spite of being called La Grande Mademoiselle, was the ancestress' of Florence Nightingale's* many pets (C. Woodham-Smith, *Florence Nightingale 1820–1910*, 1950, p. 329).
6 Dr Geoffrey Head informs us that throughout WG's period as minister, the site of Cross Street Chapel was vulnerable to a town council that wished to develop the city centre.
7 Probably cousin Mary Holland (*Letters*, p. 283)

MARIA SINGLETON

To Maria Singleton from her sincere friend,
E. C. Gaskell.
May 20th 1854

Knutsford Public Library

JOHN M. F. LUDLOW*

Plymouth Grove
Manchester,
Monday [?29 May 1854]

Dear Mr Ludlow,

I can *not* get my lawyer-friend to take any notice of my letters of enquiry as to Guyon, the great beautiful Hungarian Wolf-Hound. Either the lawyer is not at home, or Guyon is disposed of. I will go on worrying him – (i. e the lawyer,) but meantime don't suppose I'm neglectful of the Keeper[1] of the Ashmolean Museum. My little girl has got some Cochins, thank-you; a Jessy, and a Johnnie and an anonymous, & a Lily after myself. You are going to receive such a long letter (apropos to your MS) from me before very long. So be prepared. I have often wanted to make some enquiry about Mrs Ludlow;[2] I have several times felt a little anxious to know that we did not seriously knock her up that hot Sunday. I hope we did not. Will you give my affectionate regards to her? Mr Penrose never copied me out those valuable lines, so I only remember the first 'One old ox opening oysters.'[3]

I have never moved from home since the week I last saw you; but we are now going off for a fortnight or so.[4] I do *expect* to hear of Guyon, & when I do I will let you know.

Yours ever very truly
E. C. Gaskell

Annotation 1854.

Cambridge University Library, Add 7348/10/121

1 John Phillips (1800–74), Keeper of the Ashmolean Museum from early 1854 and previously Professor of Geology at Trinity College Dublin. No connection is known between him and either ECG or Ludlow.
2 Ludlow* was unmarried; this would be his mother.
3 Presumably a children's alphabet rhyme.
4 ECG was in London with her husband by Thursday, 1 June 1854 (*Letters*, p. 295).

JOHN M. F. LUDLOW*

Wednesday Noon.
[?7 June 1854]

My dear Sir,

Will you be so kind as to give the enclosed note to Mrs Ludlow? You would perhaps see that the note this morning was not in my handwriting, for I was obliged to go out very early in hopes of being back in time for the chance of *that* call of Mr Kingsley's which never will come to pass. But they tell me the omission of \ naming / Sunday as the day on which I could come is 'very characteristic' of me.

I am afraid you do not quite like my coming on that day; but I could *not* manage it otherwise. And I have named an hour which I am now half-afraid is too early, because I wanted to be allowed to join in the 'Conventicle'.[1]

Yours very truly
E. C. Gaskell

Annotation 1854

Cambridge University Library, Add 7348/10/122

1 A Sunday morning service conducted by Ludlow and Hughes. See p. 94 n. 2 above.

JOHN M. F. LUDLOW*

8 Bedford Row
Thursday [?8 June 1854]

My dear Mr Ludlow,

I find my Bradshaw is an old one, so that I cannot be quite certain of the times of the trains to Wimbledon. Those mentioned in it are 8.10, 9.50, and 10.30.

Can you tell me whether there are any alterations for this month, and also which train would suit you best, as I should be very sorry either to miss, or in any way interfere with your Sunday morning 'Conventicle'.

I am yours very truly
E C Gaskell

Annotation (forged) 1854[1]

Cambridge University Library, Add 7348/10/123
Perhaps dictated to Catherine Winkworth* (*GSN* 11, March 1991, p. 9).

1 WG and ECG were staying with the William Shaens*, ?1–13 June 1854. John Forster* came to advise ECG about the composition of *North and South* (*Letters*, p. 295 et seq.; *L & M*, I. 443). See also misplaced letter, p. 158 below.

~

Letter 147b to MA from [Manchester] redated [?22 September ?1854]

~

MRS EMILY SHAEN*

Thursday. Lea Hurst[1]
[27 October 1854]

Well! I vow I won't write letters; but it's no use; & I must answer you. You *have* done me so much good, dearest Nim[sic]; more than any one else in my life, – (that I'm aware of) except my own darling Aunt Lumb, & Miss Mitchell. I always feel raised higher when I'm near you, & *held up* in a calmer & better atmosphere than my usual anxious poor, impatient one. One person may act on some & not on others, – it's no cause for {disheartenment} \ despair / because, darling, you can't work on every body; very few *can* – only such people as F. N. I am so *sorry* to hear how weak you are. I had no idea thereof. I'll enclose you 2 pieces of Mr S. Gaskell[2] to show how *he*'s carried off his feet. When I *told* him of Miss F. N. before he saw her, he called her my 'enthusiastic young lady' & irritated me by speaking very contemptuously of her; as 'well-meaning' &c. Now here's his first piece, & his second piece, & *you need not return 'em*.

Oh! I wish I were with you my dear E. to nurse you a bit, & pour into you. But I'll do the best I can towards answering your questions. By the way I've written in such a hurry to Katie that she has misunderstood me. The Egyptian letters[3] *are* to be *printed*; only *not* [double stress] some bits, which I thought especially beautiful & touching, & telling of individual character. And before I forget I've got that poor Emma Gallagher(that girl I had in the summer,) *cleaned* most thoroughly, & decently clothed waiting for a place at our house. She is 16 but sharp & good for her age; I don't think she would do for London perhaps; but I should like her to have some nice place. She was starving at home.[4]

(Back to Miss F. N.) Mrs Nightingale says she was a 'dreamy' child. Did I tell you of her 13 dolls *all* ill in rows in bed, when she was quite a little thing. These two girls had a governess for two years & a half – from 7 to 9½ with F. N. Then she married, & they'd another, whom they did not like, so then Mr N. took his girls in hand, & taught them himself. He is a *very* superior man; full of great interests, took high honours at College, – & worked away at classics & metaphysics, & mathematics with them; especially F N who he said had quite a man's mind. She does not sound to have been wayward, – only carried away by a sense of the 'Father's work' that she ought to be about. She was early struck by all sorts of Catholic legends, – (not that she's a bit Catholic, except as feeling that *that* is a living faith. One day she said (I can't remember many of her sayings, but I'll try & recollect all I can, & then remember they're private bits.) 'There are two Churches in Europe that are dead, the Anglican & the Greek – & two that are alive, the R. Catholic & the Lutheran. The two former can be galvanized into action, but the actual living soul has departed out of them.'

I used to ask Parthe N.[5] a great deal about *F* N. Parthe is plain, clever, and *apparently* nothing out of the common way as to character; but she *is*, for all that. She is devoted – her sense of existence is lost in Florence's. I never saw such adoring love. To set F at liberty to do her great work, Parthe has annihilated herself, her own tastes, her own wishes in order to take up all the little duties of home, to parents, to poor, to society, to servants – all the small things that fritter away time & life, *all* these Parthe does, for fear if anything were neglected people might blame F., as well as from feeling them *duties* as imperative as if they were grand things. Well! but to return I was always asking Parthe about F; and I never saw such intense affection as that with whh she spoke of her. She said that she never saw any one like Florence for the natural intense love of God, – as a personal being. She says F does not care for *individuals* – (which is curiously true,) but for the whole race as being God's creatures. One little speech of Florence's Parthe told me, – 'I look to 30 as the age when our Saviour took up his work. I am trying to prepare myself to follow His steps when I am as old as he is.' Now she is 33 –

Florence takes up one thing at a time, & bends her whole soul to that. Music was it once. When they were 17 & 18 Mr & Mrs N. took them to Italy before they were presented. And F worked away at music: the Scientific part; & for the time cared for nothing *but* music. She has never cared in the least for Art. Then again the study of the truth as disguised in the myths & hieroglyphics of the old Egyptian religion, as the root of other religions, took hold of her; (you will see the exquisite beauty of her ideas on this head, when you get her letters –) & for a year & a half in Egypt & in Athens she was absorbed in this. Now all this is swept away. They were correcting the proofs of her Egyptian letters when she was here, – & had to refer to her about the myth about Thoth. She could remember nothing about it. She did not even care to *try* & remember. She never reads any book now. She has not time for it to begin with; & secondly she says life is so vivid that books seem poor.

The latter vols of Bunsen[6] are the only books that she even looked into here. She used to sit with her head bent a little forwards, one hand lying in repose over the other on her knees, looking in that steady way whch means that people are not seeing the real actual before them. The only thing she talked much about that *I* heard was suggested by Bunsen, who stated something like this – that among the Japhetic races *individuals* had not so much influence as among the Shemitic; Mr Nightingale said that that was a finer state of society when individuals were not so much ahead of those about them &c; & she took up the other side very warmly, & said that the admiration of the heroic was of itself so fine a quality, & was lost – along with epic poetry &c where heroes were none &c &c &c. It was *very* interesting, but I make a mess of it in repeating.

I'll tell you one or two more of her speeches, – only mind! I felt that I heard them as being received into the family, not as addressed to me myself, so they are rather private. Speaking of the Cholera in the Middlesex Hospital,[7] she said – 'The prostitutes came in perpetually – poor creatures staggering off their beats! – it took worse hold of them than of any. One poor girl, – loathsomely filthy came in, & was dead in four hours. I held her in my arms & I heard her saying something. I bent down to hear. 'Pray God that you may never be in the despair I am in at this time.' I said 'Oh my girl, are you not now more merciful than the God you think you are going to? Yet the real God is far more merciful than any human creature ever was, or can even imagine.' Then again, I never heard such capital mimicry as she gave of a poor woman, who was brought in one night, when F N. & a porter were the only people up – every other nurse worn out for the time. 3 medical students came up, smoking cigars, & went away. F N. undressed the woman, who was half tipsy, but kept saying 'You would not think it Ma'am but a week ago I was in silks & satins; in silks & satins Ma'am, dancing at Woolwich. Yes! Ma'am for all I'm so dirty I'm dressed in silks & satins sometimes. Real french silks & satins.' This woman was a nurse, earning her 5 guineas a week with nursing ladies. She got better.

She has very seldom told her family of her plans till they were pretty well matured; then they remember back for years little speeches (like that about our Saviour at 30,) which show that the thoughts have been in her mind for years. I saw a *little* instance of this while she was here. She had had the toothache, & an abscess in her mouth, & Mrs N. was *very* anxious about her, as she was evidently not strong. On Monday she said 'I am going tomorrow.' This took them quite by surprize as she evidently was still very poorly; & Mrs N. remonstrated; but it turned out she had written & made so many arrangements depending on her presence before she had even spoken about it to her family that they had nothing to do but to yield; & it struck me, that considering how decidedly this step of hers was against their judgement as well as against their wishes it was very beautiful to see how silently & diligently they all tried to 'speed the parting guest.' Indeed that seems their constant plan.

They can not change her determinations. Parthe one day said 'She seems led by something higher than I can see & all I can do is to move every obstacle in my power out of her path'; and so it is with them all. That text always jarred against me, that 'who is my mother & my brethren,' – and there is just that jar in F. N. to me, – She has no friend – she wants none. She stands perfectly alone, half way between God & his creatures. She used to go a great deal among the villagers here, who doat upon her. One poor woman lost a boy 7 years ago of white swelling in his knee, & F N. went twice a day to dress it. The boy shrank from death; F N. took an engraving from some Italian master, a figure of Xt as the Good Shepherd carrying a little lamb in his arms, & told the boy that so tenderly wd Xt carry him &c. The mother speaks of F N – did to me only yesterday – as of a heavenly angel. Yet the father of this dead child, – the husband of his poor woman died last 5th of September & I was witness to the extreme difficulty with which Parthe induced Florence to go & see this childless widow *once* while she was here; & though the woman entreated her to come again, she never did. She will not go among the villagers now because her heart & soul are absorbed by her hospital plans, & as she says she can only attend to one thing at once. She is so excessively soft & gentle in voice, manner, & movement that one never feels the unbendableness of her character when one is near her. Her powers are astonishing. In one way you will see that in the Egyptian letters, – in another way in what she has done in the Ladies Hospital in Harley Street. She has been night-nurse & day nurse, – housekeeper (& reduced the household expences one third from the previous housekeeper who had been accustomed to œconomy all her life –) mixer-up of medicines, secretary, attended all the operations, – & rubbed cold feet perpetually at night – which last I name because they found that one lady jumped out of bed when F. N. was coming round & stood with her feet upon the hearth stone in order to have them rubbed.

To go back to F N's previous life – I believe there is no end to the offers she has had – For nine years Mr M. Milnes[8] was at her feet; but Parthe says she never knew her care for one man[altered word] more than another in any way at any time. Mr & Mrs Bracebridge(named in S G's letter) went with her into Egypt. I long for those Egyptian letters. They *must* come out before your confinement.[9] She & I had a grand quarrel one day. She is I think, too much for institutions, sisterhoods, & associations, & she said if she had influence enough not a mother should bring up a child herself; there should be créches[*sic*] for the rich as well as the poor. If she had 20 children she would send them all to a créche, seeing of course that it was a well-managed créche. That exactly tells of what seems to me *the* want, – but then this want of love for individuals becomes a *gift*, & a very rare one, if one takes it in conjunction with her intense love for the *race:* her utter unselfishness in serving & ministering. I think I have told you all, – even to impressions, – but she is really so extraordinary a creature that impressions may be erroneous, & any thing like a judgement of her must be presumptuous. And what a letter I have written! Only if you're on the sofa it won't tire you, as it might do if you were busy. I'll even stick in a letter from Meta, which you can send back *sometime*. Only I want it back. There's no hurry; by Susanna will do; & Mr Sam Gaskell, as I told you, you may burn. I have told Meta she may begin to prepare herself for entering upon a nurse's life of devotion when she is thirty or so, by going about among sick now, & that all the help I can give in letting her see hospitals &c, if she wishes she may have. I doubt if she has purpose enough to do all this; but I have taken great care not to *damp* her, – & if she *has* purpose, I will help her as I promise, to lead such a life; tho' it is not every one who can be Miss N.[10] You will also see that she is much happier: & they seem very fond of her. Oh! I'm sorry about Sarah. Remember it is not Sarah per se that you have to consider; you have justice to do to Wells, & to your other servant whoever she may be. If you & Sarah were alone in the house it might simplify things & make it easier. I wish, my darling, you *were* here, for a day only. It is so lovely: so very lovely, & still, & out of the world: to say nothing of air more pure than I ever felt yet. You *have* done me lasting good; Emily. So there! I give you the lie. I won't speak about Sarah.

Yes! I have read Carlyle's W. M. once or twice, – & thought it wonderfully clever & suggestive, & disagreeable & I remember the Hamlet criticism particularly; the oak in the vase &c but surely Hamlet '\ fat & / scant o' breath' is in Hamlet's self, & that style of fat suggests fairness.[11] I've got to – (with Margaret,[12] – I'm off at that now following your letter,) when they've quarrelled, silently, after the lie, & she knows she loves him, & he is trying not to love her; & Frederick is gone back to Spain, & Mrs Hale is dead, & Mr Bell is just come to stay with the Hales, & Mr Thornton *ought* to be developing himself, – & Mr Hale ought to die, – & if I could get over this next piece I could swim through the London life beautifully into the sunset glory of the last scene. But *hitherto* Thornton is good; & I'm afraid of a touch marring him; & I want to keep his character consistent with itself, & yet large & strong & tender, & *yet a master*. That's my great puzzle. I am enough on not to *hurry*; & yet I don't know if waiting & thinking will bring any new ideas about him. I wish you'd give me some. I go to Captain Holland's,[13] Ashbourne Hall Derbyshire tomorrow & home on Tuesday next.

Your own grateful & affect. Lily

My duty to Will, – & dear love to Maggie, bless her.

Envelope Mrs Wm Shaen / 8 Bedford Row / London.

Postmarks GU / 27 OC 27 / 1854 *and* MATLOCK / BATH / OC 28 / 1854

Annotations [notes in ECG's hand?] Meta / Emma Gallagher / Miss F N /Mrs S[?] / W M [not in ECG's hand:] written at Lea Hurst / posted at Matlock

Pierpont Morgan Library (Gordon Ray Collection)
MS substituting GL 217, reprinted from a slightly cut version in Haldane, *Mrs. Gaskell,* pp. 90–96.

1 Derbyshire Summer home of the Nightingale family (only 15 bedrooms). Embley Park, Hampshire, was their main home.
2 WG's brother, Samuel Gaskell (1807–86), a very experienced doctor, was in 1849 appointed a Commissioner in Lunacy (like Bryan Procter and John Forster*) and based in London; at 2 St James Place in October 1854. (*Letters,* p. 313).
3 *Letters from Egypt for Private Circulation Only,* 1854. Charles Holte Bracebridge and his wife Selina ('Sigma') of Atherstone Hall, near Coventry, had rescued Florence from psychological collapse by taking her to Rome and, in the winter of 1849–50, to Egypt. She visited Kaiserswerth on he way back, arriving for a fortnight on 31 July 1850 with her baby owl from Greece, Athena, in her pocket.
4 A single, unindexed reference to Emma Gallagher in *Letters* (p. 793) is explained by these restored two sentences. See *Portrait,* p. xii.
5 Parthenope [Greek for Napoli] Nightingale (1819–90), sister of Florence* [Firenze], also a correspondent of ECG. In June 1858 she married Sir Harry Verney (1801–94), of Claydon House, Buckinghamshire. He was old, rich and active, with '4 children ready-made, which is an advantage', Florence thought.
6 Bunsen's *Hippolytus,* of late 1853.
7 F. B. Smith, *Florence Nightingale: Reputation and Power,* 1982, pp. 16–17, asserts that these stories are not supported by the hospital's archives. (Smith gives the correct name of the recipient in his footnote.)
8 After nine years of courtship Richard Monckton Milnes* made his final offer of marriage in June 1849. He was refused.
9 Willie born 4 December 1954, 'a regular little red Carib ... still far from Caucasian' (*L & M,* I. 470, 478).
10 'Her education of her daughters was remarkable for its time in that she allowed their natures to develop rather than imposing patterns upon them' (Patsy Stoneman, *Elizabeth Gaskell,* 1987, p. 33).
11 In J. W. von Goethe's *Wilhelm Meisters Lehrjarh,* trans. by T. Carlyle 1824, the hero is a member of an acting company whose performance of *Hamlet* provides for commentary on the play. See in particular Book V, chs 4–12 *passim,* where ECG's specific references occur.
12 The working title of *North and South.*
13 From 1852 the home of Captain Frederick Holland, R. N. (1814–60), son of S. C. Holland and therefore ECG's first cousin.

~

Letter 608 (undated) from [?Lea Hurst or Ashbourne] to MA now dated [late October 1854]

Letter 626 (undated) to Mrs Ouvry now dated [?c. October ?1854]

~

RICHARD COBDEN*

Plymouth Grove
[Thursday] November 23. [?1854]

My dear Mr Cobden,

I should have enjoyed meeting you at Teddesley[1] very much; but there are[altered word] all sorts of engagements and occupations to tie me fast at home just now, and so I must relinquish the pleasure. Mr Macready[2] comes here on Saturday, the 25th, time unknown; and Mr Scott (and nobody else,) will share our family dinner at four o'clock on Sunday next. Mr Gaskell and I are *almost* sure you will be unable to come, but still we ask you, by way of not losing a chance. Remember there will be only Mr Scott & Mr Macready besides ourselves; and that four o'clock dinners may go under the name of lunch if you have any late dinners in prospect. Mr Gaskell desires his kindest regards, he is just returned from Glyn Garth, where he left all well; Mrs Schwabe is going to Paris again this winter. Mrs Rich & Chevalier Neukomm[3] are her visitors[.] Will you remember me to Mrs Cobden, & believe me ever, dear Mr Cobden

Yours very truly
E. C. Gaskell.

West Sussex Record Office Cobden Papers 17

1 Home of Lord and Lady Hatherton, Staffordshire.
2 William C. Macready (1793–1873), actor. This information corrects date from typescript source, *Letters*, p. 325.
3 Chevalier Sigismund Neukomm (1778–1858), musician, friend of Geraldine Jewsbury in Manchester.

~

Letter 222 to Eliza Fox, Monday, Dec. 24, 1854, redated Monday [?4 December] 1854

~

SARAH HIGGINS[1]

Plymouth Grove
Friday Evening [?1854]

My dear Sarah,

Will you tell the other girls that I would rather they did not come on Saturday (tomorrow) but on the following Saturday, *the 18th*,) as I should prefer getting it so that we had *not* the Saturday & Sunday together[.]

Your sincere friend
E. C. Gaskell

Envelope Miss Sarah Higgins / 38 John Street / Boundary Street / Oxford Road.

Chicago University Library

1 Sarah Higgins (Mrs Richard Wade) was a Sunday School pupil of ECG. This note is found in the 5th edition of *Mary Barton* (1854). A presentation copy to another pupil, Ann Smith, is dated 20 May 1854. See *EY*, p. 434 n. 12.

MISS YATES[1]

January 1st [?1855]

My dear Miss Yates,

We are hoping to see a few friends belonging to the Congregation on Friday Evening the 12th instant, to tea, and if you should find yourself able, and be inclined to come when the time arrives, we shall be truly glad to see you; only don't trouble yourself to write either way at present. Give us the chance of having the pleasure of your company if all goes well, as I trust it may.

Yours most truly
E. C. Gaskell

Illinois University Library

1 Perhaps the senior Miss Yates of 'The Dingle', Toxteth Park, daughter of Joseph Brooks Yates (1780–1855), of a prominent Liverpool Unitarian family. The perpetual calendar gives 1838, 1844, 1849 and 1855 as possible dates. WG was with them in 1855.

MRS MARIA JAMES

Plymouth Grove
Monday, Janry 22 [1855].

My dear Mrs James,

I have a great deal to say; some of which I mean to keep till I have a chance of seeing you; i.e. when I pass through London from Febry 8 to Febry 13th,[1] when I am coming to you about advice as to a good shop to sell old point lace; of which a poor friend of mind has had a valuable legacy, – as she thinks; & as they form part of the first turn of good-fortune in her long Governess life she is anxious to make the most of it, and has requested me to get them valued, if not sold for her in London. So much for *that*. *Lace* knowledge is what I want from you. But I want a little piece of *law* knowledge (gratis) from Mr James.

We know a ci-devant dissenting minister;[2] who has a deranged wife, whom he neglects; and two little girls, whom he more than neglects. The eldest is to a certain degree cared for; the second aged 4 years is treated by him as follows; she sleeps with him \ in the same bed / in his miserable lodgings; he washes & dresses her; & begs her a sausage or a veal-pie for her breakfast; puts her to bed again at 12, when his engagements call him out. From bed at noon she dare not stir under peril of a severe beating she dare not stir[*sic*] till his return; sometime 4 sometimes ½ past 6, sometimes far later. The woman of the house works out of doors, & this little wee child is left perfectly alone without food, or power of motion, or help if it cries, or light in these dark evenings, – or any kind of companionship He has *no notion of responsibility* almost to the degree of being mad himself. If the child, walking out with him, meets any friend of his who speaks kindly to her, she puts her hand in theirs, saying 'Take me away from that man.' Otherwise she never speaks. She came out of the cheerful nursery of a friend in September, but is now becoming idiotic, & is quite unable to remember anything.

She is a lovely little creature. Her mothers friends, who are well off, would do *anything* to get her, & bring her up; but he (her father) has an aversion unspeakable to them, owing to their having opposed his marriage; and declares he would carry off his child where no one could hear of her again sooner than let her go. Meanwhile the child is becoming idiotic; if not already so; her eyes are diseased with opthalmia &c. Is the law good for anything or not in such a case? Please ask the Vice-Chancellor; & tell him how sorry we all were not to see him when he was here.

My paper is in mourning for Sir Henry Holland's father.[3] We are all well I am glad to say. I trust you are, my dear Mrs James? Yours affectionately

E C Gaskell

Princeton University Library

1 ECG hoped to see Mrs James (p. 58 n. 1 above) on her way to Paris (*Letters*, pp. 329–31).
2 The next letter gives his name as Cameron.
3 Peter Holland died 10 January 1855. June (*EY*, p. 441) is an error from Irvine's pedigree, but cp. his p. 71.

MRS MARIA JAMES

Thursday
[?25 January 1855]

My dear Mrs James,

I was both so ill with influenza, and so overwhelmed with business yesterday that I *could* not write to you, much as I longed to do so, to thank you, oh *so heartily*, for your letter, and the V. C.'s law. In the first place I had to be at the school, 2 miles from here at 9, – till 12; then on to see a family of nine children who have just lost their mother in her confinement, 5 miles from here; back at two to have a meeting by appointment with one or two friends who are taking an interest about this poor little Isabel Cameron &c &c; and so post time came before I had even written you a *line* of acknowledgement! But I know you know how grateful & obliged I was; and how delighted with the Court of Chancery.[1]

I *do* believe Mr Cameron is deranged. He came the other day to call on a Miss Acton,[2] (a very nice daily governess who takes an interest in his elder little girl, & who is almost the only person whom he allows to see either him or his children,) and wheeled a chair into a dark corner of the room, saying 'Don't look at me! Don't look at me. My nose was growing so large, I have pared it all round with my razor,' – and his face really was all blood!

Miss Acton has given me the information as to the treatment of the younger child; & not only confirmed it yesterday, but told me even worse things of the same kind, proving Mr Cameron (I shd say,) to be deranged; for at times, she says, he is very fond of this child; only he seems to have no sense of responsibility about her, and in fact he ought to be treated as a madman. She (little Isabel) has been taken for a week by a Mrs Saml Bright, sister-in law to the MP[3] And our plan at present is this. To write to the mother's friends, stating the present condition of the child, the cruel neglect to which it is exposed, & asking them, formally, if they are willing to undertake the care of the children[,] saying that if persuasion fails to obtain Mr Cameron's consent to such a measure, there are legal means &c.

We *know* of their willingness; and Mr C. has repeatedly said he would sooner see his children dead than under the care of their mother's relations; only it seemed right to take these steps in the first instance. Then I have written to Mrs S. Bright (whom I don't know,) giving a similar account to what I have told you of little Isabel's condition, and begging her to retain the child a little longer; and also for her & her husband (who employ Mr Cameron to lecture to their work-people,) to use all their influence to induce him to give up this youngest little thing to the mother's relations. Then if {all) these steps fail, as we fear they will, we intend to try law. Meanwhile little Isabel *shall* be cared for; unless indeed, what Miss Acton fears, her father, getting hold of some suspicion, carries her off on some of his mad wanderings, of which he gives no account.

The difficulty will be to obtain evidence. There is the bad rough woman with whom Mr Cameron lodges; but she is out much of the day, & cares little for the child, & much for keeping her room let. There is the elder sister, Ida, who can tell a great deal, – but is only eight years old, & in dreadful fear of her father. (Ida is placed at school by the assistance of friends, & spends her holidays with Miss Acton; and there are Mr Cameron's own admissions of his treatment of Isabel, made to Miss Acton; but she fears so his carrying off both the children, & her never hearing of them again; or at any rate his never allowing her to see Ida again, & beating Ida for telling that she begs, that, if possible she may not be named; although she says, if everything else fails she will come forwards. So these are our difficulties; & that's where it stands!

Then I will bring the lace; and *thank* you. Oh! I have been so cramped for room at the end of N & S.! They objected to more than 20 numbers; said 'the public would expect me to keep my word' &c, – a word which *they* had passed, not I. I begged hard for the interpretation of 'five months['] to include 22 nos and obtained the favour with a kind of Che sarà sarà resignation on their part, & a perpetual grumbling. So my poor story is like a pantomime figure, with a great large head, and very small trunk. And it might have been so good! I shall try to add something to the separate publication to make it less unnatural, & deformed. But I will never write for H. W. again.[4]

Yes! indeed I will come to see you very thankfully if you will have me. Meta & I go up to London on the 8th, Meta, being immediately swallowed whole by the Austins; & I, after some consideration, determining that, what with my 'Lace to sell',\ on Friday / and the necessity of going to call on the Tagarts & at Mrs Lalor's on the Saturday, I ought not to be anybody's visitor, have taken 2 rooms for 4 nights, till the 13th, at a person's house, who is under great obligations to us, & who sends a most devoted message respecting the care she will take of me 'as in duty bound'.[5] Her house has the additional recommendation of being in Bloomsbury Sq; near Mrs Shaen's for odd moments; & there Meta is to come on the Monday night, ready for a start from London Bridge with two of the Combe Hurst Smiths the next morning. I suppose we shall be in Paris about 3 weeks, during which time reviewers are earnestly requested to say all they have got to say about N. & S.; and then on my return I again deposit Meta at the Austin's; and I must spend 3 or 4 days with the Bonamy Price's, if they like to have me; & then I should very much like to spend about as many with you.

Mr Gaskell I am sorry to say, after flying about a good deal in the autumn, is tied fast now until Whitsuntide. MA says I am to be sure & tell you that when in London in September, after the Norwich Festival[6] she went up Wimpole Street, hoping to see you: but saw closed windows instead, & heard you were out of town. I wish you would not be 'afraid of asking me purposely'. MA. & I agree that yours is one of the 3 houses we like best to stay at. I have, like you, so much to say, – all about the Miss Colemans, – only that must keep[.]

Kindest regards to the V. C. & respects to the whole Chancery Bar, which I am glad to hear is growing both wise & prompt. Love to May & Will

Yours affectionately E. C. Gaskell

Brotherton Collection, Leeds University

1 W. M. James (p. 49 n. 4 above) was a Chancery barrister. One of the functions of the Court of Chancery was to protect the interests of orphaned or otherwise vulnerable children; he had perhaps advised that an appeal could be lodged in this case. In 1869 he became Vice-Chancellor of the Court of Chancery.

2 This information redates Letter 177, to Marianne (*Letters*, p. 263 and n. 2).
3 Samuel Bright (1826–73) was the youngest brother of John Bright.
4 ECG was in dispute with Dickens over the conclusion of *North and South* in *Household Words*. She expanded it for the book edition of 1855 (Smith, p. 89). She continued to send stories and shorter pieces for the magazine, but did not write for it in serial form again. Cf. *Letters*, pp. 329–31.
5 Mrs Dove, no. 36 (*Letters*, pp. 233, 238, 331).
6 A triennial music festival, held in 1854, 12–15 September.

LADY MATILDA MAXWELL[1]

[?c. 12 February 1855][2]

I am afraid not, dear Lady Matilda, and yet I should like to leave it open, if I may. I am going to dine with Mrs Stanley,[3] 6 Grosvenor Crescent, quite quietly 'at their usual dinner hour' – and I do not know what that is; but Mrs Stanley told me she should like to read me some of Miss Stanley's letters from Koulali,[4] which of course implies a quiet sit after dinner. However I am going to find out at what time they dine; but I do not think I can be with you by tea-time; only if I find that I can may I come in for half an hour or so afterwards?

Believe me to remain, dear Lady Matilda,

Yours most truly
E. C. Gaskell

Envelope The / Lady Matilda Maxwell.

Fales Library, New York University

1 Formerly Lady Harriet Bruce (d. 1857), wife of Sir John Maxwell (1791–1865), 7th Baronet.
2 See *Letters*, p. 331, and n. 4 below.
3 Catherine Stanley, née Leycester (1792–1862), wife of the late Bishop Edward Stanley (1779–1849); they were family friends of ECG and her aunt Hannah Lumb (*EY*, p. 109).
4 Mary Stanley (1814–79) took a party of 40 nurses, including fifteen Irish Roman Catholic nuns with their own superior, to the Crimea in December 1854 – much to Florence Nightingale's* dismay. In January 1855, a cavalry barracks at Koulali was turned into a hospital under Mary Stanley and run on the 'lady plan'. Mary Stanley broke down, however, and returned to England in March. She was with the Gaskells in January 1863 (*L & M*, II. 388).

~

Letter 177 to MA from [London] redated [c. 12 February 1855]

~

VERLAG B. TAUCHNITZ[1]

Chez M. Mohl,[2]
120, Rue du Bac, Paris,
February 20th, 1858[sc.1855]

< ... > Now *North and South* has appeared in *Household Words* (in 20 numbers extending from the beginning of last September to the end of January) ... I may add that I am writing a good deal in addition to the last quarter of the story which had to be very much compressed, and spoilt to suit the purposes of *Household Words*. I think it certain that there will be a sixth part of additional matter < ... >

Text from [Curt Otto], *Der Verlag Bernhard Tauchnitz, 1837–1912*, pr. pr. Leipzig, 1912.

1 Publishing firm founded in Leipzig by ChristianTauchnitz in 1837. In 1842 he initiated his Collection of British Authors, a series of pocket-sized paperback reprints. American titles were added later. From the outset he sought the authority of his authors as well as paying them, and all the major – as well as many lesser – English novelists were reprinted in a series that ran for nearly one hundred years, greatly boosted by the increasing popularity of continental rail travel.

2 Professor Julius Mohl (1800–76), Oriental scholar, surrounded by walls of books 'as to suggest almosty inevitably the idea of a mouse in a cheese, eating out the hollow it lives in' (Lesser, p. 118). He had married Mary Clarke on 11 August 1847. This important friendship has been studied by Yarrow, *GSJ* 7 (1993), pp. 17–22; Margaret Lesser, 'Madame Mohl and Mrs Gaskell', *GSJ* 13 (1999), pp. 36–53.

ANON

19 Rue d'Angoulême[1]
Friday Evening
[?late February ?1855]

My dear Madam,

I feel exceedingly obliged to you for your very kind attention, and I will very gladly avail myself of it. My daughter Marianne, and a friend of mine, (Mrs Curtis)[2] who is staying in the same house, will be ready at any time after half past eight at which it may suit you \ to call /; when I hope also to make the acquaintance of a lady who has already, without my seeing her, laid me under a very pleasant obligation.

I remain, dear Madam,
Truly yours
E. C. Gaskell

Huntington University Library

1 See this address, *Letters*, p. 335.

2 Perhaps Annie Curtis, associated with the Schwabe family (p. 187 n. 2 below).

LOUIS HACHETTE[1]

[c. 17 March 1855]

Dear Sir,

I have written out what I thought you would like to know about the novels by *living* writers. I have told you there as well as I could the place which the different novelists hold in England. But, as most of them are more or less known to me personally, and as I have told you very frankly what I think of their books, I am sure I may rely on your not allowing any one to see this paper but yourself. Where I could not give you the author's address, I have put down that of his publisher, to whose care any letters can be addressed. The only personal *friends* I have among the number are Mrs Nicholls[2] (Currer Bell,) and Miss Jewsbury; but I believe I have been quite impartial in what I have said of them. Any further information I can furnish you with on this subject is quite at your service.

I have written twice to Messrs Chapman & Hall. Mr Chapman tells me he has collected all that he can (all that is published in England,) and is only waiting for the completion of the printing of 'North and South', (which will be finished, he says, in a few days,) before sending the parcel to Baillière. But as he is rather dilatory, would you prefer my writing to desire him to send off those which are ready at once?

I am very glad to have an opportunity of reading the article on Macaulay,[3] & will take care that it is safely transmitted to him.

Yours truly
E. C. Gaskell

Name of the author, and address.
Mrs Nicholls, Haworth Parsonage Keighley Yorkshire.
Her works are

'Jane Eyre', 3 vols 8vo, 1848;

(a very remarkable book.)

'Shirley', 3 vols 8vo, 1850

(not so good, but better than the best of most other authors.)

'Villette', 3 vols 8vo 1853.

This is considered fully equal to 'Jane Eyre' as to talent, but the story is not so interesting. Nearly all the action takes place in a 'pension' at Brussels, (Villette,) amongst Belgians and French people. The authoress was English teacher formerly in a pension at Brussels, and some of the characters are portraits. There is a chapter of very fine description of Mlle Rachel, under the name of 'Vashti'.

The books of this writer are published under the pseudonyme of Currer Bell, which retains the initial letters of her maiden name, Charlotte Brontë.

Her two sisters wrote novels; but only one of them succeeded. Her book is called

'Wuthering Heights',

by Ellis Bell, (Emily Brontë) I am not sure how far the French would appreciate this tale, which is a very powerful description of the wildest provincial life in England; more like the earlier part of Mme George Sand's 'Mauprat',[4] than anything else I know. The last edition of *Wuthering Heights* in one vol: contains a short memoir of her sisters by Mrs Nicholls, which is as extraordinary, and as interesting as any of the stories she has written. Their works are published by

Smith and Elder Cornhill, London.

\ All / these books have been reviewed and criticized in every possible English review, magazine, and newspaper, & always with admiration for their wonderful talent.

address

Mrs Marsh[5] Eastbury Harrow near London.

This lady has written about thirty novels, one or two of which are very good; three or four tolerable, and the rest forgotten as soon as read. She writes for money and writes far too quickly. Her first novel was published among [line or more missing] –mously about 20 years ago, and is very fine and dramatic. It is called

'The two Old Men's tales'. 2 vols.

Seven or eight years afterwards she wrote 'Emilia Windham'.

You are probably acquainted with the writings of Mrs Gore, which are about as numerous as those of Mrs Marsh, and are of the class called in England 'Fashionable novels.' They have very little plot in them, their principal interest (for those who read them,) consisting in a lively, spirited epigrammatic description of the manners of lords and ladies. The best novel that Mrs Gore has written is called

Mrs Armytage'. 3 vols.

There was a novel published about two years ago, in one volume, which excited great attention, and the highest praise, and which was, I think, worth all Mrs Gore's, and Mrs Marsh's novels put together. I should be thankful if I could write with the glorious power of that book, with all it's many faults.

'Christie Johnstone'.

by Charles Reade Esq.

(Publisher, Bentley New Burlington Street London.)

The scene is laid at Newhaven, a small fishing-town, near Edinburgh, where the inhabitants are very proud, and only intermarry with each other. The tale is full of pathos and humour, and vivid dramatic effect; *but* the language in which all the people speak is pure Scotch, and it would require a most skilful translator. The fault of the book is it's fragmentary character; the separate events are too much disjointed, like scenes at a play. I don't know at all how it would do in French. I only know that in England we are all waiting impatiently for his next novel.

There are many ladies who come in well in the second rank of novelists;
Miss Jewsbury 3 Oakley Street King's Road Chelsea London
who has written *'Zoe'*, *'The Half-Sisters'*, *'Marian Withers'*, and has just published *'Constance Herbert'*.

'The *Half-Sisters*' is the best of hers. Her books are valued not so much for the story, as for the remarks and observations of the author contained in them. She is daring, shrewd, and amusing, and would write essays perhaps better than stories. But her books are very clever.
Miss Mulock
care of Messrs Smith and Elder Cornhill, London.

She has written six or seven pretty sentimental novels, with not much power displayed in them, but with a good deal of grace and delicacy. {Her} \ Miss Mulock's / books are great favourites with English *ladies*; but I notice that *men* get tired of them. Their titles are

'The Ogilvies'. 3 vols.
'Olive'. 3 vols
'The Head of the Family'. 3 vols.
'Agatha's husband'. 3 vols.

Of these *'The Head of the Family'* is considered the best. These books have been noticed with praise, in the Edingh Review.

About four years ago there was a good novel published, called
'Mrs Margaret Maitland'. It was a quiet story of Scottish Domestic life, among the middle class, written with a certain degree of both humour and pathos. The authoress, whose name I do not exactly know,[6] has published many since, but none so good, though all in the same genre as the first. *'Merkland'*, \3 vols. / is the only title I can remember, but there are always several advertized as 'by the author of Mrs Margaret Maitland'. Her publishers are Hurst and Blackett Great Marlborough Street London.

There is a very brilliant novel, called *'Lady Lee's Widowhood'*, \2 vols. / about a year old. It was first published in numbers in Blackwood's Magazine. The author is a Major Hamley, who has distinguished himself in the Crimea, and is said to be writing a history of the campaign. His novel is very brilliant, and clever. The scene is laid in an English country house, but great varieties of character are introduced, and admirably kept up The 'Times', newspaper, (which rarely reviews novels), noticed 'Lady Lee's Widowhood' about four months ago with high praise.
Publishers Messrs Blackwood & Co Edinburgh.
This book would require a translator almost as witty as the author.

There is a young writer, a friend of Mr Dickens', who is likely to work himself into a good place as a writer of fiction. He takes great pains, and devotes himself to novel-writing, as to a profession. His style is considered very good. I do not much admire his books myself, but many good judges do.

Wilkie Collins Esq
Publishers, Bentley & Co New Burlington Street London.
His books are

'*Antonina*', a romance of the later Roman Empire.
'*Basil*', (detestable)
'*Hide and Seek*', reckoned very good.[7]

Address à Monsieur Hachette
Annotation Paris le 18 mars 1855

Archives Hachette Livre

1 Louis Hachette (1800–64), founder of a famous Parisian publishing firm, instituted in 1853 his series of railway novels, the Bibliothèque des chemins de fer. This published many English novels in translation, including all ECG's major fiction between 1854 and 1868. See also *Letters*, p. 333.
2 Charlotte Brontë had married the Reverend Arthur Bell Nicholls on 29 June 1854.
3 The article is unidentified. See, however, *Oeuvres diverses de Lord Macaulay*, 1st series tr. Amédée Pichot with biographical memoir, 2nd series, tr. A. Joanne et E.-D. Forgues; 2 vols in 1, Paris, L. Hachette 1860.
4 *Mauprat* (1837), by George Sand (1804–76), is a story of family violence, social conflict and education in which a first-person narrator tells how he had been adopted and abused as a child; coarse and uneducated, he is reformed by his beautiful cousin, who leaves her elegant fiancé in order to marry him. See also p. 43 above.
5 Anne Marsh Caldwell (1791–1874), a relation by marriage of ECG (*EY*, p. 108), a widow with seven children since 1849. She wrote *Two Old Men's Tales* (1834); *Emilia Wyndham* (1846) – 'wherewith we are not altogether captivated (as Mrs. Gaskell had told us we should be' (Catherine Winkworth* to Eliza Paterson*, 12 May 1848: *L & M*, I. 146).
6 Margaret Oliphant (1828–97). *Passages in the Life of Margaret Maitland* (1849); *Merkland, A Study of Scottish Life* (1851).
7 ECG's recommendations provide many insights. Her misgivings about the Brontë novels, and notably about *Wuthering Heights*, anticipate comments in *CBL* (1857). Charlotte's 'short memoir' of Emily and Anne in the 2nd edition of *Wuthering Heights* defended her sister against the charge of coarseness.

Catherine Gore (1799–1861), Anne Marsh and Margaret Oliphant were astonishingly prolific. Mrs Gore wrote over 40 novels of society in the 1830s and 1840s; *Mrs Armitage, or Female Domination* was published in 1836. Marsh, Oliphant and Dinah Mulock (Mrs Craik, 1826–97) were driven by severe financial necessity. Dinah Mulock was able to negotiate very favourable contracts; her most famous novel was *John Halifax, Gentleman* (1856); her novels referred to here were published between 1849 and 1853. See also p. 184 no. 3 below.

ECG knew Geraldine Jewsbury well. *Zoë* (1845), *The Half-Sisters* (1848), *Marian Withers* (1851) and *Constance Herbert* (1855) all have an explicitly feminist agenda. Edward Hamley (1824–93) became a full general after a distinguished career. *Lady Lee's Widowhood* (1854) was his only full-length fiction, first published in *Blackwood's Magazine*, as was *The Story of the Campaign: A Complete Narrative of the War in the Southern Russia*. Charles Reade (1814–84), novelist and dramatist, published *Christie Johnstone* in 1853.

William Wilkie Collins (1824–89) was at the start of his career: *Antonina, or The Fall of Rome* (1850), *Basil, A Story of Modern Life* (1852) and *Hide and Seek* (1854) are his first three novels. *Basil* is a story of sexual intrigue: ECG's opinion is supported in the *Westminster Review:* 'The incident which forms the foundation of the whole is absolutely disgusting; and it is kept so perseveringly before the eyes of the reader in all its hateful details, that all interest is destroyed in the loathing which it occasions' (October 1853; 60. 373–3).

LOUIS HACHETTE

120 rue du Bac,
Thursday morning.
[?22 March 1855]

Dear Sir,

I am very intimate with Mrs Nicholls, and Miss Jewsbury, and I shall be very glad if I can in any way facilitate an arrangement between you and my friends. As soon as I return to England (next Wednesday,) I will write to Mrs Nicholls, and see Miss Jewsbury about your wish to enter into a treaty with them for the translation of their works.

But I think I ought to tell you how very offensive such a title-page as the one affixed to the translation of Jane Eyre,[1] which you sent me last night, would be to any English author, especially to a lady bearing the high reputation of Mrs Nicholls (Currer Bell). I am sure from my knowledge of her character that if she were aware of it she would decline entering into any negotiations with you. I allude to the words 'Imités par Old-Nick.' I am sure you are not aware of the extreme vulgarity which all the English affix to the expression 'Old-Nick'. I know that you would not have put any thing of such mauvais ton on one of your books if you had understood how offensive it is to English people. And in the next place every author of any note is anxious for a correct and faithful translation of what they do write; and, {if from}\ although from / the difference of literary taste between the two nations {ever} \ it may / become{s} desirable to abbreviate certain parts, or even to leave them out altogether, yet no author would like to have a whole volume omitted, and to have the translation of the mutilated remainder called an 'Imitation.'

I ought perhaps to apologize for speaking so plainly about this; but, as I believe it to be your wish to enter into a very fair and liberal arrangement with the English authors of reputation, it is better to say frankly that I can not ask Mrs Nicholls to give her assent to the present edition of \ the translation / Jane Eyre. If I told her, or any English novelist of character, the form of this title page, I am sure that they would not enter into any negotiation whatever, let the pecuniary advantage be what it might.

Mme Mohl will very willingly speak to Mme Belloc[2] as you desire; but she thinks that you are not aware that Mme Belloc is very poorly and seldom goes out. I do not know if 'Cranford' will be one of my works which you will select for translation but if it were, I should be very glad, as far as I am concerned, if you and Mme Belloc could come to any agreement, as I fancy she is well acquainted with the delicacies of the English language.

I was very sorry to find that I had forgotten to name Miss Young[*sic*].[3] (This is the real name of the author of the Heir of Redclyffe, although her books appear anonymously.) She has written in periodicals and for children for many years; but without much notice from the public, until she published the 'Heir of Redclyffe' about a year and a half ago. 2 thick vols. of a size smaller than 8vo Parker & Co, Strand, London. This book had an immense success in England; and secured a success for the work she has published since 'Heartsease, or the Brother's Wife.' I am not sure if these two books would be appreciated out of England. They are like delicate miniature-paintings of domestic life, with very little event or story beyond the progress of character. One reason of their great sale (independent of their beauty and labour of execution,) is that they are considered *'safe'* books, which any mother may place in the hands of her children, down to the very youngest, sure that they will receive no new ideas from them, but those relating to religion. There is very little love in these books. They are hardly to be called religious novels, and yet they {are} bear a continual reference to it, and especially to that form of it called *Puseyism* in England.
Miss Kavanagh[4]
Miss Sewell.[5]

Yours very truly
E. C. Gaskell

Archives Hachette Livre

1 *Jane Eyre, ou Mémoires d'une gouvernante, de Currer Bell (C. Brontë), imités par Old Nick*, was an abridgement, published in the Bibliothèque des chemins de fer series in 1855. 'Old Nick' was a pseudonym of Emile-Daurand Forgues for his many translations of English and American works. Ironically, he was to translate both *Sylvia's Lovers* (*Les Amoureux de Sylvie,* 1865) and *Cousin Phillis* (*Cousine Phillis,* 1866). The latter first appeared in the *Revue des deux mondes,* of which he was editor.

2 Louise Belloc, née Swanton (1796–1881). See *EY,* pp. 191–2.

3 Charlotte Mary Yonge (1823–1901), prolific High Anglican author, a disciple of Keble. *The Heir of Redclyffe* (1853) was a best-seller, published by J. W. Parker, followed by at least one hundred titles for adults and children. *Heartsease* (1854).

4 Julia Kavanagh (1824–77), a Roman Catholic, lived in France and England though of Irish extraction. Regarded as an authority on French life and culture, she wrote *Women in France in the Eighteenth Century* (1850), *Women of Christianity* (1852), novels and short stories, often with French settings. See esp. *Letters,* pp. 675–6.

5 Probably Elizabeth Sewell (1815–1906), like Yonge a Tractarian, who wrote novels to pay off her family's debts. Her best known work was *Margaret Percival* (1847). Her brother William, a clergyman who is said to have publicly burned Froude's *Nemesis of Faith* in 1849, was attributed as editor of some of her works.

MRS ANNA JAMESON[1]

11 Princes Terrace[2]
Thursday
[?12 April 1855]

My dear Mrs Jameson,

Till today I hardly knew my plans. Now I do. Tomorrow I shall be 'flitting' from here to 8 Bedford Row; at what time I do not exactly know, but pretty early in the day. On Saturday Meta & I breakfast with Lady Hatherton, and do some shopping afterwards: but Bedford Row will be my home till Monday afternoon, when I go to Mrs James, \ 47 Wimpole St / where I stay till Wednesday, and then Meta & I go off home. If, with this butterfly sort of direction, I could achieve a meeting with you, dear Mrs Jameson, believe me {if} it would give me great pleasure.

I have got our two used catalogues of the Louvre for you. 1854, both. I shall leave them with Mrs James, if I am *not* so fortunate as to see you. Mr Gaskell sends me word of your kindness about that lecture[2], respecting which I took a warm interest, and which is now amplified, is it not? I am truly obliged to you for giving it to me, & so imparting a double value to it. I read, (not *my* copy,) it at Mrs Wedgwood's the day after it came out, & I particularly thanked you for the broad basis you had taken for your noble end and true ideas. Believe me ever, dear Mrs Jameson,

Yours very truly & gratefully,
E C. Gaskell.

You don't know the good you have done me in your life-time, so I have a right to rel<ie>ve myself by signing 'gratefully'.

Pierpont Morgan Library (Gordon Ray Collection)
Letter 234, now expanded from MS; dated from address and movements.

1 Anna Brownell Jameson (1794–1860), writer and art historian. After separating from her husband, she studied art in Italy. 'Lily and she struck up warm friendship', Susanna Winkworth* wrote in December 1852 about a visit to Plymouth Grove (*L & M*, I. 372).
2 Home of T. B. Price (*Letters*, p. 336).
3 Perhaps her essay 'Sisters of Charity' (1855), or 'The Communion of Labour' (1856).

MRS MARIA JAMES

Saturday morning
8 Bedford Row.
[?14 April ?1855]

My dear Mrs James,

My courage is rather crying out about M. Hollond's, on Monday; but I do hope I shall go, as I should like to see her, and it would be very pleasant to go there with you. Only as affairs at present stand I am engaged to dine out with Mr and Mrs Shaen, an engagement which may fall through, but which is I think sufficiently probable to prevent my coming to *dinner* with you, which I should very much have liked. I will try and be with you by *ten* \ 10 o'clock / (will that do?) but if I am not, please don't wait. Is it not rather taking a liberty with her to go there without an invitation, for I don't think you know how little I know of her. I have received a great deal of kindness from her, but I have only seen her, *bodily*, twice.[1]

Mr Gaskell got in to the Crystal Palace[altered word] with an Editor<'s> ticket, as I had bethought me to ask Mr Forster if he could procure him admission; and when once inside he found a friend able & willing to show him more than he had time to see. He heard all the music rehearsed, – saw most things very agreeably if only cursorily, was introduced to many people of note, all though the medium of – hold your nose lest you sneeze at the idea! of a worthy *tobacconist* in Manchester,[2] who has contracted to supply all the drinkables; and being a very clever practical Lancashire man had evidently been able to make his value felt. Thank you for all your exertions, and kindness. I know you will be glad to hear he got in & saw so much even through such ignoble means. For my part I am so grateful I mean to take snuff for the future.

Yours affectionately
E. C. Gaskell

Mrs Lucy Magruder

1 Mrs Robert Hollond[sic]: ECG met her twice in Paris, [?February ?1855] (*Letters*, p. 335).

2 Perhaps Charles Lovatt, a 'well-known tobacconist', with a shop in Market Street (J. T. Slugg, *Reminiscences of Manchester Fifty Years Ago*, 1881; facs. repr. Shannon 1881, p. 3).

MRS MARIA JAMES

Monday [?16 April ?1855][1]
3 o'clock

My dear Mrs James,

I will certainly come. I have only just got your note, and your 'Please do come' is very irresistible. But I may be a little later than 10 as it is a late dinner, & I shall have a good way to go. Will you wait for me?

Yours affe[ctionate]ly in greatest haste
E C Gaskell

Fales Library, New York University

1 Perhaps associated with the previous letter.

LOUIS HACHETTE

Plymouth Grove,
Manchester.
April 26. 1855

Dear Sir,

I have received your kind note of the 23rd of April, and I am extremely obliged to you for it.

I am very glad to learn that you like the translation of Mlle Morel's better on further inspection. To me she was recommended by Mme Geoffroy St Hilaire,[1] but when I became personally acquainted with her, I became interested in her for her own sake, and I am very glad to learn from you that you approve of her translation of 'Mary Barton'.[2] I was not aware that the only translation of 'Ruth' with whose existence I am acquainted was by either Mme Henriette or Pauline de Witt. I knew that they had translated portions of 'Mary Barton', but I was unacquainted with the name of my translator in the 'Revue Contemporaine'.[3]

I fancy you will not find 'the Moorland Cottage' worth translating. 'North and South' is just come to a second edition.

It is very difficult, almost impossible for me to judge which of my smaller stories would please French readers. For instance I should not have imagined that French-people would have cared for 'Libbie Marsh'; yet M. Sayou[?],[4] who translated it, told me that it had been very successful. I, myself, like the *'Sexton's Hero'*, and *'Lizzie Leigh'*, the *'Heart of John Middleton'*, *'The Well of Penmorfa'*, *'The old Nurse's Story'*, and *'Moreton[sic] Hall'*, the best of all my smaller tales.

I have named your intention of applying to the principal English authors, with a view of establishing relations with them, to Mr Charles Dickens, and also to Miss Jewsbury.

My dear friend, Mrs Nicholls, died, as you are aware, very unexpectedly. Her publishers are Messrs Smith and Elder, Cornhill,

London; and Mr Smith was also her personal friend.[5] I imagine that any application, as to the right of translating her works, had better be made to *Mr Smith*; as, although the copyright belongs to her heirs, yet, as her property in them goes to her husband, the Reverend Arthur Bell Nicholls, who always disliked her writing novels, and is now, moreover, in the deepest grief for her loss, a letter on the subject of a french translation of her works would not be likely to be attended to, I fear; while Mr Smith would most honourably represent her interests, as inherited by her husband.

I have now I believe, Sir, answered all the points in your letter, and I beg you to believe what pleasure it will always give me to be of any use or service to you in my power.

I am extremely gratified by the kind assurances at the close of your letter that I shall not be forgotten by you, and Madame Hachette. I can only say how happy it will make me to have the pleasure of renewing our intercourse either here, or in Paris; and, in either case, presenting my husband to you, to share in your kindness and friendship [three words repeated], which have formed so pleasant a part of my recollections of my stay at Paris. Believe me, Sir, we shall only be too happy at some future period, if we can so arrange it as to pass a short time with Madame Hachette, and yourself at your country-house; and we hope sometime to have the pleasure of showing you our great manufacturing town.

My daughter Meta begs to recall herself to Madame Hachette's favourable recollection, and to say how much the little bag has been admired. Mr Gaskell also desires me to present his compliments to Madame Hachette, and yourself, and believe me, dear Sir, to remain

Yours truly
E. C. Gaskell

Archives Hachette Livre

1 Isidore Geoffroy Saint-Hilaire (1805–61) was a Professor of Zoology from 1850. MA was afraid that they would 'have to talk zoologically' at his home; ECG adds, '& be kissed' (*Letters*, p. 332).

2 Hachette must have sought ECG's approval prior to publication: Mlle Octavie Morel's translation appeared in the Bibliothèque des chemins de fer in 1856, a railway paperback reprint series founded in 1853 for a primarily French readership. The similar Tauchnitz series in Germany had European aims.

3 *Ruth*, translated by Mme Cornélis de Witt, daughter of François Guizot, and *Cranford*, translated by Mme Louise Belloc, were published in the same series in the same year. All of ECG's longer works and a number of her stories were translated for Hachette in the 1850s and 1860s.

4 *Trois époques de la vie de Libbie Marsh*, Paris 1854. The translator is unidentified, but 'M. Sayou' is possibly Pierre-André Sayous, a literary historian fl. 1860.

5 George Smith* (1824–91), also publisher (Smith & Elder) and an important friend of ECG.

MRS SUSAN DEANE*

Plymouth Grove,
May 7th 1855

My dearest Susan,

Emily has been misinformed, as Marianne wants me to tell her. The visitor we expected, and whose delay in answering Marianne *supposes* she must have alluded to in her note to Heathfield,[1] was Eliza Heald. Until we had a reply from her, I could not tell if we had a bed to offer Emily Green. We never for a moment thought your girls long in answering, as we knew all along about the bed-difficulty and should have made more efforts ourselves to accomodate[*sic*] them, if we had not heard from Agnes Ewart (at Southport) of the Railton's good intentions.

Will *this* note do for an autograph? If not, I will gladly send you another, and if I can send Miss Egerton Leigh any more that she will care to have (of *living* authors I have good store,) I shall be very glad indeed to send her any {of what I have}.

Ever your very affect. cousin
E. C. Gaskell.

Haworth Parsonage Museum

1 Knutsford home of the Reverend Henry and Mary Green*, parents of Emily.

MRS ANN SCOTT

Plymouth Grove
Saturday Evng
[?19 May 1855]

My dear Mrs Scott,

Mr Gaskell is gone into Wales, *and* my two eldest girls are going to Latchford[1] (in Cheshire) tomorrow, *and* my nurse is in Cornwall,[2] *and* all the other servants are expecting holidays this Whitsun Week, so I am unable to leave my two youngest little girls in the evening, and at their bed-time during this \ next / week. Partly for this reason I had previously declined accompanying Miss Shaen to Miss Winkworth's on Tuesday night, where I know she hopes to meet you and the Miss Kerrs[*sic*].[3] It is a very long time since we have seen each other, except by very tantalizing glimpses which count for nothing, but I hope it will not be so much longer. Some day (after the next ten,) when all the family have come together again I shall try to find you at home some evening by driving over in the little poney-carriage. With much kind regard believe me

Yours affectionately
E C Gaskell

 Princeton University Library

1 Near Warrington, where WG was born. See p. 33 n. 2 above.
2 Ann Hearn's first holiday in 12 or 13 years (*Letters*, p. 344).
3 Sisters of Mrs Ann Scott née Ker.

MISS HANNAH KAY[1]

Plymouth Grove
Tuesday[?Wednesday]
July 11th [1855]

My dear Miss Kay,

I write to you instead of to your brother because I think it is most probable that before this he is gone to London as he anticipated. Perhaps you know that he was kind enough to invite Mr Gaskell and me to Gawthrop, with a view of telling me such particulars & impressions arising out of his acquaintanceship with Miss Brontë, as he knew I should especially value for the purpose which I have in hand. I believe that I can not leave home again before Monday or Tuesday the 23rd or 24th of this month; and even then Mr Gaskell is uncertain if he could accompany me. However if either of those days would suit Sir James, I should be very glad to come; and Mr Gaskell perseveres in hoping to be able to accompany me. If {not, I would try} \ the time I name for my visit / does not suit you & Sir James, I wd try to come later on in August from Silverdale near Lancaster, where we shall spend that month.

Believe me my dear Miss Kay

Yours very truly
E. C. Gaskell

Princeton University Library

1 Hannah Kay (1806–69), sister of James Kay-Shuttleworth. This secret visit was replaced by one to Haworth on 23 July (*Letters*, pp. 354, 361, 364).

MARY GREEN*

Gawthorpe.[1] Friday
[?17 August 1855]

My dear Mary,

Upwards of 300 letters to read through / copy what is worth in 2 days, & every day a journey to take till I land at Silverdale again on Monday must be my excuse. Yes! to be sure we can take them in, & with us, just as of old. I shall pack them in among our girls any how – they know the old ways, so that's all settled – & I must go back to my work –

Yours very affely
ECG.

I am always so glad to hear from you & of you, – only I can hardly write back as I shd do – I have got a packet of Fox How flower seeds from Mrs Arnold to Isabella –

Oh! I do so want some quiet. I *must* be so busy at Silverdale –

Dr R. Jamison

1 On 13 August 1855 ECG wrote that she would be at Sir James Kay-Shuttleworth's from 16th (*Letters*, p. 368).

MARIA MARTINEAU

Lindeth Tower
Silverdale
[*c.* 19 August 1855]

My dear Miss Martineau,

I am very much obliged to you for both your letters. The first gives many little particulars to be enquired about, as you know we agreed that from many informants what they said was to be received as *impressions* rather than facts.[1]

Yes! I went over & saw Miss Ellen Nussey[2] for a few hours on Tuesday. I like her; she is simple, affectionate, refined & sensible. She has known Miss Brontë ever since '31, & kept up a correspondence (she has intrusted me with 300 letters to look over,) with her from '32. From one of them I gather that the *2*[alteration]nd year of Miss Brontë's residence at Mme Beck's[3] she *received* 16£ as English teacher – He*g*er [double underline] is that the name? Mr Brontë writes it, as I read He*z*er[multiple underline].

It was *Emily* & Charlotte Brontë who were at Brussels. Mr Nicholls writes me word that Emily absolutely *repelled* people by her cold sullen manner.[4] Will you be so kind as to ask Miss Dixon[5] what Emily was like personally. She must have been the most curious & mysterious of the sisters – Her extraordinary morbid development of talent – her repulsive manners, – & yet the worship she seems to have obtained from Charlotte.

Is the description of the house in Villette like the real house in the Rue d'Isabelle. – I feel very greedy in wanting every detail Miss Dixon could give of that Brussels time, though I hardly know in what direction to ask you to enquire[.] M. Heger's character & *all about him particularly*. What was the subject of 'the treatise in the French language', which Mr Brontë tells me Charlotte wrote for M. Heger, and for which he gave her a diploma. Did she ever visit in any Belgian family, so as to obtain the sort of knowledge of their domestic habits indicated in Robert Moore's sister's character & ways in Shirley.[6] *Can* you ask anything about Miss *Martha* Taylor's illness & death in Brussels, when it happened, if while the Brontës were there[7] – It made (whenever it occurred,) a *deep* impression on Miss C. Brontë – she seemed to me to have loved that girl dearly. Who was 'Ginevra'?[8]

Perhaps I may trouble you again. You are very good & kind. Many of the particulars I should like to have are not for public mention but to fill up my own idea of her character, before I attempt to draw her portrait, which grows more extraordinary & more incomprehensible, i.e. beyond *my* limits of comprehension, – every day. I have written twice to Mrs Taylor, & would go & see her; but at present her husband & child are ill. – She tells me little or nothing; her thoughts being otherwise occupied.

We remain at Silverdale till Sep 4. Oh what writing! you will excuse it, won't you. I am not well, & my hand trembles. I heard from Mrs Turner, with the Taylor's address.[9] I was glad to hear so comfortable an account of your dear Aunt. How kind she was to me![10]

Yours very truly
E. C. Gaskell

Birmingham University Library (on deposit)
We are grateful to Margaret Smith for valuable help with our notes.

1 An ironical assertion in the light of developments after the publication of ECG's *Life*. No other letters to ECG at this time from either Harriet Martineau* or her niece and companion from 1855, Maria Martineau (1827–64), seem to be known. HM had published a sketch of CB in the *Daily News* for 6 April 1855. See also *Letters*, p. 337, 449; Waller, pp. 36–7; Barker, pp. 775, 805–8.

2 Charlotte Brontë's friend Ellen Nussey (1817–97) had proposed ECG as a biographer to A. B. Nicholls on 6 June 1855, offering to be a main source if needed. ECG first went to see Miss Nussey at Brookroyd, Birstall, on 14 August 1855. See esp. *Letters*, pp. 869–90; *CB Letters*, pp. 27–33; Barbara Whitehead, *Charlotte Brontë and her 'dearest Nell'*, Otley, W. Yorks 1993, pp. 195–7.

3 ECG's research met with its greatest difficulties when she investigated CB's life at the Pensionnat Heger in Brussels during 1842–3. Mme Beck is the name of the fictional character in *Villette* (1853) based on Mme Claire Zoë Heger. She refused to see ECG in Brussels, which adds to the uncertainty surrounding CB's relationship with her husband, Constantin Heger.

4 An unexpected comment. No such letter from Nicholls to ECG is known, but cf. *Letters*, pp. 361–2.

5 Mary Dixon (1809–97), was a friend of Charlotte Brontë from Brussels (*CB Letters*, p. 297 n. 4) and knew the Martineaus well. Maria's father Robert Martineau (1798–1870) lived from late 1851 in Highfield Road, Edgebaston, close to the home of Mary's brother George Dixon (1820–98).

6 Charlotte Brontë's *Shirley* (1849), the heroine of which is based upon Emily.

7 Mary Dixon's cousins, Mary and Martha Taylor of Gomersal, were school-friends of Charlotte Brontë and Ellen Nussey at Roe Head. Martha died, probably from cholera, on 12 October 1842. Charlotte and Emily Brontë were in Brussels at the time (*CB Letters*, p. 296).

8 A fictional character, Ginevra Fanshawe, in *Villette,* said to have been based on the 'selfish, worldly and sly' Maria Miller, a fellow pupil at the Pensionat Heger. See Barker, p. 423.

9 Amelia Ringrose, married Joseph Taylor of Gomersal (?1816–1857); their daughter was Emily Martha (1851–58). See *Letters,* pp. 282–3 (the 'decent kind' of Mr Gradgrind); Barker, pp. 699–700. ECG had asked George Smith* earlier, probably in July, for the address of a brother of Mary Taylor: 'she emigrated to Melbourne, I think' (*Letters,* p. 359).

10 Another unexpected comment: ECG seems to have met Harriet Martineau* at Ambleside in 1855 (see p. 159 below).

ANON

Lindeth Tower
Silverdale
Thursday Aug. 23 [?1855][1]

My Dear Sir,

Miss Winkworth comes tomorrow for a week, or[altered from colon] so; could you come to us on Monday or Tuesday next. – I am sorry I can not offer you a bed here; but if you would not mind going to the Inn at night, we would give you every day accomodation (a room to yourself &c) with the greatest pleasure.

Believe me ever

Yours most truly
E. C. Gaskell

John Geoffrey Sharps

1 EGC was at this address on 23 August [1855] (*Letters,* p. 369).

?MARY TAYLOR[1]

Silverdale
till Sepr 4th [c. August 1855].[2]

My dear Miss Taylor,

I am so much obliged to you for your trouble[.] What you send me is good, and is a help. M. Heger *is* Paul Emmanuel,[3] – & don't you see the likeness in all that your friend says of his fulfilment of his duties as a member of the Society of S. Vincent de Paul.[4] But I crave for more – I wish I knew Brussels, – that glimpse of the Rue d'Isabelle at the foot of an escalier en pierres is picturesque, – & one wants the frame-work of locality because *she* was so much influenced by places & surroundings.

Has M. Heger written anything, – I know the school was considered 2nd rate; & I have heard that it has suffered by the publication of Villette.[5] Can you ascertain if this is true? I should like to know a pupil of Madame Becks. She had many English. Thank you. I am like Oliver Twist I 'ask for more'.

Yours most truly
E C Gaskell

Pierpont Morgan Library, MA 4308

1 Mary Taylor (1817–93), of Gomersal, Yorkshire, a school friend of Charlotte Brontë who emigrated to New Zealand, 1845–60. She answered ECG's enquiries in respect of *CBL* and defended it when published. An ardent feminist, her collection of essays, *The First Duty of Women,* was published in 1870. ECG might have been in touch with her earlier than has been realised.
2 Compare the address and dating of Letter 266 (*Letters,* p. 369).
3 Paul Emmanuel is the despotic tutor in *Villette* with whom the heroine, Lucy Snowe, falls in love.
4 The 'friend' might be the unknown French lady in Brussels who wrote to ECG about Heger at a later date; her letter had to be inserted into the manuscript of *CBL.* (See especially *CBL,* ed. Angus Easson, Oxford and New York, 1996, pp. xxiv, 176, 505–6.)
5 ECG wrote to George Smith*, 'I hear Mme Hezer[*sic*] has lost all her pupils since the publication of Villette' (*Letters,* p. 366).

WILLIAM EDWARD NIGHTINGALE[1]

286 Bath Crescent[2]
[Late September 1855]

My dear Sir,

Here is the [']Greyt Eggshibishun',[3] as dirty a copy as I threatened you with yesterday. But I only send it to you as a pledge that a cleaner copy shall be forthcoming. Mr Langshaw gave me this for you, conditionally; I was to try if by writing to the author I could procure another copy, which I believe I shall be able to do, although it is out of print; in which case you will perhaps be glad to exchange 'old lamps for new'.

The Lectures on the Lancashire dialect[4] are by my husband – and are also out of print, or else in this case also you should have had a cleaner copy.

Yours, with much respect
and regard,
E. C. Gaskell.

Columbia University Library

1 William Edward Nightingale (c. 1793–1874), father of Florence* (1820–1910) and Frances [Parthenope] (1819–90), Lady Verney from 1858.
2 Glasgow, the home of Charles Wilson, 'an extremely intelligent Scotch artist', married to a cousin (perhaps on the Stevenson side). ECG met William Whewell and R. Monckton Milnes* on 28 September 1855, there for a meeting of the British Assocation for the Advancement of Science. The latter advised her not to write Charlotte Brontë's biography whilst her father was alive. See *Letters,* pp. 456, 872; Mrs Stairs Douglas, *William Whewell* (1881), pp. 442–3.
3 ECG had told Parthenope Nightingale that she was looking for the *Ratchda' Man's Visit to th'Great Exhibition* (*Letters,* p. 359). She gave William Whewell a copy at Glasgow. *O Ful, Tru, un Pertikler Okeawnt [of the] Greyt Eggshibishun, e Lundun … Be O Felley fro Rachde.* Rochdale Public Library provided a copy of this rare work. See also *Letters*, p. 359; *GSN* 29 (2000), p. 19.

4 Two lectures on the Lancashire dialect were printed separately by Chapman and Hall, *The Lancashire Dialect, Illustrated in Two Lectures* (1854; see Smith, p. 14), and also appended to the 5th edition of *Mary Barton* (repr. Angus Easson, ed. *Mary Barton,* Halifax 1993)

~

Letter 636 (undated) to [?Robert Chambers] from [?Glasgow, September 1855]

~

MARY GREEN*

Monday night
[?15 October 1855]

My dearest Mary,

I am dressed to go to the Hallé's as your note & parcel are brought in, but I have a few minutes to spare before the others are ready, & so I shall write as hard as I can. I am so dog-tired I would far rather stay at home, agreeable as it will be, Scotts and Halle's, – but the girls want to go, & Mr Gaskell is too busy to chaperone them; so he stops at home, & I go – & only wish some one less tired were in my place to enjoy what I know *ought* to be enjoyed. This last week has been such a strain upon one's powers of doing, saying & being.

My 'mysterious journey' was to Birstall, near Leeds[1] where one of dear Miss Brontë's friends lived, whom it was necessary I should see, & who was going to winter in the South at the end of last week. I went on Monday, & went over all Miss Brontë's school-places, & the places named in Shirley, & made myself acquainted with a district of about 5 miles square, & came home, – to find that Mr Monckton Milnes had been here on Monday, offering a visit on Thursday & Friday, Mr Gaskell's two busiest days, when I had him, beside many other smaller engagements entirely on my hands; friends each coming to tea, & a housemaid leaving, & another coming, who did not know where to find a thing, –

On Saty morning when he was gone I thought I had a piece of quiet before me; but then came a letter from Mrs Chapman the Anti Slavery Mrs C. volunteering a visit that afternoon to stay till today. I am *very* fond of her, tho' I know nothing about abolition, & that great interest of hers; but I was delighted to have her in our house – & Annie Austin & Alice W who are all staying here, are charmed with her beauty sweetness & eloquence. Then last night we had a sort of Anti Slavery conference in our drawing-room, & they sighed over my apathy, but I can not get up an interest in the *measures* adopted by people so far away across the Atlantic.[2]

So you see my life seems worked up into other people's, & as if I had no time for anything, just now, anything belonging to myself, I mean. I *ought* to be copying letters &c some hours every day, I *ought* to be making flannel petticoats, as usual and just at present, I can't. Snow Wedgwood[3] comes to us on Wednesday, – & every evening till Saty we are engaged. This is always the busiest time of the year. Last Saturday I was half planning going over to take Susan Deane by surprize, & have a little quiet myself from Saty last to Monday, or Tuesday, but then came this note from Mrs Chapman, – saying she was coming here.

Tuesday morning

We shall be extremely glad of the damsons, & thank you much for thinking of them. We are all so fond of fruit, that far worse things than damsons would be more than commonly welcome. – We sometimes buy blackberries, – not to gratify my taste, for I suppose I was too country bred, to appreciate blackberries cooked: but the rest of the household are thankful for them.

I must go now; we have to struggle out to Worsley to lunch, & to be home to a six o'clock tea with some of the congregation.

Yours very affecly ECG.

I have not had time to enter on any really interesting subject. But I am glad to hear that the *differences* between you & J. P[4] are tabooed subjects. Remind me to tell you about Miss Bathurst – & her brother, the priest at Stoke – *he* a convert.

Dr R. Jamison

1 See *Letters*, pp. 872–3, for this visit to Ellen Nussey.

2 Maria Weston Chapman, née Weston (1806–85), handsome and dynamic, impressed young Annie Austin and Alice Winkworth rather more than ECG. See J. A. V. Chapple, 'An Anglo-American Story', *Conference Papers*, The Brontë Society and The Gaskell Society, 1990, pp. 95–100.

3 Snow Wedgwood had recently written, 'Mrs Gaskell too will be a great delight to me. She is one of those people whose society is a great happiness to me, much more than I shd have expected from her books ...' She found herself copying bundles of letters in a house characterised by 'perpetual feeding'. See Chapple, 'An Author's Life', *BST* 17 (1979), p. 288.

4 'I am extremely sorry to hear of John Philip Green's going over to Rome. ... It is very sad for his family' (Stephen Winkworth, *L & M*, I. 488). See also p. 210 below.

LOUIS HACHETTE

42 Plymouth Grove,
Manchester
October 22nd 1855.

Dear Sir,

A friend of mine, who is going to Paris, has kindly offered to take charge of three numbers of *'Household Words'*, in which you will find a story of mine, entitled *'Half a life-time ago'*.[1]

I send them to you in compliance with the first article of our agreement, drawn up at Paris on the 12th of last March.

I have been hoping to hear from you respecting the translation of some of my works; especially of 'North and South',[2] of which, a copy, was I believe delivered to you at the end of last April; and as four months \ see *article* 4 / have more than expired since then I shall be glad to know if you renounce your right of translating it.

I had a message delivered to me from M. Guizot,[3] through Mr Monckton Milnes to the effect that \ translations of / some of my works had already appeared in the 'Bibliothèque du Chemin du fer' [*sic*].

If there should be any money owing to me, on behalf of any of these translations, the friend, who will convey to you the numbers of Household Words, will remain a week in Paris, where he is well-known, and he is authorized by me to receive it. His name is

Mr Satterfield,

Maurice's Hotel.

I should be very much obliged to you, if (in case there is any money owing to me,) you would send me the following books, in payment, or in part payment. The same gentleman, Mr Satterfield, will give you a receipt for them on my behalf, and will convey them to me, if sent to his care at Maurice's Hotel, within a week from the 25th instant.

'Tolla', par M. About.[4] L. Hachette

'Proverbes' par M. Alfred de Musset,[5] Charpentes

'Memoires de la Vie et des Contemporains de Madame de Sévigné,' par M. Walckmaer[*sic*].[6]

'Les deux Marguerites',[7] par Mme Charles de Reybaud.

Memoires de Madame de Crécy.[8]

I sincerely hope that Madame Hachette and the rest of your family are well, and have enjoyed this splendid summer.

My daughter, who enjoyed your kind hospitality, begs to be remembered to you, and to Madame. Believe me, to remain dear Sir,

Yours very truly

E. C. Gaskell

Archives Hachette Livre

1 *Half a Life-Time Ago* appeared in *Household Words* on 6, 13 and 20 October 1855. It does not appear to have been translated for Hachette.

2 *North and South* was ultimately published by Hachette as *Nord et Sud,* 'traduit avec l'autorization de l'auteur par Mmes Loreau et H. de l'Espine', in 1859.

3 François Guizot (1787–1874), famous scholar and politician, mentioned in ECG, 'French Life', Knutsford Edn, VII. 642. His *Histoire de la révolution d'Angleterre,* 1826–56, on the development of the constitutional monarchy was his magnum opus.

4 *Tolla* (1852) was the 'first, and truly beautiful, little novel' (Henry James) of Edmond François Valentin About (1828–85). He was a journalist, novelist and playwright, whose work is said to typify the spirit of the Second Empire.

5 *Comédies et proverbes* (1840), by Alfred de Musset (1810–57).

6 *Mémoires touchant la vie et les écrits de Marie … Marquise de Sévigné,* by Charles Athanase, Baron de Walckenaer, 6 vols 1842–65.

7 *Les Deux Marguerites* (1845), a novel by Mme Charles de Reybaud.

8 Not identified.

LOUIS HACHETTE

42 Plymouth Grove
Manchester.
October 29 1855

Dear Sir,

I am very much obliged to you for your prompt and kind attention, in so soon replying to my note of enquiry respecting the translation of my books. It is perfectly satisfactory to me, and I hope that the result may be so to you. I am also very much obliged to you for your kindness, in advancing me so much of the payment in the shape of books. There are many Germans in Manchester, so German literature abounds, and is easily to be procured; but it is difficult even to hear of *good* modern French publications – and I was delighted to be made acquainted, through the Athenaeum of October the 13th, with the great beauty and merit of 'Tolla'. In London, ten days ago, there was not a copy of 'Tolla' to be had, so great had been the demand for it, I am told.

You asked me sometime ago to tell you of any works of fiction of remarkable merit, that {have} appear{ed} in England. There are three books, each in *one* volume, which have made a great sensation here, within the last two months. They are more distinguished, – the first two especially, by power, than by beauty, but they are all three of unusual merit.

'Paul Ferroll',[1] (1 vol) Hurst and Blackett,
Great Marlborough Street.

'Martha'. ?

'A lost love';[2] Smith and Elder, Corn Hill.

The first is written by a lady of good family, and very large fortune, Mrs Archer Clive. It is nineteen years of the life of an exemplary gentleman, whose only fault is that he murdered his first wife to marry his second. He lives very happily, in the practice of every virtue, till, owing to the false accusation of a poor woman of the murder of the first Mrs Paul Ferroll, he thinks it his duty to come forward, and confess that he is the murderer, but he is so good that for a long time no one will believe him. –. The great skill is in the working out of this plot. People here condemn the book as 'the work of a she-devil', but buy it, and read it, and in six weeks a second edition had to be issued.

'Martha' is the story of a woman of good family, who falls in love with, and marries a peasant. He is a bad character, and becomes involved in crime, but she screens him for a long time, until, finding that he has taken refuge with a rival she gives him up to justice.

'A lost love', is a very graceful pathetic story, made out of very common every day incidents, but told in a way that reminds one of 'Eugénie Grandet'.[3]

I do not even know the *real* names of the authors of these two last books. I have given you a sketch of the plots that you might judge how far they would suit the taste of the French Nation. My daughter joins with me in requesting you to present our kind remembrances to Mme Hachette. Meta is just now employed in making a work-bag on the model of hers.

Mr Gaskell was in Switzerland this summer, and only spent a day in Paris, otherwise he had intended to do himself the pleasure of calling upon you, and making your acquaintance. My eldest daughter and I spent a very happy three weeks in Scotland during his absence. It would give us the greatest pleasure to see you and Madame Hachette here, should our good fortune ever bring you in the direction of Manchester. Believe me, Sir, to remain

Yours truly
E. C. Gaskell

Hachette Archives Livre

1 The plot of *Paul Ferrol,* by Caroline Archer Clive (1801–73), is as ECG describes it: she omits to mention its conclusion whereby the hero escapes from the death cell on the eve of his execution.

2 Anthony Smith, *Martha: A Sketch from Life* , and Ashford Owen, *A Lost Love,* were reviewed by Geraldine Jewsbury in the *Athenaeum* for September 1 and August 25 respectively. See M. C. Fryckstedt, *Geraldine Jewsbury's 'Athenaeum' Reviews,* Uppsala 1986.

3 Confirming Philip Yarrow's suggestion that ECG had read this major novel of 1833 by Honoré de Balzac, which *Cousin Phillis* 'resembles in its main outline' (*GSJ* 7, 1993, p. 31).

ROBERT CHAMBERS

42 Plymouth Grove,
Man<chester>
[c. 17 Nov. 1855]

My dear Sir,

As all the obligation in our acquaintance lies on my side,[1] & as I have already much to thank you for, I feel rather reluctant in making to you a request, which from that circumstance alone may seem presumptuous, that you will look at the accompanying Manuscrip<t, w>hich is written by a frie<nd of m>ine,[2] who is desirous of having it admitted into your Journal.[3] You will be able to judge better, perhaps, than I can – of its merits, & suitability, but if you will kindly look through it, it will be conferring a great favour on me –

Yours truly
E. C. Gaskell.

National Library of Scotland (Chambers deposit).
Substitutes Letter 636a, printed from typescript.

1 Robert Chambers had entertained ECG in Edinburgh c. September 1855. See *Letters*, p. 547.
2 Perhaps Mrs Henrietta Jenkin, née Jackson (1807?–85), mother of H. C. Fleeming Jenkin (1833–85). See *Letters*, pp. 809–10 (redated 1856).
3 *Chambers's Edinburgh Journal*, renamed *Chambers's Journal* in 1853, published poetry, fiction and non-fiction. W. Chambers wrote retrospectively, 'The object was not merely to enlighten and amuse, but to touch the heart – to purify the affections thus, if possible, imparting to the work a character which would render it uniformly acceptible to families'.

LOUIS HACHETTE

Plymouth Grove,
Manchester
November 24, 1855

Dear Sir,

Mr Satterfield has just delivered to me your kind remittance of five hundred francs on account of the different translations, which you are publishing or printing at this present time, of my works. I suppose I had better try and write a receipt in French on a separate piece of paper which I will enclose in this envelope. He has also brought me two parcels of books, which you have kindly sent me. I am extremely obliged to you for so promptly complying with my request for the books; \ there is one of them / named in the bill, which is not included in the parcel; it is Les deux Marguerites par Madame Charles Reybaud, 2 vol: 5f. 30c. Wheras[*sic*] Tolla, (which I was much afraid lest I should not receive when I learnt from your letter that it was out of print,) is included both in the parcel and the bill; and is a book which I received with much obligation and gratitude as a present from you.[1]

You will find a list of my stories published in Household Words[2] on the other side of this page: Mr Dickens is now in Paris, and I have written a letter to Madame Mohl by this post, charging her to obtain from him the reservation of the right of translation, to be printed at the foot of the page in any future stories which I may publish in Household Words. His own story of 'Hard Times' first appeared in Household Words, *without any such reservation,* but the right of translation was reserved to the author on the title-page of Hard Times when it was published as a volume.

Yours truly
E. C. Gaskell
[Page not in ECG's hand.]

Household words
'Lizzie Leigh' in Nos 1, 2, 3
Well of Pen Morfa 34, 35
Heart of John Middleton 40
Disappearances 63 – 65
The old Nurse's story in the Christmas \Number / for 1852
Morton Hall 191 – 192
My French Master 195 – 196
Sheepshearing 148
The Squire's story in the Christmas Number for 1853

Archives Hachette Livre

1 See p. 145 above.
2 Hachette seems not to have published any of these stories.

MRS JAMES

Knutsford.
Decr 3rd [1855][1]

My dear Mrs James,

We were so sorry to miss Mr James last week! I think it was very naughty of him not just to drop us a line to let us know he was in Manchester; when some of us would so gladly have staid at home for even the chance of seeing him. However 'better luck next time,' as some one is always saying in one of Capt: Marryatt's novels. Only as we never know when our Manchester Chancery sits; *do* (once more) beg him just to tell us when he is in our neighbourhood. I have had an immense number of letters to look over, and makes notes from, of poor Miss Brontë's lately, and that has seemed to take up all my writing time; or I should sooner have acknowledged the receipt of a note from you, written about the time Mrs Browning[2] was in London, and repeating a wish which she had expressed to see me. I heartily reciprocated that wish; but with two hundred miles of distance to separate us, and neither of us willing to undertake so long a journey it could not be.

You also spoke of my visit to Sir James Kay Shuttleworth, of which you had heard through Lady Kay Shuttleworth. I thought you would be surprized to hear of my going, after all our conversations; and I have no doubt you were, though you did not express it. I had written to Lady Hatherton (who had been a good deal with Miss Brontë in the Exhibition year, as I thought, – I was mistaken;) to ask her for any particulars she might remember of that time; and she in her reply said that Sir James has perhaps been one of Miss Brontë's most confidential friends, and had seen a great deal comparatively speaking, of her after her marriage. Lady Hatherton either saw or was writing to Sir James soon after this, & named my letter & it's purport to him; and the consequence was a very kindly expressed letter from him inviting Mr Gaskell & myself to go to Gawthrop for two nights; when he said he should be able to tell me much, & show me letters about which he was not strong enough to write. Mr Gaskell was just gone into Switzerland, but I went to Gawthrop on my way back to Silverdale where the children were; and spent two nights with Miss Kay & Sir James. He seemed very poorly, and was evidently not able to say a great deal of what he had to say about Miss Brontë. He got up somewhere about 6, and rode with his boys before breakfast; and, perhaps in consequence of this early rising in the morning, he not only required a great deal of solitary rest in the day-time, but he went to bed, when I was there between ½ past eight and nine at night. The boys, Robin especially looked delicate, but are very gentle engaging lads; and Sir James appeared to devote his whole time & thoughts to them. He spoke of his wife's health requiring a residence in the South, and as if he regretted it very much.[3] But indeed he was hardly able to speak of anything but Miss Brontë, he appeared so delicate. Miss Kay too seemed out of health, and out of spirits. If you are seeing Lady Kay Shuttleworth will you give her my love, and tell her how much I should like to see her again.

I came here to my cousins on Friday last for a week. All the girls are at home, and very busy with their different employments. Marianne has been having singing lessons from Garcia,[4] who has been in Manchester for three months or more. She enjoyed her visits in Scotland, more than the Scientific Association[5] itself, and so did I, I must confess. Scientific language is quite new to me; and yet some knowledge of it is required to understand all the papers, except indeed those read in the Statistical Section.

With kindest regards to Mr James, and love & kisses to the little ones, believe me dear Mrs James,

Yours affectionately
E. C. Gaskell

How is Lady Romilly?[6]

Pierpont Morgan Library

1 A single envelope survives in the Fales Library, New York University: to Mrs [?]ames / 5 Abercrombie terrace, / Liverpool; *postmark* MANCHESTER DEC 11 1855.

2 Elizabeth Barrett Browning (1806–61). ECG was to see her in April 1857 in Florence (Uglow, p. 425).

3 In 1853 Lady Kay-Shuttleworth* separated from her husband, living in Eastbourne and the Continent. The older children, Ughtred and Robin, lived principally with their father (R. J. W. Selleck, *James Kay-Shuttleworth: Journey of an Outsider,* Ilford, Essex 1994, pp. 284–5, 292–3).

4 Manuel Patricio Rodriguez Garcia (1805–1906), from a famous Spanish musical family and the outstanding singing master of his day. He was on the staff of the Royal Academy 1858–95 (Grove).

5 The British Association for the Advancement of Science held its annual meeting in Glasgow in September 1855. Unitarians were particularly active in its affairs (*EY*, p. 142).

6 Caroline Charlotte Otter, wife of Sir John, in 1865 1st Lord Romilley (1802–74), Master of the Rolls 1851–75; sister of Mrs Maria James and Mrs Amelia Strutt.

RICHARD MONCKTON MILNES[1]

Plymouth Grove
January [?]7 th [1856]

Dear Mr Milnes,

I wonder if you received the Gilbert French intelligence, and the copy of the Guy Mannering pamphlet[1] I sent you about 3 weeks ago? For I find, from Mr Scott that I put quite a wrong address upon them; namely, *Grosvenor* – instead of *Brook* Street.

Yours very truly
E. C. Gaskell

Princeton University Library
MS of Letter 277, to a 'Mr Richies' (*Letters*, p. 379). 'Milnes'* looks something like 'Richies' in the autograph.

1 Gilbert French (1804–66), 'Parallel Passages from Two Tales Elucidating the Origin of the Plot of [W. Scott's] *Guy Mannering*' (1855). See *Letters*, pp. 376–7.

LOUIS HACHETTE

Plymouth Grove
Manchester.
January 21, 1856

Dear Sir,

I have received by post a copy of the translation of Cranford, for which I beg you to accept my best thanks. I am delighted with the grace and ease of the translation, and for this, I shall write and express my gratitude to Madame Belloc.

I was on the point of writing to you, Sir, before this, to tell you that having read 'Ruth' with much care and attention, I was extremely gratified to find my meaning so well rendered in a foreign language; and to beg you to express to Mme de Witt my sense of the pains which she must have taken. It is true that my knowledge of the French language is but imperfect, and that consequently my praise may not be of much value; but it, and my gratitude are sincere, and I should have written myself to express them to Mme de Witt, had my personal acquaintance with her been only a very little greater than it is.[1]

I continue to receive letters from French ladies, requesting my permission to translate certain of my works; Mme Edmond de Pressensé,[2] Rue de Parme is one, a friend of Mme George Sand's living with her at

Nohant[3] is another. I tell all that I have no longer any power, and I refer them to you.

You probably are aware that Mr Dickens is residing at 49 Avenue des Champs Elyssées. I remain, Sir, Yours truly

E. C. Gaskell

Archives Hachette Livre

1 See p. 135 n. 3 above.
2 Eloise-Françoise-Louise de Plessis-Gouret, Mme de Pressensé (b. 1826), poet and children's writer; translator of E. Sewell's *Amy Herbert.*
3 Nohant was Sand's country residence.

LORD STANHOPE[1]

Plymouth Grove
Manchester.
Janry 22 [1856].

My Lord,

As you implied a wish that I should not reply to the letter you addressed to me on the 28th of May last, I considered that it would be selfish presumption in me to attempt to express the gratification which I had received from your candid & friendly criticism, as well as your kind appreciation of 'North and South'. But it almost seems to me as if this obligation to silence was removed by the little present, which I have this morning received; and which bears a few words from you on it's title-page.[2] I had just been reading enough of the Addresses in the Athenæum to whet my appetite strongly; and I had determined to have them for my own as soon as I could. I have, perhaps, no right to say how much the manner of obtaining them adds to their value. I have greedily hurried through them since they came; just as one can not help doing with a book received while one is in the first flush of impatience. But I shall read them again to 'savour' them more thoroughly.

As we stand, each labourers on the same broad field, I suppose I may tell you (may I not?) how the last – the Birmingham address, has delighted me; as one who has never seen, and is never likely to see the treasures that it speaks of.[3] I suppose all educated people, who are in my case, long and yearn to form some definite, coloured, living idea of the Great City; but so few travellers care to place themselves in our position; {who} \ or / are dramatic enough to understand how such a little clause as 'It is but a stone's throw' helps us to realize what we hear and read and think (and some of us dream,) so much about. I have looked at a map of Rome by many a half-hour; I know the kind of colouring pervading the environs, and the Campagna. And all the buildings are old friends from engravings, but distances, and relative positions (such as can one be seen from the other?) &c, and the connection between the Ancient the

Mediæval & the Modern Rome are very difficult indeed to make out; and I, for one, thank very {one} \ much that person / who takes the trouble, for the time, to identify himself with the untravelled and the ignorant. To be sure it is a little provoking to come to the actual truth sometimes; & to learn for instance that the engravings of the dome of St Peters are in fact almost birds' eye views.

But I have no right to take up your time, my Lord. I beg your pardon for having said so much.

I remain

Your obedient servant
E. C. Gaskell.

Centre for Kentish Studies, Maidstone (U1590 C401/5); annot. 22 Jan. 1856.

1 Philip Henry Stanhope (1805–75), 5th Earl Stanhope.
2 *Addresses Delivered at Manchester, Leeds and Birmingham* (1856).
3 Stanhope had given his Birmingham address 'upon the antiquities and works of art, ancient and modern at Rome' on 24 November 1855. ECG was to go to Rome in February 1857.

JAMES NASMYTH[1]

[Spring 1856][2]

My dear Mr Nasmyth,

I wonder which was the proudest, and 'pleased'est, Mrs Nasmyth or I this morning. I settle the question in my own mind thus. She was in a perpetual state of pride and pleasedom at having the Artist of Fireside[3] Sketches for her husband; and I made up for such pride not being my permanent state by my vivid & active delight at having that portfolio of beautiful drawings given to me for my very own, & by you.[4] We look them over & look them over, and can't agree which we like best. Indeed that's no wonder for the 'I' of this evening can't agree with the 'I' of this afterooon.

Mr Gaskell likes Gatherin' Sticks best, – has made up his mind slowly, but is very faithful. So does Marianne. I cling to the Fairies just now. But how full of thought & fancy they all are! I feel as if *I* ought to point out their beauties to *you*, for that you can never, in the unconsciousness of creation, have found them out for yourself. Thank you & Mrs Nasmyth for promising to come on the 13th. Mr Gaskell's kindest regards and thanks.

Yours most truly
E C Gaskell

Edinburgh City Library
Dr J. A. Cantrell, author of *James Nasmyth and the Bridgewater Foundry*, Chetham Society 3S, 31 (Manchester, 1985), kindly drew this letter to our attention.

1 James Hall Nasmyth (1808–90), engineer, inventor, tool-maker and designer. Like a number of members of the Nasmyth family, and in particular his father, Alexander (1758–1840), of Edinburgh, he was a gifted artist.
2 In an autograph album collated by Ann Nasmyth (1817–93) are a number of similar letters to JHN, the earliest dated 11 February 1856. Harriet Beecher Stowe wrote on 2 April 1858 that she had first seen his drawings at Plymouth Grove in May 1857.
3 From his marriage to Ann Hartop (18170–93) in 1840 until his retirement in 1856, Nasmyth lived at Fireside, Patricroft, near Manchester. He established a foundry there in 1836; Holbrook Gaskell (1813–1909) was his commercial partner until 1850.
4 See Nasmyth's *Autobiography*, ed. Samuel Smiles (1883, rpt 1897), p. 310: '... I executed these drawings in my evening hours. They were not "published," but I drew them with lithographic ink, and had them printed by Mr. Maclure. I afterwards made presents of the series to some of my most intimate friends.'

FRANCES HOLLAND

Burrow Hall[1]
Kir[k]by Lonsdale
Thursday [13 March 1856]

My dear Fanny,

Thank you very much; it is very satisfactory[;] all I fear is that she won't take me in for only a week & yet I don't want to stay longer, (if I can afford I shall take Meta with me for her to see paintings, so any Miss Hill experiences will be useful to know.) I can get plenty of *grand* Brussels introductions from Madame Van der Weyer (Belgian ambassadress,) but I don't want to be pottered by civilities that won't help me on in my object – i e. getting to know all I can{t} of Miss B's two years in Brussels.

When I go I don't quite know yet, – about beginning of May I fancy. I am bringing up Julia & Flossy for a fortnight's sight of London; and it must be before the hot weather begins, as Julia can't stand the least bit of heat, – & then I shall send them down to Manchester, & go on to Brussels. Can any one tell the expense of getting there cheapest way, – i.e. crossing to Ostend from London I suppose? I don't care for sea, at all; only I don't like being out all night because then one has to go down stairs & that gives me a deadly headache, which lasts for days, & would incapacitate me for work.

I can refer my respectability to the Ministre de justice, (head of the Police) in Brussels if need be, as he & I have exchanged civilities already, – he wrote to me to ask if some man called Wm Gaskell, who was claiming the right of buying a house in Brussels was any relation of mine, as hed the impudence to say he was; as if he was the Ministre de justice would forward every wish of so 'illustre' an 'auteur', & went on at a great rate about the honour in which he held me; so I mean to make *him* serviceable, as I find he holds a good position for ascertaining past facts in Brussels.

Then I can get some shop-keeping introductions, through the manufacturing of *cotton* thread for the great lace shops in Brussels, but what I want are *literary & educational* introductions, without stating my *reason* for wanting them; as I want to hear the general opinions of the Hegers (Beck –) Can you help me to these last?

Yours very affecly
ECG

I will let you know when we come to London (*Chelsea.*) Meta has been there this 2 months –

My compliments to Dr & Mrs Richardson

Envelope with stamp Miss Fanny Holland/ Port Madoc / North Wales.
Postmark 20 April 1852 [wrong envelope]. See *Letters*, p. 844.

Brotherton Collection, Leeds University
Printed in J. A. V. Chapple, 'Two Unpublished Letters from Burrow Hall, Lancashire', *GSJ* 6 (1992), pp 67–72.

1 Rented by friends, the Samuel Alcocks, and close to the Clergy Daughters' School, Cowan Bridge, where two of Patrick Brontë daughters died.

HARRIET ANDERSON[1]

Burrow-Hall
March 15th [1856]

My dear Harriet,

I hardly like putting that date, because it reminds me how long it is since I received your letter, & it gave me so much pleasure that I meant to write to you almost directly in reply. I was half afraid of writing *directly* because I thought it might seem like intruding upon your letter-writing-time, which you had said was so closely filled up with Indian claims. So I put your letter aside; and almost ever since I have been putting off writing to that fatal 'convenient season' that never comes. I dare say you know how much better & more regularly indifferent and commonplace letters of civility get answered compared to those to which you really wish to send something of what you are thinking and feeling, as well as doing. So just because I wanted to write you a nice long letter I have never written to you at all; till now that I am staying for a few days in the deep quiet of an old Hall, far removed from railways and post offices and all such new-fangled inventions where nothing more interesting than the adventures of the rooks in building their nests ever happens to disturb the deep serene.

Where are you? Dalhousie? Edinburgh? How is the little boy who went to school for the first time last September <?> How is Mr Anderson? How is your head, dear Harriet? Do you suffer as you did from those terrible headaches? Have you seen Elizabeth since the autumn? I should so like to see her again, and her home, and belongings. Please to thank her for planning so kindly that we should return by Wythburn;[2] and tell her how much I should like to do so at some future time. And now I am going to tell you all about ourselves.

When all my four girls are at home we have only one large spare-room and one very small one; but between our return from Scotland and Christmas we had nineteen people staying in the house! so I think you may fancy the necessarily quick succession. It so happened that many of our friends who had been asked 'aforetime' (as the lawyers say, don't they, Mr Anderson?) found it would be convenient to them to come then; and very heartily glad we were to see one and all; but I came to the conclusion that I very very much preferred having visitors who stayed long enough to settle down into their own occupations, without disturbing {y}my daily life, – the intercourse one has, – and that one has *earned*, as it were, by the due performance of regular duties is so much more grateful and natural as well; that when for fear of losing some precious time out of two or three days, one sits down directly after breakfast to talk and be talked to as hard as possible. Among our visitors we had had Mr Monckton Milnes, and did not I often think of 'the cool of the evening'[3] that's all. But down below the coolness there is a charming nature, warm, affectionate thoughtful for others, faithful and true in friendship.

All this gaiety was but bad for the work I have in hand; the life of Charlotte Brontë (Currer Bell) the authoress of Jane Eyre, which I am writing at her father's request. I have had above four hundred letters sent me to read over, {correct} and make extracts from. And I never *did* write a biography, and I don't exactly know how to set about it; you see I have to be accurate and keep to facts; a most difficult thing for a writer of fiction. And then the style too! that is a bugbear. It must be grander and more correct, I am afraid. But in all matters of style and accuracy I have a capital helper in my husband, who has an admirable knowledge of language; and an almost fastidious taste as to style. I sometimes tell him he does not read books for the subject but for the style.

Marianne would I know desire to be remembered most kindly to you, if she were aware that I was writing to you; but I am staying here with two old friends quite by myself. One of my friends is paralytic, and the presence of young people annoys him. So my dear little Polly is housekeeping at home, and taking care of her two young*er* sisters; (young*est* I should have said, but I was just picking out a good pen if I could.) Ah! you don't know my children yet! There is Meta – two years younger than Marianne; taller, plainer, cleverer; a very great darling of her mother's, because perhaps she was very delicate and not expected to live when she was a child. She is very clever. Not a great reader; but a good understander; fond of both music and drawing; utterly different in moral characteristics from Marianne, but the two are dear fast friends, and the only thing which I believe could rouse Meta into a desperate passion would be if any one tried to presume upon Marianne's sweet temper. Meta is in London; she has been there ever since February 1st. She went to see two girls, who lost both father and mother in one fortnight;[4] they were great friends of Meta's who had also received much kindness from Colonel and Mrs Jackson. The latter was dying of cancer, the former was a strong handsome healthy man; But he dropped down dead in the street just a fortnight before his poor wife died after five year's illness; and the \ only / brother (an artillery officer,) was ordered out to the Crimea the same week![5] So the girls wrote in their distress to beg Meta to come to them; and a sorrowful visit it has been, although I think she has been a comfort to them. They are adopted by the Dean of Canterbury,[6] and are gone there now; and Meta is staying with some relations of mine at present, and going for the Easter holidays to the Charles Darwins – he the naturalist who went round the world in the Beagle. Marianne misses her sister much. She has had a piece of gaiety during her absence however in going to the wedding of an acquaintance, where she was delighted to meet some Scotch people; and from one of them she heard some intelligence of mutual friends in Glasgow. I wonder if you know this Mr Skene; I did not find out till late in the evening, that, although he knew Glasgow he lived in Edinburgh, where he is I believe an advocate.

All this time I have said nothing of my two *little* girls. We make that distinction, because, owing to the death of a little son while yet a baby there is six years difference in age between Meta and {Ju} Florence the next girl; aged twelve; then came another boy, who also died,[7] just as he had made himself a place in the hearts of all who knew him 'a child whom all who looked on, loved' – and then Julia aged eight. These two last little people make our house very full of brightness; I wish you could see them all, dear Harriet for yourself, instead of listening to mother's maunderings! Is there no chance of your and Mr Anderson's coming to Manchester, – or *through* Manchester on your way anywhere. The Darwins still live at Shrewsbury[8] if Mr Anderson would like to pay them a visit, and earn a few more golden opinions? *Do* let me know if there is ever any chance of you coming to us. I should so like it.

The Miss Bells have left Manchester and gone to live in Conway; North Wales. Their brother Dr Bell did not succeed in his practice; and indeed I fear their affairs became very much worse; though how and why I was not intimate enough with them to know. I liked them very much indeed; & one of my plans for next winter is to see if they (two of them) would not come to us for some weeks, to see something of old friends, and to have a little society. But one hardly dares to plan for 'next winter'. I do not like the putting in, D V.[9] but it is always in my heart.

Will you give my – well! my very kindest remembrances to Mr Anderson. I am glad to hear he likes me; he ought to do because I like him so much. But however I am always rather proud to feel that I *can* like people very truly and very much, even if they don't like me.

My dear Harriet I am now, as always yours affectionately

E C Gaskell

Haworth Parsonage Museum
Printed by Sally Stonehouse, 'A Letter from Mrs Gaskell', *BST* 20 (1991), pp. 217–22, and by J. A. V. Chapple, *GSJ* 6 (1992), pp 67–72.

1 Internal evidence (headaches, Matthew Anderson, a sister Elizabeth) suggests ECG's early friend, Harriet Carr*.
2 Lakeland Village drowned when Thirlmere's level was raised in 1894.
3 Sydney Smith's nickname for Monckton Milnes*.
4 Perhaps Louy Jackson and a sister. This sister is not mentioned in September 1856 (*Letters,* p. 411), nor thereafter, but Louy Jackson (and L V J) occurs frequently as a friend of Meta ('orphan', p. 538). The 'Louy & Emma' noted by Stonehouse (p. 221, n. 18) are probably Shaens.
5 No artillery officer called Jackson served in the Crimean War. The editor of the Crimean War Society Journal, Major C. D. Robins, suggests that his posting might have been rescinded on compassionate grounds. It is possible that he was a relation of Louy, Pilkington Jackson. See esp. *Letters* pp. 615, 911, and WG to ECG, 25 July 1860, *GSN,* 14 (1992), p. 10.
6 William Rowe Lyall (1788–17 February 1857, m. Catherine Brandreth of Liverpool; no issue); Dean of Canterbury 1845–57.
7 The first death is the only reference known to this infant, one of many not officially registered for some years after it became compulsory in 1839. The second boy is Willie, who died at Porthmadog. ECG misquotes Wordsworth's 'A child whom every eye that looked on, loved' from the poem he had inscribed on the tombstone of his son Thomas (d. 1812), which she could have seen in Grasmere churchyard.
8 The family home there was The Mount, Shrewsbury, though Charles Darwin lived at Down House, Bromley, Kent, from 1842.
9 Deo volente: God Willing (Latin).

MRS LUDLOW*

3 Parham Place[1]
Kings Road
Wednesday Eveng
[?30 April 1856]

My dear Mrs Ludlow,

I found your very kind note here on our return from a long day at the Sydenham Palace.[2] I should like very much to come to spend a day or two with you at Wimbledon, and if it will be convenient to you I will very gladly do so, – but not for some time yet; for every day is swallowed up in sight seeing, and while my little girls are with me I can not do anything separate from them. They go home *about* the end of next week, – it may be the beginning of the next, – and then I leave London (with my second girl) for a week or a fortnight. But on my return, – according to this reckoning about the middle of May, – may I let you know, with a hope of making some arrangement for paying you a little visit then? In the mean time any note addressed to 8 Bedford Row will always find me; but until the end of next week I am here; if it can be called being *here*, when all we do is to sleep and breakfast here, and come home to a late tea. For this reason I think, dear Mrs Ludlow, that you had better not give yourself the trouble of trying to find us, as we are never in. I should have liked you to have seen my two little girls notwithstanding.

Believe me to be
My dear Mrs Ludlow

Yours very truly
E. C. Gaskell

Princeton University Library

1 See *Letters*, pp. 387–8, for ECG's stay in Chelsea.
2 The Crystal Palace had been moved to Sydenham by 1854.

LADY HATHERTON[1]

8 Bedford Row.
Friday Evening
7. o'clock [?June ?1854]

My dear Lady Hatherton,

I am very sorry, and very much ashamed of myself; but I have been at Sydenham all day, for the first time, and I am come home so dizzy with over-fatigue as to be literally unable to stand to be dressed, & I can only go to bed, instead of coming to you as I quite hoped & intended. I am *very* sorry.

Your affectionately
E. C. Gaskell

Lord Montagu of Beaulieu, Estate Archive (M/H/C23)

1 Misplaced letter. Cp. C. to A. Winkworth, June 1854 (*L&M*, I. 443).

JEMIMA QUILLINAN[1]

Edward Holland[2] Esq
Dumbleton Hall
Evesham
Monday Aug 4th 1856

My dear Miss Quillinan,

I am think[ing] you will wonder very much at receiving a letter from me, but I am very anxious to ascertain, if you can give me any information respecting a letter Mr Branwell Brontë wrote some years ago to Mr Wordsworth. Miss Martineau told me last year when I was at Ambleside, that at Mr Wordsworth's death this letter had been offered to Miss Brontë but she had declined it. It was a letter written by Mr Branwell Brontë to Mr Wordsworth asking his opinion respecting some poems of Mr B. B's which he sent.[3] I am very anxious to know if the letter still exists and if it does {wether} whether I might have either a copy of it, or if you would kindly lend it me, and I would copy it and return it you. If you know nothing of it, I wonder if you know at all what answer Mr Wordsworth sent, and, if there is anywhere a copy of his letter. I am very sorry to give you so much trouble, but I am engaged as perhaps you may know in writing in[*sic*] Memoir of Miss Brontë (Currer Bell) and this letter will help me very much.

Again apologising for troubling you Believe me to remain

Most truly yours
E. C. Gaskell.

Wordsworth Library, Grasmere
Printed by Stephen Gill, 'A Manuscript of Branwell Brontë, with Letters of Mrs Gaskell', *BST* 15 (1970), pp. 408–11.

1 Jemima Quillinan (1819–91), elder daughter of Edward Quillinan (1791–1851), by his first wife, Jemima Brydges. After her death he married Wordsworth's daughter Dora on 11 May 1841, thus bringing his children into the Wordsworth circle.

2 See *EY*, pp. 182–3.

3 Branwell wrote to Wordsworth on 19 January 1837, enclosing poems and asking for advice about a literary career. Wordsworth did not reply. See p. 160 below.

ANON

[4–10 August 1856]

Dear Sir,

I should be extremely obliged to you if you would send a 'Manchester Examiner & Times' of last Monday week, July the 28th with the article on Free trade in Belgium[1] in it, to

Mademoiselle Helen Corr,
chez M. Corr van der Maeren,
Bruxelles,
Belgium.

We made the acquaintance of him & his daughter when we were in Brussels this spring, and I should be extremely glad to give them the pleasure of seeing the article in which M. Corr van der Maeren is so honourably mentioned.

If you will kindly let me know what I shall owe you for the paper & postage, I shall be extremely obliged to you, & will remit it in stamps immediately.

Believe me, dear Sir,

Yours truly
E. C. Gaskell.

P S. I shall be away from Manchester for some time longer – my present address is

Edd Holland's Esq. M. P / Dumbleton Hall, /Evesham.

Torquay Museum (AR 684)

1 The article declares, 'There is no state in Europe so hampered with obstacles to Free Trade as Belgium. But ... some men with intelligence and influence are actively bestirring themselves in this matter.' Corr Van der Maeren was a leading member of the Belgian Association of Free Trade and author of a circular promoting free trade.

JEMIMA QUILLINAN[1]

Edward Holland Esq MP
Dumbleton Hall
Evesham
Wednesday August 13th [1856]

My dear Miss Quillinan

I am very much obliged to you indeed for your kindness in taking so much trouble to procure me Mr Patrick Brontë's letter.[2] I have been attending the British Association Meetings[3] which has prevented my sending it back to you as soon as I otherwise should have done. What a curious letter it is, the first part is most powerful writing but it falls off very much when he attempts to draw a simile. Will you be kind enough to give the enclosed note from me to Mrs Wordsworth. My daughter was at the dance you name, but had no idea you were there, or she says she certainly should not have allowed the evening to pass away without being introduced to you for though she herself has but an indistinct recollection of having seen {to} you at Fox How, she has often heard of you from those of us who are acquainted with you, and would have much liked making your acquaintance herself. With kind remembrances to your sister Rotha and many thanks for the trouble you have taken for me

Believe me to remain

Yours very truly
E C Gaskell.

Wordsworth Library, Grasmere

1 See p. 159 above.
2 Branwell's full name was Patrick Branwell. His letter was printed in *CBL*, I, chapter 8. Stephen Gill indicates certain errors in the account there given.
3 Edward Holland was a leading agriculturalist. The British Association for the Advancement of Science met in Cheltenham, 6–13 August 1856.

MR STEWART[1]

Plymouth Grove
November 11th [1856]

My dear Sir,

I am very sorry to say that in spite of your care & beautiful packing the glass over the Photograph is broken: and I am consequently not *quite* so well able as I should otherwise have been to judge of the merit of the Photograph. But we all think, from what we can see, that it is most beautiful, and correct & pleasing. It is very like her; and a very good copy of the drawing. I am going as soon as I have finished this note to take the Photograph down to Dancer's, who is our great resource here in all such matters [altered from *manners*], and I have no doubt he can replace the glass without injuring the Photograph; but at any rate he will tell me truly whether he can or no. I am *very very* much obliged to you. There is no hurry (before February) as to time. But I am very sorry you had to wait so long at the Parsonage before Mr Nicholls' return. – I am very sorry you will have to go again. – In short I am very sorry *really* for all your trouble, but \ I am / so delighted to have got you to do it, and so charmed with your success that I am afraid my gladness and gratitude over-top my regret for your trouble. Thank you over & over again, and do let me have the pleasure of doing something for you some time. It *is* a place to have seen, & people to have seen, is it not?

Yours very gratefully & truly
E C Gaskell.

Princeton University Library

1 An unidentified professional who photographed the George Richmond portrait of Charlotte Brontë, used for an engraved frontispiece to the 1st edition of ECG's *Life*. Cf. *Letters*, p. 421.

JOHN M. F. LUDLOW*

Plymouth Grove
Novr 17th [?1856]

My dear Mr Ludlow,

I want a little *gratis* law, please, so I come to you. I have a poor friend who has embarked his savings long ago in Fergus O'Connor's Land Scheme.[1] Last Spring (March I think) 'four counsellors' came to the 'King's Arms' (a small public house in a poor part of the town-) and made all the working-men concerned in the Land Scheme come and give 'the Counsellors their affidavy, *and* a shilling.' *Now*, the said Counsellors want half a crown: and in this way, says my informant, 'they will get many a hundred of pounds; and how are we to tell if we are being *done*, or not. It's hard sending good money after bad, and yet we should be loath to lose a chance of getting the money paid down again'. So I have begged this piece of paper from him and send it and his statement. He sets great value on this piece of paper, and I have promised it shall be carefully returned to him again. In great haste, and with many regrets for not having seen you and Mrs Ludlow this summer,

Ever yours most truly
E C Gaskell

Annotations 1856 ?1854 [in pencil].

Cambridge University Library, Add 7348/10/124

1 A scheme to remove industrial population from the slums by selling shares in a land company at a preferential rate. The capital of £5000 raised from 2000 shares would purchase 120 acres of good arable land at £18. 15s an acre to provide 60 allotments; the rest would purchases cottages and stock. Allotments could be let to members in perpetuity for £5 a year, and from this income further land might be purchased. By 1847 there were 600 branches of the Chartist Land Company, but it was wound up by Act of Parliament in 1851, most investors suffering financially. See *L & M*, I. 107; A. M. Hadfield, *The Chartist Land Company* (1970).

JOHN M. F. LUDLOW*

Plymouth Grove
Novr 27 [1856].

My dear Mr Ludlow,

You must not think I have been ungrateful for your kindness about my poor friend's claims. I have been in North Wales[1] for a week, and only returned last night to find your two letters, the second enclosing the 'piece of paper'. (Is it not a piece of paper, that you invert commas about the expression?) I am glad he has even so much chance as you say he has of obtaining a little of his money back again; and I will try and find out what the second claim of half-a-crown can be, and defend him from imposition if I can. Only to think of your being a grand-uncle! Does the baby who brings you this honour belong to the niece who was staying with you a year & a half ago; a West Indian?[2]

I am not strong, – and much tired with my yesterday's journey, & today's letter writing. But you will know how truly obliged to you I am, from few words as well as from many.

Do, please, give my kind remembrances to Mrs Ludlow.

Ever yours very truly
E. C. Gaskell.

Annotations 1856 ?1854 [in pencil].

Cambridge University Library, Add 7348/10/125

1 At Pendyffryn Hall, near Conway, 'the lovely and romantic residence of Mr R. Dukinfield Darbishire', where he used to invite Unitarian ministers of Lancashire and Cheshire to take Sunday services in his drawing room. See Henry Solly, *'These Eighty Years', or, The Story of an Unfininished Life,* 1893, II. 179; *Letters,* p. 422.

2 Ludlow's niece (b. in France, 1834) was the daughter of his sister Maria and Charles List, a Frenchman who went out as Treasurer of Martinique in 1836. See Ludlow, *Autobiography,* pp. 31–33.

MRS SPENCER

Plymouth Grove
Wednesday [?late 1856]

My dear Mrs Spencer,

I have been looking over my letters from Miss Brontë; & I am sorry to say *all* the notes, & shorter letters have been weeded out for the purpose of autographs. There are absolutely none left, but long & characteristic letters, which I shall require for the purposes of biography. If, after that is written, you will remind me again I will see if I can not spare you one. I have been more entreated for her autograph that[*sic*] for that of any other person. Whose else do you want? Send me a list, please, & I will look & see that *you* have them, if *I* have duplicates. Or come & see my book – that would be best of all, & I will show you 4 good reasons why that unfortunate cousin of Mr Gaskell's does not look as young as she did.

Yours very truly
E C Gaskell

Princeton University Library

LOUIS HACHETTE

Plymouth Grove
Manchester
February 8th 1857

Dear Sir,

I beg to present you with my best thanks for your letter, received this morning.

We have finally arranged to leave home on Friday morning next, and we hope to arrive in Paris at five on Sunday Evening, (the 15th) We remain there until Tuesday Evening. We shall be at the Hotel des Missions Etrangéres[*sic*], Rue du Bac, for the convenience and pleasure of being near M. and Madame Mohl.[1]

If it is convenient and agreeable to you and Madame Hachette, we shall have very great pleasure in spending Monday Evening with you; but should I be taking too great a liberty, if, in this case, I requested leave to bring a young lady[2] with us, who is travelling under our escort to Rome? Her father is one of our principal merchants in Manchester, and she herself is highly cultivated, and a great friend of the Chevalier Bunsen, and his family.[3]

Pray present our kind compliments to Madame Hachette, and believe me to remain

Yours truly
E. C. Gaskell

Archives Hachette Livre

1 ECG was to stay with her friend Mary Clarke Mohl* in her upper-stories apartment at 120 rue du Bac, which overlooked the garden of the Missions Etrangères, a seminary for missionary priests in the Far East. See the photograph by Brenda Colloms (*GSJ* 13 ,1999, p. 45).
2 Catherine Winkworth* accompanied ECG, MA and ME to Rome.
3 Bunsen had resigned as Prussian ambassador, retiring to the Villa Charlottenburg, Heidelberg in 1854 (*L & M,* I. 442 n., 461)

EDWARD E. HALE[1]

Plymouth Grove
Manchester
Febry 11th / 57

My dear Mr Hale,

(It is such a pleasure to write upon respectable paper, instead of foreign flimsiness.) I have an opportunity through my kind friend Mr Henry Bright, of sending you what papers I have been able to collect, by a 'Mate's Check'.[2] N.B I have not a notion what it is but Mr Bright says it will ensure the safety of my papers. You will perhaps think I make them of more consequence than they are worth, when you see how little definite information they give; but the fact is every body here is 'in a fix', to use what we call an Americanism on the subject. We can't get *parents* to attend the merry active amusements of the young; now family gatherings are the natural purifying restraints upon over-excitement. We in our class have chaperonage – abroad the \ active or *passive* / love for amusement seems to run through all ages, & fathers & mothers are as glad to go out to the theatre or a dance as their children – it is not, as here, a selfish enjoyment on the part of the young, for abroad I *know* one member of a family often earns[?] the moderate prices of admission for *all*. However I am too tired to be very sensible tonight.

The Mr *Weigall* [3] whose letter is one of those *I* most value, – from knowing the man, – is a clergyman of the Church of England; always among our manufacturing population. – Oh! such a man! I *will* enclose another letter of his, nothing bearing on the question, – but a couple of years ago I was asked to recommend a clergyman to a living, & named Mr Weigall, toiling away with 7 children for 150£ a year; he listened to the proposal made him of removing from Macclesfield at first, and then declined \ explaining why / in the letter I send, marked with a little x.

You will have heard I hope from Charles Buxton,[4] & his character will have told itself, – good strong religious man! a brewer by trade in the worst part of London. Mr Spottiswoode[5] too is a '*brick*', (do you Americans know what bricks are?) He is son of Spottiswoode *of* Spottiswoode, 'of' being equivalent to the aristocratic 'de' or 'von', in whose family the 'King's Printership' has been a sinecure for years; i.e. they have a right to print all Parliamentary Papers, Blue books &c, and may charge the nation what they like for it. *My* Mr Spottiswoode took the highest honours at Cambridge, and had a comfortable young-man-of-family-&-fortune life open to him; when he bethought him of wondering what was the root of the family wealth; & examining into the responsibility that *must* accompany all pleasures & blessings. Well! to cut a very long story short, – he & his brother left the 'West-End' –, and went to live in the old queer house in the City belonging to the King's Printer ages ago, {of} and have taken *all* the apprentices, sent from the country to learn the business under their roof – eating, walking, living with them like wiser elder brothers resuming the mastership in the Printing-house (where these two fine young men have already learnt every detail of the business, & can set up a frame quicker then any of their men –)

The day opens with prayer (C. of England morning service) read in a great attic fitted up as a chapel, with organ, religious engravings (*outlines* from the great old pictures –) by one of the Mr Spottiswoodes, then all to breakfast &c. They don't urge any knowledge upon them. A Whitsuntide or two ago they took their boys (young men) a walk to the Isle of Wight – they saw Carisbrook Castle- 'What is that place' said one, & wanted the *story* about it – 'No' said Mr S. 'don't pick out the *plums*; those who want really to know what makes some of us look with so much more interest at C. Castle than others hold up their hands, if they are brave thorough fellows, & we'll have a history class when we get home.' Now mind you value Mr Spottiswoode's scraps of letters, – he's a *doer* – Then Mr Wilson – Price's Patent Candle Works – *you* know him. He is another brick. Yet with all these bricks I've got so little! But I can't help it. I don't believe there is more *to* be got, – and 'It's ill taking the breeks aff a Hielandman!'[6]

Now thank you – yes, right down thank you. *The* American parcel came – (price only 2 shillings, are you *sure* you did not pay anything?) on Saturday, only about five minutes after I had finished my life of Miss Brontë. Oh *how* it gave me the right turn away from what had been pressing on brain & heart too hardly & heavily for months! I plunged into Madame Ossoli,[7] – and – it is Tuesday Evng, have given all my spare time (precious little!) to her, – for you see we are setting off for Rome on Friday next, & I saw her book would not be admitted into the Papal States at half a glance, – and so began right away upon her Italian life. But thank you for all. I feel quite rich in books I want to read now. Margaret Percival in America[8] is the book you and your sister wrote, is not it?

No! I never met your Uncle! I don't know (to begin with) what his name is; but I never was in any Mr Grenville's house in my life. There are many other Mrs Gaskells afloat in London. I can count the Americans I know on my fingers.[9] Hales (to start with.) Mr & Mrs Bradford of Roxbury. Mr Theodore Parker. Mr Wight (a man who translated \ V / Cousin,)[10] Mrs Chapman, Westons & Russell Sturgis, my dear Mrs Shaw, and Anna Shaw, Greens, Storys, – a Mr Somebody I have seen this year, rummaging in the Records, whose name I never caught, a Mr Kennedy Southern State Slave-holder, *but* I could not help liking him Mrs Twisleton, Miss Dwight.[11] I like both these last extremely – and now you have every American I ever spoke to in my life, except our Mr Channing. Choose your Uncle out! Oh! Mr & Mrs Abbot Lawrence I have just spoken to.[12]

But are not you astonished that we, (I, Marianne & Meta our two eldest girls,) are going to Rome! I am, I can assure you. We are going first to the Story's,[13] good kind friends as they are, they have begged us to go there until we can meet with apartments; we stay over Holy Week, & come home by land or sea, according as our money holds out. We shall be at home by May 1st. I hear Mrs Perkins & Mrs Stowe[14] are to be in Rome; I shall much like to see them, if we chance to meet; I like to think of seeing an actual *pinchable* relation of Mrs Hale's. America seems to me like the moon; I am sure it is somewhere, but quite untouchable in this mortal state. I hope I shall see everything, *even Grim Tartary hereafter*. I am so busy *that* I go writing on; you don't see why there is that *that*. Why, if I left off writing I should have to puzzle myself sorely which of the 200 duties I ought to do first and next; and perhaps I should begin to think; & that would never do, – as so far is fixed, for I should begin to feel my heart ache very sorely about those we are leaving behind us; it does already, & I wonder (oh! strange friend, whose face I have never seen, and never shall see! yet to whom I write so freely) whether I am doing right, – Oh how hard I wish at times for this world to be over & that light come in which we shall see light, & know more clearly than we ever, I at least – seem now to do, what is right & be able – without morbid introspection to find out how much is mere pleasure-seeking, & how much is needful recreation – However we are going, & there's an end of it:-

Yes! I know Jacob Abbott's books,[15] & like them much. I fancy I can't care for doctrine so much as most people, it never hurts me much, except *high* Calvinism. I did so like receiving your parcel. I have told you so, once, but there it comes again! I like to have a parcel from America; it is the first I ever had in my life. And I like the books and I like the sender.

I hope you will like the Life of Miss Brontë; I think you ought to – for her sake. Messrs Appletons did purchase (not the right but) the complimentary power of republishing it.[16] I am so tired out I must stop. Kind love to your wife; and a kiss apiece to the two little ones (there are *two* are not they) and please tell your Father I should very much like sometime to see Mr Webster's private letters.[17]

Yours very truly indeed
E C Gaskell

Mr Gaskell sends his kindest regards.

Princeton University Library

1 Edward Everett Hale (1822–1909), Unitarian minister of South Congregational Church, Boston, and a prominent abolitionist. He was the author of short stories, memoirs and miscellaneous journalism. '*Such* an American-looking American' (*Letters,* p. 663).
2 Usually 'mate's receipt', issued to guarantee material sent by ship. This letter makes it clear that the 'papers' are accounts of philanthropic employers.
3 ECG met Mr Weigall at Capesthorne in 1852.
4 Charles Buxton (1823–71), partner in a brewing firm, elected Independent Liberal MP for Newark in 1857.
5 William Spottiswoode (1825–83), a distinguished physicist, and George Andrew Spottiswoode (1827-99) separately inherited the family publishing firms, Eyre & Spottiswoode and Spottiswoode & Co. The family traced its descent back to the Middle Ages. The former were licensed to print Bibles and Anglican Prayer Books. Both organised their workers as described here, providing recreational and educational facilities (including scientific lectures), a schoolmaster and a chaplain.
6 James Pillans Wilson. Quotation from Walter Scott, *The Fortunes of Nigel* (1822), chapter 5.
7 Sarah Margaret Fuller (1810–50), American journalist and essayist best known

for her *Woman in the Nineteenth Century* (1845). She had clandestinely married the Marchese Giovanni Angelo Ossoli, a supporter of the Italian republican, Giuseppe Mazzini. ECG probably refers to her *Memoirs* (1852), edited by her Boston associates, James F. Clarke, William Henry Channing and R. W. Emerson.

8 *Margaret Percival in America* (Boston 1850) was a sequel to Elizabeth Sewell's successful novel of 1847. The sequel, 'edited' by E. E. Hale, was in fact written by him with his sister Lucretia.

9 Probably beginning with Manchester-Liverpool-Boston Unitarian connections (*EY*, pp. 392, 422), ECG came across many others from distinguished families. Samuel Dexter and Julia Bradford were early friends, after whom ECG's youngest daughter was named (*Letters*, p. 18; Chapple, *GSN* 17, 1994, pp. 7–8). Theodore Parker (1810–60), Unitarian Clergyman of Boston; anti-slavery campaigner.

10 Orlando W. Wight (1824–88), Unitarian minister and author, arrived in Liverpool in 1853; translated Victor Cousin.

11 Maria Weston Chapman (1806–85) was one of five Weston sisters of Weymouth, Mass. ECG had met Emma Forbes Weston by 1855 (*Letters*, p. 352). Russell Sturgis (1805–87), banker and father of the novelist Julian Russell Sturgis, was the brother of Mrs Sarah Shaw (1815–1902). Her son, Robert Gould Shaw, died in the American Civil War commanding a black regiment. ECG published an article on him in *Macmillan's Magazine* for December 1863. See Marianne McLeod Gilchrist, 'The Shaw family of Staten Island: Elizabeth Gaskell's American Friends', *GSJ* 9 (1995), pp. 1–12. ECG met 'a very agreeable American Kennedy', 'a very charming Mrs Edward Twisleton and a Miss Dwight, her sister' in London in 1856; Mrs Twisleton (1820–93) was a cousin of Charles Eliot Norton* (*Letters*, pp. 416, 581).

12 William Henry Channing (1810–84), Unitarian minister at Renshaw Street Chapel in Liverpool 1854–57, who then succeeded J. Martineau at Hope street Chapel, Liverpool. Abbott Lawrence (1792–1855) had five sons.

13 William Wetmore Story* (1819–95) and his wife Emelyn*, with whom ECG was to stay in Rome in 1857. At her daughters' request, Henry James destroyed ECG's letters to the Storys after using them for his biography of Story.

14 Harriet Beecher Stowe (1811–96), famous author of *Uncle Tom's Cabin* (1851–52). Mrs Perkins was her sister. See *Letters*, p. 237, and *L & M*, II. 112.

15 Jacob Abbott (1803–79), Unitarian clergyman, Professor at Amherst College and author of children's books.

16 D. Appleton & Co. published the 1st American edition of *CBL* (1857).

17 Noah Webster (1758–1843), whose famous *An American Dictionary of the English Language* was published in 1828.

LADY HATHERTON[1]

[c. February 1857]

< ... > but I did not mean any one to know it, because people are always so scandalized at the reopening of Superstition.

Two years ago we used to see the Dow[age]r Lady Elgin at Paris a good deal; & she delighted in wild stories. It was in her vast half lighted room that I heard the germ of that story from a M. Bonette – He told it as having happened to some one he knew in the South of France, as far as the Man's falling in love with a mysterious Girl at a watering place, & her telling him of the Fiendish Double by which she was haunted for some sin of her Father's.

The Grandmother Witch is a pure Invention: The History of the poor Clares & their ringing the bell in extremity of famine I heard this year from a Flemish Lady in {Belgium} Antwerp who had a Sister a poor Clare.

Brotherton Collection, Leeds University
Printed in J. A. V. Chapple, 'Elizabeth Gaskell's *Morton Hall* and *The Poor Clare'*, *BST* 20 (1990), pp. 47–49. Copy entitled 'The Poor Clare, a story in Household Words Janry 1857 [13–27 December 1856]', found in Jane Adeane's notebook.

1 Extract of a letter fm Ly Hatherton in reply to an enquiry I had made Febry 13th, 1857: 'I can gratify your Curiosity about the poor Clare, Mrs Gaskell writes me word that it is her's.'

LOUIS HACHETTE

120 Rue du Bac
Monday Evening.
[?16 February 1857]

Dear Sir,

I forgot to enumerate among the names of the books that I gave you this morning, the titles of *'The Moorland Cottage'*, a Christmas Story[1] about the length of Mr Dickens' Christmas Stories, published separately in a duodecimo volume of about 150 pages in December 1850; and a story nearly as long as the Moorland Cottage, which appeared \ 1851 / in numbers in a periodical, the title of which I forget, but which I can ascertain directly from Mr Chorley the Editor.[2]

These stories are *ex*clusive of the American publications.

I remain, Sir,
Yours truly
E. C. Gaskell

Archives Hachette Livre

1 Published in December 1850 with illustrations by Birket Foster. See Alan Shelston, '*The Moorland Cottage*: Elizabeth Gaskell and Myles Birket Forster', *GSJ* 2 (1988), pp. 41–58.

2 'Mr Harrison's Confessions', *The Ladies' Companion and Monthly Magazine,* Feb-Apr 1851, then edited by Henry Chorley (*Howitt Autobiography*, II. 57).

SIR RUTHERFORD —?

120 Rue du Bac
Saturday, Feby 21 [?1857]

Dear Sir Rutherford,

I am only too happy to tell you that my address is *Plymouth Grove, Manchester* when I think of the pleasant consequences likely to accrue to me from writing these few words.

Yours very truly
E. C. Gaskell

Location and addressee unknown
Autograph, sold at Sotheby's, 11 July 1996, Lot 191.

MRS MARY PUTNAM[1]

Via di S. Isidoro[2]
Wednesday
[23 February – 14 April 1857]

My dear Mrs Putman[sic],

It will give my daughters and myself very great pleasure to spend tomorrow evening with you –

Very truly yours
E. C. Gaskell.

Huntington University Library, SL 249 (2), dictated?

1 Mary Traill Spencer Lowell Putnam (1810–98), sister of the writer J. R. Lowell (1819–91). With visiting card inscribed 'For Mrs Putnam'; underneath, 'Mrs W Gaskell'[engraved] 'Miss Gaskells' [MS].

2 The Gaskells intended to stay with the Storys* for a few days, before finding lodgings (*Letters*, pp. 447–8, 714). See especially Henry James, *William Wetmore Story and His Friends*, 1903, I. 353, 355–9.

MRS HOZIER[1]

43 Via di San Isidoro
March 15th [1857]

Dear Mrs Hozier,

I am very sorry and so are my daughters that we were so dreadfully fatigued with sight seeing on Saturday Eveng, as to be unable to do anything after our late dinner but go to bed. Indeed dinner was not ended until nearly nine o'clock; and as we had come in only just in time for it, and had another party to go to before coming to you, I believe it would have been later before we should have arrived that[sic] you would have liked to receive us.

I am very penitent & sorry, & hardly dare call in person to apologize; but indeed I could not help it. – Please forgive me, & believe me, dear Mrs Hozier, yours very truly

E C Gaskell.

Envelope Mrs Hozier / 3 Porta del Popolo.

Princeton University Library

1 Not identified. ECG letters are rare from this period. Two letters about return travel arrangements survive: MA to C. E. Norton*, 43 Via di San Isidoro, [April, 1857] (Harvard bMS Am1088 3485–6); also, one from Meta to CEN, n. d. (bMS Am1088 2599). The best source of information remains *L & M*, II, 108–41.

ANON

Plymouth Grove
Manchester –
September 2nd 1857.

< … > I am very fond of collecting autographs myself, so I can enter into the feeling which makes you wish for mine.

E. C. Gaskell.

Pierpont Morgan Library (Gordon Ray Collection).

WILLIAM DEARDEN[1]

Plymouth Grove.
Septr 9th 1857.

Mrs Gaskell presents her compliments to Mr Dearden, who, she concludes, has sent her the enclosed extract, and begs to return it him with many thanks. She never reads anything printed in papers or reviews about herself, from want of time and inclination, and therefore fancies that it may be of more use to Mr Dearden than herself.

Envelope W Dearden Esq. / Brunswick Place / Bradford / Yorksh:
Stamp; postmarks MANCHESTER / 8S[?] / SP 9 / 57 *and* STOCKP<ORT>

West Yorkshire Archive Service: Kirklees (DD /DW16)

1 Yorkshire schoolmaster and lecturer who defended Patrick Brontë's reputation against the *CBL* account in the *Bradford Observer*. Patrick Brontë dissociated himself in letters to ECG of 20 and 31 August 1857, but Dearden was not to be silenced. See *Letters*, p. 468; Barker, pp. 803–5.

DUKE OF DEVONSHIRE

42 Plymouth Grove
Sepr 17th, 1857.

Dear Duke,

I have the greatest pleasure in the world in sending you the enclosed letter from Charlotte Brontë to me, which I have chosen out as being, in my opinion, the most interesting I ever received from her, and consequently the one I like best to offer to your Grace.[1] For it makes me so glad to think I can give you anything you would care for, after all the kindness you have shown to me, in sympathizing words, and thoughtful deeds.

I did not like detaining your Grace the other morning when I feared that you might be tired, for any selfish purpose of gratification on my part; or else neither Meta nor I liked leaving Chatsworth without expressing to you once again how very much pleasure we had derived from our visit there, and \ thanking your Grace for / the opportunity of a leisurely inspection of so many of the rare treasures in your possession.

May I now assure you of our gratitude, and request you to believe me, your Grace's humble servant, Elizabeth C. Gaskell.

I am sending a copy of the Third Edition of the Life of Charlotte Brontë to Chatsworth.

Chatsworth (MS Devonshire Collections 2nd Series)
Printed by J. A. V. Chapple and Margaret Smith, 'Charlotte Brontë and Elizabeth Gaskell in Society', *BST* 21 (1995), pp 162–3.

1 A few days before this letter, ECG and Meta were visiting Chatsworth, the Duke's seat in Derbyshire, and had unexpectedly been invited to stay (*Letters*, pp. 470–73).

R. MONCKTON MILNES*

42 Plymouth Grove
Saturday Sepr 19 [1857]

My dear Sir

I have only just obtained the information you wanted about Sir John Potter, and have barely time to send it you before post time, otherwise I have so much to say to you that this would be extended into a very long letter. Sir John Potter's face is considerably drawn on one side, & he is ordered to live very carefully & abstemiously; but his mind is not at all affected, nor is he, I believe conscious in what a critical state he has been, & is still by some of his friends, considered[.] He is at home, and is giving ' a series of dinner parties', much to the regret of some of the more cautious of his well-wishers, who think that he should only have a 'little quiet society'. But he attends town-councils &c &c, so that he has not assumed any of the habits of an invalid. That is all we can learn, as Mr Gaskell did not *see* him yesterday when he called, & as perhaps you know, Sir John & his brother are the only two people I am aware of who have not forgiven 'Mary Barton'[1] so, owing to him, & his having *expressed* a dislike to meeting me, we never see each other in society. Mr Gaskell thinks, from what he heard yesterday, that Sir John would much be[altered word] grieved & disappointed if he expects you, and you do not come, as he is 'said to be' very jealous of any allusion to his attack.

I want to see you very much to have a long 'confidential' talk with you, & to ask your advice on a subject, which is any thing but literary. I hardly know if I can begin upon it now; it is however purely personal, & can wait as it only refers to myself & my daughter & her affairs. It is my second girl, who is engaged to an Indian Officer,[2] a son of the late Genl Sir Dudley Hill, an old peninsular officer. Capt Hill was at home on furlough when he offered; he was accepted by Meta, & Mr Gaskell sanctioned the engagement on condition that Capt Hill tried & succeeded in getting an appointment in *England,* a thing which he fancied it would not be hard for him to do, as he had some good connexions, Mackinnons & others, and is himself a very clever & hardworking officer in the Madras *Engineers*; who volunteered to serve in the Punjab under his great friend poor Sir H. Lawrence. Capt Hill took a first class at Woolwich, & had \ in consequence / the liberty of antedating his commission &c.

Well! all was going on pretty happily, when this first terrible Indian news came, & all officers on furlough had to return – of course if the best appointment in the world had *then* be[en] offered to him, he cd not have accepted with honour, – he had to go out directly, feeling that once out his return under the \ [?addition] / *five* years (dating from last May,) which are required to entitle him to a 200£ a year pension, – would be very imprudent unless an appointment could be procured for him in England. – Mr Gaskell objects to his going out to India not merely now, but at all, and the only thing which could reconcile him to the marriage even in a couple of years' time wd be if in any way he could get an appointment *promised* to Capt Hill.

He speaks French like a native, Italian pretty well & German enough to understand it, – he has been highly promoted in the East from his knowledge of languages, so I suppose he would find any others easy to acquire; – I have heard – (but you must know how little I am in the way of knowing such things,) that Foreign Office Messengers are not unsuitable appointments for active, clever men, able to speak many languages; and we *know* of two Foreign Office Messengers going to retire. But of course Captain Hill's honour pledges him to remain {at} \ in / Madras until poor India is quiet, – only *would* you sometime read over the accompanying list of the \civil/ appointments he has held, the gentlemen who are most kind & ready to give him testimonials & the situations he thought himself qualified for; & then – sometime – quite at yr leisure, – tell me if I can do *any* thing in the case?

With very kind regards to Mrs Milnes, believe me ever

Yours most truly
E. C. Gaskell.

[In Meta Gaskell's hand]
Appointments held by Capt: C. E. Hill. Madras Engrs
2nd Assistant Civil Engineer, 7th Division.
Executive Officer in charge of the Palghaut, and Ponamy Road.
1st Assistant Civil Engineer, Mysore District.
Superintendent Mungerabad Ghaut Road.
Assistant to the Civil Engineers – Punjaub.
In charge of Civil Engineers' Office. Superintendent of Civil Buildings in the Punjaub.
Superintendent of the [?Hukee] canal in the Punjaub, with powers of a joint Magistrate.
Superintendent of the Timber Agency of the Ranee in connexion with the Rajah of Chumba.

References to
Marquis of Dalhousie – Marquis of Tweeddale – Earl Gifford – Sir H. Lawrence.
C. G. Mansel Esq. Financial Commissioners in the Punjaub.
R. Mongomery Esq. Judicial Comr in the Punjaub –
Colonel Napier – Chief Engineer – Punjaub –
Colonel F. Colton, Superintending Engineer, Madras –
Colonel Peace – Superintending Engineer of Railway Madras
Foreign-Office Messenger. County Constable. Inspector of Prisons. Stipendiary Magistrate. Inspector of Railroad. Manager of a Railway – &c – &c – &c

Trinity College, Cambridge

1 Sir John Potter (1814–58), MP, three times Mayor of Manchester, and his brother Thomas Bayley Potter (1817–98), MP, felt that ECG had deliberately revived memories of the murder of Mrs T. B. Potter's brother in 1831. See esp. *Letters*, p. 196 n. and Michael Wheeler, 'Two Tales of Manchester Life', *GSJ* 3 (1989), pp. 6–28.

2 ECG and Meta met Captain Charles Hill in February 1857 on their voyage to Italy. Meta's rapid engagement to Hill, a widower aged 40 with two children, is one of the more intriguing stories in Gaskell biography. Coinciding with the events leading up to the Indian Mutiny, the engagement was a source of great anxiety; it came to a head when Meta heard accusations of dishonesty which Hill failed to refute and the engagement was broken off. See *Letters*, pp. 474–5, 505–6, 898–9; J. A. V. Chapple, 'Elizabeth Gaskell's *Six Weeks at Heppenheim:* Art and Life', *Rivista di Studi Vittoriani* 3 (1997), pp. 15–16.

WILLIAM STIRLING[1]

42 Plymouth Grove
Manchester
Tuesday Sepr 22. [1857]

My dear Sir,

Lady Hatherton has asked one of my daughters to make a sketch for her, in water-colour, of your Murillo[2] 'Woman Drinking' – She went accordingly yesterday, but was very properly (now one thinks of it) refused to make even a small imperfect sketch without your written permission. May she have it? Meta Gaskell by name, – fond of drawing but not likely to endanger the value of your painting by anything like too faithful a replica.

Yours very truly
E C Gaskell.

Glasgow City Archives (T-SK29/ 28/101).

1 William Stirling (1818–78), nephew of Lady Matilda Maxwell; later Sir William Maxwell-Stirling, scholar-collector.

2 Bartolomé Murillo (*c.* 1617–82), Spanish painter of religious subjects. His 'Woman Drinking' was exhibited in the Manchester Art Treasures Exhibition of 1857.

SAMPSON LOW

42 Plymouth Grove,
Tuesday, October 2nd 1857

My dear Sir,

Many thanks for the check for 50£ quite safely received last night. (Should I send you a stamped receipt?) I am so overwhelmed with visitors, that I have had no time to finish copying the 'Doom of the Griffiths', which being written upwards of 12 years[1] ago, required some alterations. I will indeed send it as soon as possible. In greatest haste

Yours very truly
E C Gaskell

Open University (Low Deposit)

1 A mistake for 22 years? Cp. Letters, p. 488; p. 179 n. 3 below.

?H. MARY CHURCH

Manchester,
October 10, 1857

'The word 'holy' which people in our day repeat as if they were quite sure that they knew what it means, and could assume that every one else knew what it means, must, it seems to me, be interpreted by the Scripture itself, & not by any notions or practices of ours'

From Sermons, by the Revd F. D. Maurice, on the Sabbath

E. C. Gaskell

Annotation Recd direct from Mrs Gaskell. / [?]H Mary Church.

Mrs Lucy Magruder

WILLIAM STIRLING

42 Plymouth Grove
Manchester
October 10th [1857]

My dear Sir,

I seem to myself to have been very ungrateful in not having sooner thanked you for your very kind permission to allow Meta to copy your 'Woman Drinking'. I suppose I have a fresh afflux of obligation to you, now I see how successful she has been. She finished her copy yesterday.[1] Thank you very much.

I was indeed most truly grieved when I saw dear Lady Matilda's death[2] in the newspaper. I do not think I ever knew any person more truly 'holy'. I am very thankful that I have known her. I shall always think of her when I pass the York Gate of the Regent's Park; the place where I last saw her, – and looking back after her carriage, saw her too looking after me, & caught the grave kindly smile which I shall never see again. I forgot that you were her nephew when I wrote last.

Yours truly & gratefully
E. C. Gaskell.

Glasgow City Archives (T-SK29/ 28/101).

1 Meta rose early on 28 September to begin copying the Murillo before the Art Treasures Exhibition opened. See *Letters*, pp. 473–4.

2 Lady Matilda Maxwell died in August 1857.

JOHN M. F. LUDLOW*

42 Plymouth Grove
Manchester
October 29 [1857]

My dear Mr Ludlow,

It is not five minutes since I have put down Tom Brown;[1] just finished it. God bless Mr Hughes! for of course now I know, as every body does that it is his. But I ought to thank you first – I *am* so vexed &

sorry I have not done so sooner, only it cd not be helped[.] Perhaps you know I was in Italy or somewhere till May 28th – then home, our Exhibition;[2] no end of pleasant but very tiring duties of hospitality; & much to make me very anxious. (Do you know my second daughter (the little girl you & Mr Hughes saw here years ago) is engaged to be married to an officer in the Madras Engineers.) – Well! I had no time for reading – no one in our house had; or heart for it with our terrible Indian anxieties, – one of my dear friends was that Mrs Ewart, whose letters, without her name, appeared in the Times of Wednesday 7th Octr the Humiliation Day – called 'most affecting letters of a lady' – and later, since we all know she is dead – two more letters of hers from Cawnpore have been published with her name.[3] – (I am working at a point, though perhaps you don't see what).

Well I began Tom Brown in August – & saw enough to see it was too good to read with half a heart, & in broken snatches of time – don't you know the feeling of wanting to keep a book (or an almond) till the very choicest bit of time for enjoying it? Then Mr Gaskell, very full of Tom whom he had read right early in the day, – lent it unbeknownst to me to an old Rugboean, Adam Fairbairn by name, whose father, a gallant old man, who has worked his way up from being a common blacksmith, took it – *my* copy – and I was not going to read any other – up into Scotland, & there wickedly lent it to grandsons – & it only came back this week; very dirty & dogs-eared like a highly popular book, – & so I never read it – not a bit or a line of it *really* – till this week, & that is why I have not thanked you sooner. Thank you right heartily now. I dislike putting my feelings into words, – because spoken praise of such a book is so poor – but I *mean* to be the better for it – and thank Mr Hughes for writing it – and shut him up in a room with a well barred window till he has written his next, will you. You have fine opportunities you know – never mind Mrs Hughes.

My kindest regards to Mrs Ludlow. What is the best public school for a boy full of good & evil \ age 9 /, & sure to be no half & half character – motherless, father in India, going into the army, not much money, & 'who wants to go to Rugby that he may get into all the scrapes Tom Brown got into??' I shall make you & Mr Hughes into consulting physicians about this lad; in whom I take a great interest.

Please don't think me ungrateful. If I *have* been, I *am* not; and am penitent into the bargain.

Yours most truly
E C Gaskell

Annotation 1857.

Cambridge University Library, Add 7348/10/126

1 *Tom Brown's Schooldays* (1857) was by Thomas Hughes. WG acknowledged its arrival on 30 April [1857] (Add 7348/10/131). It was dedicated to 'Mrs

Arnold of Fox Howe[sic]', and thus brings together a number of Gaskell connections.

2 The Manchester Art Treasures Exhibition, held from May to 11 October 1857, was a sequel to the Great Exhibition of 1851. Concentrated entirely on the fine arts, it was the first such exhibition to bring together works from private collections in a purpose-built exhibition hall. It was patronised by royalty and achieved an international reputation.

3 The massacre at Cawnpore, in which ECG's friends Lt-Col. and Mrs Ewart were killed, occurred in early June 1857 (*Letters,* pp. 468, 899). Mrs Ewart's letters were published anonymously in *The Times* on 7 October 1857, appointed by Queen Victoria as a day for special prayers to be said in churches: 'The whole country meets on this day to deplore in the presence of God the national visitation involved in the Indian Mutiny. It is a day of National Humiliation, and its suitable accompaniment, national self-examination' (*Times,* 7 October 1857). Two further letters – one by Mrs Ewart and one by her husband – appeared under their names on 22 October.

CHARLES ELIOT NORTON[1]

[by Marianne Gaskell for her mother]

42 Plymouth Grove
Friday Oct 30th 1857.

My Dear Mr Norton

I am not writing an answer to your charming letter received this week, that I shall do very soon. This letter is a business one for Mama. Do you remember her telling you that she had undertaken to write a story for Harper? She finished it on Monday and sent it off to Sampson Low the American {book} publisher in London.[2] He did not acknowledge the receipt of the parcel till this morning (Friday) I enclose his letter in which he says that Harper like the rest of the American world is suffering from money difficulties.[3] Mama is very much afraid that Mr Low has delayed answering her letter that he might be able to send the story off tomorrow by the packet which sails then, without Mama's having the power to stop it [.]

She says he has \ done / one or two *'dodgy'* things of the kind before. She is afraid that her story will be lost altogether, having got into Harper's hands. What she wants, is to know if you would be so very kind as to see a little about it, if you having all particulars think it necessary. She is afraid she is very troublesome but she knows you will be so kind as to help her out of her difficulty if you think there is likely to be any. The name of the story is 'The doom of the Griffiths'[4] It is about 53 folio pages.

I am writing in great haste to catch the post. Tomorrow I mean to write you an answer to yours for which very many thanks.

Yours ever affectionately
Marianne Gaskell.

Every one joins me in love to you.

Harvard University (bMS Am1088 3491)

1 Charles Eliot Norton* (1827–1908), American scholar, man of letters and important correspondent. See esp. Jane Whitehill, *Letters of Mrs. Gaskell and Charles Eliot Norton,* 1932; repr. 1973, Hildesheim and New York. His correspondence at Harvard with ME is also extensive.
2 A smaller Victorian publishing house, which also acted for Harper's of New York. Sampson Low (1797–1886) founded the firm in the 1830s and probably dealt with ECG, though his son of the same name (1822–71) joined him in the 1850s. ECG wrote a preface for the firm's edition of *Mabel Vaughan* by the American novelist Maria Cummins in 1857. Low published two collections of ECG's stories, *Round the Sofa* in 1859 and *Right at Last and Other Tales* in 1860, but offended her by advertising the former as made up of new material when it was made up of previously published stories.
3 SL to ECG, 29 October 1857. See Sharps, p. 257 n. 1.
4 'The Doom of the Griffiths' was first published in *Harper's Magazine* for January 1858.

MARY GREEN*

[c. November 1857]

My dear Mary,

I am sure you will excuse my taking the readiest scrap on hand just to write a line or two. Messrs Smith & Elder always send me the 'Homeward Mail' – a copy of which I send on to you by this post. It is edited by Kaye,[1] the historian of Christianity in India author of Life of Sir J. Malcolm, Ld Medcalfe[?] &c, – *not* an exaggerating but a judicious man, from all accounts. We will always send this paper on to you, on the day on whh we receive it, – it is very speedy news; and much more to be relied on than local papers. We don't want it, & they send it me gratis, so you need have no scruple in taking it.

Next. Please thank Emily very much for her note. I am so glad she & Isabella are going to Paris. I do not know at present of anything I want to send, but perhaps I may think of something to trouble them with before 10 o'clk on Xmas day.

Poor little Johnnie Langshaw![2] What is he going to do in India! I seem to have heard no Knutsford news for a long time; and I am always so glad to hear. I hope Mr Gaskell will go to Pendyffryn for a week at Christmas; but as yet he won't promise. This damp weather is bringing back Marianne's indigestion I fear. She is longing for mornings when she can walk out before breakfast without fear of catching cold –

Our kind love to you all.

Your ever affec friend
E C Gaskell

Dr R. Jamison

1 Sir John W. Kaye (1814–76), military historian. See *Letters,* p. 483 n.
2 Son of J. P. and Emily Langshaw, b. 17 October 1845.

MARY GREEN*

Saturday
[?12 December ?1857][1]

My dear Mary,

Please will you and Mr Green come to us for next week but one; i.e. the week beginning on Monday the 21st? The Home-Mission[2] meetings take place that week, which Mr Green will have to attend I believe; and it will be a very great pleasure to us to have you & him with us then. So please come, dear Mary.

Meta & I are looking forward very much to having Annie & Ellen with us on Monday for the rest of their holidays. Owing to the long delay in receiving their reply we have made several engagements, some of which we are glad of, some of which we are sorry for; but decisions have to be come to pretty promptly, here; and we had not time to refer to them. Firstly Florence is at the Wilmot's at Buxton;[3] went there yesterday for a week. (Marianne & Julia will be at Boughton[4] & Oxford, you know?) Secondly, I drink tea with Mrs Robberds on Monday; but Meta will be glad to have the quiet coming with the dear friends of her childhood. Thirdly, one of your girls, is to go with us to a dinner at Mr Carvers on Tuesday \ Meta & the other quiet at home /. Fourthly, Annie & Ellen are to go to the Hallé Concert on Wednesday, while Meta accompanies Mr Gaskell & me to dinner at Mr Bazley's. On Friday too there is a dance at the Charles Souchay's (expected to be very pleasant,) to which we are some of us going, so Annie and Ellen had better come prepared. A dance at the Gaddum's on the 23rd.[5]

We shall dine early (1 o'clk) on Monday; I hope they will come before then. We want to hear Knutsford, Paris, & Indian news very much, so they must bring us a carpet-bag full of gossip.

Our dear love to you all.

Yours very affectionately
E. C. Gaskell.

Dr R. Jamison

1 Dated from previous letter of [November 1857].

2 The Domestic Mission Society was founded in 1833 at Cross Street Chapel. WG was on its committee, acting as secretary from 1841. See esp. M. C. Fryckstedt, *Elizabeth Gaskell's 'Mary Barton' and 'Ruth': A Challenge to Christian England,* Uppsala 1982, pp. 71ff.

3 Edward and Emma Wilmot of Hulme Warfield had gone to live at Buxton.

4 Boughton, Worcester, the home of ECG's first cousin Charlotte Isaac, née Holland (b. 1808).

5 Wealthy manufacturers of German origin like Henry Gaddum, Salis Schwabe*, Carl Souchay and Martin Schunck*, though 'assimilated into the local élite', retained cultural identity. See Alan Kidd, *Manchester,* Keele 1993, p.162.

JOHN M. F. LUDLOW*

42 Plymouth Grove,
Tuesday, Janry 19 [1858]

Dear Mr Ludlow,

I think it was very kind of you, *very* kind indeed, to send me your Lectures on India.[1] I meant at first to have read them before I wrote to acknowledge them, as I always like to do with friend's books; but I find it will be good close reading, and so interesting too that I don't like to hurry or skim over it; indeed I *could* not. So I just write to say thank you heartily, not merely for the book itself, but for thinking of me, as a person interested in India;[2] as well – as just let me say, – in all you write & do, however much it may be, or it might be (for I don't remember that it ever *was*) that I may differ from you. –

We have started our Working Men's College[3] here – my husband was somewhat dismayed, but at the same time very much pleased last night to find that the names \ down / for his class (English language & literature,) were already 57 – I say I think you Londoners have some limit to your numbers, have you not? However you won't answer me if I question you ever so much so I shall leave you alone.

My very kind regards to Mrs Ludlow, & ever believe me yours very truly

E C Gaskell.

Annotation 1858.

Cambridge University Library, Add 7348/10/127

1 Delivered at the London Working Men's College, and published with other material in 2 vols in 1858.
2 By this time Captain Hill was in India, at Dowlaisheram, where he was making improvements, 'from building a Roman Catholic chapel like the church at Ambleside, to a billiard room like a Swiss chalet' (MA to C. E. Norton*, Plymouth Grove, 25 January 1858, Harvard bMS Am1088 3489).
3 This college, founded in 1858, was also based on Christian Socialist principles. Students had to be over 16; classes took place in the evening; the fee was half-a-crown for a term of ten weeks. William Gaskell was both lecturer in English and on the Board of Management.

?DAVID MASSON[1]

42 Plymouth Grove
Manchester
Monday, March 15th [1858][2]

Dear Sir,

Many thanks for your letter. Of course you know that Spenser is *said* to have inhabited an old house, yet existing near Burnley, Lancashire, called Hurst-Wood, – and to have written his Shepherd's Calendar there. At any rate that is the tradition among the old families in the neighbourhood, – a curious one enough, with manufacturing wealth jostling old landowners, who date from the Saxon times. Hurst Wood is now little more than \ an / old farmhouse and out-buildings (the whole giving the idea of a much larger mansion built round a square, – but there are only fragments of the Square remaining, –) the rooms are small, & heavy with rude timber beams, with armorial bearings here & there. The situation of the place is fine & good, though almost inaccessible now, from the badness of the roads (or no-roads) leading to it; it stands on the edge of the sweeping moors looking down into a ravine, through which a little brook, fringed with alders &c, trembles.

The people about Burnley (who care to do so,) claim many of Spenser's words as still existing there. I send by this post a lecture, delivered by my husband on the Lancashire dialect, which is reckoned curious & interesting by some; and also a Sermon of his on Milton. *He* has, at any rate, been for some time on the look-out for your promised edition of Milton, and has often expressed his wonder that it did not appear.[3]

Yours very truly
E C Gaskell

Annotation D. Masson?

Princeton University Library

1 David Masson (1822–1907), prolific writer and scholar. A Scot, he moved to London in 1847 and was appointed Professor of English Literature at University College London in 1853. In 1865 he became Professor of Rhetoric and English Literature at the University of Edinburgh. A pioneer of higher education for woman, his daughter Flora (d. 1937) wrote an early study of ECG and her writings for the 9th edn of the *Encyclopaedia Britannica* in 1879.

2 Dated by perpetual calendar and 5th edition of *Mary Barton,*

3 WG's *Sermon for Milton's Death Day* (1857). Masson's *Life of Milton,* 7 vols 1859–94; edition of Milton, 1874.

LADY MARY FEILDING[1]

42 Plymouth Grove
April 13th [1858]

My dear Lady Mary,

Your last letter came when I was ill in bed, and I only remember that there was the Garcia[2] question to reply to, which Marianne did; but although I can only remember this one question I know there was something else to reply to. Now this sounds very careless in me; but I have been very ill; and I dare say you know how thoughts become confused, and papers mislaid, on a sick bed. And I know it was something I wanted very much indeed to reply to; so if you can remember what it was, will you tell it {m } me again?

To make my letter worth having I am going to copy you out those lines[3] which I think I spoke to you about last year, as admiring so much. I wonder if you will do so too.

Philip, my King.
Look at me with thy large brown eyes,
Philip, my King!
For round thee the purple shadow lies
Of babyhood's regal dignities.
Lay on my neck thy tiny hand,
With love's invisible sceptre laden,
I am thine Esther to command
Till thou shalt find thy queen-handmaiden
Philip, my King!
Ah the day that thou goest a-wooing
Philip, my King!
When those beautiful lips are suing
And some gentle heart's bars undoing
Thou dost enter love-crowned, and there
Sittest all glorified – rule kindly
Tenderly over thy kingdom fair –
For we that love, ah! we love so blindly
Philip, my King!

I gaze from thy sweet mouth, up to thy brow,
Philip, my King!
Ay there lies the spirit, all sleeping now,
That may rise like a giant, and make men bow
As to one high-throned among his peers.
My son! than thy brethren higher & fairer
Let me behold thee in coming years!
Yet thy head needeth a circlet rarer
Philip, my King!
A wreath, not of gold, but palm, one day,
Philip, my King!

Thou too must tread, as we tread, a way
Thorny, and bitter, and cold and gray:
Rebels within thee, and foes without
Will snatch at thy crown. But go on, glorious
Martyr, yet monarch, till angels shout
As thou sitt'st at the feet of God, victorious,
'Philip, my King!'

There are some things in this I like extremely; and some things I don't. I miss and need a great deal in it; and yet I like it much, supposing the person were very young and untried, who wrote it: but there is a sort of exaggerated confidence in human strength to do right, – and an idea that we can ever feel satisfied with what we have done, – that makes me turn from copying this, to the 'Lead Thou me on' of the Lyra Apostolica,[4] with a great feeling of rest.

I wonder how I come to be writing all this to you just now. I suppose because I had often reproached myself with not having kept my promise about 'Philip my King' – and then, in the quiet of my half-invalid life, – one goes on from thought to thought, forgetting how, in the hurry of London, notes & letters are troublesome in proportion to their length.

Please tell me what it was you wanted to know: if, indeed, I can still be of use in answering. It is not yet certain whether our friends will send their daughter to school or not. I do not even know if they have written to Miss Maclean. Meta says Holman's[*sic*] Hunt's picture for the forthcoming exhibition[5] is most beautiful.

Yours ever most truly
E. C. Gaskell.

Warwickshire County Record Office (CR2017/ C479/ 1)

1 Lady Mary Catherine Frances Feilding (b. 1823), twin sister to the 8th Earl of Denbigh. ECG spells Fielding elsewhere (*Letters*, p. 334: sic MS).

2 See p. 149 n. 4 above.

3 'I have found out who "Philip my king" is by. It is by Miss Mulock the authoress of John Halifax &c &c Mr Henry Bright told us, he had seen it in a book of autographs in her handwriting and was told by the owner of the book that it was by her' (MA to C. E. Norton*, Plymouth Grove, 25 January 1858, Harvard bMS Am1088 3489). Dr Shirley Forster informs us that it was written to Dinah Mulock Craik's godson, Philip Bourke Marston, and first appeared in her *Poems* (1859).

4 From John Henry Newman's 'Lead Kindly Light', first published as 'Faith' and reprinted without title in the *Lyra Apostolica,* a collection of poems by Newman and Tractarian asssociates, in 1836.

5 In March 1858 John Ruskin arranged for Meta to see Hunt's unfinished 'Christ Disputing with the Doctors' (*Letters*, p. 507).

JACOB GRIMM[1]

Rhodes House[2]
near Manchester
16ten Mai [1858][3]

Uebersetzung

Liebe Mrs Curtis

Könnte ich Deutsch schreiben so würde ich Professor Grimm selbst schreiben – ja ich hätte dies schon längst gethan – um ihm für das durch Sie geschickte Portrait zu danken – um ihm zu sagen wie sehr es mich erfreute, daß er meiner gedenke.[4] – Da ich leider kein Deutsch kann so bitte ich Sie ihm folgende Frage von mir zu stellen. –

Es giebt mehrere Oerter in England in welchen die Syllbe Knut mit dem Localnamen vereinigt wird z. b. Knutsford (eine Stadt in der Grafschaft Cheshire) ist einer. – In jedem dieser Oerter *fließen zwei oder mehrere Flüsse zusammen.* – Die Sage aber verbindet den Namen des Ortes mit dem des Königs Knut – da das Wort Knut in alten Ausgaben der Dichtungen Chaucers als Mittelwort der Vergangenheit des Zeitworts to knit (einigen) 'knit in bonds of friendship' – vorkommt, so fragt man: ob König Knut vielleicht seinen Namen durch sein *Amt* als *Verbinder der Königreiche* bekommen hat. – und ob der Zuname anstatt des ursprünglichen Namens gebraucht worden wäre – als wäre z. b. König Harold *Hasenfuß* – nur *Hasen* Fuß genannt worden – mit dem Unterschiede, daß die Bedeutung Knuts ein allgemeineres Interesse besaß, und darum allgemeiner angenommen. – Es liegt mir viel daran dies zu wissen und da Professor Grimm in solchen Sachen die allerbeste Autorität ist so würden Sie mich sehr verpflichten wenn Sie ihm diese Fragen von mir machen würden.

[Translation

Dear Mrs Curtis

If I could write in German, I would myself write to Professor Grimm. In fact, I would have done so long since, to thank him for the portrait he sent through you and to say how very pleasing it was that he thought of me.[4] Unfortunately, I know no German, so I ask you to put the following question to him for me, please.

There are various places in England where the syllable Knut is joined with the local name – Knutsford (a town in the county of Cheshire) is one example. In each of these places *two or more rivers flow together.* Tradition, however, associates the name of the place with that of King Knut – as the word Knut appears in old editions of Chaucer's poems as the past participle of the verb to knit (einigen) 'knit in bonds of friendship', one wonders whether perhaps King Knut got his name through his *office* as *uniter [unifyer?] of the kingdom*, and whether the surname or epithet was used instead of the original name. Thus, for instance,

King Harold *Harefoot* might simply have been called *Hare* foot, with the distinction, however, that the meaning of Knut possessed a more general interest, and was therefore assumed more generally.

I would really like to know about this, and since Professor Grimm is in such matters the best authority, it would greatly oblige me if you were to put these questions to him on my behalf.]

Staatsbibliothek zu Berlin, Preußicher Kulturbesitz: Nachlaß Grimm 1025
We are most grateful to Professors Peter Skrine and Frank Shaw for transcription of the difficult, old-fashioned German handwriting, together with commentary on the two letters and our translations. The covering letter reads:

Verehrter Herr Professor

Die Schriftstellerin Mrs Gaskell hat mich gebeten Ihnen zu schreiben und da ihr Brief alles klar und deutlich ausdrückte was sie wissen wollte glaubte ich nichts besseres thun zu können als denselben übersetzen. –

Die Uebersetzung lege ich ein obgleich ich überzeugt bin, daß Sie es Englisch eben so gut verstehen können und ich thue es nur ihrem Wunsche gemäß. – Mir ist es unendlich angenehm mich in Ihr Gedächtniß zurückzurufen und wenn ich auf eine Antwort auf einliegende Fragen hoffen dürfte so würde es mich beglücken –

Ich habe so schöne Stunden in Ihrem Hause verlebt,[5] daß ich zu gern einen Augenblick in Ihrem lieben Familienkreise verweile und frage ob es Mme Grimm, Professor Wilhelm, Auguste und Herrn Hermann gut gehe: bitte grüßen Sie Alle[6] herzlich von mir und erhalten Sie im freundschaftlichen Andenken

Ihr
Sie hochschätzende
Annie Curtis

Dürft ich Sie bitten einliegenden Brief Mme Ger<h>art zu überreichen.

[Dear Professor,

Mrs Gaskell the authoress has asked me to write to you, and as her letter expressed clearly and plainly what she wanted to know, I thought I could not do better than translate it. –

I enclose the translation even though I am convinced that you are able to understand it just as well in English and I only do it in accordance with her wish. It is exceptionally pleasant for me to remind you of myself, and if I might hope for an answer to the enclosed questions, I would be delighted.

I have spent such pleasant times in your house[5] that I willingly linger a moment with you and your family and ask if everything is well with Mme Grimm, Professor Wilhelm, Auguste and Mr Hermann. Please greet them[6] heartily for me and spare a kindly thought for your respectful

Annie Curtis

May I ask you to pass the enclosed letter to Mme [?]Gerhart]

1 Jacob (1785–1863) and his brother Wilhelm (1786–1859) became famous as learned collectors of folk tales; their *Kinder- und Hausmärchen [Nursery and Household Tales]* were published in 3 vols in 1812, 1814 and 1822. Jacob was Professor of Philology and Librarian at Göttingen 1817–37, when both brothers were dismissed from their academic posts for political reasons. In 1841 they were invited to settle in Berlin.

2 Annie Curtis (not yet identified) sends her translation into German of a letter from ECG to Jacob Grimm, together with her own covering letter, which is printed above with English translations. Rhodes House, near Middleton, Lancashire, was owned by the Salis Schwabes* from 1832, part of the site of their calico printing business.

3 An English translation of Grimm's reply from Berlin, dated 22 May 1858 (not known to be extant), is printed in the Reverend Henry Green's *Knutsford Its Traditions and History with Reminiscences, Anecdotes, and Notices of the Neighbourhood* (1859), pp. 27–8. Manchester merchants had many connections with Germany, and Victorian postal services were remarkable by today's standards.

4 In about May 1854 ECG told John Forster* that Jacob Grimm had asked for a copy of WG's pamphlet, *The Lancashire Dialect, Illustrated in Two Lectures*, 1854 (*Letters*, p. 283). Presumably Grimm had sent a portrait in response.

5 She had evidently been a guest of the Grimms in the Linkstraße, Berlin, where Jacob Grimm lived with his brother and family from 1847.

6 Herman[sic] (1828–1901) was the son, and Auguste (b. 1832) the daughter, of Wilhelm Grimm. Herman became a distinguished art historian.

LOUIS HACHETTE

42 Plymouth Grove
Manchester.
May 25th [1858]

Dear Sir,

My daughters and I were all so much pleased to receive a letter from you again, and to hear something of you and Madame Hachette (who have always been so kind and hospitable to us,) that I hope you will allow me to write immediately and tell you what pleasure your letter, (received {)} this evening) has given us.

Twice this week, – on Sunday and yesterday, – we have been wondering at your silence; and regretting extremely that – owing to M. Alfred Hachette[1] not having left his address on his card, we had no opportunity of giving ourselves the pleasure of seeing him in our house, and endeavouring to show our sense of the kind hospitality with which you have always received us in Paris. Once more let me say: how much pleasure your letter gave me as it relieved me from the apprehension that anything had occurred to disturb our good understanding.

You are quite right in supposing that I should be glad to know any details of your progress, and literary plans which you may give me. I am particularly interested in all you tell me. If the journalist you have employed to keep you 'au courant' in English literature does not tell you of any good novels, it is because none are written. I never knew so few *good* romances published. 'Year after Year' by the Author of 'Paul Ferroll'[2] is considered a failure. Dickens reads aloud, instead of writing, and is said to earn more money in this way. Thackeray writes the 'Virginians',[3] a monthly serial of which doubtless you have heard. The cleverest novel that has appeared during the last six months is 'Guy Livingstone'[4] (in one volume.) It is the story of a 'fast' young man; but it is a very brilliant clever book. I do not know how it would bear translation; but I am inclined to think that, if well done, it would be popular in France. It is rather melodramatic; but every scene is highly interesting in itself. The author is a Mr Lawrence, an Oxford man, and not above thirty years of age. During the winter every one was absorbed in the Indian news; and we read only books about India. And now the parliamentary debates take up all our reading time. I will always let you know when any romance or novel has a great success in England.

I shall be very much obliged to you for one or two copies of the translation of 'North and South'. If Madame Loreau be the lady I had the pleasure of meeting at your house last year I am sure she would translate it well.

You do not mention how much I am indebted to you for the dozen pair of gloves, which arrived quite safely?

I should be delighted to think that there was an opportunity of our availing ourselves of your kind invitation to visit you at Plessis, and renew our friendship with Madame Hachette. We are going abroad this autumn; but we English are afraid of you French, and are uncertain what you mean by being so strict about passports.

Pray present our affectionate compliments to Madame Hachette, and do not allow your daughters to forget us. As for Monsieur Alfred I do not forgive him for not leaving his address, and so giving us the pleasure of seeing him.

Believe me to remain,
dear Sir
Yours very truly
E. C. Gaskell

Annotation Repondu le 2me[?] aout[sic] 1858

Archives Hachette Livre

1 Hachette's* son, who was to have succeeded him in the firm, but who left Paris in 1863 because of ill-health.

2 C. A. Clive's *Year After Year* (1858), as ECG says, was not as successful.

3 *The Virginians* had reached its seventh monthly instalment at this point.

4 *Guy Livingstone* (1857) was the first novel of George Alfred Lawrence (1827–76). Its hero, like its author and Hughes's Tom Brown, is the product of Rugby and Oxford: in this case the novel deals with his whole life – romantic betrayal, a broken engagement, a protracted death and a death-bed reconciliation with his lost lover.

LOUIS HACHETTE

42 Plymouth Grove
August 16th 1858.

Dear Sir,

I have never received any answer from you to my last note, nor has the copy of the French translation of 'North and South' ever reached me; which, when you last wrote, you kindly said you would send me soon – the publication being shortly to take place.

This makes me a little scrupulous about writing to you \ again; but as it is / for the purpose of acquainting you, according to our agreement, with the nature of a book of mine that {h} is about to be published, I shall do so.

This work is to consist of a republication of any stray tales[1] of mine that may have appeared in different periodicals during the last few years, *set in a slight framework*; which, of course, as it is to link them all together, will be freshly written. Messrs Sampson Lowe[*sic*] and Co. \ of Ludgate Hill, London, / have made me a very good offer for it, and I expect it will be published in November, and that it will {consist of} \ make / two volumes. All the tales have appeared in the 'Household Words', with the exception of one called the 'Doom of the Griffiths', which was printed in the American periodical \ 'Harper's Magazine' /, and another, which was published by Fulcher of Ipswich. I will send you the sheets, as soon as I can obtain them. The right of translation of the stories is reserved, in the English edition.

With best compliments to Mme Hachette, believe me to remain,

Yours very truly
E C Gaskell

Annotation Repondu le 2me[?] Aout[sic] 1858

Archives Hachette Livre

1 *Round the Sofa* (1859) was translated by Mme Loreau and published as *Autour du Sofa* (1860), but omitting 'Half a Lifetime Ago' and 'The Poor Clare'.

VERLAG B. TAUCHNITZ

42 Plymouth Grove,
Manchester
August 16th, 1858

< ... > With one of whom I had always heard agreeable and respectful things said, and who has always behaved so kindly and liberally to me. ... The English publication of these tales[1] is undertaken by Sampson Low, Ludgate Hill, and I will direct him to send you the two that I have named to you < ... >

Text from [Curt Otto], *Der Verlag Tauchnitz*

1 i. e., *Round the Sofa.*

MRS FRANCES WEDGWOOD[1]

Plymouth Grove
Tuesday
[17 August 1858]

My dear Mrs Wedgwood,

I shall be delighted to see you, any time tomorrow or Thursday as best suits you. I am to have two blisters on my spine on[*sic*] tonight for 12 hours; and though I don't much mind them (as they always relieve me from worse pain,) yet they will prevent my being much of a gad-about for two or three days, and will make me a 'figure to be seen'. But you will I know excuse that. We dine (which you can make your lunch,) at one; and drink tea whenever any body wishes, as Mr Gaskell is from home, and we have none of the regularity of a family with a man at the head.

I do so want to see you. So only arrange to stay as long as you can. You *could* not come & stay *with* us, could you? I have nothing whatever to offer except that we should so enjoy having you. But you would find it dull, I'm afraid. *Should* you? Do come & stay with us if you can.

Your ever affect.
E C Gaskell

Keele University Library (Wedgwood MSS., Mosley Collection)

1 This letter is enclosed in one from Mrs Hensleigh Wedgwood to her daughter Katherine, [c. 20 August 1858], describing a visit to ECG at home. 'She had not been well with back pain – you know her constant attention to tidyness & comfort under all Circumstances'; adding, 'She almost timidly told me that M's engagement was finally broken off ... she spoke much of course of the great intense relief that it was at an end.'

LOUIS HACHETTE

42 Plymouth Grove
Manchester.
September 2nd [1858?]

My dear Sir,

I write in great haste, as the post leaves shortly; but I do not want another day to pass without my answering the kind note I have received from you during the past week. I am afraid I shall only have time now to tell you a little about the books of which you have sent me a list, to make a few observations upon. Many of the London publishers, such as Charles Skeet, Newby & Co.[1] publish books on the following terms only; accepting *from the author* a certain sum at the outset 'to cover the risk of the publication', as they call it, which sum they repay if the work is profitable, and they gain \ instead of lose / upon it.[2] This makes them anxious rather for the *pecuniary* success of the books they publish; than for the *matter of the book's* being such as does them credit to have put in circulation. Pray do not think that, in saying this, I make invidious distinctions: the fact is pretty generally known – and the books that emanate from the hands of the wealthiest publishers, & those who pay highest, usually are the works of most merit. I, and two of my daughters are going next week to Germany. We may return (in November) through Paris. If so, we shall hope to see you, Mme Hachette, & your family. Till then I remain With much respect

Yours truly
E. C. Gaskell.

Archives Hachette Livre

1 Charles Joseph Skeet (1812–92), bookseller and publisher in London 1850–84. Thomas Cautley Newby, ECG's 'mean publisher to be gibbetted' (*Letters*, p. 418), tricked the Brontës, Anthony Trollope, Julia Kavanagh and other authors. Newby & Co. 1843–74.
2 Eliza Lynn Linton paid Newby £50, standard for a young author.

CHARLES BOSANQUET[1]

106 Haupt strasse
Tuesday Morning [?26 Oct. 1858]

My dear Sir,

I have fixed to go by the train tomorrow that leaves Heidelberg at 9–30 – and which arrives at Carlsruhe at 11–20: and to go on from there to Strasburg at 2–7; so you see, (if you still find that it suits you to accompany me to Carlsruhe,) we should have plenty of time for seeing the Deaconesses,[2] after I have procured my visa. I name my times, because I think it is possible that you may like to make some arrangement with Miss Graham. But please don't think yourself in any way *engaged* to go with me to Carlsruhe; for already I am afraid lest my not going till Wednesday may have cut into your week's excursion; and I am sorry I did not think of this more fully yesterday, but I was almost stupified by a bad head ache: which has not yet quite left me, & makes me write confusedly I am afraid.

This gist of my note is this. You are not to go with me, please, if it is in the very least interfering with any other plan or wish of yours; but *if* you go, we should have time to see the Deaconesses.

Yours very truly
E C Gaskell

Address Chas Bosanquet Esqr / Prinz Carl.

Formerly Leeds City Archives

1 Charles Bertie Pulleine Bosanquet (b. 1835), barrister, a well connected and

deeply religious young man from a Low Church or Evangelical family who met ECG and her daughters on her visit to Germany in 1858. See *Letters*, pp. 647–50, for religious difficulties caused by the Gaskell's Unitarianism.

2 Members of a religious order, the 'Diakonissenwerk', devoted to educational and hospital work, founded by Pastor Theodor Fliedner in 1836. Their 'Mutterhaus' in his parish of Kaiserswerth was a model. Florence Nightingale* spent three months there in 1851; Catherine Winkworth*, who later wrote a life of Fleidner (1867), also visited it. ECG probably proposed a visit to Kaiserswerth itself, though other houses were possible.

FLORENCE NIGHTINGALE*

Manchester,
Decr 31 [1858].

My dear Miss Nightingale,

I was in Paris, as you would hear when your letter & the 'Confidential' Notes & Subsidiary Notes[1] arrived. I thought you would not care for the mere form of acknowledgement which I could have sent immediately on my coming home, so I waited until I had read something of them.

And now may I say what is in my heart; or will you snub me à la Dr Johnson? I don't believe you will, because it is so very true, & moreover I will try not to praise or honour you a bit. *Don't* I remember you? – and *haven't* I thought of you? – & your soldiers, & your army matters. Little bits that your sister told me long ago about your soldiers come up in my mind in the dead of night often & often, & one can't be strongly interested in individuals without learning to care for the class to which they belong. Besides you know I live in the very midst of what was once called the Peace party[2] – (Manchester has really as pretty a fighting spirit as any one could wish to see, –) & formerly, before the Crimea, I constantly heard the 'army' spoken lightly of, if not positively sneered at, – now all speak with respect of soldiers, – since that winter in the trenches. It is a great change in \ the / manner of speaking & thinking, & as good a testimony as I think can be brought to the gradual acknowledgement of the noble qualities called out by the discipline & dangers of a soldier's life.

I read the Subsidiary Notes first. It was so interesting I could not leave it; I finished it at one long morning's sitting, – hardly stirring between breakfast & dinner. I cannot tell you how much I like it, & for such numbers of reasons. First because you know of a varnish, which is as good or better than black lead for grates: (only I wonder what it is, –) Next because of the little sentences of real deep wisdom, which from their depth & true foundation may be real helps in every direction, & to every person; and for the quiet continual devout references to God, which make the book a holy one – – Now all this has nothing to do with your soldiers, but don't think the book thrown away upon me, because I have not sooner said that I had no conception *what* those poor poor fellows had had to go through till I read the larger book of notes. – One can hardly believe it – much less realize it. That larger book should have been read first; it is both a tougher subject, & or infinitely the most painful; {&} the other fortunately, will bear reading over & over again, & gives one a glimpse into blue sky. Now I am only going to say one thing more. You have done nobly the disagreeable work you had in your way; you have not shirked it but given it simply & plainly out.

My dear Miss Nightingale, you once directed an envelope (about a poor woman at the Establishment for invalid gentlewomen,) & put two words & your initials inside – do you think I have parted with it, – I only wish you could ever tell me what I might or could do to serve you & yr interests. *Mind* you do, if I ever can. And don't think this letter impertinent, because you don't know how much I have restrained & kept back.

No one shall see those books but my own family. Nor does any one know that I have them.

May God bless you!

Yours very truly
E. C. Gaskell.

Brotherton Collection, Leeds University
From 'I read the *Subsidiary Notes*' to 'a holy one' was reprinted in *Letters*, p. 522.

1 Two documents written for the Royal Commission on the Health of the Army (1857), which she had printed 'for private circulation among influential people' (Cook, I. 343). The first was called *Notes on Matters affecting the Health, Efficiency, and Hospital Administration of the British Army,* and the second, *Subsidiary Notes as to the Introduction of Female Nursing into Military Hospitals in Peace and War.*
2 Opposition to the Crimean War had been led by John Bright, MP for Manchester 1847–57; he was supported by Richard Cobden* and other Manchester Free Traders.

?H. A. BRIGHT*

Plymouth Grove
Manchester.
Friday 7th January [?1859].

Dear Sir,

As I have not the least wish to join in a testimonial to Mr Hawthorne,[1] and[*sic*] must therefore decline adding my name to the subscription list.

Yrs &c
E. C. Gaskell

Princeton University Library (Dictated?)

1 N. Hawthorne resigned as U.S. consul in Liverpool, February 1857. He intended to leave Britain in July 1859, after a European trip.

MRS SARAH NICHOLLS[1]

42 Plymouth Grove
January 27th [1859]

My dear Mrs Nicholls,

Mr Gaskell & I will very gladly accept your kind invitation to dinner on *Wednesday,* if that will suit you. If not on *Monday,* only our Flossy goes to school[2] on Wednesday I do not like losing an evening of her *before* she goes.

Ever yours affectionately
E C Gaskell.

John Geoffrey Sharps

1 Probably the wife (née Ashton, d. 1881) of Benjamin Nicholls (1790–1877), a Manchester cotton-spinner; member of Cross Street Chapel's congregation and Mayor in 1853. WG published his funeral sermon and memoir.
2 Florence Gaskell went to school with the Miss Greens, daughters of Henry and Mary Green, in Knutsford (*Letters,* pp. 530, 537).

CHARLES ELIOT NORTON*

[by Meta Gaskell for her mother][1]

42 Plymouth Grove,
Manchester
January 27th [1859]

My dear Mr Norton,

As Mama's deputy I write to you, to beg you to enquire if Messrs Ticknor and Fields[2] will buy the copyright of a story which she is now writing for the 'Household Words',[3] and which she expects to be about the length of 'Lady Ludlow'. She has been very badly treated abt the latter – *Mr Sampson Lowe*[*sic*] must have behaved badly, she thinks. Without one word of application to her, either directly, or through Mr Lowe, \ at least none has ever reached her / Messrs Harper have republished Lady Ludlow; the authorship of which they can have learnt only through him – Mr Lowe. Mama has written to Messrs Harpers abt this piracy, sending her letter through Mr Curtis[4] that attention may be paid to her complaint. Of course she has been unable to accept Messrs Ticknor and Field's offer; in consequence of Messrs Harper's having snatched at it \ (Lady L) / so dishonorably. Of course, too, it brings her dealings with the Harper-firm to an end – for ever.

If Messrs Ticknor and Field[sic] will give her a certain sum for this new story, and in addition to the price of the story enough more to pay for the copying of it, – (which she can get done by a poor lame cripple) – and if you will let Mama know by return of post, Mama will see that they have a copy of the story in time for them to have the start of any other American publisher with it. She is not quite sure whether the Household Words-people will allow of its publication in America before its conclusion in their paper; but she will enquire. At any rate she supposes that its appearance as a whole story in America simultaneously with the publication of the *last* chapters in Household Words is allowable. Perhaps you know how this is – ?

I hope you are pretty well now. We look forward much to seeing Thurstan Holland[5] soon, and hearing a vivâ voce account of you all.

Pray do not think I forget the portrait of Mama for which you asked. I am waiting till she will and can sit for a fresh one, in preference to copying the old one, as I hope I have improved sufficiently during the last three years in my drawing to be able to succeed better.

I have seen a great deal lately of your friends Lady Elgin and Lady Augusta Bruce.[6] I never could speak of you to the latter without thinking of how we talked to *you* of *her* that dark, snowy evening as we came down the Appenines – Bologna-bound. They both desired their affe[ctionate] remembrances to you. Poor Lady Elgin is now almost lifeless, *physically,* but her eyes glance, and the expression of her face varies, with all the old sweetness and intelligence. They say her memory and her power of understanding are as good as ever; but she cannot utter a word, and seems often in sad distress from wanting the power of expression, which occasionally she replaces with terrible cries like those of an animal in pain. Lady Augusta's meekness & patience, you who know her, may guess – but it is far beyond description.

Mama is very well just now – I hope not merely *for* just now, though so is Papa –

With our united affectionate remembrances,

Believe me, my dear Mr Norton,

Most truly yours
Meta Emily Gaskell

Harvard University (bMS Am1088 2644)

1 The older daughters wrote many letters for their parents (*Letters,* p. 530).

2 Boston firm founded by William Davis Ticknor (1810–64) in 1832, which published Hawthorne, Longfellow, Thoreau and Emerson, and also the *Atlantic Monthly.* J. T. Fields (1817–81) rose from office boy to be Ticknor's partner. See also p. 197 below.

3 'Lois the Witch', *All the Year Round,* 8 to 22 October 1859, is the only story of this length published serially by Dickens in this year. *Household Words* was superseded by *All the Year Round* in April-May 1859, but ECG could not have anticipated this so early. See also ECG to C. E. Norton*, 9 March 1859, where she again seeks his help for a story then consisting of 'upwards of 100'

pages (*Letters*, p. 535). But see Sharps, pp. 579–85, who argues convincingly for 'A Dark Night's Work'.

4 George W. Curtis (1824–92), author and editor, who married in 1856 Anna Shaw, a 'marriage of true minds' for ECG.

5 Edward Thurstan Holland (1836–84), just back from America (*Letters*, p. 524). His MS account of his experiences is in the Brotherton Library, Leeds University, deposited by Mrs Portia Holland. He was to marry Marianne in 1866.

6 Dowager Lady Elgin (d. 1860), the mother of Lady Augusta Bruce (1822–76), was known to ECG through Mme Mohl*. Arthur Stanley, who married Lady Bruce in 1863, met her at the Mohl's house. See p. 169 above for ECG's 'The Poor Clare' connection.

MRS MARY ARNOLD*

Plymouth Grove
Manchester
April 16th [1859]

My dear dear Mrs Arnold,

May I say how deeply we are grieved by what we see in the Times? and how we are thinking of you & yours? We are *so* sorry, – Meta is sitting grave and sad, and recalling our days with him at Fox How, – but yesterday it seems, – and yet how much has happened since, – his wife's death, and the poor little children.[1]

Meta has just roused herself – (it is not five minutes since we saw it –) to say 'But he is better off *there* than *here*', and though this thought is put in a homely fashion, yet there is deep and blessed truth in it, is there not, dear Mrs Arnold? But oh! I am so sorry for you, and I can do you no good, except by praying that God will send down His Comforter, as indeed I know He will.

Don't think it necessary to write, – *much* as I should like to hear from some of you.

I am so glad I knew him, even that little bit; do you remember his \ and his wife's / sending me the £5 for the poor of Manchester,[2] long ago, when they were a new-married couple up at Simla?

Poor Rowlands too!

Ever dear Mrs Arnold,
Yours affectionately
E. C. Gaskell

Trinity College, Dublin

1 William Delafield Arnold (1828–59), fourth son of Thomas and Mary Arnold*, went to India for a second time in 1855. His Anglo-Indian novel of development, *Oakfield, Or Fellowship in the East* (1853), is called a 'strange, quixotic, disillusioned work' by E. M. Forster. In *Letters*, pp. 551–2, ECG quotes Fanny Arnold's sad account of her brother's swift courtship of Frances Hodgson, their marriage in 1850 and her death in 1858, leaving a baby and

three small children. They were sent back to England by ship with their governess in January 1859. Broken in health, WDA followed not long after, but died at Gibraltar in early April 1859. His sister Jane, wife of the Liberal politician W. E. Forster, adopted the children.

2 In 1854 ECG referred to a gift of £10, and fancied, ironically, that 'Oakfield is a very literal piece of his own life, except that he recovered instead of dying on returning home' (*Letters,* p. 326).

CHARLES ELIOT NORTON*
[by Meta Gaskell for her mother][1]

Ashbourne Hall,[2] Derbyshire
May the Ninth 1859.

Dear Mr Norton,

I am staying here alone with some cousins of mine. Mama went home this morning for two days. Before she went she left it in charge to me to write and thank you very much indeed for your kindness in enquiring about the price that she could get for a tale in America.[3]

She hopes you will not regret your trouble, but forgive her having caused it you; when you hear that it {is} \ has been / useless. The offer that Messrs Ticknor and Fields make is so *very* small in comparison with what she gains here that she does not think it worth accepting.[4]

Mr Sampson Lowe[sic] has just offered her £1000 for a tale but little longer than the one Messrs T. & F. bid for.

Privately speaking I am so glad that she should thus give up the resolution she formed in 1857 of publishing for the future in America. It always pained me, when she mentioned it. Her abandoning her natural and wonted *publishing field* for a new and foreign one, would, I thought seem like an attempt to revenge on the English reading-public (who have so warmly received and appreciated her works) the sorrow caused her by a small party – or rather by two families – in consequence of the publication of her last book. C. B.

I dare say that I am mistaken; and see it in too narrow a light; but I cannot help feeling glad at this termination to the negotiations which you have so very kindly conducted. I should so like to know what you think about it; but pray do not mention the *unofficial* part of what I have written in your next letter; for any allusion to what happened in 1857 about the Life of C. B. seems to open the old wound. ...

Harvard University (bMS Am1088 2600)

1 After the opening paragraphs printed above, Meta continues at length with purely personal details of her activities at Ashbourne Hall. See *GSN* 18 (1994), pp. 3–4.

2 Home of the Frederick Hollands (*EY,* p. 444).

3 ECG to CEN, 9 March [1859] (*Letters,* p. 536).

4 See ECG to J. T. Fields, 14 June [1859] (*Letters,* p. 560; cf. p. 581).

LORD STANHOPE

17 Cumberland Terrace[1]
Regts Park
May 31st [1859]

Dear Lord Stanhope,

You were so kind as to ask me to let you know if I came to London this year, as if I did you might possibly be at leisure to go to the National Portrait Gallery with me.

I am here with my daughter for a week or ten days, and have therefore ventured to write this note.

I remain, dear Lord Stanhope,

Yours truly
E. C. Gaskell

Princeton University Library

1 ECG writes from this address on a number of occasions, notably to George Eliot, and to John Greenwood when he informed her of Charlotte Brontë's death.

DUCHESS OF SUTHERLAND[1]

11 Kildare terrace[2] W
June 18 [?1859]

Dear Duchess,

I must apologiz<e> for not sooner acknowledging your note, and the permission you so kindly sent me to see Stafford House; but we have been at the Crystal Palace all day, and I only found your Grace's letter on our return at nine this evening.

May I beg you to accept my best thanks for the pleasure we expect to receive through your kind courtesy.

Believe me to remain, dear Duchess,

Yours respectfully
E. C. Gaskell

Mrs Lucy Magruder

1 Harriet, Duchess of Sutherland, Mistress of the Robes, Queen Victoria's closest confidante. ECG had already been to Stafford house with Emily Winkworth* in May 1849 (*Letters*, p. 828; *L & M*, I. 183). An undated note from the Duke to an unnamed correspondent (amongst EGC's autographs in the John Rylands UL, Manchester), welcomes her visit, 'I hope that the sun may shine – Pictures as well as plants require it.'

2 ECG was at this address, 14 June [1859] until the 27th (*Letters*, p. 560).

R. MONCKTON MILNES*

Bank-end
Auchencairn[1]
By (ie. 22 miles off) Dumfries
N.B.
Wednesday, June 29 [1859]

My dear Sir,

This date will tell you why we cannot breakfast with you tomorrow. We came here yesterday straight from London; and a greater change can hardly be imagined. We are in the Covenanters Country, – Guy Mannering's country,[2] – but not the country of potatoes, seeing that I have just found out that we must send for them to Castle Douglas, nine miles off. And books and news of any kind are if possible still greater rarities; I am half tempted to claim your promise of a book in lieu of Elder's Life of Kane, which you carried off last year; and were, as I must confess, most welcome to.[3]

With kind regards to Mrs Milnes, believe me to remain

Yours very truly
E. C. Gaskell.

Trinity College, Cambridge

1 By the Solway Firth, in south-west Scotland.
2 *Guy Mannering* (1815) was set in eighteenth-century Dumfrieshire.
3 ECG wrote that 'Dr Kane's life is *murdered'* (*Letters*, p. 506). She refers to *Biography of Elisha Kent Kane,* by William Elder (1806–85), American physician. Kane (1820–57), a U. S. naval officer, was a pioneer of the American route to the North Pole.

DANTE GABRIEL ROSSETTI[1]

{Back}
Back End, Auchencairn,
near Dumfries, N.B.
Friday. [22 July 1859]

Dear Mr Rossetti,

The real address is Ba*n*k End, only twice over my pen would make Ba*c*k End instead, which signifies the less as we leave here (alas the day) for \ 42 Plymouth Grove – / Manchester on Monday next, so I hope you will take all this long explanation of the error in the direction, as a proof of my very preraphaelite love of accuracy.

Thank you very much for your proof sheets. I do know the Vita Nuova a little, – as much by Mr Norton's translation (have you seen it? in the Atlantic Magazine?)[2] as anything; but I have known the original in a sort of way[3] for some time, & it is well, for it stands a[s] a centre to all the other poems.

You would receive I hope M. de Circourts Papers[4] on Cavalcanti and Cino da Pistoga by yesterday's post? I did not like to delay them for the chance of my letter today, – nor do I like to delay this \ enclosed / letter of M. de Circourt's for one or two criticisms which I should like to make if I may on what appear to me to be slightly defective lines in the Sonnets. I like your translations so very much that I want them to be perfect, – and I think the reconsideration of a word or two here & there, which cause the line to strike upon my ear as unrhythmical, would be worthwhile. I remember such a pretty story dear Mrs Wordsworth told me[5] of her husband, – which I think emboldens me to stick my two or three fancied defects, in words on a bit of paper, enclosed.

Mr & Mrs Wordsworth & his sister Dora were all living at Grasmere 5 or 6 miles away from Ambleside, the nearest post town; and they were very poor & lived in a cottage, & in the mornings Wordsworth wrote, & Miss Wordsworth cooked, & helped Mrs Wordsworth to make the beds & nurse, for they had no servant, & they had, I think *one* little child, – and then they dined, & then they locked up the house, & walked, carrying the child among them. And one day a proof came of one of the Lyrical ballads, – postage to be paid back, – & postage from Ambleside to London 13d. In the afternoon the three walked to Ambleside to post & pay for the proof. – then they walked home, & at tea Wordsworth who had been silent for some time culminated into an exclamation of how bad some one word in the sent-off ballad was, – did not answer to his meaning a bit. So he & Miss Wordsworth set off *again* to Ambleside, got in after the Post Mistress had gone to bed, for they keep early hours there, – stated the case, – they are good friendly people those Lake country folk, – got the letter out of the post box, – for you see they could not afford a second 13d; had a candle lighted, sent the Post Mistress to bed, – sate up till the mail went out at 4 am, – & as the guard was blowing his horn, *the* word came into Wordsworth's head – (or Dora's,) and it was written down, sent off, candle put out, and they trudged back to breakfast at Grasmere with merry hearts.

Do, if you think M. de Circourt can give you any help, write to him. He is a member of the Institut, so I always direct to him there. He is Genevite, & has been Ambassador up & down in former days, & married a Russian lady,[6] – they are neither of them young, – two or three years ago she set herself on fire & was dreadfully burnt, & then there came out such beautiful patience & heroic cheerfulness out of the \ Russo / Parisian lady of fashion, that it was quite a lesson against judging. And he is a *thoroughly* kind, & very accomplished man. I am *very* glad you like Adam Bede; – do read 'Janet's Repentance' in Scenes of Clerical Life, – by the same author. But the man or woman[7] is a noble creature, whoever he or she be, – I thought I knew who wrote it, when I saw your brother; but I believe I don't.

I have not seen Tennyson's new poems,[8] – but I have smelt oh *such* honeysuckle today, and you have only smelt the Thames.

Yours very truly
E C Gaskell.

My daughters' kindest regards.

Princeton University Library

1 Dante Gabriel Rossetti (1828–82), Pre-Raphaelite poet and painter. As well as his English works, he published translations of the classic Italian poets, notably of Dante's *Vita Nuova.* DGR wrote to ECG on 18 July 1859, envying her freedom in Scotland when he himself felt 'bottled and corked down in Thames water' (*Letters of Dante Gabriel Rossetti*, ed. O. Doughty and J. R. Watt, Oxford 1965–7, I. 355).
2 Charles Eliot Norton*, ' "The New Life" of Dante', *The Atlantic Monthly,* January – March 1859, consisted of translated extracts from Dante's *Vita Nuova* linked by an extended commentary. ECG had read it in MS (*Letters,* p. 607).
3 Italian was available at ECG's school, Avonbank (*EY,* p. 242).
4 Count Adolphe de Circourt (1801–79), diplomat and historian, author of *Poètes de la première renaissance Italienne: Guido Cavalcanti* (1855), extracts having appeared previously in *Revue contemporaine.* ECG met him in Paris in 1855 (*Letters,* p. 334). See also Waller, pp. 54–5, 67–8.
5 Cf. *Letters,* pp. 207–8, where John Foster is told the same story. See also Alan Shelston, 'Elizabeth Gaskell, Dante Gabriel Rossetti and Wordsworth', *Notes & Queries,* n.s. 46.4, December 1999, pp. 470–3.
6 See ECG's 'French Life' (Knutsford Edn, VII. 643–5) for his wife, a celebrated salonnière. See also Sharps, p. 462.
7 For speculation about George Eliot's identity, see Uglow, pp. 242–3, 462–3.
8 Tennyson's *Idylls of the King* were published in June 1859.

ANON

[?late August 1859]

< ... > I am afraid I cannot given the exact dates but I will put down as much as I can remember about 'Thomas Glover', and the clergyman at Silverdale – (the revd Alfred Hatfield, Silverdale nr Lancaster;) would send every particular, and would, I am sure, speak very highly of the boy.[1]

His father was a fisherman, drowned by the coming up of the tide on the sands, five or six years ago. He left a widow, & 3 children, two girls besides Thomas, who must now be 14. Mrs [altered word] Glover is very much respected & liked. She has had a hard struggle to live – 'has been welly hungered to death' many a time; but owing to the kindness of Peggy Hatton, a washerwoman, she has pulled through, though she is often 'hard put to it' in the winter, when there is much less to do. A gentleman whose name I forget offered to pay for Thomas's schooling; and he has profited well by the privilege. He writes well, is a great way on in arithmetic; and is generally an intelligent quiet & gentlemanly boy,

– with a kind of thoughtful dignity about him, that comes I should think, from his having been his mother's confidant & comforter during all her hard days. About Silverdale there is very little work, even of an agricultural kind; people live on fish, and their potatoe grounds in a kind of primitive fashion; and there is nothing much done in the winter; & low wages in the summer. Besides the boy's talents & acquirements fit him to be something more than a labourer; and I want him to earn money somehow, so as to be able to help his mother. Apprenticeship costs money, & though that might [be] got over, yet there would be his living to be found all the time he was an apprentice. I should be *very* much obliged to any one who would help him to employment, & I feel pretty sure that he would do me credit.

E C Gaskell.

Princeton University Library

1 By the end of August ECG had 'bagged' two places for the lad, 'one agricultural, one in Manchester' (*Letters*, pp. 572, 605).

BESSIE RAYNER PARKES[1]

42 Plymouth Grove
Saturday [1 October 1859]

My dear Miss Parkes,

Miss Hannah Behrens[2] can*not* come on Tuesday Evng (and even Miss Winkworth is I regret to say doubtful,) but Miss Behrens hopes *you* will go there to luncheon on Tuesday, as, I believe she has asked you to do in her note. There will be there no one of those I planned but ourselves, so if you have any engagement offered to you that you would prefer, don't scruple throwing us overboard; & if not, come to us.

In greatest haste

Yours most truly
E C Gaskell

Envelope Miss Bessie R. Parkes / Palatine Hotel / Manchester
Postmark MANCHESTER / 5X / OC 22 / 59

Girton College, Cambridge (BRP IX: 29)

1 Bessie Rayner Parkes (1829–1923), active feminist. In 1867 she became a Roman Catholic and married Louis Belloc, the son of Louise Swanton Belloc. After his early death, she abandoned feminism; ironically, her son Hilaire Belloc was to become a strident anti-feminist. See *Letters,* p. 902; *EY,* p. 192.

2 Hannah Behrens* is mentioned in *Letters,* p. 605. See also *Letters,* pp. 545–6 for the high life led by the family at Worleston, Cheshire.

JOHN ROTHERHAM[1]

42 Plymouth Grove
Manchester
Wednesday, October 5th [1859]

Dear Sir,

I dare say you will be surprized at receiving a letter from a complete stranger, but I saw Mrs Nicholls last night, and she asked me if I would reply to your letter to her from Lynton[?], as she felt quite unable to do so herself at present. I conclude from your letter (which she allowed me to see,) that you know nothing about John[2] after he wrote to you 'about a fortnight ago.' But I suppose you know that he has never been quite strong since the Election, about which he took (as you must know) a very active interest. In the early part of July he dined out once or twice to meet a Governor Seward,[3] (an American, – and probable candidate for the next Presidency, –) and caught cold. A kind of low intermittent fever hung about him, for which he went to the sea; to Fleetwood for a week. He did not come home much better. Mrs Nicholls said he lost his interest in public affairs, and indeed in things in general. He did not eat much, or sleep well, and was altogether what people call 'out of health' without having any distinct ailment. In the last week of August he was obliged to be present at some private meeting of the Athenæum, – auditing accounts I think, – and after sitting in a heated room there he walked home at ten o'clock at night. He was never out of doors again; I do not think he was ever up; or rather down-stairs again.

The attack of fever came on at stated times (3 o'clock in the afternoon), – showing it's aguish character; and he extremely objected to taking quinine, yet *would* always know what Mr Fletcher, – the medical man he had chosen out for himself years ago, – prescribed for him. Dr Ashton, his uncle, was in Manchester at the beginning of his illness, – but at the end of a week the pain which {he} \ John / complained of{,} was alleviated by the use of leeches, and as he only seemed *very* weak Dr Ashton left, to go to Ludlow on business; & hearing a good account on the Wednesday he went to the Archæological Socy meeting in Berkshire, and travelled about in that county, so that no letter reached him till he heard of John's death.

I called frequently during the fortnight of his illness, & generally saw Mrs Nicholls. The *first* time I saw her she said 'He is so weak he does not care to eat, or speak, but lies just like a log of wood, as if moving his finger was an exertion.' Then the next time 'He was a little better – but it was very slow work' – in answer to my saying she looked ill 'Oh! if John was well I should be well,' – and so on – never really making much ground till on the Friday before his death (on Sunday,) she said 'Well! I think he really *is* better now, – he was in terrible agony yesterday morning before it was light, – I said 'John! I shall send for Mr Fletcher!' he said 'No!

Wait till 6 o'clock, Mama' but I wouldn't, and when Mr Fletcher came he said it was very well I didn't for inflammation had set in. He put 20 leeches & a blister on directly.' I thought it sounded ill to have to use such violent measures after the weakness she had spoken of; but she went on to say that the leeches & blister (applied to the lower part of the back) had done him so much good, that they had lifted him out of bed on to the sofa \ on the Thursday aft / while his bed was made, & that he had lain there an hour & a half, that he had begun to take a little interest in the Chinese affairs[4] (it was just after the \ news of the / attack on the Peiho,) and told her to keep the newspapers for him for it would be nice reading while he was getting better &c. She was in *very* hopeful spirits that day.

On Saturday I could not go – I sent, & heard that 'the doctor had been with him from very early that morning,' and it was then 5 o'clock in the aftn. We all felt that this was bad, – the fact was I believe that the pain – (inflammation of the bowels) which had seemed subdued by the blister & leeches on Thursday, had returned; and he was too weak now, to bear any active remedies. Still I don't think Mrs Nicholls knew it to be so bad, – she says how shocked she was when, Mr N. returning from the mill at 2, said what a change for the worse he saw. All that night 'that night of agony' as Mrs Nicholls calls it, they hoped and feared, – he did not speak much – once he said something, as they gave him food, – and they asked what it was, – he smiled & said 'Only a line from Virgil that came into my head' – then again, when his father was feeding him with a tea-spoon, he looked towards his mother, and said 'Papa likes doing things for me, does he not?' – {Towa} Once in the night they said that Mrs Nicholls must be worn out, & that they had better get a nurse – he put his arms round her neck & said 'I don't want anybody but my own dear Mama,' – Towards 4 a m she thought he was a little better for he had been dozing, – & said 'Why John we shall have you downstairs to dinner next Sunday' – She says the wistful earnest look in his eyes as he looked at her and said 'No! mama, you will not,' took away all hope, – and after that I think he spoke very little. When we came back from Chapel at about ½ past 12, a groom came to summon Mr Gaskell, who went & remained to the last, – but he does not think John knew him, – he moaned, & dozed & once he wakened up & tossed his arm out & said Where am I? & Mr Nicholls said 'Here in your own bed, John, with your father & mother by you.' –

The blow to poor Mr & Mrs Nicholls is, as you will fancy, more than words can tell. Her sister Mrs Anderson[5] is with her, & I go as often as I can; I don't think she has seen many other people yet. I always delighted in her society, she was so full of humour, – but I now almost reverence her, she is bearing it so beautifully. She means to try & carry on all his plans; his school &c &c &c. – so does Mr Nicholls, – in that they say will be their great comfort. Mr Nicholls is restless, – more passionate in his expressions of grief; & more easily turned away to other subjects. She likes nothing better than to talk of him, to plan the distribution of his things – (she bade me say you are to have something of his, –) She looks grey and white; she has not \ realized / – but indeed her life won't be long enough for her to realize the full extent of her loss. I wish she would go out. – She does not sleep, & dreads sleeping, for if she sleeps she dreams of *him*, and then there is the awakening.

I cannot think of anything more to tell you, but if there is any thing else you would like to know please ask me. You know how the *town* has recognized him? how the working people by a 1d subscription are going to have an obelisk & drinking fountain put up to his memory? We met poor men coming away from the house, & crying as if their hearts wd break the day of his death.

Yours truly
E. C. Gaskell

Girton College, Cambridge

1 Born *c.* 1837. Travelling companion of J. A. Nicholls in USA, August 1857 to February 1858.

2 John Ashton Nicholls (1823–59), son of Benjamin and Sarah Nicholls (p. 194 n. 1 above). A selection of his letters, edited by his mother, was published as a memorial volume in 1862. See *Letters,* pp. 574–5.

3 William Henry Seward (1801–72), Governor of New York State 1838–42, Secretary of State under Abraham Lincoln from 1861.

4 In the late 1850s Chinese naval action and bombardment of Chinese forts on the Canton river escalated into war. In 1858 the British seized forts on the Peiho river, after which the Chinese then acceded to the demands of Western powers to legitimise the opium trade.

5 See *Letters*, p. 652.

?DAVID GRUNDY[1]

42 Plymouth Grove.
Decr 4 [?1859]

[ECG, Marianne and Meta beg 'a few fents & scraps of cloth' to 'manage a cape or cloak apiece for Xmas day', on behalf of ten old women who receive parish relief of '2s. *in* money, 2s. *worth* in food'. ECG concludes by writing that poor old women,]
< ... . shivering to the Union in a worn bombazine petticoat, & calico gown & shawl equally worn, won't be particular if they have a covering of many colours, so that it is warm.

Believe me to remain ever

Yours very truly
E. C. Gaskell.

Holybourne, Hampshire

1 Letter 609, now dated. A portion of the MS holograph is to be found in a frame at 'The Lawn', the house that ECG bought in 1865.

?FREDERIC CHAPMAN[1]

Mrs Lyall's
The Close
Winchester
February 25 [1860]

Dear Sir,

Have you been able to muster me up an autograph of Carlyle's yet? *or* of Mr *or* of Mrs Browning's – &c &c &c. I should be very much obliged to you for them as soon as possible if you have.

Also, do you think it would be advisable to take any further steps (about the missing copy of Richard Peverell[*sic*],[2] by applying to the Gt Malvern post-master; as you are certain it was despatched on a particular day, – (date forgotten-), – & the Belle Vue Terrace[3] people are equally certain it was not received by them.

Do you think it would *pay* to have some of my smaller stories, – such as the 'Well of Pen Morfa' (in the Lizzie Leigh collection, printed separately – I am often asked for them, by people who wish to have them for circulation among the poor). I shall be here till Thursday next; after that, for a week, at Mrs Thompson's 4 Upper Belgrave Street[4] –

Yours very truly
E C Gaskell.

Princeton University Library

1 Frederic Chapman (1823–95) succeeded his cousin Edward as head of Chapman and Hall in 1864.

2 Perhaps George Meredith's *The Ordeal of Richard Feverel*, published 1859.

3 Catherine Winkworth* was ill at Great Malvern, Worcestershire, in the winter of 1859. She moved down from Belle Vue Terrace to 'more comfortable lodgings in Portland Place' on 16 December 1859 (*L & M*, II. 288).

4 ECG writes from here on 1 March [1860], to George Smith* about autographs (*Letters*, p. 602).

~

Letter 498 to Emelyn Story* from [?Manchester] redated [post-February 1860]

~

SAMPSON LOW

42 Plymouth Grove –
April 23rd [1860]

My dear Sir,

I cannot help feeling that my two last letters to you,[1] the first the one to be shown to Mr Harper, the second the one enclosing the few lines I had written as an introduction to the volume of Tales[2] \ have never reached you /. I should be very much obliged to you, if you would kindly send me a line to say if you have received them.

Believe me to remain

yours truly
E C Gaskell.

Wigan Archives, Leigh

1 See Letter 463, 42 Plymouth Grove, 16 April 1860, for the second letter to Sampson Low (*Letters*, p. 613).

2 *Right at Last, and Other Tales* (1860) was published by Low in Britain and by Harper's in the U. S. In both, the title story was accompanied by 'The Manchester Marriage', 'Lois the Witch' and 'The Crooked Branch'.

SAMPSON LOW

42 Plymouth Grove
Manchester –
April 25th 1860

Dear Sir,

I return you the papers, duly signed; and I beg to return you my best thanks for the 100£, and also to Messrs Harper for their additional 25£, (all safely received this morning), as payment for the English copyright of 'Right at Last &c' – and also as payment for the right of republication in America.

I think this is a proper acknowledgement; if not perhaps you will be so kind as to let me know?

Would you be so kind as to send copies 'from the author' to

E. S. Fulcher Esq. Sudbury, Suffolk
J. Russel Esq, Office of the 'Scotsman' Edinburgh
Miss M. Gaskell, care of Miss Darwin[1] 19 York Terrace, Regent's Park, London
Mrs Lyall, The Close, Winchester.

and if I might have two copies for myself I should be much obliged. I don't think the reviews need be troubled, as they never notice reprints. Can you tell me how to get a parcel (containing 2 sermons[2] of Dr Stanley's of Oxford, & a small drawing,) to America. I tried the sermons by the post, and found[altered word] that my[?] price 1s. here, would be charged six shillings for conveyance to America! Believe me to remain

Yours very truly
E C Gaskell –

With stamp endorsed April 25 /60.

Trinity College, Cambridge

1 Meta was soon to go on a sketching tour in Switzerland with 'an oldish Miss Darwin', one of Charles Darwin's three sisters, in 'quiet respectable luxury'

(*Letters,* pp. 630–33). It also turned out to be 'a 4 month's-long fight for Miss Darwin', who could not bear John Ruskin or his writings (ME to C. E. Norton*, 46 Plymouth Grove, 20 September 1860, Harvard bMS Am1088 2601). Either Susan (1803–66) or Emily (1810–66) Darwin is possible.

2 A. P. Stanley (1815–81), Dean of Westminster 1864–81, son of Bishop Edward and Mrs Catherine Stanley. ECG had heard one of his controversial sermons preached in the University Church two months before ('it was curious to see how many [of the Dons] shut their eyes, as if going to sleep'). See *Letters,* pp. 608–10.

?FREDERIC CHAPMAN[1]

46 Plymouth Grove
Manchester
April 27th [?1860]

Dear Sir,

I should be very much obliged to you for a speedy answer to this letter; my last (from Winchester, at the end of February) has remained unanswered till now, although there were several questions in it to which I should have been glad to have received early replies.

Would you be so kind as to ascertain, and let me know as soon as you conveniently can, how my account with Messrs Chapman with regard to the 'Moorland Cottage,' published in 1850, stands. Mr Edward Chapman gave me £50 for { } \ 1,000 I *think* – / copies, after which I was to have a share in the profits of all copies sold above that number. On this account he sent me 20£ in 1853 (I believe,) and then said something about this payment (of 20£) being made *before* the requisite number of *surplus* (above the \ ? / *1*,000 for which he had paid 50£ at first) were disposed of. That is the last I have heard of it; but the copyright remains with me, and if the first edition is all disposed of I am anxious to include it with some other tales, \ in a vol / for which Messrs S. Lowe &c wish to make me an offer.

I conclude from your silence that you no longer desire to republish 'Cranford', &c. – But will you be so kind as to give me an explicit answer.[2] I remain dear Sir

Yours very truly
E. C. Gaskell

Fales Library, New York University
Letter 486, from MS copy, redated 1860 from 1861.

1 See p. 206 n. 1 above.

2 ECG had forgotten that until her husband gave three months' notice to terminate a formal agreement dated 8 May 1855, Chapman still retained the right to publish *Cranford* in a cheap edition. In 1863 her husband, 'in clearing [sic] out his desk', found the signed agreement. 'What can I do?', she cried to George Smith,'*please* let me pay for the horrid old stereotypes, or what ever they are' (*Letters,* p. 721). See Collin, *BJRUL* 69 (1986), pp. 68–9, 74–5.

SAMPSON LOW[1]

42 Plymouth Grove
April 30th / 60.

My dear Sir,

Thank you much for the two copies of 'Right at last' which you have forwarded to me; also for sending the presentation copies. I am extremely obliged to you for sending me the information about the American postage.

Believe me to remain

Yours very truly
E C Gaskell.

University of California, Los Angeles

1 Letter as extra-illustration in a copy of J. Forster's* *Life of Charles Dickens* (1872–74), vol. 3 (Univ. of California, LA, collection #170/404).

MARY HOLLAND

[c. late May 1860]

My dear Mary,

Cooks are dearer to me than cousins,
Of cousins I'll get many an one
Of cooks perhaps ne'er anither.

and a cook is coming to see me on Friday afternoon.

I am sorry: for I like Frank, & I love Sybil. Captain Jackson[1] turned up yesterday, and staid till today.

Your affect. cousin
E C Gaskell

Princeton University Library

1 Pilkington Jackson (b. c. 1836), a young army officer, approached ECG for advice about stocking a reading room for his men stationed in Gibraltar. Florence Nightingale* assisted him, too, with a Soldiers' Home (FN to ECG, 28 September 1860: Waller, p. 23). See *Letters,* pp. 615, 640, 911.

MARY GREEN*

43 Eaton Place.[1]
Thursday [?14 June 1860]

My dear Mary,

Philip only left about an hour ago, after sitting here nearly two hours, & carrying off with him a letter to Mr[?] Smith (& Elder) who promises me 'a very strong letter of recommendation to the first solicitor's house in Bombay' & any others he may find Mr Green desires when he sees him. I do not think Philip is out of spirits. I think on the contrary he must have been long depressed by his small success, & the tedious waiting, and that the prospect of going where he really seems to have a good prospect of immediate employment. He gave me all his reasons for thinking that he had this prospect; and I must say it appeared to me that he had sufficient grounds for the step he was going to take. As he has probably told them all to you there is no use recapitulating them. The only quarter from which I could see a cloud, was from the fact of his being a Roman Catholic, which, as I know the *religious* people in India, are all Evangelical or Low Church, seemed to me unpromising, as *far as it went*. But then again he had evidently encouragement from several people, high up in legal position in Bombay, who were well qualified to judge of his probabilities of success.

He thinks he *may* return, if all is successful – as successful as he hopes, – for a *visit* in three years – that if he is *very* successful he may come home for good with a sufficient fortune to live upon, in *twelve* years time. He reckons his *necessary* expenses at 300£ a year, (*more* than in England,) but his chances of speedy success as *far* greater. At the *very* worst he says he can return & take up his *English* barrister's life, *where he leaves it now*. He speaks cheerfully and looks well. I do not think he has an idea (when had children ever!) of how much you suffer at the prospect of separation, – he spoke of 'telegrams' as 'diminishing the distance[']; – which showed me how little he understood what the pain of absence *really* is, – I remember Meta did the same. – But then it is as well, if one can feel but *really* sure that the step our children are going to take is for their true happiness. For Philips success in his profession I should say his chances are as 100 to 1, against what they would be if he remained in England. I saw Mr James yesterday, & had a long talk with him about Philip He said Philip was doing 'nothing in his profession here', – but might do much at Bombay, where he believed there was a good opening &c.

I asked Philip when he thought he should sail – he said on the 27th *or*, if he could persuade Dunbar (whom he is going to accompany,) on July 12th. But he does not wish Dunbar to get the start. He is going to write to him tonight to ask if he will delay his voyage till the 12th. I am telling you as much as ever I can, because I feel as if it was the only little thing I can do for you.

Do not ever doubt us, dear friends – don't you, dearest Ellen, ever doubt Marianne. We can not help, – it is as much God's ordering as any other event of our lives, – having a very large circle of acquaintance and many occupations which come upon us unexpectedly, & prevent our keeping our time & thoughts so free, as others, who do not know so many. But I am quite sure no one that I know of ever needed our sympathy, but what we gave it with true hearts. Dear Ellen Marianne loves you dearly, & has many a time said this week 'Oh! I cannot get this sorrow of the Greens out of my head', – indeed we have thought of it more than of anything else. So often one means to write, or to say things, & the time & opportunity slip by; – but believe this, we do love you dearly, as dear true friends of long ago; – and trust us always, please –

I must go – Ever your most affectionate E C Gaskell

Marianne goes to the Price's at Brighton for a little sea-air on Saturday, for a week, – I go to B. C. Brodie's Cowley House Oxford – until I see how she is, & what she can bear in the way of fatigue.[2]

Dr R. Jamison

1 Home of (Sir) John Hawkshaw (1811–91). See *Letters,* pp. 619 n. 2, 622.

2 Marianne's sudden illness, theatening small pox, was announced on 6 June 1860. See *Letters,* pp. 622, 631.

MARY GREEN*

Müller's Hotel
anlagen
viâ Calais. Heidelberg, Baden
Sunday, July 8th [1860]

My dear Mary,

We have been thinking a great deal of you all; and wondering much all about what you are doing. It must be a sad week, we know, with all of you, if the plans hold which Philip had when we left of sailing on the 12th. We shall be so glad to hear from you, or one of you, some account of all of your goings on, and how you all are.

The one thing I write about now, (in a hurry to catch the post) is this. We are so comfortable here, & the place is so lovely that we think it would be very nice indeed if two of your girls could join us here.[1] The expense of living here, – (they would have a double-bed[?] bedded room to themselves, & share our large airy sitting-room, with piano &c would be 3 {?} gulden (or florins) a day each. A florin is 1s – 8d$^{1/}$2; so it comes to rather more than 5s a day. For this they would have breakfast in our sitting-room, (tea, \ or / coffee, eggs bread & butter-) dinner at the table d'hote), and[?] tea with cold meat or fruit{,} in our room. The place is thoroughly clean comfortable & airy.

We shall stay here, certainly, a fortnight after Wednesday the 18th, by which day we think they could join us. Leaving London (as Ellinor Bonham-Carter[2] who is here has just done –) by the Antwerp Steamer Baron Osy on Sunday at 12 \ Monday / (1£ – 8s) fare. – It arrives at Antwerp before 8 the next (Monday) morning; & the train leaves for Cologne at 9: – there is just time for breakfast, {either} if you have not taken it on board, either at an inn (*Hotel du Parc* we always go to – the landlady is a very nice English *lady* –) or at the Railway Station. The fares by the Cologne train to C. are \ about / 30fr. exp (1st class) {18 francs 40 cent 2nd class)\ which that train is – *Change* \ *carriages* / *at Malines* / and it reaches Cologne at 4 PM.

The Hotel Disch is a very good one, strongly recommended by Marianne. (They cd go & see the Cathedral that aft: table d'hote[*sic*] is at *one*, so they would be too late for that, – order *one* [double underline] portion of meat \ to tea / (one portion is enough for two always in Germany). Next morning ({ ? } there is always an omnibus meets every train at the Station, & sets you down at any hotel you like, – name your hotel at once, as there may be an omnibus especially belonging to that hotel. Next morning leave Cologne at *nine* o'clock by *train* (along banks of the Rhine.) Reach Mayence at 10 mi. past *2*. {Take the} The train leaves Mayence *for* Ludwigshaven at *2 – 50*; (Ludwigshaven is just on the opposite side of the Rhine to *Mannheim*.) Cross the Rhine by the bridge to Mannheim Station; the train leaves for Heidelberg at 7; and gets in to Heidelberg at *7 – 36*, where we would meet her. Fare from Cologne [Sentence breaks off at this point.]

Leave London on Sunday 15th
Arrive at Antwerp on Monday at 8 a m.
Leave for Cologne at 9 a m. arrive there at 4 p m
Leave Cologne \ Tuesday / at *9.a.m*, via Mayence, Ludwigshaven, Mannheim, & reach Heidelberg at 7 – 30; Fare from Cologne *not more* than 1£ – 10s; less as far as we can make out in a hasty calculation of German money. *English* speaking carries you the whole way except at the railway station.

French & English gold (25 francs a sovereign) for travelling – Change to *German* money at Mayence; but *not* at the Railway Station – 11 florins 36 Kreutzers a sovereign, 9 florins odd Kreutzers for a napoleon.

Do please let them come! I have no time for more. You will find my letter *correct*, though incoherent.

Yours ever affect E C Gaskell

Dr R. Jamison

1 This invitation was not taken up. ECG's third visit to Heidelberg, with three daughters and Hearn, was complicated by Marianne going to Kreuznach for medical treatment. See *Letters*, pp. 630–32; WG to ECG, 25 July 1860 (*GSN* 14, 1992, p. 9).

2 Elinor (1837–1923), daughter of John Bonham Carter (1788–1838) and Joanna, née Smith; and sister of Hilary Bonham Carter (1821–65). Elinor also went to Kreuznach: 'their little ménage with Hearn for duenna' (*Letters*, p. 632). They were cousins of Florence Nightingale*.

?FREDERIC CHAPMAN

42 Plymouth Grove
Manchester –
Tuesday, August 21st 1860.

Dear Sir,

As far as I understand your proposal, made on Messrs Smith's behalf, I shall be very glad to accede to it.

I understand from you that Messrs Smith wish to take off your hands the remainder of the 2s edition of Cranford & Lizzie Leigh,[1] for which they would at once pay me £44–13s–9d for Royalty.

They also wish me to promise them the right of reprinting fresh editions of these works, when the stock in hand, as named above, is disposed of: and for this \ right /, when the editions were required, they would make me an offer for the power[altered word] of republication.

If I have rightly stated these requests, I give my consent to both. But I do not understand your last paragraph \ taken in connexion with the foregoing / in which you say 'we publish a very successful five shillings series, the one that North & South is in, and we are of opinion that, after a while Cranford & Lizzie Leigh would come in this series[altered word] to advantage. We should like therefore (if you think well of this,) to have your consent; in this case the royalty would have to be increased in proportion from the 2s series to the 5s series.' I shall be glad to have this more fully explained. I remain dear Sir,

Yours truly
E C Gaskell

New York Public Library, Carl and Lily Pforzheimer Collection of Shelley & His Circle
Printed by D. Collin, op. cit., pp. 73–74.

1 Both were published in the two-shilling series of Chapman and Hall's Select Library of Fiction in 1855. *North and South* was published by Chapman and Hall in a 'Cheap edition', costing 5s, on 30 June 1859 (Smith, p. 100).

FREDERIC CHAPMAN

42 Plymouth Grove
Augt 22. [1860]

Dear Sir,

I am glad to recognize an individual in your signature, instead of a mere firm, which is the dullest of all possible signatures to my mind. Only – having been out of England for 3 months – a little more literary gossip would have been most acceptable, especially as my daughter heard from Major Chippendale that you are *the* best authority for such gossip in London. Perhaps however it will come with the cheque; and then it will be a question which is most acceptable. Can you send me an autograph of Anthony Trollope's into the bargain? (I am an autograph collector, as I wish all my friends to know.) Where are Mr Lewes & Miss Evans now? My daughter, travelling between Basle & Berne three weeks ago – (about,) *fancied* they were in the railway carriage with her.[1] The gentleman had fine eyes, a clever, disagreeable, bearded face. The lady looking older, worn, and travel-tired & evidently *her* wishes were law to the gentleman.

How excellent & good & clever 'Framley Parsonage'[2] is, – I *never* read anything in the way of fiction so true & deep!

Please to send me his autograph.

Yours very truly
E C Gaskell.

Are you a brother of Mr Edward Chapman's; and if so, where are the Sewells, once of Santander. *Any* information about them & theirs will be most welcome.

Princeton University Library

1 Meta was in Switzerland from 6 May to 10 August; George Eliot and G. H. Lewes passed though in June 1860 on their return from Italy and stayed in Berne. It is possible that Meta saw them, but not 'three weeks ago'.
2 Serialised in the *Cornhill Magazine*, January 1860–April 1861.

VERLAG B. TAUCHNITZ

42 Plymouth Grove,
Manchester.
October 4th, 1860.

Though I put the above address, I am writing from a little village in Yorkshire ... *Lois the Witch* and the *Crooked Branch* were both published subsequently in *All the Year Round* ...

I have a little daughter of eighteen years of age[1] who is so very German, that she declares 'she was born in England by *mistake*' ...

Text from [Curt Otto], *Der Verlag Tauchnitz*

1 i. e., Florence, born 1842.

SAMPSON LOW

46 Plymouth Grove
October 14th [?1860]

Dear Sir,

You would oblige me very much if you would send a copy of that volume of 'Round the Sofa', *or* 'Right at Last' which contains the

'*Manches[ter] Marriage*' to '*Mrs Wm Story, care of Messrs Chapman & Hall* 193 Piccadilly.[']

I have to thank you much for constantly sending me the 'Publisher's[altered word] Circular'[1] in which I always find much to interest me. I remain, dear Sir,

Yours very truly
E. C. Gaskell

Haverford College, Pennsylvania

1 A trade journal listing current publications, founded by Sampson Low in 1837.

ANON

46 Plymouth Grove
Novr 1st 1860

Dear Sir,

In turning over my 'docketed' letters today, I have met with yours, inquiring after Mr Brontë, and, I am ashamed to say, I have forgotten whether I ever answered it or not. Deeming it the less of two evils to send you a second answer: I will {ans} reply to the questions contained in your note, feeling specially disposed and qualified to do so, from having gone over \ to Haworth / only last Saturday, and spent some time with Mr Brontë.[1] He is now confined entirely to bed; and very weak – but retains all his *mental* powers completely. He is touchingly softened in his old age; and most gentle and tender – tho' he has lost none of his vigour & energy of thought & speech.

I cannot help thinking that he wd be much pleased if you wrote to him; expressing your interest in his daughter, & *in himself* – tho', I think that you must hardly expect an answer, & consider your note as good seed sown, merely in as much as it wd serve to lighten some of the long, lonely days he now spends (as I said) entirely in bed.

He has a marvellous appetite for political news; & any crumbs of information with regard to the local feelings abt politics near Newcastle wd be a real treat to him I am sure; or if you know any of the English volunteers for Garibaldi,[2] & cd send him extracts from their letters, he – & may I say I also? – sd feel grateful.

Yours truly
E. C. Gaskell.

Columbia University Library

1 Visit on Thursday [not Saturday], 25 October? Meta, then with ECG in Gargrave, near Skipton, Yorkshire, describes this visit (ME to Ellen Nussey, 25 October 1860, MS Berg, NYPL). See also Barker, p. 818.

2 In May 1860 Garibaldi landed in Sicily with 1000 volunteers and overthrew the Bourbon government. A Garibaldi Fund Committee was formed in

London with about 1000 supporters, many of whom arrived in Italy in October, though by this time his campaign to unite Italy under King Victor Emmanuel was virtually over.

Letter 600 to MA (undated) from Plymouth Grove now dated [?c. November ? 1860]

VERLAG B. TAUCHNITZ

46 Plymouth Grove,
Manchester.
December 11th, 1860.

In reply to your enquiry as to the terms I should wish to obtain for its republication [*Lois the Witch*] in your Series, I can only say I feel quite confident, from former experience, that what you think fit to offer me for the power of republication, will be both just and liberal, and that therefore I will gladly leave the decision on this point to you ... I am afraid that all this negotiation about the translation[1] of an unwritten book is rather in the spirit of an English proverb, which speaks of 'reckoning one's chickens before they are hatched.' But I do mean to set to with vigour, and finish my book this winter.

Text from [Curt Otto], *Der Verlag Tauchnitz*

1 Footnote to 'translation' reads 'Verhandlungen über die deutsche Übersetzung mit einem andern Verleger.' *Lois the Witch, and Other Tales* was published by Tauchnitz in 1861, but translated for publication by another publisher. Generosity in the matter of fees sprang from the firm's policy of paying for all works reprinted in its series.

EDWARD E. HALE

46 Plymouth Grove
Manchester –
Friday, December 14th 1860

My dear Mr Hale,

You are not, by no means, to suppose yourself forgotten; tho' we have been so lazy, or so busy all this year. And now Xmas is coming round again, and we do so wish you were likely to turn up again, 'all promiscuous' as our English servants say, & share our turkey, and have a merry round game at cards, and altogether make us young and happy again. Please, *are* you coming. If not, will you accept my very best wishes for a happy Christmas, and a merry New Year, and give the same from me to 'Emily' and the bairns, King Arthur not forgotten. Oh dear! how long it is, and yet how short it is since last Christmas. I may give you a short chronicle of our year's events, but it won't set it before you;

it will be more like headings to chapters, which are hardly dry bones, – only bits of bones, that don't even fall into shape. However suppose we try, as even that kind of account of our year's proceedings as[*sic*] better than none. You left us – Meta in Edinburgh, – Mr Gaskell just going to have a new colleague, a Mr Drummond,[1] aged 25, at whose ordination you were to have assisted, only you didn't.

Well! Mr Drummond came; a small slight young man, with a lovely complexion, beautiful, steady-looking eyes, and an expression of goodness such as I have seldom seen equalled. He stayed with us till he could meet with lodgings; he was shy & reserved in society, but when he got into the pulpit he became bold and outspoken from the very fervour of his convictions; and yet he is so tender as well as so earnest in his religious feelings. I think him very sweet and good in private life, but rather feel as if I were his mother, & might advise and order him about; but in the pulpit I feel like a child learning from a disciple. So much for our Mr Drummond. Then Marianne went to Worcester, to a dance at the house of some cousins, at the end of January; and Meta came back from Scotland, and Mr Gaskell, she & I set off for Oxford in the first week of February, picking up Marianne on the way. The water was out in the meadows for miles round Oxford, making the place look very beautiful as we came near it, in the red light of a winter setting sun, all the buildings reflected in the smooth clear waters. But I dare say it was very unhealthy. Mr Gaskell and I went to the Brodies, just beyond Magdalen Bridge. Marianne & Meta to the Smiths (he a 'coach' at Balliol.) That very first night we went off all to dine at Arthur Stanley's, and that was the beginning of a week of charming Oxford dissipation – dinner at Queens, Ch. Ch. Balliol &c &c, & breakfasts & lunches everywhere. I like the society in Paris *very* best of all; & then Oxford, and then comes London. At the end of our ten days Mr Gaskell had to come back to Manchester & we went on to Eton for two days.

Perhaps we should have taken Eton first, for it is not unfit to go with Oxford; but should be a preparation for it, rather than a supplement to it. We saw nobody there, as we were staying in the house of a widower, who was not visiting. Then we again separated [-] Marianne going to stay with some friends near London, Meta & I to Winchester,[2] where I fell ill of bronchitis, and had to burrow into bed within two hours of my arriving at the house we were going to stay at. I was there for several weeks, lying in bed, and looking out into the beautiful Cathedral Close, with the branches of its great trees sweeping slowly across my windows as the wind swayed them, and the sound of the chanted services in the Cathedral came to me faintly, morning & evening. My hostess was the widow of the Dean of Canterbury, who preceded Alford, and I felt it very curious, how I became not more clerical, but canonical in my way of thinking, before I left the Close. I found myself inclined to resent any disturbance of the vested interest of the dignified clergy[3] by whom I was surrounded, & to consider enquiry as to the distribution of the Church funds, as sacrilegious impertinence. Then I worked my way home under Meta's care & nursing, by slow weary degrees; and was shut up in the house for a long time after my return.

The next family event was Meta's being invited to go for a tour in S. France & N. Italy by a distant relation, a Miss Darwin, sister of Mr Charles Darwin ('origin of Species.') So she set off on the 3rd of May, and two or three days later Marianne followed her {to} \ as far as / London; and as Florence was at a boarding-school, & Julia at her day school and Mr Gaskell *very* busy, I had plenty of time in those long days to myself: & I went on famously, writing away at my book;[4] till – at the beginning of June, I had a letter, one morning after Mr Gaskell had gone into town, saying that Marianne had been taken ill of small pox at the friend's house with whom she was staying in London, & that the family had left the house. Of course I could only pack up my things & be off directly. I found her that evening ill, but it was not the genuine small pox, only a spurious kind, very prevalent in London, just then. However I staid in the house for 10 days, nursing her, for she was very poorly, & not going out, for fear of giving infection. Then she was ordered to Brighton for a week, and I went back to our friends at Oxford, in order to be near at hand if she was not so well. (She was staying at Brighton with friends, who could not take me in – the Bonamy Prices, Dr Arnold's friend & correspondent.) So I came in for Commemoration in Oxford, which is a very gay and pretty sight. Then Marianne was advised to go to the German Baths; so Mr Gaskell brought Florence & Julia up to London, for by this time their holidays had begun,) and Marianne, Florence[,] Julia, I, and the girl's nurse, Hearn, (who has lived with us nearly 19 years) set off via Ostend Brussels, Cologne Rhine to Heidelberg, where I meant to consult a very famous German doctor about Marianne. He ordered her to Kreuznach, near Bingen on the Rhine; so I took her there, & found accomodation[sic] most scarce; so, leaving Hearn with her, & a young friend of hers in very comfortable lodgings, I went back to my two youngest in Heidelberg, where we stayed the rest of their holidays, enjoying ourselves exceedingly.

We have many friends there; & we used to take long walks on the summer afternoons into the lovely country all round the equally lovely town; and drink coffee in some of the pretty primitive 'gast-hausen' – and then walk home, or be rowed home on the Neckar in the summer evening twilight. But holidays will come to an end; and at the end of July I summoned Marianne to meet me at Bingen, that I might see if she was profiting by her *cure* – before we returned home. She was looking and feeling so much better that I had no scruple in leaving her under Hearn's care. She had to get up at 6; go out to walk & drink 10 oz of whey, – indoors to breakfast at 8 on bread and milk & eggs. Then a bath – a lying down, another walk, dinner, without wine or potatoes or fruit or spice or butter – another lying down another walk, tea (a repetition of breakfast, – tea & coffee being forbidden,) & to bed at ½ past 8. To be sure she did nothing but attend to her health but it is astonishing how much good it did her. When she came home about the middle of September she looked better than she had done for years. Meta gave us – (*first* – returning German party) the meeting at home. We had hoped it would have been at Heidelberg; but that did not suit Miss Darwin's plans. Mr Gaskell (who dislikes the Continent very much) had been staying with some friends in Scotland, during the time of our absence.

Since then we have been at home and very busy in one way or another; friends stopping in the house principally. And all this time I have never had the grace to thank you for all the useful information you gave me about the lodging houses.[5] I was & am so much obliged to you for it; it was immediately made available for the assistance of the 5 young barrister friends of mine in London, who, as I think I told you, are hard at work altering some of the dwellings in St Giles; they are anxious to build a model lodging house that shd *pay* 4 per cent, but as yet they have not been able to meet with any builder & architect willing to erect a new building on their terms; so they are thinking of getting and remodelling an old house. Has this plan been tried in America? I have not got my sewing machine yet – the outlay at first daunts me; besides which we have so many poor people in Manchester, always begging for the employment of plain work, that I wonder sometimes if it would be *individually* right to take a machine instead. Today is the last day on which I can send off a letter to arrive in America by Xmas day – so I must close. The girls mean to write to you soon. Mine & Mr Gaskell's kind love

Your affectionate friend
E C Gaskell

Smith College, Massachusetts

1 James Drummond (1835–1918) was a gifted theologian, who served at Cross Street Chapel until 1869, when he went to Manchester New College (Principal 1885–1906). Hale had spent Christmas 1859 with the Gaskells (*Letters,* p. 607).

2 With Catherine Lyall (née Brandreth, d. 1863), widow of Dean W. R. Lyall. See *Letters,* pp. 602–3 (both Meta and ECG '*scarified* raw by mustard plaisters').

3 Since 1854 dissenters had been admitted to Oxford and allowed to take bachelors' degrees, but College Fellows were required to subscribe to the 39 articles of the Church of England. Dissenters still had to pay church rates, and privileges accruing from the disposition of charitable bequests remained contentious.

4 Possibly 'The Specksioneer' [harpooner], a December 1859 title for *Sylvia's Lovers;* by August 1861 it was 'Philip's Idol' (*Letters,* p. 667). Ward (Knutsford Edn VI, pp. xiv-xv) claims ECG's authority for two other rejected titles: 'Too Late' and 'Monkshaven'.

5 Cf. ECG to C. E. Norton*, 5 April [1860], describing '5 young men (all Oxford or Cambridge)', including Thurstan Holland, planning to buy land in Holborn for a lodging house for 40 families. Norton gave her details of lodging houses in Boston and New York (*CEN Letters,* pp. 46–7, 50–51).

HENRY A. BRIGHT[1]

[c. 28 December 1860]

My dear Mr Bright,

(A merry Xmas to you, & a very happy New Year.)

Mr Gaskell gone from home for Xmas holidays – does not come back till the end of next week – & I am 'not to forward any letters except on *indispensable* business['], that he may have the *complete* rest he needs so very much. He does not *wish to have [to be?] writing a letter to any one* – Under these circumstances shall I forward yours?

Yours most truly
E C Gaskell

He will be overwhelmed with business when he comes back – on Saturday 5th – So *please,* if you can help it don't give him any more just now – you can have no idea how over-worked he is.

Address Henry A. Bright Esq / Sand Heys / West Derby near Liverpool.
Postmarks MANCHESTER 28 Dec 60; LIVERPOOL 29 Dec 60.

Northumberland Record Office (Brooks Collection)
Society of Antiquaries of Newcastle upon Tyne; transcribed by Professor Philip Yarrow and Frank Whitehead.

1 Henry Arthur Bright*, probably also the recipient of Letter 593, undated (*Letters*, p. 784).

ANON

46 Plymouth Grove
January 11th 1861

Sir,

I am sorry that I have not got any remnant of Miss Brontë's writing left. I am constantly applied to for some but have given all away long ago. I remain, Sir,

Yours &c
E. C Gaskell

Princeton University Library (AM 19797; dictated?)
Printed by J. A. V. Chapple and Margaret Smith, 'Charlotte Brontë and Elizabeth Gaskell in Society', *BST* 21 (1995), p. 161.

Letter 429a to MA from [?near London] redated [25 March 1861]

DANTE GABRIEL ROSSETTI

1 Cumberland Place[1]
Regents Park NW
[March 1861]

Dear Mr Rossetti,

Here is M. de Circourt's address. I am sure he will be so very much pleased by your sending him a copy of your work[2] that I am very anxious you should fulfil your kind intention of doing so.
Winter address
M. le Comte de Circourt 11, Rue des Saussaies Paris.
Summer address
aux Bruyères par Bougiral Seine et Oise.

I hope Mrs Rossetti did not suffer from her long day of fatigue? My daughter has had the very unpleasant operation of having her tonsils cut out,[3] and is a prisoner in the house. Her weariness is charmingly beguiled by studying your sketch of the triptych for Llandaff Castle, sent us by Mr Lushington[.] Thank you afresh for this pleasure.

Yours very truly
E. C. Gaskell

University of Texas at Austin

1 The new home of Hensleigh and Frances Wedgwood. He had recently published *A Dictionary of English Etymology,* with an introduction 'On the Origin of Language'.
2 *The Early Italian Poets* (1861). Rossetti refers to this in a letter of 17 December 1861, and De Circourt in a letter of 27 August[sic] 1861. See esp. Sharps, p. 462 n. 34; ECG, 'French Life', Knutsford Edn, VII. 644–6; Waller, pp. 54–7.
3 See *Letters,* pp. 646, 919.

ANON

42 Plymouth Grove
Manchester
April 21st [?1861][1]

Dear Sir,

We once spent a day with the Dean of Salisbury,[2] & went to see the places in the neighbourhood, among which I particularly remember Bemerton as being the place which I cared for the most, for George Herbert's sake.[3] They told us there that the small old-fashioned church was that built in his day; and it then looked as if it were not calculated to hold the parishioners, if the limits of the parish were rightly pointed out to us.

I have very gladly made out as good a list as I can of those who may I think contribute to this good work; it is a little difficult to pick out *literature*-loving 'capitalists' in this district, where the present and the future claim more attention than the past with many of us. And then again many of those who are rich have a very strong feeling that they ought to spend what they appropriate to such works as that about which I am writing, in South Lancashire, and Manchester, where they make their money. So though I dare say you think I have a great range of choice it is not so in fact; and in one or two cases I have put down the names of the wives, as more likely from their knowledge of G. Herbert to feel reverence & gratitude to his memory. Some of the people whose names I send are I know from home just now, in Paris & in London. I think it possible I may remember some others, and if so I will send them to you. I am truly glad – (I have had so much help from his poems) that you have given me the opportunity of sending the accompanying order, which is made out in the name of yours very truly

Elizabeth Cleghorn Gaskell

April 25th Owing to my being obliged to go suddenly from home this letter has been delayed, as I forgot to leave orders about the Post Office Order.

Princeton University Library

1 See Sharps, p. 367 n. 77, for this visit.
2 Henry P. Hamilton (1794–1880), Dean of Salisbury from 1850.
3 George Herbert (1593–1633) was Vicar of Bermerton, Wiltshire. He was buried in the parish church (restoration completed 1866 by T. H. Wyatt).

EDWARD E. HALE

Monday April 22 [1861]

My dear Mr Hale,

Are not you getting tired of thanks & Gaskell letters – (this is the mother of the family, – and your original correspondent, writing on the final scrap allowed me.)[1] If you are not I am going to thank you very heartily for *my share of the* pleasure – for my 90 days – (it seems to me that Mr Gaskell has been intruding on my province, & thanking for it too – you can't think how we English always like to know what you Americans think of us & Europe; & the flavour of Hale-ism all through the 90 days was very agreeable as suggesting a remembrance of the original article. Since the others have written theirs we have seen in the newspapers the sad news that you Northeners, are likely to be at war when this reaches you.[2] I do hope it may not be true; & *why* should it? If the South secedes you would not wish to *compel* Southern & Slavery States to be united with you, would I[?]. I should think (to use a country phrase here) 'it was good riddance of bad rubbish'. But I am very sorry for you all any-how. And I wish I could understand American politics which are *the* most complicated things I know. If you were here, or I were there, I have no end of questions to ask you. We have not set up a sewing machine because we know so many poor people, who are always begging for needle-work as an employment. How does Mrs Hale's go on? I have not been very strong of late; I went up to London with Meta to have her tonsils cut out, as she had been suffering very much from sore-throat, – and somehow I got upset in my health, and have never quite come round. Otherwise I am going to finish my book,[3] 3 vols, very soon; though after seeing what Miss Evans (George Eliot) does I feel as if nothing of mine would be worth reading ever-more. And that takes the pith out of one. Then Meta says 'But Mama remember the burying the *one* talent,' – so I cheer up, & mean to get strong & do the best I *can*. All the world in London was agog about 'Essays and Reviews'.[4] 1st edition 1,000 copies. 2nd after some discussion as to whether there *should* be a 2nd 750. Bishops abused. 3rd edit 2, 000, 4th 3, 000 5th 3, 000, 6th 6th[alteration] (edition) of Essays & Reviews 4, 000, & now they are at the 8th edition. My love to Mrs Hale, & the children, not forgetting 'King Arthur.'

Your affectionate friend
E C Gaskell

Smith College, Massachusetts

1 ECG takes over a letter by Florence Gaskell, dated 19 April 1861, referring to a gift of poems of James Russell Lowell (1819–91). There are associated letters by William Gaskell [mentioning Hale's *Ninety Days' Worth of Europe,* Boston 1861], Marianne, Meta and Julia.
2 The first shots of the American Civil War were fired by southern troops on 12 April 1861. The northern response was delayed as other states seceded, but war was probably inevitable.
3 *Sylvia's Lovers*, published in early 1863. William Shaen* had heard 'a good bit of it in London and thought it would be her best' (Catherine Winkworth* to Agnes Paterson*, [May 1860], MS Mrs Susan Kearney).
4 A volume by broad church theologians, challenging biblical authority on historical and scientific grounds. It provoked violent reactions; some contributors were charged with heresy in the ecclesiastical courts.

HENRY J. S. SMITH[1]

46 Plymouth Grove
Manchester
April 27th [1861]

My dear Mr Smith,

Will you give us the great pleasure of receiving you at our house at the time of the British Association – (Sepr 4th) for we begin to fear that at any other time we shall not have attractions enough for you?

We hope to see the Brodies, possibly Mr Harcourt,[2] Mr and Mrs

Hensleigh Wedgwood – and then if you will come our house will be full. Do not be too grand a Savillian Professor for us poor unmathematical creatures.

With kindest regards from us all to you and Miss Smith, & Mr Gaskell's especial hopes that we may tempt you here at last –

Ever yours very truly –
E. C. Gaskell –

an answer requested – some time

Manchester Central Library

1 Henry J. S. Smith (1826–83), Savilian Professor of Geometry at Oxford from 1860. On 29 September 1861 he was to send ECG a copy of Francis Palgrave's recently published *Golden Treasury*, 'which I did *not* see lying on your drawingroom table' (Waller, p. 63).
2 See *Letters*, p. 667 and p. 242 n. 3 below.

ROBERT von MOHL[1]

Plymouth Grove
Manchester
May 5th [1861]

My dear Mr Mohl,

Will you allow me to introduce to you and Madame v. Mohl, Mr Mrs and Miss Walker of Oxford.[2] He is Professor of Natural Science in that University, and is obliged to recruit his health by a visit to Heidelberg of some months. He is already acquainted with two of the 'First Men', (Bunsen, & Kirschoff[*sic*] –)[3] and now I hope to make him acquainted with a third, and Professor Helmholz[4] will make a fourth. Are there any more 'First Men' in Heidelberg; if so, will you be so very kind as to make Professor Walker known to them; as I am sure from the specimens I have seen, that acquaintance with 'First Men' will add considerably to his pleasure in his residence at Heidelberg. I should formally introduce Mrs and Miss Walker to my dear Anna; but that I do not know if I am to address her as Fraulein v. Mohl or Frau Professorinn[*sic*] &c &c Helmholz. So will you kindly do it for me if she is still under your roof; and, if not, I must trouble Professor Helmholz.

Please give our kind love to Madame v. Mohl, and ever believe me, dear Mr Mohl, with the warmest recollections of the happy time we have spent at your house.

Yours most truly
E. C. Gaskell.

Tubingen University Library

1 Robert Von Mohl (1799–1875), jurist and politician, brother of Julius. He wore 'a swallow tail coat & primrose coloured gloves' when ECG met him

and his daughters Anna and Ida in 1858 (*Letters*, pp. 517, 893).

2 Robert Walker, FRS (1801–65), Professor of Experimental Philosophy at Oxford 1839–65; author of works on mechanics and of *The Physical Constitution of the Sun* (1860).

3 Robert Wilhelm Bunsen (1811–99) was Professor of Experimental Chemistry from 1852; his technician Peter Desdega seems to have designed the Bunsen burner. Gustav Robert Kirchhoff (1824–87), Ordinary Professor of Physics from 1854, founded the science of spectroscopy in collaboration with Bunsen.

4 R. von Mohl's daughter Anna (1834–99) married in 1861 one of the greatest all-round scientists of the century, Hermann L. F. von Helmholz (1821–94), Professor of Physiology from 1858. ECG had met him in London in 1859 (*Letters*, p. 557).

MRS MARY ROBBERDS*

Monday [?June ?1861][1]

My dear Mrs Robberds,

I was hurrying over my work to go this afternoon to join Meta at Mary Holland's, when you were so good as to call; I *was* so sorry not to see you, if only for a few minutes, when I heard who it was, who had been so good as to call[.] I did hope to have got time to go and see you before starting; but it is now within half an hour of railway time. I opened your note to Mr Gaskell, (who went last night with Mr Charles Beard[2] to London for a fortnight,) and thank you for it, and it's enclosure, very much on his behalf. He shall have both as soon as he comes back.

Please thank Mr Herford too for his pamphlet on the Education of Pauper Children.[3] It seems to me both very interesting & very well reasoned. I have often heard in Scotland of the strong attachment between decent families & the sort of *foster child* brought up {am} in the midst of the family; and every approximation to God's ordinance of a '*family*' is surely to be desired. But I must stop

Yours affectionately
E. C. Gaskell.

Annotation Letter from Mrs Gaskell to Grandmama about 1860

Harris Manchester College, Oxford
Printed by Anna Unsworth, 'A New Gaskell Letter', *N & Q* 37 (1990), p. 37.

1 For date, see *Letters*, p. 653.

2 A son of J. R. Beard, Charles Beard (1827–88), minister of Hyde Chapel, Gee Cross, east of Manchester, from 1850, and a close friend of WG.

3 Perhaps Charles Herford (1817–1901), who married Mary Jane Robberds in 1852 (*Letters*, p. 191). He was a wine merchant and an important Unitarian layman.

MRS HALL[1]

Plymouth Grove
Manchester
July [?]19th [?1861]

My dear Mrs Hall,

I wonder whether I am already too deeply in your debt for me further to tax your kindness; or whether you will allow me to introduce to you Mr Cosmo Innes,[2] a friend of mind, who with his wife and daughters are proposing to stop sometime at Heidelberg this autumn. I have so very often lately sent acquaintances of mine with letters of introduction to you, that I feel almost ashamed of adding another to the list; but in this case I have this 'sop' for my conscience – that I am sure it will be a real pleasure to you to make Mr Innes' acquaintance, and that you will have many interests in common. To him I am promising not a little, in giving him this note.

We were quite charmed to see your friend M. \ Auguste / de Bonstettin[?] again, as I dare say he would tell you \ we had done /. He has developed into one of the finest and most attractive characters possible, as far as I could judge, and his faithful remembrance of our former intimacy touched me much.

Ever yours affecly
E. C. Gaskell.

My daughters join me in love to yourself, and Miss [?]S Hall.

Royal Institution of Cornwall (Enys Autograph Collection 596)

1 Presumably a Mrs Hall, 'oh! *so clever, & scandalously* bitter', a friend of 'dear sweet' Henriette Benecke (Mrs William, née Souchay). See *Letters*, p. 629; Marquardt, I. 15, II. 103.

2 Cosmo Innes (1798–1874), Professor of Constitutional Law and History at Edinburgh from 1846 to his death. He was also introduced to A. de Circourt in March, and arrived in Paris by 15 April 1862 (Waller, p. 67).

ANTONIO PANIZZI[1]

Plymouth Grove
Manchester
July 26 [?1861].

Mrs Gaskell presents her compliments to Mr Panizzi, and trusts that her remembrance of the pleasure she has had in meeting him at Mr W. M. James', & at Lady Coltman's will be considered by him as a sufficient excuse for the trouble she {will} is afraid she shall give him. Mrs Gaskell is very anxious to meet with a (*privately printed*) translation by Wiffen of the religious works of Valdez or Valdesso,[2] the Spanish courtier & friend of Charles Vth. Nicholas Farrer[*sic*] of Little Gidding published a translation of Valdesso's works,[3] – but it is defective, which Wiffen's translation is *not*, as Mrs Gaskell has been told.

If Mr Panizzi could inform Mrs Gaskell where she could meet with a copy of Wiffen's translation she would feel extremely obliged to hi<m.>

Richard Hobbs (Villiers) MSS.

1 Antonio Panizzi (1797–1879). Born in Italy, he came to England as a political exile in 1822 and was appointed Professor of Italian at the new University of London in 1828. At the British Museum from 1831, he became Principal Librarian in 1856, establishing the book catalogue and supervising the building of the famous domed Reading Room He was knighted in 1869.
2 The works of Juan de Valdes (c. 1500–41), whose writings evidenced elements of mysticism and personal piety, were translated by Benjamin Barron Wiffen (1794–1867) in 1861 and 1865.
3 Nicholas Ferrar's translation of Valdes' *Divine Considerations* was published in 1846.

HARRIET MARTINEAU*

46 Plymouth Grove
Manchester.
Septr 13 [1861]

My dear Miss Martineau,

I am afraid if I tell you the real reason of my not sooner replying to you, you will think me a bad manager; but the truth is we have had our house full for the British Association,[1] (some sleeping out of the house,) besides an invalid to attend to, that until today I have not had a minute of time to reply to any of my letters received during the past ten days. I was very much gratified by Mr Lucas's kind expression of his wish that I should write for 'Once a week';[2] but certainly at present it is quite out of my power; for I am already behind hand with engagements which will occupy me (more or less,) for a year to come; and beyond that space of time I do not like to look.

I have very lately declined a very liberal proposal of Mr Dickens to write a story of some length for Household Words.[3] Indeed I do not like writing a *long* story to be broken up into little bits in a serial publication; but even if I preferred this mode of publication I could not find time to prepare anything for the next twelvemonths.

We are all at home, and well; a little fagged and < ... >

Pierpont Morgan Library (Gordon Ray Collection).

1 The annual meeting of the British Association for the Advancement of Science was held in Manchester from 4 to 11 September 1861. The president on this occasion was a friend of ECG, Sir William Fairbairn, the distinguished engineer.

2 *Once a Week,* ed. Samuel Lucas, a periodical founded in 1859 by Bradbury and Evans, with a serial novel in every issue. They included Charles Reade's *A Good Fight* and George Meredith's *Evan Harrington.*

3 see p. 195 n. 3 above.

?MRS EDMUND GRUNDY[1]

46 Plymouth Grove.
Novr 8th [?1861]

My dear Mrs Grundy,

I enclose you a note of introduction to Mrs Winkworth;[2] hoping that it may be of service to you: but I think I ought to warn you in what very delicate health Mr Winkworth is, and Miss Kate Winkworth still \ is / a complete invalid.[3]

But I cannot help fancying that seeing you and Mr Grundy may form a bright spot in their present life which is sadly clouded with anxieties just at present, owing to the ill-health of so many of the family.

Hoping that St Leonards (or Hastings?) may do you good, and that you will come back to Manchester much stronger. I remain

Yrs most sincerely
E. C. Gaskell.

I do not know whether I have spelt Whiterock Place[4] rightly: it is pronounced white – rock.

Cheltenham Ladies' College (gift of Miss F. A. Brancker)

1 WG had recently dined with a Mrs Edmund Grundy of Manchester, a Garibaldi supporter. 'The evening ended with a few Christy Minstrel songs, in which Mrs G, two of the girls, and one of the sons took part' (WG to ECG, 25 July 1860; *GSN* 14, 1992, p. 10).

2 Mrs Henry Winkworth, née Eliza Leyburne.

3 Henry Winkworth had a stroke in February 1861; his daughters Catherine* and Susanna* were also ill in this year (*L & M*, II. 327–8, 337, 345, 354).

4 8 White Rock Place, Hastings (*L & M*, II. 356).

EDWARD E. HALE[1]

Friday December 13th [1861]

My dear Mr Hale,

We are so grateful to you! and to Mr Charles Hale, who must have been noticing all our little speeches of wonder, or wishing, in such a pretty delicate manner! Canvass back ducks![2] two barrels of apples; box of books, – all come and come safely and *gloated* upon in their separate ways. They arrived this morning (canvass-back ducks yesterday,) the apples in very good condition in spite of a frightening note from Mr

Stewart this morning; but the Gilliflower apples, are hardly spotted, & the Northern *Spy*?[3] (January) not at all. We have plunged into them at once, Mr Gaskell (after enjoying them at meals) carrying one off in his pocket to eat at odd hours, and Florence (trying them in all sorts of ways [-] with *cheese* at last,) suddenly exclaimed 'Shall we have to send them all back if we go to war with America?'[4] We are sadly afraid of your (American) answer, – it is privately believed by many people (though of course it does not get into the papers) that the Emperor of the French is having *great* influence in your cabinet, wanting to foment the differences between Gt Britain & the U. S. into a war, for *several* purposes of his own, – one to weaken us; another is that (I had it from a gentleman who is related to the present prime minister) {that} he (L N)[5] has been urging us to break the blockade, which we have refused to do; so, (as they are in desperate want of cotton in France, & of corn too,) he has influenced Mr Seward in his treatment of Gt Britain. Every one in England was up in arms when they heard that a *shell* had been fired across the bow of the Trent, even before they knew if it would be judged illegal, – but the feeling is cooling down; & it will be with deep sorrow that the nation will now go to war. No one here cares 2d if Mason & Slidell be hanged or not; indeed the personal feeling is rather against them. Meanwhile there are the most active preparations for war; all naval officers {sent} \ summoned / back from from[*sic*] furlough &c; but every one dreads the day when the President's answer will come. We were staying with Mr & Mrs Adams at Mr Monckton Milnes in Yorkshire[6] when the telegram announcing the stoppage of the Trent came, – & Mr Adams was much distressed & depressed tho' he said but very little. What a very nice person he is! Don't you like him very much?

Please thank Mr Fields for sending us the Atlantic;[7] we have always wished to see it. I seem as if I were not half telling you anything; but don't you know those kind of fine days when every body comes to call on every body? It is so today with us. But I only[altered word] wish you had been here to have heard the screams of joy & approbation with which each separate thing was received, & the constant 'Is not it sweet of Mr Hale' – ['] How good of them,' &c &c &c. We did so like having yr brother here; and I think he was a great deal better for it, – he was so good, and one-of-the-familyish, – he would tell you our great family event – Marianne going to Rome for the winter – she is there safe & sound, & enjoying herself much. You don't know what an incubus this dread of a war with you is! I think of it almost the last thing at night, & the first in the morning. I wish you were here to be talked to, for it seems to me as if I could not get a single sentence in writing finished without an interruption today. We liked Mr [?]Emersons[8] very much. He came to us (Meta Florence & me[-] Mr Gaskell was out) one eveng & we passed him on to the Wedgewoods[sic], connexions of ours, & descendants of 'Wedgewood ware', at the Potteries in Staffordshire, as he wished to see the manufacture; they asked him to their house to give him some advice about Paris, & were equally pleased with him. Tomorrow I shall write to your brother Charles, (care of T Wiggins) & thank him for all his thoughtful fairy god-father discovery of what would give us pleasure; only I want to send this off by tomorrow's packet.

Florence is plunged into the novel by Winthrop[9] – I have < > dead since the begi<nni>ng of this war, which seems but yesterday! and poor Mrs Putnam, Lowell's sister – we met her in Paris & in Rome taking such care of the education of this boy, – do you know her – if you do & meet her please tell her how often I have thought of her. {I wish} Poor Dr Oliver Holmes too – he has lost a son has he not.[10] We are telling that pretty story of your showman who wanted to put a frame on the engraving 'because it was to go to England' to every one, – for we hear just the opposite side from most people – 'The Americans have got up a complete hatred against the English &c &c.' But we don't hate each other, do we? My love to 'Emily' & the little ones, (not forgetting King Arthur, and to Susy, – in great haste yours ever affec[tionate] friend[sic]

E C Gaskell

Smith College, Massachusetts

1 With letters from ME and from WG, mentioning a visit of Hale's brother Charles. E. E. Hale had written to Sarah P. Hale from 'Mrs Gaskell's' on 'Haworth stationery', 11 November 1861 (see *Portrait,* illustration 15).
2 North American duck (*Fuligula valisneriana*).
3 Cf. WG's letter: 'apples from the tree of Nathan Spry and Gilliflower'.
4 In May 1861 news was received of the blockade of Southern ports by the North. On 13 May Britain declared its neutrality, but a British ship, the *Trent,* was boarded by northern troops and two Southern agents, James M. Mason and John Slidell, on their way to argue the Southern case in Europe, were taken off. William Henry Seward was Lincoln's Secretary of State and very anti-European.
5 Louis-Napoleon (1808–73), French Emperor 1852–70, whose coup d'état of 1 December 1851 had confirmed 'the Mohl's worst suspicions' (Lesser, p. 132).
6 Henry Brooks Adams (1838–1918), historian and novelist, met when EGC was staying at Fryston Hall for four days in November 1861 (*Letters,* p. 673).
7 James T. Fields edited the *Atlantic Monthly* 1861–71. It was then well known for articles on politics and contemporary affairs.
8 Ralph Waldo Emerson was not in England at the time.
9 Probably *Cecil Dreeme* (1861), a novel by Theodore Winthrop (1828–61), posthumously published.
10 Oliver Wendell Holmes (1809–94) was a New England writer and physician. His son and namesake was in fact wounded three times, but lived on till 1935.

FLORENCE NIGHTINGALE*

46, Plymouth Grove
Janry 22. 62.

My dear Miss Nightingale,

Thank you very much for letting me see your letter to Captain Jackson.[1] Thank you very much, and more than I can tell you, for every thing. I do believe that your appreciation and respect for what he has done will make him wise in many ways: more ways than you imagine.

I spoke yesterday to Mr Bazley[2] our MP about the transmigration of Country weavers.[3] He has had 12 girls, recommended by Mr Bracebridge – and they have been well received, and are doing well. He 'could have done' with as many as forty, – but the trade jealousy would, in case of his importing so large a number, have been aroused, and instead of a pitying welcome, they would have been treated as intruders. This, Mr Bazley says, is one great reason for the S. Lancashire manufacturers not importing any great number of either Spitalfields or Country weavers. And now comes in the shadow in the distance – the temporary evil to be apprehended from the probable cessation of the American supply of cotton; whh naturally makes the manufacturers chary of bringing too great a supply of labour to depend upon cotton alone.

I send you a note from a young man, – who, I fancy, is not overrich, – it may be destroyed as soon as read; but I think it will please you. Dear Miss Nightingale, God bless you.

Yours ever respectfully & truly
E C Gaskell

Brotherton Collection, Leeds University

1 See p. 209 n. 1 above.
2 Thomas Bazley (1797–1885), philanthropic mill-owner of Bolton and Manchester, MP for Manchester 1858–80. He proposed expansion of the Indian cotton trade to avoid exclusive dependence upon American imports.
3 Probably handloom weavers brought in for specialist work; handlooms remained in operation, if in severely declining numbers.

ALEXANDER MACMILLAN[1]

46, Plymouth Grove
Feb. 13th 1862.

My dear Sir,

I send you the preface for Colonel Vecchj's journal,[2] which I have just completed. I think that it had better be printed as speedily as possibly [sic], so as to prevent the possibility of any fresh alterations & additions.

Yrs very truly
E. C. Gaskell.

Princeton University Library (Dictated?)

1 Alexander Macmillan (1818–96), publisher in Covent Garden.
2 A translation of C. Augusto Vecchi, *Garibaldi at Caprera* (March 1862), a memoir of the Italian patriot. See *Letters,* p. 680, where she tells Henry Morley that 'the task of editing the book' was not voluntary, and WG to ECG, 25 July 1860, *GSJ* 14 (1992), p. 10.

JOHN WILSON

46 Plymouth Grove
Manchester
Febry 14 [?1862]

Mrs Gaskell presents her compliments to Mr John Wilson, & will be very glad to purchase the book {named} \ numbered / in his Catalogue of Janry 1, 1862 *232*, viz

La Maison des jeux Académiques[1] contenant un recueil general de tous les jeux divertissans pour se réjouir et passer le temps &c – 12mo, 3s–6d, Paris 1665.

University of Texas at Austin

1 A revision of a similar work of 1642 by Charles Sorel (c. 1599–1674), novelist, critic and historiographer. 'A unique and fascinating blend of imaginative literature and social analysis, which examines the creation of fiction(s) in the broader context of game' (Peter France, *The New Oxford Companion to Literature in French,* Oxford 1995, p. 773)

HENRY A. BRIGHT*

46 Plymouth Grove
Tuesday, Febry 25 [?1862]

My dear Mr Bright,

Do you know you have never sent me an introductory letter to Hawthorne[1] for Mr Edward Dicey[2] (Trin. Coll. Camb. nephew of Sir James Stephen[3] author of 'Rome', 'Cavour', commissioned by Macmillan to go out to America & represent the views of the Northern side &c &c &c.) However if you will do me a favour I will forgive you this omission; provided always you *do* send me the letter to Hawthorne.

The favour is this; my third daughter, Florence, has been for some time engaged to go to the Wellington Ball on Thursday with the Lewin Mozleys; Mrs Mozley being a Manchester acquaintance of ours. It is Florence's first visit anywhere by herself; and she is feeling both shy & strange, especially as we learnt last night that Mrs L Mozley will probably be unable to go to the Ball, & that Florence may have to go with Mr L. Mozley & his mother; both of whom are all but strangers to her. Now will you kindly look her out & speak a few friendly words to her? I don't think she very much minds about dancing; but she would be glad to have a known friend to speak to her. She will be in blue, with pink roses in her hair. She is very small & little & looks younger than she is, (19.)[4]

Yours ever very truly
E. C. Gaskell

Trinity College, Cambridge

1 Nathaniel Hawthorne was a great friend of Bright* and known to ECG's first cousin, Charles Holland. Hawthorne was in the USA from 1860 to his death in 1864.
2 Edward J. S. Dicey (1832–1911), author of *Six Months in the Federal States,* 1863, and an obituary of Hawthorne in *Macmillan's Magazine* for July 1864.
3 Sir James Stephen (1789–1859) was Professor of History at Cambridge 1849–59.
4 FE was born 7 October 1842, so not yet twenty.

ANON

Plymouth Grove
Feby 27[?1862]

Dear Sir,

I send you two letters to forward to Mr Dicey; perhaps more will follow. One, (as you will see,) is to Hawthorne from an intimate friend of his. The other is from me to Mr Ticknor;[1] but I do not remember his Christian names; would you please find them out and insert them on the address?

He is the Author of the History of Spanish Literature &c, and a very distinguished man, although rather formal and pedantic in manner.

Yours very truly
E C Gaskell

Princeton University Library

1 George Ticknor (1791–1871), Harvard Professor of French and Spanish, author of *History of Spanish Literature* (1849).

VERNON LUSHINGTON[1]

46 Plymouth Grove
Tuesday, April 1st [1862]

Dear Mr Lushington,

I think I shall parody part of your letter and say 'I am a mother, I know it'; and therefore I suppose I cannot help spoiling my children a little; which means to say I am sending your most kind letter on to Florence by tonight's post – (it only came just now,–6[?] PM.) and telling her that if she has no particular reason for wishing to stay longer (& Thursday or Friday was the limit fixed for her stay at the Thompson's) at Wimbledon, I should like her to avail herself of your offer; but that if she does wish to, – anyhow she is to send her decision to you immediately; and I rather expect that she will accept your escort; and if so she will take care to be at Euston Square at the time named. She is so young-looking, and has never yet travelled alone, or else we should not have felt anxious to put her under some friendly charge, – I thank you for remembering our wish. I did once think that if she came with you she might be left to travel on here alone from Crewe; but on consideration I believe I must trouble you, if it is not really inconvenient to bring her on here as it will be dark, & often the most disagreeable people get [on] in the evening for short distances; it is on a hunting-line.[2] Of course you understand *that* only means if you should not find that there is any one with whom you think, she may be trusted coming straight on to Manchester. I hope all this is clear tho' I am writing in the greatest possible hurry. You will find your room and a welcome ready for you, if you are so very good as to bring Florence on to Manchester and any how our thanks are most truly yours, & the room & the welcome whenever you choose to come for them.

I am so glad you like Mr Fairbairn – but I have not time for a word more.

Yours very truly
E. C. Gaskell

Envelope postmarked MANCHESTER /AP1 /62

British Library reserved photocopy
Text from H. W. McCready, 'Elizabeth Gaskell and the Cotton Famine in Manchester: Some Unpublished Letters', *Transactions of the Historic Society of Lancashire and Cheshire* 123 (1972), pp. 144–150.

1 Vernon Lushington* (1823–1912), lawyer and Christian Socialist. ECG preferred 'Cousin V' to 'Mr G. L.', i. e. his twin brother Godfrey, Fellow of Oriel (*Letters*, p. 686). See also Irvine, p. 159.

2 Hunts seem to have met at railway stations. Mrs Joan Leach drew our attention to a later instance in *Thirty Years a Hunt Servant: Being the Memories of Jack Molyneux,* ed. J. Fairfaix-Blakeborough, 1900, p. 63: 'We boxed our horses to Chester Station ...'

VERNON LUSHINGTON*

[4 April 1862]

Dear Mr Lushington,

Do you know you left your copy of 'Good Words'[1] here? Meta is full of guilty feelings because of her unconscious 'kleptomania' last night; and would fain have it sent after you; but I say I shall keep it until you come again, at any rate,

Yours very truly,
E. C. Gaskell

Friday Morning – ½ past 9 – dated in order to show how soon our consciences began to smite us with a sense of dishonesty.

Envelope postmarked MANCHESTER /AP4 /62.

British Library reserved photocopy [McCready text]

1 *Good Words* (1860–1906), a monthly magazine carrying articles and improving fiction. The issue for March 1862 contains Mrs Craik's running serial *Mistress and Maid* and J. M. W. Ludlow's 'A Year of the Slavery Question in the United States 1859–60'.

VERNON LUSHINGTON*

46 Plymouth Grove.
Wednesday, April ? [c. 9 April 1862]

Dear Mr Lushington,

I do thank you heartily for your cheque. I do not think you know how much good it will do, – at least I hope so; and we will do our best to make it do so. We have been talking over how to make it go the farthest, & wondering – oh! it is of no use wearying you with all our long conversation as to what we had better do with it. I will give you the results in brief. {May[?] } We think of using part of it in allowing 6d or 8d a week to {so} the poor old women, whom my daughters know *well*, – & who at present have only the work-house allowance; barely enough for the cheapest poorest food, – only just enough to keep life in. They have worked hard all their working-yrs, poor old friendless women, and now often crave and sicken after a 'taste of bacon' or something different to the perpetual oat-meal. Meta says 'her old women will bless you all their lives long' if, through you, they gain the power of adding to their food. This sounds very carnal; but I feel sure you can understand it: and I feel equally sure that not a penny will be wasted or given where it will go in drink. Then some of it will go in paying \ some poor / for work done for other poor, – occasionally it is such real help to both parties to {get} pay one woman, wanting employment, to nurse another \ who is / sick, {woman}, – overpowered besides her illness, by the care of her family, – or a man, laid by for a time, while there is no one to look after him. Again I can give sewing-employment, – as I told you but I was not sure if you quite liked that plan from your silence, – only we have found it to work well; & the work to be begged and *implored for*, as if it was the greatest boon, – & it is so pathetic to have that asking for work, –. However, I know you will trust us, won't you – and (though I see all I have said seems to relate only to *women*,) there are many ways surging up in my mind in which I know that at this time, \ i. e of slackness of employment / *men* can benefit by money or money's worth (without having their just sense of independence injured) by help which comes as from friend to friend. So thank you again; & deeply. Was not yesterday a lovely day – with just a touch of north wind to give the air a fresh sharpness? We had little 'Mabel' in the garden for part of our morning's occupation.

As I hope you know you are always welcome, if it is only for the pleasure of 'bullying you', – and playing Chopin *at* you, – which is called 'educating your taste' by some people.

Yours very truly,
E. C. Gaskell.

Envelope <Vern>on LushingtonEsq / St George's Hall/ Liverpool.
Stamp, postmark AP 9 / MANCHESTER / 1862 / S.

Manchester Central Library

VERNON LUSHINGTON*

Wednesday Aft
[9 April 1862]

Dear Mr Lushington,

Don't be frightened; I shall not worry you with letters; but I must give you your first blessing. Before lunch Meta marched off to an old woman to give her her first 8d a week. Of course she cd not take the gratitude to herself – but told the white trembling old woman it was 'a gentleman' &c. The poor creature lifted up her hand and said 'Lord help him! Lord help him – and *land him safe in heaven*' – and then wanted to know all about you, & why you did not come and see her, *before* planning out her 8d \ worth /. She has 1s a week for food, so you may fancy what an addition 8d is! Was it not a pretty blessing 'Land him safe in heaven!'

Now you shall not be troubled with perpetual thanks; but I will remain

Yrs ungratefully
E C Gaskell

Envelope postmarked MANCHESTER /AP 9 /1862

Manchester Central Library

HENRY A. BRIGHT*

Saturday [?12 April 1862]

My dear Mr Bright,

It is not *my* doing that I can't answer your questions about the Unitarian (not to have that name) Hall; but Mr Gaskell's, who wants to write to you himself, about it.[1] No! you may abuse Mr Dicey's paper as much as you like, and I won't be savage: but oh! I *should* like to tar and feather you for the way in which you speak of the Northerne[r]s. You, who were so full of them once upon a time!

However I dare not abuse you too much, for fear of Mrs Henry Bright, who I want to like me sometime, and I am afraid she will not if I am too savage with you.

Yes! I do like Mr Lushington very much; and it is a conquest of prejudice on my part; for when I first knew him he rubbed my fur (mentally speaking,) all the wrong way.[2] But I think it best to begin with a little aversion. Do come and see us soon: and let me abuse you vivâvoce; and then you never can be so mean as to go and repeat it to Mrs Bright! We go to Oxford at the end of this month.

Yours, with kindest regards to your wife from us all,

Ever most truly
E C Gaskell

Trinity College, Cambridge

1 With letter from WG to HAB, [Saturday], 12 April 1862, about Bi-Centenary of Ejected Ministers Appeal, printed March 1862. The Memorial Hall was finally opened in 1865 (*Letters*, p. 758; B. Brill, *William Gaskell 1805–84: A Portrait,* Manchester 1984, pp. 75–6).

2 Perhaps c. 1853 (*Letters,* p. 235).

VERNON LUSHINGTON*

Tuesday [?15 April 1862]

Dear Mr Lushington,

Thank you very much for many and various things: more than I have time now to go into at length. My mouth sympathetically waters at the idea of the anenomes[*sic*]. I am so busy I shd not write to you now but for two things; No! not even gratitude would compel me.

1st It is said & believed by every one here that the 'Lancashire lad's' letters[1] are fictitious; – there is strong internal evidence for supposing them so, at any rate. But there is no doubt about the distress;[2] bad enough in Manchester; infinitely worse at Blackburn and Preston: \ & in / South Lancashire generally. Here, *as it is*, if it does not become worse, we have had it worse before; in 1857, (American panic,-) and 1847 – (railways.) But we fear its becoming worse; – it will be; if the

American War \ is likely to / come to a speedy conclusion; so one's interests clash terribly. If there is a prospect of American cotton in the next 2 years, people won't encourage the growth of Indian, – (thereby dwarfing a good market for their manufactured goods, – for if the Indians have no work in canal-making, cotton picking &c, they can't buy our Manchester goods,) nor will the manufacturers alter their machinery so as to use up Indian cotton, at a great expense; \ if / the said machinery has to be re-altered at the end of next year. The cotton harvest comes in in July. Some people say we have touched our worst as to the distress: but I fear not, – very much.

Next as to {how far} in what manner any sum you might send *cd* be best distributed, – most wisely as well as most kindly, – for a *very* public thing for the *whole* of S. Lancashire there is to be a great collection through the district, & the Mayor of Manchester would most probably head our Manchester subscriptions; & would receive contributions \ or Mr Gaskell of course /. Next, if you wished to give to Manchester *proper*, the District Provident Society is taking the supplementary work of the Poor Law Guardians;[3] { } educated men are working hard at distributing relief after enquiry; – the office is open from 6 A M. till 11 P.M; and the utmost pains & kindness is shown in the distribution of relief by private individuals, friends of ours on the Committee – I enclose the address of one,

Charles J. Herford Esq –
Acomb Street/
Green Heys
Manchester.

he is on the Committee and would conscientiously make your money go as far as he cd. I enclose a paper slip about the Society & another paper, sent to subscribers, showing how they are meeting cases with private exertion.

Again if you would like to have it given to any particular *class* of cases – Travers Madge,[4] living right amongst them, would, I am sure, undertake to distribute any money to any *specified set of people* – factory girls, able-bodied men seeking work & getting none, – or to whomsoever you liked in fact; and in a thoroughly wise & conscientious spirit –

Travers Madge Esq.
2 Trafford Place
Stretford Road
Manchester.

He was here yesterday; {and} So here are 3 ways; I, myself being Manchester, should prefer either of the last; but there is no doubt that there are other towns far worse off, which would be included in the general *S. Lancashire* subscription.

Please, Meta wants to read Mr Harrison[5] (she is honour & secrecy itself –) & has no time here; so I am going to take it to Oxford to give her a chance; & I will either send it to you, or give it you on Sunday, which will be better.

Yours truly,
E C Gaskell

Envelope missing [McCready III]

Manchester Central Library

1 A series of letters to the *Times,* from 14 April 1862, signed 'A Lancashire Lad', in fact by John Relly Beard.
2 Manchester, now more of a commercial than an industrial centre, was less vulnerable than Lancashire factory towns to trade cycle fluctuations. The 1861–65 cotton famine was created by the Northern blockade when over-production in the South had created the conditions for yet another depression. In 1860 Indian production was as yet undeveloped and eighty percent of raw cotton imports were from the US. After the blockade total imports were more than halved.
3 The famine placed severe strains on the provisions of the Poor Law; other private and philanthropic institutions were called into action.
4 Travers Madge (1823–66), charismatic son of a Unitarian minister, preached as a Unitarian layman. See esp. Easson, *Gaskell,* pp. 15–16.
5 Frederic Harrison (1831–1923), London barrister and leading Positivist, whose MS account of an 1861 tour of Lancashire and Yorkshire manufacturing districts was seen by ECG. Letter 503 perhaps to Vernon* rather than Godfrey Lushington (*Letters,* pp 680–1 & n.)

HENRY A. BRIGHT

46, Plymouth Grove
April 24th 1862.

My dear Mr Bright,

I return you your very interesting account with best thanks. If anything had been wanting to convince me of Forster's imposture, this would have been invaluable.

Ever yrs most truly
E. C. Gaskell.

Princeton University Library

FLORENCE NIGHTINGALE*

Plymouth Grove
April the 25th 1862

My dear Miss Nightingale,

It will be a *real* pleasure to me if I can help {you} in any way in providing you with women who would make suitable nurses.[1] This is the very time of all others, when *Manchester* ought to furnish them readily and gratefully; for there is very great dearth of employment for women of every trade, as all are more or less affected by the cotton-crisis.

I will mention your plan of training nurses to any of my friends, who may seem likely to assist in it; but I fancy, from what you say, that you would like some wider publication of it and \ to have / advertisements inserted in the papers. This I will gladly undertake to do, if you will let me know one thing which I cannot quite understand either in your note or the papers of regulations: – that is whether the applicants must be sent by parishes – (i.e. by the clergyman or vestries?) – or whether any individual lady or gentleman might get a woman admitted whom they believed capable of turning out a thoroughly good, efficient nurse. In the former case, I suppose that the women, when trained, would be expected to return to the parish which had sent them, to work *there* under the clergymen – ? I am sending a copy of the regulations down to a Clerical Library & Reading-room, frequented daily by most of the Manchester Clergymen; thinking that in this way it will come most directly under their notice.

I have heard so many clergymen just lately speaking of the great advantage of having regularly-trained nurses officially attached to the parishes, that I have no doubt of their assistance in catering for the suitable women, if the plan is once brought fairly before them.

I hope, dear Miss Nightingale, that what you say of having written so little lately, does not mean that you are suffering[2] more than usual – ?

Ever yours sincerely
E. C. Gaskell.

Brotherton Collection, Leeds University

1 The Nightingale Training School for Nurses at St Thomas's Hospital opened on 24 June 1860 (Sir Edward Cook, *The Life of Florence Nightingale,* I. 456).

2 'I am always praying for you', wrote Sister Gonzaga, 'and your health is no credit to my piety' (Cook, *Nightingale,* I. 449).

VERNON LUSHINGTON*

46 Plymouth Grove,
April 25th [1862]

Dear Mr Lushington,

Will you do me a favour, and call on your neighbour Mr W. (I think) *Thackeray* Marriott, 7, King's Bank Walk, Temple? He would like extremely to know you; if you have the leisure to spare for a new acquaintance. I think I told you about him; a Cambridge man who came to one of our Manchester parishes as curate; and did every kind of good in his power for two or three yrs; a popular preacher &c &c; all the time declining to take priest's orders, and at last breaking with his profession entirely, on acct of difference of doctrine (*Fais ce que dois advienne que pourra*,) and *not* feeling 'what will my parish do without me' – working by faith and not by sight; and now he is struggling at law, close by you. So will you know him?

We go to Oxford on Wednesday in time for May morning after all; – and will send back Mr Harrison's Diary before that day.

In the usual greatest haste.

Yours very truly,
E. C. Gaskell.

Envelope missing [McCready VI]

British Library reserved photocopy [McCready text]

VERNON LUSHINGTON*

Cowley House,[1]
Oxford
Tuesday [6 May 1862]

Dear Mr Lushington,

I am sending you back Mr Harrison's Diary by today's post; though we are not quite sure if you meant either Mr or Mrs Brodie to see it; you said something about this to Meta as you were going away; but she did not quite understand you, and we have agreed that it will be better to return it straight to you; and leave it to you to lend it to them, if they wish to see it. Meta says she does not think she ever read anything more interesting; and I almost agree with her; it is like a set of well-drawn and life-like portraits which it is always so pleasant & absorbing to study; and I cannot help liking (you know I *would* have helped it, if I could) all that Mr Harrison says and deduces from what he saw. May Meta keep the W. M. C. Magazine[2] entirely? If[*sic*] is it to be returned? I do not forget that we have several of your things which are to be returned.

Thank you too for your note; I hope we shall manage to see your brother's rooms before we leave; and we are very much obliged to him for his kind permission. I was particularly glad of your note; as I think we, (Gaskells) rather felt that the claims of other friends had somehow prevented our seeing as much of you as at a quieter time. We have had a rainy morning, but we are hoping it will be fine in the afternoon, when Meta and I are going to hear the organ played in Exeter Chapel, & Mr Harcourt[3] is going to take Florence, Margaret and Ida over several colleges. We leave on Monday I am sorry to say; Meta takes Florence to Winchester & then joins me in London, & we shall have a day's hard hunting for airy lodgings not too far from the Exhibition, & then we two go for a fortnight abroad; to Paris on business in the first instance; & then to sketch in Normandy & Brittany. That reminds me of something I forgot to ask you on Sunday; a friend of ours, half an artist himself, wants very much to know Mr Rossetti, and has asked me for an introduction to him. At any other time I should not have scrupled to give it; especially as Mr Darbishire is well able to buy pictures; as well as being I think quite a person to appreciate Mr Rossetti; but do you think I may give a stranger an introduction to him just now; one would be so sorry to seem to intrude impertinently on his grief?[4] And also, what is his address?

Yours very truly,
E. C. Gaskell

Envelope postmarked OXFORD / MAY 6 / 62

British Library reserved photocopy [McCready text]

1 ECG was staying with the Brodies at a time when Oxford was 'quite empty & shut up' (*Letters*, p. 685).
2 i. e., the *Working Men's College Magazine.*
3 Augustus John Vernon Harcourt (1834–1919), pupil, then assistant to B. C. Brodie the younger at Oxford from 1855.
4 Rossetti's wife, Lizzie Siddal, was found dying, presumably by her own hand, on 19 February 1862.

LORD AND LADY STANHOPE[1]

43 Eaton Place[2]
Friday. June 6th [?1862]

Mrs Gaskell will have great pleasure in availing herself of Lord and Lady Stanhope's kind invitation to breakfast on Thursday morning next.

Centre for Kentish Studies, Maidstone (U1590 C481)

1 Lord Stanhope had married Emily Harriet Kerrison in 1834.
2 Address of John Hawkshaw in May 1860 (*Letters*, p. 619 n. 2).

MR BICKNELL[1]

32, Belgrave Road[2] – S. W.
June 7th 1862

My dear Sir,

You most kindly gave me permission to write and announce our coming to London to you, and to remind you of your promise of giving us the entrée to the Crystal Palace[3] on Tuesday Afternoons, and also a card of admission to some private collection of pictures – the name of the owner I have stupidly forgotten.

You see I am troubling you with very little ceremony; but you must take it, please, as a proof merely of how much we should relish the two privileges you offered us. With my daughter's and my own kind remembrances to Mrs Bicknell and yourself, believe me

Ever truly yours
E. C. Gaskell.

Princeton University Library (Dictated?)

1 Not identified.
2 Lodgings (*Letters*, p. 688).
2 Now at Sydenham.

?HARRIET SOPHIA HOLLAND[1]

32, Belgrave Road, S. W.
June 21st 1862.

My dear Sophy,

Will you please give my kind regards and best thanks to Mrs George Holland[2] and tell her how very much obliged to her we are for the trouble that she has taken in procuring us the tickets for the Lady Mayoress's Ball on Tuesday.

We are looking forward to it extremely – I had often and often wished to see one –

We will receive your dress – and keep a hearty welcome for yourself.

Ever your affectionate cousin
E. C. Gaskell.

Mrs Lucy Magruder

1 Probably the daughter, Harriet Sophia, of ECG's first cousin Edward Holland (1806–75) and his wife Sophia, née Isaac (1813–51).
2 Née Charlotte Dorothy Gifford, wife of Edward Holland's brother George Henry (1816–91).

HENRY A. BRIGHT*

46 Plymouth Grove
Sunday. [?post-August 1862]

My dear Mr Bright,

I hope you did not think me very unceremonious, – but the case was this. A very charming young man (cousin to your Cambridge Vernon Harcourt,[1] – who is not 'charming' is he?) wrote to offer to come to us on Friday till Monday. Mr Gaskell is in Cornwall, – and nearly every person *in* Manchester is *out* of it, if that is not Irish. We had asked Mr Fairbairn to dine with Mr Vernon Harcourt last night; but he was telegraphed for, yesterday to London; and we, women, did not like inviting any *gentleman* with whom we were not tolerably intimate. So Marianne & Meta both repeated the wish they had expressed before, that I would ask you to come and stay with us during Mr V. Harcourt's visit. But you could not come, more's the pity; for we *are* very agreeable, though we are principally of the feminine gender. Fate however sent us Mr Vernon Lushington. I did not even know he was in the North, when at six o clk last night he walked in; and you may fancy what a welcome he had, – both on his own account, & as a friend of Mr Harcourts. With you our party would have been very nearly perfect!

I am *very* sorry indeed to hear that your wife still continues delicate; I hear your little boy is a splendid fellow. We go to Smithills[2] tomorrow evening for two nights, so don't come to lunch while we are away. Any other time you are always most welcome. With our united kind regards

Yours most truly
E. C. Gaskell

Annotation After Aug 4 1862

Trinity College, Cambridge

1 The Cambridge cousin was William G. G. Vernon Harcourt (1827–1904), B. A. Cambridge 1851; called to the Bar 1854.

2 Smithills Hall, near Bolton, occupied at this time by Peter Ainsworth (1790–1870) and his wife Elizabeth, née Byrom (see *Letters,* p. 637). Peter did not take part in the family business; he was MP for Bolton and a JP.

MARIA SUSAN RYE[1]

Gros[v]enor Hotel
London SW
Septr *15*, 10 P M [?1862][2]

Dear Miss Rye,

We brought 3 factory girls (going service) by the same train by which yr Emigrant girls came to King's Cross tonight. Our poor girls have lost their box containing all their best clothes; we have telegraphed along the line for it back to Manchester, but can any of your emigrant girls have taken it, by mistake?

It was a light-coloured paper \ covered / – box, 2½ feet long, about 1½ broad & deep; directed to Mary Stead, Rt Honble Dr Lushington's, 18 Eaton Place, London; – directed very legibly. If you would kindly look over yr {s ..} girls boxes for any resembling & directed as above, & send it (if there) as soon as possible by parcels delivery to 18 Eaton Place you wd be doing a great kindness.

Yours very truly
E. C. Gaskell (of
(Plymouth Grove, Manchester)

Annotation Ansr

Brotherton Collection, Leeds University

1 Maria Susan Rye (1829–1903), of Langham Place Group, founded the Female Middle Class Emigration Society 1861.

2 Address makes 1865 possible (*Letters,* p. 777), but a letter of 22 September 1862 to Miss Rye, dealing with emigration, was once mounted on the same page in an album.

SMITH & ELDER

[35 Marine Parade
Eastbourne[1]
c. 2 October 1862]

Directions to the Printer.

Mrs Gaskell would be very much obliged to the Printer of 'Sylvia's Lovers' if he would *break the line, and begin a fresh one*, wherever this mark occurs // in the returned proofs, or the MSS.

She would also be very much obliged to him if he would look over the proofs of the 1st & 2nd volumes; and see whether the name Jonathan or Jeremiah was decided upon in them, for that of the brother of *John* Foster; and if he would then correct the wrong name in the *3rd* vol.

She would be very much obliged to him if he would insert the MSS written on the other side of this sheet of paper, in the proofs of vol III, page 30; in the middle of the 6th line, after the words

'all this time.'

Vol III, Page 30, 6th line

(*Fresh Line*)

an uncle of his mother's, a Cumberland Statesman of whose existence he was barely conscious, died about this time leaving to his unknown great-nephew {some} four or five hundred {s of} pounds, which put him at once in a different position with regard to his business. {[Then?]} Henceforward his ambition was roused, – such humble ambition as befitted &c

Address Messrs Smith & Elder / 65 Corn-Hill / London. EC
Postmarks EASTBOURNE / B[?] / OC 2 / 62 *and* LONDON / XD / OC 3 / 62

Brotherton Collection, Leeds University

1 ECG was staying near William Shaen* (*Letters*, pp. 693, 696).

VERLAG B. TAUCHNITZ

46 Plymouth Grove,
Manchester.
October 14th, 1862.

I cannot help wishing that sometime or other you would collect *Cranford* [1] out of *Household Words*, and publish it in your Series. Many of my friends, and several people who are unknown to me, have expressed their great wish to be able to purchase it when abroad.

Text from [Curt Otto], *Der Verlag Tauchnitz*

1 A footnote reads 'Mrs. Gaskells berühmtestes Werk, das 1867 in der Tauchnitz Edition erschien und noch jetzt populär ist', i.e. ECG's most famous work, first published in a single volume by Tauchnitz in 1867, and still popular.

LORD LANSDOWNE[1]

[Gothic letter stamp]
46 Plymouth Grove.
Manchester.
October 16 1862

Dear Lord Lansdowne,

I am very glad to be able to reply in the most satisfactory manner with regard to Mr Birch, and his schools.[2] I did not notice the report of them which you allude to in the Daily News, but the facts of the case are these.

Last June, when the coming distress in South Lancashire first became startlingly evident, a young man in a warehouse (much in the same position as to influence and money as a shopmen at a great London shop, would be,) set up a sewing-school in the district where he lived, *Hulme*, an adjoining suburb of Manchester. He had been honorary secretary to a small local Working Man's Institute, and the society let him use their room for his school; the money was at first furnished by a rich humble friend, whose name no one knows, but who placed 1, 000£ in Mr Birch's hands last winter in order that he might use it for purposes of charity. (This anonymous donor is always said to be a small shop-keeper in the neighbourhood.) With what remained in June of this money Mr Birch began his first sewing-school; and the doors to it were soon so much thronged with factory girls, (who walked from one to six miles to entreat to be taken in,) that { } \ all the / money was expended in the purchase of material, and in payment of wages; (8d a day of six hours.) He then spent some of his own small savings; but, although he is but 28 years of age he has a wife and two children, and it soon became necessary for him to make a public appeal.

This was answered very liberally; but the number of the girls who came to him increased, and increased, till now he had upwards of a thousand dependent on him; and has established seventeen sewing-schools, all of which are under his supervision, though of course now other people have come forwards to assist. His hours of occupation at the warehouse are from half past nine till six or seven at night, allowing one hour for dinner, and half an hour for tea. This small daily leisure he employs in visiting his schools; he also gets up at five every morning in order to get through the business imposed upon him by this voluntary work.

The expense of providing *material* for sewing is a very heavy one, especially at this time, and assistance is much needed. I beg to call your

Lordship's attention to some 'Letters from our own Correspondent' which are now appearing in the Daily News, and which give a very interesting, and in my opinion a most correct account of the state of things in South Lancashire. The writer is well known to me,[3] and is a person on whose word & sources of information thorough reliance may be placed. It would give me extreme pleasure if I were ever able to avail myself of your very kind invitation to Bowood. It was not without feelings of envy that I saw my dear friends Mr and Mrs Story[4] into the Great Western railway last Monday week.

I remain, my dear Lord,
Yours respectfully and truly
E. C. Gaskell.

Brotherton Collection, Leeds University

1 Henry Petty-Fitzmaurice (1780–1863), 3rd Marquis of Lansdowne. A moderate reformer, he served in a number of administrations, both before and during the Victorian period, but when invited to form a government on his own account during the political crisis of 1852, declined to do so.

2 Established to provide relief for unemployed female operatives, who received materials and a small wage. William Birch was a young clerk who set up his first school at the Hulme Working Men's Institute. The expansion of his schools was typical of the movement as a whole: by February 1863 over 40, 000 women were involved. Most were organised by a Central Relief Committee.

3 Charles Beard.

4 W. W. and Emelyn Story* (*Letters*, pp. 696–7).

THOMAS WRIGHT

46 Plymouth Grove
December 2nd [?1862]

Dear Mr Wright

If you like some *women's* clothing for Woolfold (or elsewhere, in yr own personal knowledge,) you may go to the Central Relief Office[1] in a day or two, and take *one* of two parcels, bales, or packages addressed as before i.e. *To Mrs Gaskell, to be had on application.* Or you might do as before, – take both bales to Cross St Chapel rooms, & choose out what articles are most serviceable to *your* \ Woolfold, & Lane Ends &c / people, making up the rest for me to send for.

In greatest haste
Yours very truly
E C Gaskell.

Princeton University Library

1 Set up in June 1862, it consisted of prominent Manchester business men, mayors and ex-mayors of the cotton districts, and co-ordinated philanthropic activities supplementary to Poor Law provisions.

ANON

46 Plymouth Grove
Manchester
December 10th [?c.1862]

Dear Madam,

I am very much obliged to you for your letter of Decr 8th enclosing 3s worth of stamps, as a weekly contribution from yourself and some of your friends. If it is more trouble for you to send it *weekly*, I could take it *monthly*; in which case I would acknowledge it by *letter*; in case of its being sent weekly, I might be a little more irregular in acknowledging the receipt of the stamps, as I have very much to do just now. But in any case, and in the name of the poor people here I thank you and your friends extremely for your so kindly thinking of them in their need. I have very little doubt that the two parcels of clothes will arrive at the Central Relief Office today, where I mean to call for them. Once more thank you.

Yours respectfully
E. C. Gaskell

Princeton University Library

MRS BOSTOCK[1]

46 Plymouth Grove
Dec. 16th [1862]

My dear Mrs Bostock,

I remember you, and my pleasant visit to West Dingle perfectly, and had no need of a reminder to tell me who you were. Thank you and your husband very much for the money you have sent me. I shall do my very best to spend it well and usefully. I am so busy that you must forgive me for not writing more – Believe me to remain

Yours most truly
E C Gaskell

Annotation [?]1862.

Princeton University Library (Dictated?)

1 Not identified.

ANON

46 Plymouth Grove
Manchester
Janry 7 [?1863]

Sir,

I have received your letter asking me to contribute to your volume of stories published for the Lancashire Relief Fund.[1] I am so much occupied with Sewing Schools &c – that I really hardly know if I can find time to write anything, as it takes an unfatigued *body*, as well as a willing *mind*, to write even a short story.

You do not say when you expect to have your book published? and the time at which you would require my story would have a great deal to do with my decision. If I am able to write anything, I should never think of taking any remuneration; I should like to show my sympathy with your effort, – which is the only reason why I do not at once refuse.

Yours truly
E. C. Gaskell

?Chester Record Office (from Knutsford)
Letter 519a, now from MS.

1 The Lancashire and Cheshire Operatives Relief Fund was known also as the Mansion House Fund, London: its existence indicates that the distress was regarded as a national issue. No likely volume of stories has been identified (*Letters*, p. 930 n. 2).

MISS JAMES

46 Plymouth Grove
Manchester
Janry 28 [1863]

My dear *Madam* (for you see I am not quite sure if you are *Mrs*, or *Miss James* – or else I should be only too glad to address you in the pleasant, friendly way you do to me –)

I have received your letter this morning and I will, thankfully find out some deserving recipient of your kind mother's counterpane. I have already three or four deserving cases in my mind; and when I have received the counterpane, and quite decided to which of my poor people it ought to go, I will write & give you the full particulars that your mother may not feel that it has gone 'vaguely' into an indiscriminate quick-sand of distress; but may learn enough to identify the kind of people and household to whom the counterpane will give warmth and comfor<t.> Perhaps, if you will allow me, I shall come and see you some day; for I have a friend in Clifton *Place* (and I fancy Clifton *Garden<ns>* must be somewhere near,) on whom I ofte<n> call when in London<.>

I remain, dear Miss James – (for you see I have decided on your being a Miss James.)

Yours very truly
E C Gaskell

Please thank your mother *very* much, both on my own account & on behalf of some starving people.

Envelope Miss James, / 43 Clifton Gardens / London
Postmark MANCHESTER / 9.00 / FE 2 / 63

Norfolk Record Office (MS 11351, p. 23)
Wordsworth Museum (envelope only)

VERNON LUSHINGTON*

Tuesday[*sic*] night
4th. F'by [sc. 8 February 1863]

My dear Mr Lushington,

If you knew the fright we have been in you would not have wondered at my ingratitude, – as you *ought* to have been doing, when you never received any thanks for all your kindness! But last night – 10 PM. – Saturday too – and many posts shut up, – Marianne startled us all by reading out an advertisement 'Merrie England sails on the morning of the *10th* (Tuesday)'.[1]

Ship papers, & Mr Walcott's letter all said *11th*; but if she missed her passage! money paid, &c! Yet she was a great way off, & her final outfit not completed, her boxes here, & not painted with her name, – & before we could settle what to do, bedtime had come. However, it is of no use worrying you with details; by dint of telegraphing, sending for her, packing up, & unpacking, & repacking all is right, and we have got our breaths and our moral feelings back again; and now I have time to say how all through the day I have been thinking of your untiring goodness & helpfulness. I wish I could do something for you; but I will, if ever you will give me the opportunity.

Will you direct, – you may read if you like for perhaps you may know something of the subject, – the enclosed letter to Mr Furnivall?[2]

Yours really gratefully & truly,
E. C. Gaskell.

Envelope postmarked MANCHESTER /FE 9 / 63

British Library reserved photocopy [McCready text]

1 The Gaskells were paying for the passage of a Mrs Regan and child to Australia (*Letters*, p. 699).

2 F. J. Furnivall (1825–1910), Christian Socialist and founder member of the London Working Men's College; he was also a philological and literary

scholar. In 1858 he had wanted to know the secret of WG's success with teaching English Literature at the Manchester W. M. C. (*L & M,* II. 230).

JOHN M. F. LUDLOW*

46 Plymouth Grove
February 9th [1863]

My dear Mr Ludlow,

I am very glad you liked my paper;[1] and please do what you think best with the rest of the MSS. If you think its being published will do any good, please let it be published where you think best, – but if it is superfluous and unneeded, equally please, burn it. Only don't let *me* see its face again[.] I am very glad about the Reader's steady progress. I know I like it!

Yours very truly
E. C. Gaskell

Cambridge University Library, Add 7348/10/128

1 Presumably submitted to the Christian Socialist journal, *The Reader* (1863–67), edited by Ludlow* for a short time, with 'a list of contributors such as was never known for a newspaper'. ECG was an early contributor (*CH Gaskell,* p. 435).

~

Letter 178 to Williams & Norgate redated 46 Plymouth Grove, 12 February [?1863]

~

MARY GREEN*

Avignon
March 18th [1863]

My dear Mary,

We are detained here for a few days by the Mistral, a violent wind which is preventing the boats from leaving Marseilles; and we are not sorry; as it gives us a little time for quiet, and rest; as you may fancy that we were all a good deal upset by the event of last week. – I hardly knew Mr Crompton, – I mean we knew each other to speak to – and Mr Gaskell had stayed with him in Scotland; and Carry Crompton had stayed with us in the autumn; and we liked her[altered from 'him'] very much indeed; – but I had no idea whatever that there was an attachment between Mr Crompton and Florence;[1] and at first I was more surprized than pleased, as I knew nothing of him. But Lady C. sent *such* a pleasant account of him, – he was brought up at home till he went to Cambridge, (where he took high honours,) and has always lived under his father's roof since then, 'making the Sun of the household' – and the Judge sends word he 'has never cost them a moment's anxiety since he was born', so that I already began to like the idea before I saw him on Saturday (when he brought Florence & Meta over to Paris, & stayed a day there.)

Do you know dear Mrs Green he has once or twice reminded me of *you*, in moral qualities? His careful accuracy in speaking the truth; and his extreme unwillingness to give pain (even to tiresome & vulgar people, are like you –) Meta and I expected that they – (i-e. Mr Gaskell, Mr Crompton or Florence,) would like us to 'give up our journey[']; but Mr Gaskell had no wish about the matter; and both Mr C and Florence wished that the plan might be carried out. So as soon as the wind changes we go straight on to Rome.

I am so glad to hear such pleasant news of dear Annie.[2] Pray give my kind love to her, and the rest of the girls, especially to Emily; and Mr Green –

Ever yours very affecly
E C Gaskell

Mrs Green / Knutford [written over p. 4].
Dr R. Jamison

1 ECG was at first shocked by Florence's engagement to Charles Crompton (1833–90), a barrister ten years older, 'not exactly a Unitarian, nor exactly broad Church' (*Letters*, pp. 705–6); WG was very pleased (*L & M*, II. 391). 'In a quiet, 19th century sort of way, there has been a *vendetta* between the Cromptons & Mama's family, dating from some past ill-usage – each says on the part of the other of course' (ME to CEN, Hotel d'Allemagne, Rome, 17 April [1963], Harvard bMS Am1088 2641).

2 See p. 261 below, recording the birth of Annie Green's first child.

WILLIAM WETMORE STORY*

Hôtel d'Allemagne[1]
Thursday [early April 1863]

My dear Mr Story,

(just to plague you with a question or two, – the bearer awaits the answers, but can wait as long as you like.)

What do you think would be the *best* ceremonies to go to next week? by '*best*'' I mean most likely to be decently accessible at so late a time of applying for tickets, and without too much fighting on our feminine parts.

Next. We have circular notes (10£) negociable at any bankers. Macbean, Cholmley [two crushed words] – but have not \had / any occasion to use them at present –

Who *is* our banker then? to <whom[?]> may we apply for tickets?

Last question – Is *tonight* the French ambassador's reception – Indiscriminate but respectable English people say it *is*. If so at what time do you go, & may our carriage fall into your train?[2]

Ever yrs affecly
E C Gaskell

Harvard University Library, bMS Am 1702 (15)

1 See *Letters,* p. 931, for this address in Rome.

2 The Storys had moved to 'a splendid suite of rooms at the [Palazzo] Barberini' (Meta to Norton, Hotel d'Allemagne, Rome, 17 April [1863], Harvard MS Am 1088 2641). See Henry James, *William Wetmore Story and His Friends* (1903), I. 353, 355–9. ECG's passport indicates she left Rome for Florence on 26 April 1863.

MRS FANE

Hôtel d'Allemagne –
Saturday Morning
[?April 1863]

Dear Mrs Fane,

I am heartily ashamed of myself for never having either written or called to explain our never joining you at Frascati last Tuesday; but we have been very busy indeed during this (our last) week in Rome, and I have been thus prevented from doing what I fully intended should have been done long since. We went our 'giro' by Mandragone, quite hoping to return by the villa, and to have an hour or two there with you all; but an accident that happened to one of my daughters made us hurry back to Rome that she might have a little quiet rest as soon as possible.[1]

The girths of the donkey on which she was riding suddenly broke, and as it was not a side-saddle, but one of the chairs on which she was sitting {and} she was {therefore} thrown straight back on her head, and rather stunned. Will you give our united kind regards to your daughters, and hoping that we may soon meet again.

I remain ever yours very truly
E. C. Gaskell.

Address Miss [?]Allice

Mrs Lucy Magruder

1 Immediately south-east of Rome are the towns and vineyards of the Alban Hills, locally known as Castelli Romani. Mandragone was perhaps the villa where this unidentified Mrs Fane was staying.

MRS FANE

Hôtel d'Allemagne.
Sunday.
[?April 1863]

My dear Mrs Fane,

Our plans have at length got a little into shape, and as we at present propose going for tomorrow to Albano[1] and sleeping at the little inn there to have the next day at Frascati, I am afraid that we cannot join you in your excursion to Tivoli[2] on Tuesday. For this I am very sorry indeed, as it would have given me such pleasure to have had your companionship in the expedition. If we were certain of going to Tivoli, I would {name} \ propose to you / another day for a joint excursion to it; but I cannot speak positively about it.

In great haste,

very truly yours,
E. C. Gaskell.

Mrs Lucy Magruder

1 On the shores of the crater Lake Albano; the Pope has his summer palace nearby, at Castel Gandolfo.

2 Picturesque town about twenty miles east of Rome near the ruins of Hadrian's Villa, and famous for the sixteenth-century Villa D'Este and its many baroque fountains.

VERLAG B. TAUCHNITZ

Plymouth Grove,
Manchester.
April 24th, 1863.[1]

I am very glad that *A Dark Night's Work* has reached you safely. I am afraid it is rather short for one volume. I am very sorry, but alas! I had no more to say about them, having at last married Elinor happily ... My daughters and I are anxiously looking forward to paying you a visit < ... >

Text from [Curt Otto], *Der Verlag Tauchnitz*

1 Written as from Plymouth Grove? ECG was actually in Italy. *A Dark Night's Work* was published by Tauchnitz in 1863.

LOUIS HACHETTE

Poste restante,
Florence.
May 22nd [1863]

Dear Monsieur Hachette,

I only received your second letter this morning; and I am afraid that your first must be lost, as it has not yet reached me. \ I am so sorry that you had the trouble of writing another. / I agree to your proposal of making one volume out of 'Sylvia's Lovers', 'The Sin of a Father', and 'A Dark Night's Work';[1] for I feel sure that whatever you suggest is best and right.

I am disappointed that you send me no news of Monsieur Alfred Hachette's health; but I trust that *'no news is good news'*, as we say in England, and that he is recovering as surely as you wish.

We shall be passing through Paris sometime about June the 8th, and I shall call on you and Madame Hachette, and hope that I may have the true pleasure – that it always is to me – of seeing you both.

With many thanks for your letter, I am most truly yours,

E. C. Gaskell –

Archives Hachette Livre

1 In fact, *Sylvia's Lovers* was published on its own by Hachette, translated by E.-D. Forges, 1865.

AUGUSTUS VERNON HARCOURT

120 Rue du Bac
Paris
Wednesday [? *c.* 14 June ?1863]

My dear Mr Harcourt,

Will you kindly obtain for me and answer to the following enquiry? M. de Haussonville, (son-in-law to the Duc de Broglie, consequently *grand-son-in-law* to Madame de Stael[*sic*],) wants to know if he can send his son (& his son's tutor) to Oxford, or the neighbourhood; and, placing them in some clergyman's household, (now comes *the* question) procure for the young man the liberty of attending certain courses of lectures, *without*[double stress] entering him as a member of the University; – & making him formally go through terms, examinations &c &c. I am afraid he can*not*; but I said he would enquire. If he cannot attend courses of lectures without being formally entered as a member, can you send me word what would be the necessary preliminaries – Matriculation Examination, I suppose – (of what does it consist?) and payment of certain fees? and what else?

You will probably know how high and distinguished a name M. de Haussonville's is; and he seems most anxious to secure all possible educational advantages for this only son; but the question is what *is* possible for a young foreigner at Oxford. I think Dr Stanley would be able to tell me, only I do not know where he is at present; if at Oxford I am sure he would solve any difficult question on this subject you asked him about; and I shall be very much obliged to you for a full answer.

And now pray put my mind at ease by telling me you got your gun at last? Mr Gaskell grew afraid of it's rusting, or suffering some injury from our damp weather; – we, women, all maintained that that was your responsibility, and that, if you feared any harm you would send an imperative order for it to be sent, or come for it yourself; but when an opportunity (as it seemed) presented itself we deferred to the masculine judgment, – and will never do so again, if it has either been lost, or suffered injury.

I was so sorry to be so poorly when you were at Worthing;[1] but I could not help myself; and I was again fast falling into the same state of ill-health when I can here last Saturday, with Julia, whose first visit to Paris it is. Every one here is full of anxiety as to this Polish insurrection,[2] which seems to be extending itself widely. They fear that if Prussia forms an alliance with Russia, – two despotisms, – for Russia is, I suppose considered despotic at this time, – Hungary will rise, and this Emperor take advantage of the general commotion to 'throw his cap over the Rhine:' and that a great European war will be inevitable. Every one here (Russians, & French –) that we have seen, seems to be extremely interested and unusually well informed about all the disturbances occasioned by Essays & Reviews, Colenso's book &c; & are greedy for news about the prosecution instituted against Mr Jowett.[3] I am struck by the extreme interest the Russians seem to take in English literature, especially in theological works, but, all those whom I have met, seem to be acquainted with Dr Stanley – whose Lectures on the Eastern Church[4] have been translated into Russ, – and that may perhaps account for[altered word] their interest in all his pursuits.

Pray believe me to remain, dear Mr Harcourt,

Yours most truly
E. C. Gaskell

Julia sends you her kind regards.

Annotation Mrs Gaskell 1864 [doubtful]

Pierpont Morgan Library (Gordon Ray Collection)

1 See p. 242 n. 3 above for A. Harcourt. In September 1862, haunted by 'Poor on the Brain' in Manchester (*Letters*, p. 698), ECG had gone to Eastbourne, not far along the south coast from Worthing, Sussex.

2 The January rising of 1862–63 was a guerilla conflict between Polish nationalists and their Russian rulers. Lasting sixteen months, it was suppressed by

February 1863 when Bismark signed a military agreement with the Tsar. This Russo-Prussian alliance alarmed Western European powers. In Britain the *Times* led strong anti-Russian feeling.

3 In February 1863 Benjamin Jowett, Master of Bailliol, was prosecuted in the Oxford Vice-Chancellor's Court, for his essay 'The Interpretation of Scripture' in *Essays and Reviews*. Though this prosecution was dropped, controversy was added to with the *Pentateuch and Book of Joshua Critically Examined* (1862), by J. W. Colenso, Bishop of Natal and therefore outside the authority of the established church. He questioned the authority of Old Testament books by arguing that they were derived from historically different sources. For WG's discussions with F. W. Newman and J. A. Froude at this time, see *L & M*, II. 391–3.

4 A. P. Stanley, *Lectures on the Eastern Church* (1861).

HENRY A. BRIGHT[*]

[?Summer 1863]

My dear Mr Bright

Sunday as it is we are so anxious about our dear Florence \ (city) / - box that I must write a line or two. I *think* you will find that the name of the Ship is the *Esperance, not* the Enterprize as you have written it. We gave the box in charge to Carlo Brini, banker at Florence on May 27. He said it *might* be *nearly* 3 months going by *sailing* vessel from Leghorn, – but we preferred it to the expense of a quicker passage. Not hearing anything of it's arrival we wrote to Brini about a fortnight ago; and in reply we got the paper forwarded to you; which, with many apologies, he said his clerk had neglected to send. In it I think you will find a date June 11th, as the day on which the box was delivered up to the ship 'now at anchor' in the port of Leghorn. (Hendersons of Leghorn, owners.)

Ought we to write to < ... >

Trinity College, Cambridge

FLORENCE NIGHTINGALE[*]

[Gothic letter stamp]
42 Plymouth Grove.
Manchester.
Augt 22nd [1863]

My dear Miss Nightingale,

Nothing could have made me more pleased to think that I had written 'Sylvia' than to know that it had given *you* one hour's enjoyment or timely change of thought – Thank you for accepting it so kindly.[1]

I accept the offer of your Report[2] gladly. I think fuller knowledge of suffering, like added loss, only opens one's heart, instead of filling it; and the sight of all this great Distress here sharpens the edge of my interest for any plan for meeting & conquering evil anywhere –

It is very pleasant to feel how Capt. Jackson's work at Homes has been his salvation, and has – I do believe, strengthened his character for life – a character, which was always charmingly sweet and tender, & only wanted a little ballast. Hoping that you are as well as you can be, I am ever

affectely yrs
E. C. Gaskell.

Brotherton Collection, Leeds University

1 FN's cousin Hilary Bonham Carter had told ECG on 6 Sept. 1859 that FN had just re-read *Ruth* ('a beautiful novel') and 'bids me ask now for North and South, which also she read of old' (Cook, *Nightingale,* I. 500).

2 The *Report of the Royal Commission on the Sanitary State of the Army in India,* 1863), by FN and Dr John Sutherland, had a complicated publishing history. Advance copies were sent to influential friends, and FN's important 'Observations on the Evidence' was circulated in a separate, cheaper edition. See Cook, pp. 31–9, 442–3.

FLORENCE NIGHTINGALE*

46, Plymouth Grove,
Septr 17th 1863.

My dear Miss Nightingale,

At any other time I should have felt most negligent in waiting so long before thanking you for your pamphlet; but I think that you will understand how busy I have been, and how full my heart, when I tell you that during this past week my little daughter Florence (who, I like to think, bears your name) has *been being* married.[1] The parting from a child *stuns* one; and it is very strange and difficult to turn back to the home-life and feel that she will never be there as before – as one's own *possession.*

I feel as if it would be quite presumptuous in[altered word] me to tell you what I thought in reading your book, or how it seemed to me, as the 'Reader' said, 'not a literary work, but a great action'.[2] How soon and surely will redress follow this exposure of the evil, one longs to know now; \ and / when will people see that these sanitary matters are – most literally – matters of life or death. Public attention seems well roused by your pamphlet, and one hopes will enforce active measures.

With true love, ever yours affectionately
E. C. Gaskell.

 Brotherton Collection, Leeds University

1 Florence Gaskell married Charles Crompton on 8 September 1863 (*Letters*, p.725)
2 The *Reader* 2 (1863), p. 271.

~

Letter 535 to W. W. Story* from 46 Plymouth Grove redated 22 October [1863]

~

GEORGE SMITH*

December 10th [1863]
46 P G.

My dear Mr Smith,

I have followed your advice to the letter; I have sent the (signed & dated) agreement to Mr Shaen, & copies of all the *late* correspondence since Novr 6th \ between Mr F. C. & me / to Mr Shaen;[1] & begged him to call upon you; & given him directions to write to Mr F Chapman in my name &c, exactly as you bid me. I don't quite understand what you mean about Phillis ending[2] – & my putting a few lines in addition to the Proofs, which I now return. Do you want it to *end with the year*? I shall be sorry for it is, at present, such a complete fragment; but, if you wish it, I will send you up a line or two, or else I think I had two more nos in my head, {&} one of which is part written & would have been wholly written by now, if I had not been so much annoyed about this Chapman & Hall business. On looking it over I cannot see how it *is* to be made to end now, even with any exculpatory 'few lines'[.] I will tell you the story in brief, as it is in my head.

I (writer) get a letter from Holdsworth saying he is going to be married directly to some Canadian lady. I have to tell {Sylvia.} Phillis. She comforts *me* at first for the blunder I made in telling her; but becomes irritable for the first time in her life – her father gets uneasy questions me, when every one is gone to bed. I confess my having told her, – he (irritable too) is angry with me. Phillis hearing her father's loud voice comes down, a cloak over her night dress, & exculpates me by telling out how I had seen her fretting & read her heart. But the telling &c &c, brings on a brain fever & she lies at death's door. Stupid brother ministers come (like Job's friends,) to *comfort the* Minister. He rebels against *them*, & is very humble in private. She recovers, & asks for a change – goes to my fathers – & in a town, among utterly different people & scenery, cures herself, – but it is a sort of moral 'Tis better to have loved & lost, than never to have loved at all – last scene long years after. The Minister dead, I married – we hear of the typhus fever in the village where Phillis lives, & I go to persuade her & her bedridden mother to come to us. I find her making practical use of the knowledge she had learnt from Holdsworth and, with the help of common labourers, levelling & draining the undrained village – a child (orphaned by the fever) in her arms another plucking at her gown – we hear afterwards that she has adopted these to be her own.

I think it will be a pity to cut it short but on the other side you will find the ending that I suppose *must* do if you want to end it this year. I like the illustrations to Sylvia[3] *much* – but I must end

Yours most truly
E C Gaskell

... Alas! this was the last time I ever saw Phillis radiant & happy; the last time I ever saw the girlish bliss shine out upon her face. I had raised her high in hope; it fell to my lot to dash her down from her height. Not many weeks after I heard from Holdsworth, telling me of his approaching marriage to one Lucille Ventadour, – a french Canadian. I had to go, and tell Phillis this – I cannot bear to think of the piteous scene; all the more piteous because she was so patient. Spare me the recital ...

National Library of Scotland
Discussed and printed in J. A. V. Chapple, 'Elizabeth Gaskell: Two Unpublished Letters to George Smith', *Etudes Anglaises* 33.2 (1980), pp. 183–7.

1 See p. 208 above and *Letters,* pp. 719–24. This recent correspondence with Frederic Chapman is not known. William Shaen* acted as ECG's lawyer.
2 The confusion was resolved when Smith adopted the shorter of ECG's proposals: the 'two more numbers' which would have extended the narrative remained unwritten.
3 ECG, *Sylvia's Lovers* (February 1863). The Illustrated Edition of December 1863 in one volume was illustrated by George Du Maurier (Smith, pp. 174–7).

ELLEN ?GREEN

46 Plymouth Grove,
Jan. 11th [?1864]

My dear Ellen,

You can not think how much your note and invitation pleased me; nor how much the latter tempts me to break through all standing engagements that would prevent my coming to you. I am *coiled* round and round with plans and engagements of other people's; but I feel inclined to cut my way roughly through, and come to you – coute qui coute[*sic*]. Would you be so very kind, dear Ellen, as to let me know, *by return of post*, how *late* I may defer my visit to you, without clashing with any other visitors whom you may be hoping to have. The later, the more chance for me, I think. Florence's plans for the spring have suddenly changed, owing to Mr Crompton's giving up his intention of being 'called' this January; and this has thrown all ours into confusion.

Plans are like a card-house: – if one gives way, all the others come rattling about your head.

It sounds so *girlish* – Minnie[1] skating –

Ever yrs very affly
E. C. Gaskell.

Mrs Lucy Magruder

1 ECG sometimes used Minnie as a pet name for her daughter Marianne; also 'Polly'. See, e. g., *Letters*, pp. 178, 736–7.

WILLIAM STIRLING[1]

[?27 January-Feb. ?1864][2]

Mrs Gaskell presents her compliments to Mr Stirling, and begs to thank him most sincerely for his kind invitation to her and her daughter. She regrets much that a previous engagement in Edinburgh prevents them from availing [them]selves of Mr Stirling's agreeable proposal for Wednesday next, but if the plan proposed by Mr Wilson for Friday next should be agreeable to Mr Stirling, Mrs and Miss Gaskell will be most happy to visit Keir[3] on that day.

Princeton University Library

1 William Stirling (1818–78). Cf. p. 175 n. 1 above.
2 See *Letters*, p. 726, for a possible Scottish visit. Charles Wilson, married to a cousin, lived in Glasgow (*Letters*. p. 456).
3 The Keir estate is at Bridge of Allan, Stirling.

MARY GREEN*

[c. January 1864]

My dear Mary,

We are all so very very glad to hear of your grand-son; and of dear Annie's well-doing! Mary Holland brought the news last night; and Emily's letter confirms it[*sic*] this morning; and brings a little later intelligence of the dear mother & son.

Pray give our best love and congratulations to Annie; and best regards to Mr Falcon.[1] Indeed I think all the Aunts ought to have letters of congratulation. However they will be given in our own persons tomorrow night. I do hope the new little one may be a great comfort to you all, dear Mary.

Your affectionate friend,
E C Gaskell

Dr R. Jamison

1 Ann Louisa married Charles Falcon 4 February 1863. Their little boy died by accident aged 17 months, c. May 1865 (*Letters*, p. 761).

MRS STORY*

Manchester.
Feb. 10th [1864]

My dearest Mrs Story

I really hope that I shall safely *turn Mr Gaskell out of England* on February the 23rd; and as in this cold weather there will be no temptation to loiter on the way, and as moreover he will be in all haste to reach Rome, I expect that he will arrive there on Sunday, the 28th. He may miss the boat that would bring him in on that day, in which case he will come on the next day Monday the 29th.

Would you then, dear Mrs Story, \ kindly / secure him a bedroom for *the 28th* at the Angleterre; warm, & comfortable. *Snug* in fact. I suppose that Rome is very full this year, but I hope that there will be this one room still vacant.

You cannot think how we are all envying him, both for his visit to Rome and for the pleasure that he is to have on seeing you all, dear, dear friends. We shall look forward so much to his report of you.

If the weather is very cold at the end of this month, would you order a fire to be lighted in the room for Mr Gaskell.

Ever yours
E. C. Gaskell.

Castle Howard Archives (J23/ 491/ fol. 36)

1 'Mr Gaskell ... has been to Rome & come back, and is a different creature in consequence' (*Letters*, p. 733).

A. VOGUE[1]

89, Oxford Terrace[2]
Hyde Park
March 8th 1864

Sir,

I regret much that my absence from home has occasioned this delay in complying with your request for my autograph

Yours very truly
E. C. Gaskell

Envelope A: Vogue Esq / Park Row / Nottingham
Postmark W / 6 / Mr 8 / 64

Wordsworth Museum (Stanger MS vol. 2, 104)

1 On 24 January 1867 WG sent this unidentified correspondent a copy in his own hand of the poem, 'What a single word can do', claiming authorship and saying that it had 'been thought worth setting to music by various hands' (Stanger MS vol. 2, 105) The poem appears in chapter 8 of *Mary Barton*.

2 ECG was staying with her married daughter, Florence Crompton. This supports the conjectural date of Letter 549 (*Letters*, p. 728).

WILLIAM FAIRBAIRN[1]

89 Oxford Terrace
March 9th [1864]

My dear Mr Fairbairn,

The bearer of this note will be the Mr Martin,[2] (nephew to Madame Mohl,) about whom you expressed yourself so kindly in your letter to me the other day, for which thank you very much.

I need only remind you that he is the son of a clergyman in Leicestershire, was twentieth wrangler of his year at Cambridge; and is very anxious now to see and learn as much as he can of civil engineering, with a view of directing his mechanical talents into that {direction} course of life.

I only wish I were at home in order to introduce him personally to you. \ He has been at Glasgow to see the different works there. /

Florence and Meta beg me to give you their love.

Yours most truly
E. C. Gaskell

John Geoffrey Sharps

1 (Sir) William Fairbairn (1789–1874), major engineering employer and inventor, awarded a Royal Society Gold medal in 1860 (Kidd, *Manchester,* pp. 31–2). He belonged to Cross Street Chapel's congregation, but was by this time 'withdrawn from any active share in business'.

2 A previously unknown correspondent (see *Letters,* p. 729): Robert Frewin Martin (1842–1912), son of the Reverend Robert Martin of Anstey Pastures, Leicestershire, and Selina (b. 1809), Mme Mohl's* niece.

GEORGE SMITH*

Thursday Morg
[?5 May 1864]

My dear Sir,

(You have got my pen-mender with you at Hampstead so I cannot write tidily –) I am rather disheartened at your 'regretting the Two Mothers'[1] – will you talk over my present story (i.-e of modern life, 40 years ago in a country town,) – with Meta, & then tell me which you would prefer – it or the Two Mothers – *as soon as you can. August* [double stress] for me (if you please) to begin it. I am dismayed to find how many of my pages 24 of yours will take.

Meta says you are so good 'and thoughtful of \ your / my peace of mind about the affair with Mr Fred Chapman.' She does not go into details, but *thank you very much.* I write in a hurry to try & catch you at your own house this evening, – when Meta can tell you something of the new plot; and please let me know your decision as to which it is to be as soon as you can. Does it really take 864 of my pages to make a 3 vol novel.

Yours most truly
E C Gaskell

National Library of Scotland
Printed by Chapple, *Etudes Anglaises* 33. 2 (1980), pp. 185–6.

1 An abandoned story (see *Letters*, pp. 712, 731).
2 ECG's most substantial novel, *Wives and Daughters*, which appeared in the *Cornhill Magazine* between August 1864 and January 1866; 2 vols, 1866.

MRS EMMA WILMOT[1]

[*c.* 25 June 1864]

My dear dear Mrs Wilmot

I must put a line or two into Marianne's note to say how *very* sorry I am for you. One can say nothing more at such a time. I, who have not been tried, can only faintly imagine what must be the depth of your grief – but God knows, and He will comfort you, as you know well dear friend, – in a way which makes all human sympathy seem poor and vain. Yet oh! I am so sorry for you – & Emma & Fanny – & the dear affectionate boys! I can hardly fancy a loss that will be more deeply felt, or by a larger number of people. I used to fancy when I was a child, that when I grew older I should understand the sad and mysterious things of this life; but somehow the older I grow the more sadness and the mystery deepen. 'The night is darkest before the dawn', May we see Light in God's Light when that time comes!

Your true and affectionate friend
E C. Gaskell.

Pierpont Morgan Library (Gordon Ray Collection)

1 Edward Wilmot died at Buxton on 25 June 1864.

ABIGAIL B. ADAMS[1]

Manchester
July 7th 1864

My dear Mrs Adams,

You see I am making no end of little notes to you; but this is to ask if there are any more *especial* autographs you would like to have? I think I have remembered all those you mentioned. Pray believe me remain ever yours very truly

E. C. Gaskell

Princeton University Library

1 A second letter (see *Letters,* p. 735) to Abigail B. Adams, née Brooks (1808–89), wife of Charles Francis Adams (1807–86), American ambassador to Britain 1861–8 during the American Civil War.

MRS FRANCES WEDGWOOD

Oak-Hill Lodge
Hampstead
Monday [July 1864]

My dear Mrs Wedgwood,

I am feeling so deeply for all of you, that I can hardly find words to express it. I only heard this morning from Meta. I could not help fancying that after all he might rally; if only for a time, as he did before when he had to go to Algeria; but now that all is ended one feels and *knows* how much happier, inconceivably so – it is for him, than a few more years of earthly struggle very probably through pain and suffering.[1] And now all that is over – and 'eye hath not seen, heart of man hath not conceived' the peace and blessedness of the home where he is. These last eight weeks must have been \ an / unspeakably precious time of intercourse to you, dear Mrs Wedgwood! It seems almost as if it was a blessing equal to the whole of his previous existence. And how good, & pure, and thoughtful that was! I think one read it in his face and ways, – and heard it in his clear and lofty opinions, whenever any point of duty was involved. Indeed his whole standard was, as far as I could judge, higher, than that of almost any *young* person I know. My dear love to Mr Wedgwood. We think so often of you both, – and of the solemn household of friends, whom we love so dearly. God bless and comfort you all; the comfort that will come in time is *quite sure*; the more you think about him that is 'gone before'.

Yours truly & most affectionately
E. C. Gaskell

Annotation ansd fm Ilfracombe / Aug 2 1864

Keele University Library (Wedgwood deposit)

1 James Mackintosh (1834–64), brother of Snow* and son of Hensleigh and Frances Wedgwood*, died from cancer on 24 June 1864.

FLORENCE NIGHTINGALE*

Plymouth Grove.
Manchester.
Decr 22. [1864]

My dear Miss Nightingale,

I have been very ill nearly all autumn, or you would have sooner had some acknowledgment of what you have so kindly sent me; ending today with your letters about Pastor Fliedner's family.[1] It is in vain that you put *'not* to beg' – No other words of \ even / yours could prevent one's longing to give one's mite to help those of whom you tell one such noble things.

It is indeed almost more for one's own sake than Madame Fliedner's that one wishes to give: as a safety-valve for one's deep admiration, and grateful recognition of such an example as she and her husband have set –

Hoping that you are not suffering much, and that it is not a mockery to wish you a Happy New Year,

I am ever affly yours,
E. C. Gaskell.

Brotherton Library, Leeds University

1 *Death of Pastor Fliedner, of Kaiserwerth*: three letters, dated 21 Oct., 21 Nov., 10 Dec. 1864.

VERNON LUSHINGTON*

46 Plymouth Grove
Manchester
January 11th [1865]

My dear Mr Lushington,

Your news, as you conjectured has given us all great pleasure, for, though we never heard of Miss Mowatt[1] before, your account of her charming qualities makes us feel as if you had indeed drawn a prize; only, please, we want to know ever so much more. Where does she live? How long have you known her? Do we know any one that knows her, so that we may have a chance of hearing an *impartial* account of one who is going to become the wife of a valued friend.

I dare say you will not find time to answer all these enquiries; but if you will, we shall be so very glad to have our real interest in you gratified by hearing something more about your future wife. What a pleasant hopeful time of the year to begin a new relationship! I always feel as if with the new year come new hopes, new life, new light!

We all send you our kindest regards, & best wishes.

Ever yours very truly
E. C. Gaskell.

P S. We shall keep you to your promise of making us known to her.

Address Vernon Lushington / King's Bench Walk / Temple / *E. C.* / London.
Stamp, postmarks MANCHESTER / Z12 / JA 11 / 65 *and* A /. <LON>DON / <JA>12 / 65.
Annotation 1865.

Princeton University Library

1 In 1865 Lushingon married one of the daughters of F. Mowatt, formerly MP for Penrhyn and Cambridge.

GEORGE SMITH*

46 Plymouth Grove
Monday, January 16 [1865]

My dear Mr Smith,

Thank you very much for your prompt attention in the matter of Cranfords.[1] – I am sorry to plague you with any business, – but, if you will allow one of your clerks to ack[now]ledge a registered *post* parcel of MSS I am sending off today, you[altered word] may put this letter away, until 'Wives and Daughters' comes before your notice again. (How I wish the wretched story could be[altered word] put out of *my* head as easily[altered word] as you can put away this note.)[2]

You know I dare say that you have several times exceeded the 'about 24 pages' you told me at first you would like to publish in each number. That is the reason I send you *119*[double stress] pages now. If I don't the March (or February) Nos will fall short, as the last did, (only 22 pages, if I remember rightly.) But would you please put *all*[double stress]*the Ball* into one number, – and if you can, – end one no just after the Squire's quarrel with Mr Preston *about* page 516 or 17 – I have made a mark.

Am I limited[word double stressed] to *16* numbers? I am afraid the story is getting on so slowly tha<t> I must either condense, (& spoil it,) or put more in a number, or have more numbers. But I will *try* not. I wish it was ended & done with. So I dare say you do with this letter, consequently I am ever yours most truly

E C Gaskell

Eton College Library

1 Smith Elder took over the copyright in *Cranford* in 1860, and published an illustrated edition in 1864. See also *Letters*, p. 719 n.,

2 E. Haldane, *Mrs. Gaskell and Her Friends*, p. 300, quotes a sentence that may come from an unknown letter by ECG: 'Oh, I am so tired of my story ... I dream about it'.

JOHN RUSKIN[1]

46 Plymouth Grove
February 24 [1865]

My dear Mr Ruskin

Thank you so very much for what you have done. We sent off your last note, – enclosing Mr Cowper's, – to Mr Waterhouse,[2] within ten minutes after receiving it. I can't tell you how grateful I am. I want to do something for you, straight, slap-away. You can't tell me what, – can you?

And then again about 'Cranford[']. I am so much pleased you like it. It is the only one of my own books that I can read again; but whenever I am ailing or ill, I take 'Cranford' and – I was going to say '*enjoy*' it, but that would not be pretty, – laugh over it afresh. And it is true too, for I have seen the cow that wore the grey flannel jacket, and I knew the cat that swallowed the lace, that belonged to the lady, that sent for the doctor, that gave the emetic &c &c.

I am so glad your mother likes it too. I will tell her a bit more of 'Cranford' that I did not dare to put in, because I thought people would say it was too ridiculous, and yet which really happened in Knutsford.

Two good old ladies, friends of mine in my girlhood, had a niece who had made a grand marriage, as grand marriages went in those days & that place: (to Sir Ed. Cust.)[3] The bride & bridegroom came to stay with the two Aunts – who had bought a new dining room carpet as a sort of wedding welcome to the young couple. But I am afraid it was rather lost upon them, for the first time they found it out was after dinner the day after they came. All dinner time they had noticed that the neat maid-servant had performed a sort of 'pas-de-basque' hopping & sliding with more grace than security to the dishes she held. When she had left the room one lady said to the other 'Sister! I think she'll do.' 'Yes!' said the other 'she managed very nicely'. And then they began to explain that she was a fresh servant, & they had just had laid down a new carpet with white spots or spaces on it; and that they had been teaching this girl to vault or jump gracefully over these white places, for fear lest her feet might dirty them.

The beginning of Cranford was *one* paper in Household Words,[4] – and I never meant to write more; so killed poor Capt Brown, – very much against my will. See what you have drawn down upon yourself, by gratifying me so much. I'll stop now, however.

Yours gratefully & truly
E. C. Gaskell

Envelope John Ruskin Esq / Denmark Hill / London

Stamp, Postmarks K / FE 24 / MANCHESTER / 1865 / 30 *and* LONDON / 7J / FE 25 / 65

Harvard University Library, Murdoch ms 17
Full text of Letter 562, from MS.

1 John Ruskin (1819–1900), artist, thinker and critic. His career as author of major works on art history and his incisive social commentary earned him legendary status among his contemporaries and ever since.
2 See *Letters*, pp. 742–3, and p. 270 n. 1 below.
3 Sir Edward Cust (1794–1878), general and military historian. He married in 1821 Mary Anne Boode (c. 1800–82) of Peover Hall, Cheshire, who 'wrote a book on cats being a great fancier of those animals' (*DNB*).
4 The germ of *Cranford*, a story-article, appeared in *Sartain's Union Magazine* for July 1849.

LORD HOUGHTON [R. MONCKTON MILNES*]

46 Plymouth Grove
Manchester.
Febry 20 [?1865]

My dear Lord Houghton,

I am afraid you have never seen our Manchester Assize Courts; but I hope you have heard of them. Of course we are proud of them; and we value extremely the friendship of their architect, a young man of the name of Alfred Waterhouse, (who married a great friend of the Miss Sterlings, one of the Foxs of Cornwall.) {Both} The Times, the Saturday Review, Mr Gladstone, Mr Ruskin have expressed their great admiration for this work; the judges \ and Bar / have valued it's utility and perfect adaptation to it's ends. Mr Waterhouse has told me today, in great dismay, that he had been given to understand that his name is *ex*cluded from the limited number of competitors, (6 he believes) who are to try for the *London* Law Courts. These architects are appointed by Mr W. Cowper (the Commissioner? of Woods & Forests, or Board of Works or something.)[1]

Mr Waterhouse is gone up to London this afternoon to try and get the liberty of competing; but his best hope is in Mr Bazley,[2] our good inartistic M P. For Mr Waterhouse is delicate, and does not like asking Mr Gladstone to speak to Mr Cowper, 'for it is not right to ask one minister to apply any pressure on another.' Mr Gladstone has seen the Assize Courts and admires them extremely. Can you help Mr Waterhouse? He is such a first-rate fellow, in more ways than architecture; and we have known for some years that his great ambition was to try for the London Law Courts. He knows nothing about my writing in his behalf, so please if you blame any one for troubling you with this request let it be me.

I will {enclo} send you by this post a remarkable pamphlet of his, which has had the effect of converting a Trades Union! It is not every architect who would offer to withdraw himself from the completion of his work so that the work might be completed.

Yours very truly
E. C. Gaskell

Trinity College, Cambridge

1 Alfred Waterhouse (1830–1905) practised in Manchester 1853–65. His Assize Courts date from 1859; his Manchester Town Hall was opened in 1877. In 1866 he was selected as a competitor for the London Law Courts, but the the commission was awarded to George Edmund Street. William Cowper(-Temple) was the appointing politician.
2 Cf. p. 231 n. 2.

EMILY SHAEN*

120 Rue du Bac
Sunday
[c. 26 March 1865]

My dearest Emily,

I think you will like to hear how I am going on in Paris. It is a very amusing life; and I'll try and describe a day to you. Mme Mohl lives on the fourth and fifth stories of a great large hotel built about 150 years ago, entre cour et jardin, – 'cour' opening into the narrow busy rue du Bac, 'jardin' being a very large (10 acres) plot of ground given by Cardinal Richelieu to the Missions Etrangeres[*sic*], – and so not built upon, but surrounded by great houses like this. It is as stiffly laid out in kitchen gardens square walks &c as possible; but there are great trees in it, and altogether it is really very pretty. That's at the *back* of the house, and some of the rooms look on to it. [Small diagram showing 'Rue du Bac, Porte Cochere[*sic*], Madame Mohl's rooms, Garden'.]

On the *fourth* story are four lowish sitting rooms & Mme Mohl's bedroom. On the *fifth* sloping in the roof, kitchen grénier[*sic*], servant's bedrooms, my bedroom, wood-room &c; all brick floors, which *is* cold to the feet. My bedroom is very funny & picturesque, – I like sloping roofs, & plenty of windows stuffed into their roof any how; and in every corner of this room (& it's the same all over the house) french & English books are *crammed*. I have no watch, there is no clock in the house, & so I have to guess the time by the monk's singing & bells ringing, (all night-long but) especially in the morning. So I get up, & come down into the smallest & shabbiest of the sitting rooms, in which we live & eat all day long, and find that M. Mohl has had his breakfast of chocolate in *his* room (library) at ½ past 6, & Mme Mohl hers of tea at 7, and I am late having not come down (to coffee) at a little past eight. However I take it coolly, and M & Mme come in and talk to me; she in dressing gown & curlpapers; very very amusing he, very sensible & agreeable, & full of humour too.

I'll give you one or two specimens of Mme Mohl's witty expressions – Speaking of *men*-cooks in great families she calls them '*tom*-cooks'. Another day 'Let me see what year it was in – 1860 I went to see the play in the Ammergau 1861, Mr Mohl *worried the baker*' 'What do you mean?' oh you know we stayed with Hilary Carter[1] at Kensington – & a baker kept the post office, & he never had any foreign stamps, and M. Mohl wanted them every day, & was always going for them, till at last the baker said 'Sir Sir! you will worry me to death', – and he *did die* soon after – (M. Mohl the most goodnatured of men stands by & smiles –) 1862 I was eaten by bugs \ at Mrs Schwabe's house /, 1863 &c &c.

Then after my breakfast – which lingers long because of all this talk I get my writing 'Wives & Daughters', and write, as well as I can, for Mme Mohl's talking till 'second' breakfast, about 11. – Cold meat, bread, wine & water, & sometimes an omelette, – what we should call lunch in fact, – only it comes too soon after my breakfast, & too long before dinner for my English habits. After breakfast no 2 I *try* to write again; and very often callers come; always on Wednesdays on which day Mme Mohl receives. I go out a walk \ by myself / in the afternoons; & when we dine at home it is at six *sharp*. No dressing required. Soup, meat, one dish of vegetables, & roasted apples are what we have in general. After dinner M. & Mme Mohl go to sleep; & I have fallen into their habit; and at eight exactly M Mohl wakens up, and makes a cup of *very* weak tea for Mme Mohl & me – nothing to eat after dinner, ever; not even if we have been to the Play. Then Mme Mohl rouses herself up, & is very amusing & brilliant; stops up till one, & would stop up later, if encouraged by her listeners.

She has not been well, but for all that she has seen a good number of people since I came; she has generally a dinner party of 10 or 12 every Friday, when we spread out into all the rooms (& I am so glad; for continual living & eating in this room, & no open windows makes it very stuffy,) and '*receive*' in the evening. Guizot has dined here, & Mignet, & Montalambert since I came; & many other notabilities of less fame.[2] But every body stays up the first half of the night, as I should call it. When we go out for the evening we go to dress directly after our after dinner nap & tea; and first cross the court-yard in snow or slop, to the Porter's lodge, opening into the Rue du Bac, & send him for a coach. We jigget to some *very* smart house (for all Mme Mohl's friends are very smart people & live in very grand houses, –) curtsey as low as we possibly can to the Master of the house, & shake hands with the Missus; sit down, & in general, have a great deal of very beautiful music from the Masters of the Conservatoire, quartetts & quintetts; make a buzz of talk, look at the fine dresses, & come home as hungry as a hawk about one AM.

I am going out a great deal to dinner; last night I dined at a Russian house, a real Russian dinner. First soup, made of mutton and sourkraut[*sic*]; very nasty & horrible to smell. Then balls or rissolles very good; fish, rice, eggs, & *cabbage* all chopped up together, and cased in bread. Then caviar, & smoked fish handed round, with bread & butter. Then sweetbreads done in some extraordinary fashion – then eels, chopped up with mushrooms, lemon juice & mustard. – Then rôti of some common sort; then gelinottes[*sic*] or Russian partridges, which feed on the young sprouts of the pine trees, & taste strong of turpentine. Then a sweet soup, full of raisins & currants like plum-pudding boiled in orange-flower water. I think that was all, – it was all I took at any rate.

The gentlemen hand the ladies back to the drawing-room just as they have handed them *in* to dinner. The other night M. Guizot and M. de Montalambert dined here; the latter speaks English as easily as he does French; and was very eager about the american war; abusing the English for their conduct towards the Northerners & professing the warmest interest in the North. We never see any newspapers here, so we don't know what is going on. Guizot (who is 78) looks *much* older since I saw him last. Goodbye my dearest Emily; for I am suddenly called off.

Your own affect friend ECG.

[On envelope, in ECG's hand:]You *must* eat some meat.[3] /francs / I've no read it yet.

Envelope Mrs W. Shaen / The Red House / Upper Phillimore Gardens / Kensington / *London.*
Stamp; postmarks PARIS / 5e 27 / MARS / 65 *and* LONDON / MR28/65.

Haworth Parsonage Museum
MS substituting Letter 564, printed from Elizabeth Haldane, *Mrs. Gaskell and Her Friends,* 1930, pp. 296–300.

1 Hilary Bonham Carter (1821–9 September 1865), a friend of Mme Mohl* from 1842 (Lesser, p. 110), became Florence Nightingale's* confidante.
2 François Mignet (1796–1884) wrote a history of the French Revolution, 1824, and *Mémoires historiques*, 1843. Charles, Comte de Montalambert was a Catholic controversialist who proposed the restriction of the influence of the Church beyond religious matters.
3 From late 1862, Emily Shaen's health was precarious (*L & M,* II. 387, 421).

MADAME SCHERER[1]

120 Rue du Bac
Tuesday morng [11 April 1865]

My dear Madame Scherer,

I *am* so overdone with the heat, and our going to Passy yesterday, and to the Lyrique at night that I am afraid I shall be quite ill, if I go off again in the heat of the day to Versailles. I am only sorry to think you will have the trouble of sending to meet me! I have nothing but winter clothes here; and I am really afraid of being completely incapacitated for writing my story unless I take care of my precious and troublesome head; which begins to ache so very easily; & to be so much affected by glare and heat.

I am very sorry for it on all accounts: for I should very much have enjoyed spending an hour or two with you all, & seeing you & possibly M. Scherer again. Pray accept of my love, & believe me always yours most truly

E C Gaskell.

Envelope À Madame / Madame Schérer / Rue Royale 92 / *Versailles* / (Seine et Oise).
Stamp, postmarks PARIS / 11 / AVRIL / 65 *and* VERSAILLES 6 DIST. / 11 / AVRIL / 65.

Princeton University Library

1 Wife of Edmond Schérer (1815–89), philosopher and critic.

GEORGIANA, LADY CHATTERTON[1]

Plymouth Grove
Manchester
June 16 [1865].

Dear Madam,

When you were good enough to send me your translation of Plato,[2] I was abroad: and ... (I am ashamed to tell it of my own children!) my daughters who were receiving my letters &c for me at home, not only forgot to tell me of the fact, but cunningly hid the book away in some safe place so that it was only last night that I \ first / heard of it! I am so grieved for the appearance of ingratitude that I must have worn: but indeed I am far from feeling it. I have always had the greatest interest in Plato's works, but being no Greek scholar, have to depend on other people's labour for my acquaintance with them. I promise myself the greatest treat in reading your extracts; which I see at a glance are first rate translations, inasmuch as that fact is nowhere apparent.

Ever with much regret for the delay that there has been in my acknowledgment of your most kind present, I remain sincerely yours

E. C. Gaskell.

Endorsed 16 June 1865 / Mrs Gaskell

The Shakespeare Birthplace Trust, Stratford (DR 495 / 99)

1 Georgiana, Lady Chatterton (1806–76), author of fiction, poetry and travel literature.

2 *Selections from the Works of Plato* (1862).

~

Letter 578 from 46 Plymouth Grove, 24 August [?1865] probably to R. Monckton Miles

~

ROUTLEDGE & WARNE[1]

The Lawn,
Holybourn
Alton, Hants
October 30. [1865]

3/6 Stamps

Mrs Gaskell presents her compliments to Messrs Routledge & Warne, and begs to acknowledge the safe receipt of 'Susan Hopley', and 'Lilly Dawson, for which, & for the postage she encloses 3s–6d worth of postage stamps. But she *particularly* wanted 'Linny Lockwood'[2] which she has never read, & for which she has many times enquired from different booksellers; and she would be *very* much obliged to Messrs Routledge, if they would find her a copy, – (if not clean she does not *much* mind) & send it her *at once*[.]

Princeton University Library

1 George Routledge (1812–88) began publishing in London with his brother-in-law W. H. Warne and, from 1851, Frederick Warne. In 1848 began their successful 'Railway Library' of 1s. reprints, often of pirated American works like *Uncle Tom's Cabin*.

2 Three novels of the 1850s in the series by Mrs Catherine Crowe (1790–1876), novelist, children's writer and spiritualist. They were published in 1841, 1847 and 1853 respectively. The first two embody the Cinderella theme of an apparently working-class girl who discovers her concealed gentility, and true love; it may have some general application to *Wives and Daughters*.

MRS HOLLAND[1]

89 Oxford Terrace[2]
Friday [?1865]

My dear Mrs Holland,

I am very sorry to say an unforeseen engagement will prevent my coming to lunch with you on Sunday next

Yours most truly
E. C. Gaskell

Fitzwilliam Museum, Cambridge

1 In a Sir Henry Holland album; transcribed by Bella Stewart. His wife Saba (née Smith) would have been Lady Holland by this date.

2 The address of ECG's daughter, Mrs Florence Crompton (*Letters*, p. 766).

?EMIL or JAMES REISS[1]

[?1865]

My dear Mr Reiss,

I have sent you another note besides that to Ly Brodie. It is to Mr Harcourt, a great friend of ours, an old Balliol man, – that is to say he is now 28,[2] – but a Ch. Ch. Student now. He is the eldest son of Admiral Vernon-Harcourt, but has rather surprized his father by taking warmly to natural science, instead of to any profession. We all like him extremely and so I think you will too, if you care to present this note. He is Harrow, of Dr Vaughan's days; I don't know if you care for an introduction to any of the dons, – Canon Stanley Ch. Ch? – Dr Acland? the Max Müllers? Mr Henry Smith? the Liddells, – who however confine themselves pretty much to Ch. Ch. The Brodies will be at Cowley for some time, owing to Sir Benjamin's health.

Yours very truly
E C Gaskell

Pierpont Morgan Library

1 'Beiss', in *Letters*, p. 720, is an error.
2 Augustus Vernon Harcourt. Cf. p. 242 n. 3.

UNDATED LETTERS

MR & MRS VALENTINE BARTHOLOMEW[1]

39 Green Street,[2]
Grosvenor Sq.
January 23. [?1864–65][3]

Mrs Gaskell regrets very much that a previous engagement will prevent her accepting Mr and Mrs Valentine Bartholomew's very kind invitation for the evening of the 29th instant.

Pierpont Morgan Library (Gordon Ray Collection)

1 Not identified.
2 ECG is not known to have stayed at this address.
3 A carte de visite photograph of WG in later years accompanies this note.

GEORGINA [?BEHRENS]*[1]

Saturday Evening
Octr 29

My dear Georgina,

The enclosed packet *is* the watches, (Flossy's & Julias) with letters enclosed both from M. [?]Oudin and myself, explaining matters. I shall be very much obliged to you if you can get them conveyed by a private hand *to Mr Martin's*, before the year of guarantee expires, in December.

Yours ever affectionately
E C Gaskell

Manchester Central Library

1 ECG seems to have known the Behrens family since 1858. See *Letters*, pp. 513, 784.

MISS BELL[1]

121, Upper Rumford St
[1842 – July 1850]
Saturday.

My dear Miss Bell,

It will give Mr Gaskell and myself great pleasure to avail ourselves of your very kind invitation to meet Lady Bell[3] at your house, on the evening of Friday, the 30th. Pray give my very kind regards to your sisters, and believe me to remain

Very truly yours
E. C. Gaskell

Princeton University Library

1 Probably one of Dr Charles W. Bell's sisters; they lived at 94 Mosley Street, Manchester.

2 The Manchester directory for 1841 shows the Gaskells were still living in Dover Street.

3 Wife of Sir Charles Bell? ECG was with her in London in 1853 (*Letters*, p. 232). See p. 73 above.

HENRY A. BRIGHT*

42 Plymouth Grove
Wednesday

My dear Mr Bright,

I am very glad to hear from you again, as I half feared you might still have been annoyed by my fault-finding letter about the Tuesday Committee. Thank you for the very interesting details in your letter. Why should you not come up & see us tomorrow – to have luncheon (at one) or dinner at \ 5 *or* / 6, & go with us to a Congregational party, – & sleep here, – (or if you liked it better \ to / return to Liverpool when we go to our Congregational party). \ only you *ought* to take a little Unitarianism *pure*, now & then. / Any time however you are welcome, & should be either fed or starved as you liked best. – In greatest haste, please bring back L. G.'s repentance

Yours very truly
E C Gaskell

Princeton University Library

RICHARD COBDEN*

46 Plymouth Grove
Manchester
July 28 [?1862–64][1]

My dear Mr Cobden,

I wonder if you are over-done with letters asking for your advice & influence, but if you are, I am still going to add one to them. Please we are very much interested in an orphan-boy named Edwin Wood, who has been brought up as a pupil-teacher in the Lower-Mosely St school, and who showed both an uncommon character, and unusual ability until (three years ago, and he is now 17,) his health broke down, partly from hereditary tendency, partly from too confined an employment and over-study. He has been in the consumptive Hospital at Broughton for some time, and has come back so much better that the doctor now says a few years of sea-life would make a strong man of him. So we are trying every possible person to get him some *sea*-employment. He is as trustworthy intelligent and good a lad as ever lived; pretty well grown, but of course not up to feats of strength. I could trust him with – not merely untold gold, but my interests; for I think his judgement bids fair to keep apace with his other talents. He knows French – (*book*-french) is a good accountant, and generally remarkable for intelligence.

Is there any way of getting him employment in the P & O. Company's Service? or as a purser's clerk, – or any where on sea, or at a (warm) \ Southern / sea-port where a lad of *character* [double underline] and education could be useful. I am sorry to say we must try for him to earn money, as well as to strengthen his health; for he has an Aunt, as well as a little brother & sister who may become dependent on him in a few years. He is very anxious himself to go to sea.

With kind remembrances to Mrs Cobden and your daughter believe me to be

Yours most truly
E. C. Gaskell

West Sussex Record Office (Cobden Papers 17)

1 The Plymouth Grove number changed to 46 c. April 1860; Richard Cobden* died in April 1865. In July 1860 ECG was in Heidelberg; in July 1861 in Silverdale. The County Archivist, R. J. Childs, reports that the watermark may be 1862 or 1863.

LADY CREWE[1]

< ... > the funeral &c depend on me: so that our going is really quite out of the question. I am very sorry; for I should have liked it much. Never mind. 'Better luck next time.' The next time the Miss Grevilles[2] come

to Crewe, we must plan early in their visit for you all to come over here. – I am afraid it is impossible from what you say, this time. And will you thank Lord Crewe *really*, for me:- & fully explain to him my seeming rudeness, & how gladly, under other circumstances I would have come. I am writing any how & way; for I find a bewilderment of work of all kinds awaiting me, – & shall have to be very busy; a fit payment for pleasure. – I *wish* we could meet – and 'my cousin Kate Greville' too.

Yours ever most truly
E C Gaskell

Annotation To Lady Crewe incomplete.

Princeton University Library

1 Henrietta Crewe (died unmarried 1874); Annabel m. Monckton Milnes* in 1851. They were sisters of Hungerford Crewe, 3rd Baron Crewe (1812–94, unmarried).
2 Not identified.

MISS HALL[1]

46 Plymouth Grove
April 12th [?1861–62, 1864][2]

My dear Miss Hall,

I am very sorry that I cannot attend the Committee of the Clinical Hospital this morning; but I am in the doctor's hands, and quite incapable of it. I regret it the less, however, as I have failed to hear of a Housekeeper, though I have written in several directions, and therefore should have been of less use than I had hoped to be.

Ever yours most truly
E. C. Gaskell.

Princeton University Library (Dictated?)

1 Not identified.
2 Change of house number suggests post–1861. ECG was abroad in April 1863 and April 1865.

LOUISA CROFT (née HOLLAND)[1]

[?1861–65][2]

< ... > universal signs of depression are very sad to look upon.

Marianne & Meta desire their very kind love to you, dear Louisa.

Your very affect cousin
E. C. Gaskell.

Pierpont Morgan Library (Gordon Ray Collection)

1 ECG's schoolfellow and first cousin Louisa (1810–98), daughter of Swinton Colthurst and Anne Holland; she married the Reverend Richard Croft[*sic*], Vicar of Hillingdon in 1857. See *EY*, pp. 245, 333, 444.

2 Perhaps a reference to the Lancashire Cotton Famine.

LUCY HOLLAND[1]

Wednesday Aft:

My dear Lucy

I begin to be anxious about the Refrigerator; it has never made it's appearance; and as, although it is not hot weather, yet we are going to be a large party in the house soon, I should be very glad to have it soon.

Your affect. cousin
E. C. Gaskell

Princeton University Library

1 Lucy (1800–83), older Knutsford cousin, daughter of Peter and Mary Holland.

A. MIGSON

BL, Department of MSS, RP 5312. Photocopy: access reserved until August 2000.

MRS J. D. MORELL[1]

Tuesday afternoon ½ p. 2.

My dearest Mrs Morell,

I have put it off to the last minute but now my cold is so bad, and growing so much worse that I am afraid it would not be prudent for me to go to you this afternoon, so I am sending a messenger over to tell you so. *You know* how very sorry I am, don't you, – but please you must let me come some other time, & before long. My conversation would have consisted of sneezes and blowings of the nose. My love to Dr Morell –

Yours ever affectionately
E C Gaskell

John Geoffrey Sharps

1 Wife of John D. Morell (1816–91), Inspector of Schools. In April 1851 ECG, Mrs Davenport* of Capesthorne and Dr Morell 'joggled in a coach to Swinton', Lancashire, to inspect the school there. Afterwards, Mr and Mrs Morell came to tea. See *Letters*, p. 150.

?MRS BONAMY PRICE

<... > weary of the splendid view.

Now, if I have omitted anything in my 'screed' that you think I can tell you, and that you want to know, please write and ask for the further information. It is a *real* pleasure to be able to help you, dear Mrs Price.

Ever yours affe,
E. C. Gaskell.

Princeton University Library (incomplete).

MRS SUSANNA SCHUNCK[*]

Thursday morning.

My dear Mrs Schunck,

My little girls are very anxious to go and thank you for your two beautiful presents, which quite formed the ornament of our table; and Mr Gaskell and I quite intended to call, and thank you yesterday morning, but I was too poorly to leave the sofa. You must allow us to say how very much as parents we were touched and gratified by your kind recollection of our dear little maidens. With kindest wishes for a merry Christmas and a happy new year to all your circle, I remain,

Your sincere & obliged friend
E. C. Gaskell.

Huntington University Library, Irvine Collection

MRS SUSANNA SCHUNCK[*]

< ... > them, before undertaking so long a journey; he will not leave them till Frida<y,> in time to return for his duties on Sunday. Marianne, Meta and I will come by the 3 <[lower portion cut off]> may be a happy new year to both you and Mr Schunck, and all in whom you are interested.

I remain dear Mrs Schunck

Yours very truly
E. C. Gaskell.

Huntington University Library, Irvine Collection

WILLIAM SHAEN*

Wednesday Afternoon
[1851–58][1]

My dearest Will,

If Mr Gaskell comes to you, *tomorrow* \ Thursday / night can you give him a bed? He has to preach in Todmorden, Yorkshire, on Sunday morning. I must leave Crix[1] in time to get either home here, (in whh case he would go on to Todmorden on Sunday morng,) or by Great Northern to Todmorden on Saturday Evening. He has telegraphed to Crix (just before leaving home for a day & a night) to say he would be there on Friday evening, 6–48 train; but I do so dislike the idea of the long day's journey on Friday, then again on Saturday, & hard work on Sunday, that I shall urge him to break the journey by getting as far as Bedford Row tomorrow.

He is at the Edmund Potters[2] at Dinting until tomorrow morning. My dear Will, I think a great deal of you all this week.

Yours affectionate Lily

Haworth Parsonage Museum

1 William and Emily Shaen went to live at 8 Bedford Row c. June 1851 (*L & M,* I. 292); Crix was sold at the end of August 1858 (*L & M,* II. 209 and n.)

2 Edmund Potter (1802–83), MP, calico printer, of Dinting Vale, near Glossop. In 1865 ECG wrote that her husband '*always* goes to the Edmund Potters in his holidays'. Mrs Potter said she had asked him to bring his wife, 'but if she has, he has never told me of it' (*Letters,* p. 759).

MRS ?CATHERINE STANLEY[1]

36 Bloomsbury Sq
Saturday Eveng
[?1853–55][2]

My dear Mrs Stanley,

I shall be most happy to breakfast with you on Friday morning at 10 o'clock. Will you allow me to leave Mr Gaskell acceptance open, as he is dining with his brother,[3] and I do not know what engagements he may make with him; the two brothers have not many opportunities of meeting each other, and are glad to be as much together as possible.

Yours very sincerely
E. C. Gaskell

Princeton University Library

1 Probably the widow of Bishop Edward Stanley.

2 ECG was with Mrs Dove, 36 Bloomsbury Square in summer 1853 and in February 1855 (*Letters,* pp. 233, 238, 331).

3 Dr Samuel Gaskell.

MRS STUART[1]

46, Plymouth Grove.
November the 15th
[?post-April 1860][2]

My dear Mrs Stuart,

It would give Mr Gaskell and myself great pleasure if you and Mr Stuart and your daughter would think it worth while to spend next Friday Evening very quietly with us, to meet a few friends – at 8 o'clock.

With Mr Gaskell's kind regards I remain

Yours sincerely
E C Gaskell

Princeton University Library (Dictated?)

1 Not identified.

2 Address now *46* Plymouth Grove.

MRS J. J. TAYLER[1]

[1855–65]

My dear Mrs Tayler,

Though I have never offered myself to you for two days as Mr Tayler so very kindly begged me to do, yet indeed I have often remembered the invitation with pleasure, & wished that it had been in my power to avail myself of it – I left London almost directly after that day when you called & found me out at Mrs[altered word] Wedgwood's. I was obliged to leave the day I did, as I had promised some friends in Staffordshire[2] not to delay my visit to them later than that date, as they were on the point of leaving their house, & could only have received me at great inconvenience if I had stayed on in London for even two days. However I hope you will allow me to consider my visit to you \ as / postponed merely; & I must beg you not to { } \ think / that I have lost the right of being asked again by my delay in writing to explain why I did not take advantage of Mr Tayler's invitation this Spring.

I have been thinking much of your arrangement of the 'Brook' which I had the pleasure of hearing you sing when I dined with you. I wonder whether you will allow me to ask if you do not think that the perpetuity of motion of a Brook would not be well[?] given by repeating that pretty refrain

'For[altered word] men may come
And men may go &c

Princeton University Library (incomplete) [Tennyson's 'The Brook': refrain]

1 Wife of John James Tayler (p. 26 n. 11); moved to London in 1853.

2 Perhaps Lord and Lady Hatherton (married in 1852) at Teddesley Park.

MRS TAYLOR[1]

Plymouth Grove
Manchester
May 24.

My dear Mrs Taylor,

I don't know when I have been more gratified than I was yesterday by your note. In the first place you must know that I 'highly approved' of your engagement, which I heard of about a month ago from Miss Chorley: and which made me feel just as glad & as happy as a piece of personal good news would have done. Last year I planned it in my own mind; and thought it most fitting, and hoped for it, without feeling in the least sure that there was any real likelihood of it's coming to pass. But independently of all this gladness of mine in your engagement, I think it was so kind of you & Mr Taylor to remember me on your wedding-tour, and to send me that little note along with the cards. You see I conclude you are on your wedding-tour but I am right, am I not? I always meant to try and tempt you to come & see me, when we had an unusually good concert; and now you won't care for our Manchester music, or gaieties, or shows, or anything! Never mind! that is only a momentary feeling of rather selfish disappointment. I give you my heartiest good wishes. And I hope to come and see you both in your own home some day; but not this summer. I have eaten my cake for this year; I passed through London and stayed there a fortnight about a month ago; when I heard of your engagement. I thought of writing to you then to congratulate you, – (though I am not quite sure if Mr Taylor is not *the* person to be congratulated,) and then I hesitated, & wondered if you would like it, & 'thought better' of it; i.e. thought that I had once rather forced myself upon you, and that now you would be so full of new interests that I had no right to intrude.{)} So don't you see how charmingly your note came[altered word] upon this frame of mind?

My very kind regards to your husband. I was disappointed not to see him this year till I knew the reason why.

Ever yours very truly
E. C. Gaskell

Princeton University Library

1 Not identified.

MRS TRUEMAN[1]

Plymouth Grove,
Febry 22nd

Mrs Gaskell presents her compliments to Mrs Trueman, and is afraid she must plead guilty to the unconscious theft of the pocket-handkerchief which Mrs Trueman missed last night.

Mrs Gaskell *found* it in her hand, and can only hope that Mrs Trueman will put a kind interpretation on that very suspicious fact.

Princeton University Library

1 Not identified.

MRS VAUGHAN[1]

42 Plymouth Grove
Decr 10.

Mrs Gaskell presents her compliments to Mrs Vaughan, and begs to enclose her the accompanying autographs; with a request that if any of them shd happen to be duplicates of those already in Mrs Vaughan's possession, she will return these.

Princeton University Library (Dictated?)

1 Perhaps the wife of Robert Vaughan (1795–1868), President of Lancashire Independent College, Manchester, 1843–57. ECG met the Vaughans at a party in [Late December ?1853], 'every body out of tune with each other & with the piano' (*Letters*. p. 261).

?WINKWORTH[1]

Do you take? You're to *give* Susanna* 4s – 5d & a book left for me at your house.

Ever your affect.
E C Gaskell

Haworth Parsonage Museum

1 Winkworth / Shaen material from Leeds Archives (see Sharps, p. 688) This is written at the end of a note by Sydney Williams, which mentions a payment to Mr Shaw.

S–?

[c. 1850–55]

Dearest S.

(This is the only bit of paper I can find.) I can't get those two things for myself – but I think the best places to *try* would be, *Sexton's Hero.*[1] Either Johnson & Rawson[2] Corporation St Manchester or a Macclesfield Bookseller.

Libbie Marsh.[3] Either Hale & Howorth[*sic*][4] *here*, or Marples Lord St Liverpool. We are in a royal commotion

Yours ever very affecly
E C Gaskell

John Geoffrey Sharps
Written on both sides of an undated scrap.

1 'The Sexton's Hero' was first published in *Howitt's Journal* in 1847, and later sold as a sixpenny pamphlet at Capesthorne Fête, published by Johnson, Rawson and Co. in 1850. See Smith, p. 228.
2 Johnson and Rawson were former apprentices of Thomas Forrest, 'the only bookseller who would allow the publications of the Unitarian body to lie on his counter'. They took over in 1853. See Slugg, *Reminiscences of Manchester,* p. 80.
3 'Libbie Marsh's Three Eras' appeared first in *Howitt's Journal,* and was published separately in [1850] by David Marples in Liverpool. ECG's cousin Fanny Holland arranged this; then 'that wretched man at Liverpool' went on 'republishing ad infinitum' (*Letters,* pp. 122, 172). See Smith, pp. 227–30.
4 William Hale and Thomas Roworth (d. 1881), apprentices who formed a partnership, first in King Street, then Cross Street (Slugg, pp. 85, 333).

ANON

Madam,

I was extremely obliged to you for the little Crotchet books, which my daughters hope to find very useful. I should have acknowledged them sooner but have been in Scotland until today.

The complimentary paragraph only amused me, as it did not apply to me; if it had, I should not have liked your sending it to me. The portrait in question was of a Mrs Gaskell in Oxfordshire.

Yours truly
E C Gaskell

Princeton University Library

ANON

46 Plymouth Grove
Manchester
Decr 6th [April 1860–64]

Dear Sir,

I have very much pleasure in sending you an autograph. I only wish I could mend pens, and then you should see how beautifully I could write!

Yours very truly
Elizabeth Cleghorn Gaskell.

Princeton University Library

ANON

My dear Sir,

We shall be very glad indeed to see you on Saturday next, – and only regret that you are wicked enough to think of leaving us on the Sunday.

With kind regards to your family circle. Believe me

Yours very sincerely
E. C. Gaskell

Princeton University Library

ANON

46 Plymouth Grove
Saturday Evening [April 1860–65]

< ... > thoughts, and we could not have a pleasanter one than you will supply. In great haste,

Yours most truly
E. C. Gaskell

Fales Library, New York University (transcribed by Stephen Gill)

ANON

46 Plymouth Grove
January 16th [1861–65]

My dear Sir,

I am quite ashamed to find this morning that you have received no word of acknowledgement or thanks for the tickets you so kindly sent us for Mr Hallé's Park Concert – Mr Gaskell understood that I should write to you, while I fancied that he was doing so; in fact the thing 'fell between two stools'. But I hope that the week's delay will not prevent your believing in the heartiest of our thanks for your kind remembrance of my daughters. They enjoyed the Concert extremely, and beg me to tell you how much pleasure they received.

With many apologies for not having written sooner,

I remain very truly yours
E. C. Gaskell

Newcastle University Library (GOT 183, autographs)

ANON[1]

[1850–1860]

< ... > With my best thanks, and kind regards
Ever yours very truly
E. C. Gaskell

42 Plymouth Grove, May 3d

Manchester Central Library

1 Fragment in Griffith Autograph Collection, transcribed by J. G. Baldry.

ANON

Monday *Morning*
Plymouth Grove

My dear Sir,

I cannot tell you how *extremely* grateful to you I feel for the great trouble which you have so kindly taken about this order for St Mary's Hospital. I am sending at once to consult the poor woman's friends as to which they would prefer – her admittance to the Infirmary, or still the order on St Mary's Hospital[1] – and directly that I have their reply I will forward you her full address.

And now what I can do for you! Do you know that feeling of warm gratitude which longs to return some { } kindness for what has been received, however little may be in its power? I shall not feel quite happy till you have given me the opportunity of some practical proof of this, my present gratitude.

In great haste, believe me, dear Sir,
very truly yours
E. C. Gaskell.

Pierpont Morgan Library (Gordon Ray Collection)

1 Probably St Mary's Hospital for Sick Children, Manchester, founded 1854.

ANON

Goodbye; it is time to go to the Railway Station.
Elizabeth C. Gaskell.

Princeton University Library

ANON

< ... > dread their effect upon your health . Do seek that strength and Protection without which nothing is strong nothing is holy.

Mrs Coolidge (Jane Whitehill): copy of an extract from an unidentified letter. Cp. *Letters*, pp. 693–6, ECG to ?, Eastbourne, 25 September [?1862].

ADDENDA

MRS ARCHER CLIVE[1]

42 Plymouth Grove
February 9th [?1856]

My dear Mrs Clive,

I am writing now at my friend Mr Smith's request, as he particularly wishes to be introduced to you, in hopes that you will allow him to enter into a negotiation with you for the publication of a cheap edition of Paul Ferroll. I give him my best wishes, and can speak very pleasantly of all my intercourse with him, as he has shown himself very liberal and obliging, – and finally very 'comfortable' to have to do with, in more uncomfortable circumstances than will, I hope, ever befall you, dear Mrs Clive.[2]

Yours very truly
E. C. Gaskell

Edward Clive

1 See p. 145 above.
2 ECG thanked George Smith on 17 March [1858] for his 'good & kind behaviour, under mortification & disappointment caused by me, to Mrs Clive'. See *Letters*, p. 495.

MRS ARCHER CLIVE

17 Cumberland Terrace[1]
Monday, June 16th [?1862]

It is with extreme regret that Mrs Gaskell finds herself compelled to decline Mrs Archer's[*sic*] Clive's invitation for Friday Evening next. There are very few arrangements depending upon her own will which would have prevented Mrs Gaskell availing herself of the pleasure offered, but she promised Miss Ellen Tollet some time ago to go and see her at Betley[2] once more; and on Saturday last Miss Tollet wrote to say that, as they were leaving on the 25th, Wednesday the 18th would be the most convenient day on which to receive Mrs Gaskell.

She is very sorry indeed. With a very sincere sympathy with Mrs Clive on the subject of paper visits she was yet tempted to go to Chapel S<t[?]> in the hope that Mrs Cli<ve> might not be gone out.

Edward Clive

1 See p. 198 n. 1 above.
2 Betley-Hall, near Newcastle, Staffordshire (*Letters*, p. 294).

MISCELLANEA

I

The Gaskell Society's collection of letters from ECG to Miss Barbara Fergusson* also contains two letters from ME to her former governess.

The first letter, in an envelope (stamp missing) addressed to Miss Fergusson, J. A. Turner Esqr, Cross Street, is postmarked Manchester 23 April 1848.

My dearest Miss Fergusson,

We did so wish you to come in that day you called a little while since with Miss Macfee. Mama has got a bad headache, & did not get up this morning, as early as usual. Last Tuesday Cousin Anne \ came /, and will leave us here rather soon, I believe. Miss Mason, went to Heathfield (intending to spend \ her Easter holidays / at Knutsford) last Thursday. I hope she will enjoy them.

Florence is growing so tall, taller even than my shoulder, & really she looks quite a big girl; before we were ill, she usually had two lessons, (one of spelling, the other of reading), on Saturday and also on Wednesdays, but just now (and Mrs Leisler child even having not had the measles, it is on that account, she at present wishes Miss Hooley not to come).

Annie and Ellen Green, will remain a few days, (for their Easter holidays) here, and yet there is a great chance of their coming, as we have been unable to go there for the fear which Mrs Green has, that either of us should give the infection to any of the boys. Papa went to Rivington on Good Friday, & enjoyed himself very much, quite different did he look from usual the next morning in consequence of his trip, he brought some very early spring flowers home with him, which Florence and Marianne arranged in the little glasses, and now with a love from Marianne believe me your affecte Meta.

Please to notice what the first letters of each line in this letter spell beginning at the word 'did' in this first page, and ending at the word 'love' in the last. [*It spells,* Dear Miss Fergusson how are you we are quite well].

The second letter, in an envelope (stamp missing) addressed to Miss Fergusson*, Miss Burnett, 146 Princess Street, Edinburgh, N. B., is postmarked Manchester 14 July 1849.

Wednesday –
Upper Rumford Street.

My dear Miss Fergusson,

I hope you will excuse my not having written to you sooner. I am really very sorry, and I will make up for it by writing to you very often during the holidays.

We are going to the Lakes in the holidays – next Thursday week [19 July 1849]. We are going to an old farm, called Mill-Brow, in the village of Skelwith. We shall have three bedrooms, a small parlour, and what is called in the Lake country 'the house'. It is a large sort of hall[,] slated. [See *NED,* 1 c.]

Papa is not going with us. He is going abroad, I believe, but I don't think he has any fixed plans. Baby is such a darling and I think she is getting so pretty. Flossie is writing you a letter, but as she cannot write very fast, you won't perhaps get it for several days. She does regular lessons with Mama it is so nice.

I don't know whether you care for riddles or not, but Mrs Shuttleworth told me of one so good from its badness, that I can't help asking it you. 'What two characters from Shakespeare express a Jew confessing his debts, and paying them?' 'Cash I owe (Cassio) & 'Der's de money (Desdemona).'

Mama said I was to tell you that Mrs Soly's address was Samuel Solly (or Soly) Esquire Bishop Street London. If you would like *our* direction at the Lakes, this is it Mrs Gaskell Mrs Preston's Mill-Brow Skelwith Bridge Near Ambleside Cumberland. Rather a long one is not it?

Marianne & Mamma join me in love to you. Believe me to be dear, darling Miss Fergusson

Yours very very affectionately
Meta Gaskell

Don't mind answering if your[*sic*] busy –

The Gaskell Society's collection also includes an envelope (stamp missing) postmarked 18 September 1889 to Mrs Macleod of Newpark Clynder by Helensburgh, Dumbartonshire. Other letters, receipts and documents identify the husband, William Ross Macleod, as 'Scholar Reginus Edinensis, Alumnus 1839–40'. His brother, J. Maclead, served on *HMS Actæon* in 1840 and as a ship's surgeon *c.* 1852–55. See also pp. 303–4 below.

2

The Brotherton Library, Leeds, holds an envelope of 1859, addressed to ECG from France, on which she has written, 'John Stuart Mill's handwriting. ECG.'

3

ANON

Sun of my soul! Thou Saviour dear
It is not night if Thou art near.
Oh! may no earth-born thought arise
To hide Thee from Thy servant's eyes.

Abide with me from morn to eve
For without Thee I dare not live;
Abide with me when night is nigh,
For without Thee I dare not die.

(From Keble's evening Hymn in the 'Christian[altered word] Year'.)
Heidelberg, November 10th [1858]
Elizabeth Gaskell.

Princeton University Library

4

Harvard slip, dated 29 November 1864 and signed, quotation [from Wordsworth, *The Excursion* IX, 238 ff.] of 4 lines:

The primal duties shine aloft, like Stars,
The charities that soothe, and heal, and bless,
Are scattered at the feet of men, like flowers.

Brotherton, same date, quotation of 4 lines:

Every hour that fleets so slowly
Has its task to do or bear,
Luxurious the crown & holy
If there set each gem with care.

See collection sold at Sotheby's 11 July 1996, lot 191.

5

June 14th 1865.
Manchester

Be the day weary, or be the day long,
At length it ringeth to even-song.[1]
E. C. Gaskell

Annotation [perhaps in Meta's hand] From Mr [*or* Mrs] Robson [WG's sister Nancy and her husband William, of Warrington] – July / 65.

Princeton University Library
Other copies: Society of Antiquaries, London, dated June 12th 1864; Chester R. O. (Knutsford), from: Fryston-Hall (that happy place, –) [R. Monckton Milnes, Yorkshire] August 21st 1865.

1 See Rubenius, p 305, who cites Stephen Hawes *Passetyme of Pleasure* (ed. Southey, 1831). There are also proverbial variants.

LOCATIONS AND ACKNOWLEDGEMENTS

Once again, we express our gratitude to the individuals and institutions who have so generously enabled us to prepare this edition.

Staatsbibliothek zu Berlin, Preußicher Kulturbesitz
Birmingham University Library
    Courtesy of A. D. Martineau
British Library and Royal Literary Fund (case file 1247)
Brotherton Collection, Leeds University Library
University of California, Los Angeles
    Department of Special Collections, Charles E. Young Research Library
Cambridge University Library
    Courtesy of the Syndics
Chatsworth (MS Devonshire Collections 2nd Series)
    M. A. Pearman and the Trustees of the Chatsworth Settlement
Cheltenham Ladies' College
Cheshire Record Office (Knutsford MSS)
Chicago University Library
Edward Clive
Columbia University Library
Royal Institution of Cornwall
Duke University Library
    Rare Book, Manuscript, & Special Collections
Edinburgh City Library
Eton College Library
Fales Library, Special Collections, New York University
Fitzwilliam Museum, Cambridge
    Miss Delia Butcher
Girton College, Cambridge
    The Mistress and Fellows, Girton College, Cambridge
Glasgow City Archives
    Courtesy of A. Clive Stirling of Keir.
Archives Hachette Livre
    Courtesy of M. Georges Lanthoinnette
Harris Manchester College, Oxford
Harvard University
    By permission of the Houghton Library

Haverford College, Pennsylvania
Haworth Parsonage Museum
Richard Hobbs (Villiers) MSS.
Castle Howard Archive
    By kind permission of the Howard family
The Huntington Library, Art Collections, and Botanical Gardens
Illinois University Library
Dr R. Jamison
Mrs Susan Kearney
Keele University Library
    Courtesy of the Trustees of the Wedgwood Museum, Barlaston, Staffordshire
Centre for Kentish Studies, Maidstone (U1590 C401/5)
    Courtesy of the Board of Trustees of the Chevening Estate
Mrs Lucy Magruder
Lord Montagu of Beaulieu, Estate Archive
Leicester University Library
Manchester Central Library
Mitchell Library, New South Wales
National Library of Scotland
    Courtesy of Chambers Harrap Publishers.
New York Public Library
    Carl H. Pforzheimer Collection of Shelley & His Circle
    Aster, Lenox and Tilden Foundations
New York Public Library
    Henry W. and Albert A. Berg Collection of English and American Literature
Newcastle Literary and Philosophical Society
Newcastle University Library
    Courtesy of the Trevelyan Family
Norfolk Record Office
Northumberland Record Office (Brooks Collection)
    Society of Antiquaries of Newcastle upon Tyne
Open University (G. Low deposit)
    Book History and Bibliographical Research Group, Parsifal College
[Curt Otto], *Der Verlag Bernhard Tauchnitz*
Pennsylvania State University Libraries
Pierpont Morgan Library, New York
Princeton University Library
The Shakespeare Birthplace Trust, Stratford
    The National Trust and T. W. Ferrers-Walker Esq.
John Geoffrey Sharps
Smith College, Northampton, Massachusetts
    Hale family Papers, Sophia Smith Collection
University of Texas at Austin
    Harry Ransom Humanities Research Center
Torquay Museum
Trinity College, Cambridge
    Courtesy of the Master and Fellows
Trinity College, Dublin
Tubingen University Library
Warrington Public Library
Warwickshire County Record Office

Wellcome Institute Library
West Sussex Record Office
    County Archivist, courtesy of the Trustees of Dunford House
Wigan Archives, Leigh
Wordsworth Museum, Grasmere

ABBREVIATIONS AND SHORT TITLES

We have often consulted silently standard reference works like *The Dictionary of National Biography, Dictionary of American Biography, Biographie Nationale, Deutsche Biographische Encyclopädie,* Frederick Boase's *Modern English Biography, The Catalogue of Printed Music in the British Library to 1980* and *The Hutchinson Dictionary of Scientific Biography*. Similarly, Anne Lohrli' s list of contributors and their contributions to *Household Words: A Weekly Journal 1850–1859* (Toronto and Buffalo 1973) and John Sutherland's *The Longman Companion to Victorian Fiction* (Harlow 1988), have been valuable sources of information.

Barker Juliet Barker, *The Brontës,* 1994
BJRUL Bulletin of the John Rylands (University) Library, Manchester
BST Brontë Society Transactions
CB Letters *The Letters of Charlotte Brontë with a Selection of Letters by Family and Friends,* ed. Margaret Smith, I (1829–47), Oxford 1995
CBL E. C. Gaskell, *The Life of Charlotte Brontë,* 2 vols 1857
CD Corresp. *The Correspondence of Charles Darwin,* ed. Frederick Burkhardt, Sydney Smith et al., Cambridge, etc. 1985 – continuing
CD Letters *The Letters of Charles Dickens,* ed. Madeline House, Graham Story and Kathleen Tillotson, Oxford, 1965 – continuing (The Pilgrim Edition)
CEN Letters *Letters of Mrs. Gaskell and Charles Eliot Norton 1855–1865,* ed. Jane Whitehill [1932], repr. Hildesheim, New York 1973
CH Gaskell *Elizabeth Gaskell: The Critical Heritage,* ed. Angus Easson, London and New York 1991
ECG Elizabeth Cleghorn Gaskell
EY John Chapple, *Elizabeth Gaskell: The Early Years,* Manchester and New York 1997
GSJ *The Gaskell Society Journal*
GSN *The Gaskell Society Newsletter*
Irvine Wm Fergusson Irvine, ed. *A History of the Family of Holland of Mobberley and Knutsford, etc.,* pr. pr. Edinburgh 1902
Knutsford Edn *The Works of Mrs Gaskell,* ed. A. W. Ward, 8 vols, 1906
L & M *Letters and Memorials of Catherine Winkworth,* ed. [Susannah Winkworth and Margaret J. Shaen], 2 vols, pr. pr., Clifton 1883–86
Lesser Margaret Lesser, *Clarkey: A Portrait in Letters of Mary Clarke Mohl (1793–1883),* Oxford 1984

Letters *The Letters of Mrs Gaskell*, ed. J. A. V. Chapple and Arthur Pollard, Manchester 1966; Cambridge, Mass. 1967; repr. 1997

MA Marianne Gaskell

Marquardt Hertha Marquardt, *Henry Crabb Robinson und Seine Deutschen Freunde: Brücke zwischen England und Deutschland im Zeitalter der Romantik*, 2 vols, Göttingen 1964

ME Margaret Emily (Meta) Gaskell

MS Manuscript

NED *New English Dictionary*

N & Q *Notes & Queries*

Portrait J. A. V. Chapple, *Elizabeth Gaskell : A Portrait in Letters*, Manchester 1980

Private Voices *Private Voices: The Diaries of Elizabeth Gaskell and Sophia Holland*, ed. J. A. V. Chapple and Anita Wilson, Keele 1996 [Edinburgh U. P.]

Rubenius Aina Rubenius, *The Woman Question in Mrs. Gaskell's Life and Works*, Upsala Studies 1950, repr. New York 1973

Sharps John Geoffrey Sharps, *Mrs. Gaskell's Obsevation and Invention: A Study of Her Non-Biographic Works*, Fontwell, Sussex 1970

Smith Walter E. Smith, *Elizabeth Gaskell: A Bibliographical Catalogue of First and Early Editions 1848–1866*, Los Angeles 1998

Uglow Jenny Uglow, *Elizabeth Gaskell: A Habit of Stories*, London and Boston 1993

UL University Library

Vickery Amanda Vickery, *The Gentleman's Daughter: Women's Lives in Georgian England*, New Haven and London 1998

Waller Ross D. Waller, 'Letters Addressed to Mrs Gaskell by Celebrated Contemporaries', repr. from *BJRL* 19 (1935)

WG William Gaskell

BIOGRAPHICAL INDEX

In this index we give biographical details of a number of ECG's personal and professional acquaintances who feature in her correspondence as a whole. Correspondents and other figures not included here have been identified wherever possible in our notes to individual letters.

Mary Arnold, née Penrose (1791–1873), was the widow of Thomas Arnold (1795–1842), the pioneering headmaster of Rugby public school. There were nine surviving children, the most famous being Matthew Arnold (1822—88). After her husband's death she continued to live at Fox How near Windermere, where she was the centre of a circle that included Elizabeth Fletcher* and her daughters, Margaret Davy* and Lady Richardson, together with members of the Wordsworth and Quillinan families. At one time ECG thought of retiring to the Lake District.

Georgina and Hannah Behrens (1823–71; 1829–1904), daughters of Solomon Levi Behrens (1788–1873). The family came from Hamburg to Manchester in the early nineteenth century. Solomon lived in Plymouth Grove, 'for over a quarter of a century the main pivot of Jewish settlement' in south Manchester (Bill Williams, *The Making of Manchester Jewry,* 1976, p. 74), but had moved by the time ECG came there in 1850. His nephews, Louis and Jacob, established a branch of the family firm in Manchester in 1840, whilst another member of the family, Lionel Behrens, lived at the Polygon, Ardwick.

Henry Arthur Bright (1830–84), of Sandheys, West Derby, Liverpool, a Unitarian and a partner in Gibbs, Bright and Co. He travelled in the USA and, like Francis Bennoch, became a friend of Nathaniel Hawthorne when he was American consul in Liverpool from 1853. Bright published a number of hymns and poems, together with literary and other essays on American subjects. His sister Harriette (1836–1916) was a friend of MA, 'one of the noblest most conscientious girls I have ever met with', she told C. E. Norton in 1858.

Harriet Carr, daughter of George Carr (d. December 1836, aged 77), former Russia merchant and Branch Bank of England Agent in Newcastle 1828–36. In Newcastle she was a good friend of ECG, but was not known to earlier biographers of ECG. Later, she seems to have married a Matthew Anderson of Newcastle and Jesmond.

Richard Cobden (1804–65), Manchester manufacturer and business man. Largely self-educated, he was a life-long advocate of free trade and a founding member of the Anti-Corn Law League in 1838. First elected to Parliament as member for Stockport in 1841, famous as a parliamentarian and public speaker. Identified with the 'Manchester school' of politics and economics, he was a notable opponent of any foreign policy venture that risked war.

Ann Coltman, née Byerley (d. 1865, aged 76), of Duffield, Derbyshire, was one of the Byerley sisters who taught ECG at Barford and Avonbank, Stratford-upon-Avon 1821–6. A 'good Italian scholar, but deaf as a post' (*EY,* p. 242), she married Samuel Coltman in 1836. See especially Phyllis D. Hicks. *A Quest of Ladies: The Story of a Warwickshire School,* [1949], pp. 102–129.

Mary Darbishire, née Blackmore ('aged 35', 1831), of Emden Street, Greenheys; Rivington, Lancashire, and Pendyffryn, N. Wales, Wife of Samuel Dukinfield Darbishire (1796–1870), rich Manchester solicitor and Trustee of Cross Street Chapel from August 1821 to September 1839. The Darbishires were to become long-standing family friends, though there was a time of estrangement in the early 1850s, owing to the 'uncertainty of her saying and doings' (*Letters,* pp. 147, 175–6, 225).

Caroline Anne Davenport, née Hurt (d. 1897), of Capesthorne, Cheshire. She was greatly admired by ECG and was perhaps a model for her character Lady Ludlow (Sharps, p. 282). This '*dama* of a lady' (*Letters,* p. 91) married (1) Edward Davies Davenport (d. 1847); (2) Edward John Lyttleton (1792–1863), 1st Baron Hatherton, of Teddesley Park, Staffordshire, in 1852, becoming Lady Hatherton.

Margaret Davy (1798–1869), daughter of Elizabeth Fletcher* and wife of Dr John Davy, brother of the scientist Sir Humphry Davy. ECG met her and her sister Lady Richardson, third wife of the Arctic explorer Sir John Richardson (1787–1865), through their mother when she was living in the Lake District. She later wrote an unpublished memoir of Wordsworth.

Susan Deane (1811–89), daughter of Peter Holland, surgeon of Knutsford. A first cousin of ECG, she was a bridesmaid at her wedding. She married her father's partner, Richard T. Deane, a widower with three surviving children, in 1844. These children, Emily, Arthur and Margaret, lived on, but Susan was to lose her own five children (*EY,* p. 126).

William Ewart (1798–1869), of Broadleas, Devizes, Wiltshire, MP for Dumfries, but previously for Liverpool and for Wigan. A supporter of Free Trade, he became a close friend of the Gaskell family.

Barbara Fergusson (b. *c.* 1823), is known only from passing references in *Letters* ('Daddy' not recognised by Chapple and Pollard) and from the newly discovered letters printed above. She was governess to MA and ME from before ?6 June 1845 to 20 March 1847, when she went by mutual agreement to the family of James A. Turner, a relation of William Turner* of Newcastle. She apparently had a father living, a twin brother called Charles, who later owned a slate quarry on Anglesey, and a sick brother (J. Fergusson) at Kirriemuir, according to a letter from him of 14 June 1847 (MS, The Gaskell Society). Both ECG and ME wrote to her after she had left them, and the family remained in touch until at least 1852. During the 1850s she married the Reverend William Ross Maclead, a free church minister, of 4 Eyre Place, Edinburgh, c. 1855–62. There were no children and he predeceased her, dying in 1865. She later lived on the Wirral and, during the early 1890s, with her twin brother at 3 Dundonald Street, Edinburgh. See pp. 293–4 above; *Letters,* pp. 181, 823–5, 833; Jean Lindsay, 'Who Was Miss Fergusson?', *GSN* 29 (2000), pp. 6–8.

Elizabeth Fletcher, née Dawson (1770–1858), of Lancrigg, Westmorland, widow of advocate and reformer Archibald Fletcher (1746–1828). Her life interconnects with ECG's in a number of ways. A noted Edinburgh hostess in the early nineteenth century, her salon was known to ECG's father William Stevenson and her cousin Henry Holland. She initiated a meeting with ECG after discovering the authorship of *Mary Barton,* 'at once struck with its power and pathos'. She and her daughters, Margaret Davy* and Lady Richardson, became firm friends. ECG visited her on a number of occasions in the Lake District in the 1850s, where she was connected with the Wordsworth circle.

John Forster (1812–76), a non-practising lawyer, editor, biographer, historian and man of letters. He acted as business and literary adviser to ECG and many other Victorian writers, notably Dickens from 1836. He wrote the first full-length biography of Dickens and assisted him with *Household Words.*

Eliza ('Tottie') Fox (?1823–1903), of 5 Charlotte Street, Bedford Square, etc., daughter of W. J. Fox, who wrote in 1834, 'Man has crippled female intellect, and thereby enfeebled his own.' She was a very important friend of ECG from May 1849. After an unconventional childhood she trained in art at Sass's school and exhibited at the Royal Academy several times in the early 1850s. An advocate for women's rights, she married a fellow-artist, Frederick Lee Bridell, in 1859. After his death of consumption in Rome four years later, she continued to paint, and campaign for women's rights, well into her old age.

Gaskell Family Elizabeth Cleghorn Stevenson was born in Chelsea on 29 September 1810, daughter of Elizabeth, née Holland (1771–1811). Her father William Stevenson (1770–1829) was successively a Unitarian minister, a tutor in classics, farmer, historian and a learned contributor to major Reviews like the *Edinburgh* and the *Westminster.* On her mother's death she was taken to Knutsford in Cheshire, and her childhood was spent mainly in the care of her mother's widowed sister, Mrs Hannah Lumb. She was educated at the Miss Byerleys' school at Barford and Stratford-upon-Avon from 1821 to 1826. In 1832, she married William Gaskell (1805–84), a Unitarian clergyman, second minister at Cross Street Chapel, Manchester. They lived at 1 (later 14) Dover Street ; at 121 Upper Rumford Street from 1842, and from 1850, at 42 (later 46) Plymouth Grove, Manchester.

ECG had seven pregnancies, one of which, a girl, miscarried. Four daughters survived: Marianne ('MA' 1834–1920), Margaret Emily ('Meta' 1837–1913), Florence Elizabeth ('Flossy' 1842–81) and Julia Bradford (1846–1908). Marianne married (Edward) Thurstan Holland (1836–84) in 1866, and Florence, Charles Crompton (1833–90) in 1863. Meta and Julia remained unmarried, although Meta suffered a broken engagement. There were two sons: 'Willie' (1844–45), who died aged ten months, and an unnamed child who lived 'for only a week', c. 1837–38. For fifty years the family were served by their nurse and de facto housekeeper, Ann Hearn, on whom a great deal of domestic responsibility devolved. Elizabeth Gaskell died on 12 November 1865 at Holybourne, Hampshire; William Gaskell died in Manchester on 11 June 1884.

Mary Green, née Brandreth (d. 14 June 1871, aged 68), wife of Henry Green, Unitarian minister of the Old Dissenting Chapel, Brook Street, Knutsford, 1827–72. She became one of ECG's most intimate and trusted correspondents. They had five surviving children: Emily (b. 10 Aug. 1828), John Philip (b. 2 Jan. 1830), Ann Louisa (b. 26 Aug. 1833), Mary Ellen (b. 28 Jan. 1835) and Isa-bella (b. 13 Jan. 1831). The children were friends of the Gaskell daughters, and stayed at each others' houses. Annie, Ellen and Emily often figure in ECG's letters.

Holland family ECG's mother, also called Elizabeth (1771–1811), was the daughter of Samuel and Ann Holland of Sandlebridge, near Knutsford, Cheshire. ECG was brought up by her mother's sister, Mrs Hannah Lumb (1767–1837), a widow living at The Heath, Knutsford. Mrs Lumb's own daughter Marianne died not long after the baby's arrival in 1811. ECG would have known two of her Holland spinster aunts, Catherine and Abigail, and their three brothers – Peter, surgeon of Knutsford; Samuel, entrepreneur of Liverpool and Plas yn Penrhyn, North Wales; and Swinton, banker with Baring Brothers, of London. Peter married (1) Mary Willets (d. 1803, aged 37) and (2) Mary Whittaker; Samuel married Catherine Menzies, and Swinton, Anne Willets. There were very many cousins from these three marriages, all of whom ECG knew well, especially Samuel's son Charles ('a great quiz, and a great Radical'), who married the sister of William Gaskell, Elizabeth ('very clever, energetic, and animated'). See especially *EY,* Appendix B, 'Hollands of Cheshire'.

Lady Janet Kay-Shuttleworth (1817–72), of Gawthorp Hall, Lancashire. She married Dr James P. Kay (1804–77) in 1842; he adopted her family name. ECG met her first at Capesthorne (she was a cousin of Caroline Davenport*) and then at Brierly Close, Windermere in 1850, where she was introduced to Charlotte Brontë. After her separation from her husband in 1853, she lived mainly in Germany and Italy as an invalid. See R. J. W. Sellek, *James Kay-Shuttleworth: Journey of an Outsider,* Ilford, Essex, 1994.

John Malcolm Forbes Ludlow (1821–1911), founder of the Christian Socialist movement with F. D. Maurice, Charles Kingsley and Thomas Hughes. Called to the Bar in 1843, Ludlow followed a legal career until the 1870s. He visited Manchester in 1841, when he became involved in the Anti-Corn Law League; and also during a tour of Lancashire and Yorkshire in Autumn 1851, when he 'had the pleasure of calling on Mrs Gaskell' (*John Ludlow: The Autobiography of a Christian Socialist,* ed. A. D. Murray, 1981, p. 201). He promoted educational and welfare activities for young men, and helped found the Working Men's College in 1854.

Vernon Lushington (1823–1912), one of twin brothers educated at Rugby and Cambridge (Godfrey became a Fellow of Oriel). Vernon combined a successful career in the law with philanthropic activities, becoming a Christian Socialist and a teacher at the Working Men's College. His pamphlet 'How shall the strong man know his strength?' addressed the issue of industrial relations. A follower of Auguste Comte, he also wrote and lectured upon Positivism, which maintained the importance of a scientific rather than a religious outlook.

Harriet Martineau (1802–76), of The Knoll, near Ambleside. Daughter of a Unitarian textile manufacturer of Norwich, she became a pioneering woman writer and journalist. She wrote fiction, political and other essays, and a long autobiography, eventually edited by her friend, the American abolitionist Maria Weston Chapman. She was devoted to her brother, the Reverend James Martineau (1805–1900), but quarrelled with him, first over her advocacy of mesmerism, from which she claimed to have benefited personally, and then, irrevocably, as a consequence of her anti-religious *Letters on the Laws of Man's Nature and Development* (1851).

Richard Monckton Milnes (1809–85), of Fryston, Yorkshire, he became Lord Houghton in 1800. Reformer, socialite, traveller and man of letters. Despite an auspicious career as an undergraduate at Cambridge, where with Arthur Hallam and Tennyson he was one of the select 'Apostles', he achieved only limited success in later life.

Mary Mohl, née Clarke (1793–1883), she lived most of her life in France. After a relationship with the writer and thinker Claude Fauriel, she resided permanently from 1838 at 120 rue du Bac, Paris, where she instituted her salon. In 1847 she married an orientalist of German extraction, Julius von Mohl. ECG first met her in 1853 and became a regular visitor, composing some of *Wives and Daughters* in her apartment.

Florence Nightingale (1820–1910), of Lea Hurst, Derbyshire, and Embley, Hampshire. Hospital reformer, most famous for her work in the Crimean war, the high point of a life devoted to reform of the whole practice of hospital nursing and health administration. ECG also corresponded with her elder sister Parthenope and wrote part of *North and South* at Lea Hurst.

Charles Eliot Norton (1827–1908), American scholar and man of letters. A member of the Boston intellectual élite and an active abolitionist, he met ECG first in London in 1850 at the Procters' (*CEN Letters,* p. 1) and then in Rome in 1857, becoming a warm and important correspondent of both ECG and her older daughters. Amongst his extensive writings he translated Dante and edited Carlyle; he also pioneered the study of Art History at Harvard for over twenty years later in the century.

Agnes and Eliza Paterson (1822–89; d. 1856), 'such nice, simple-hearted, intelligent, merry girls' (*L & M,* I. 74). They lived with their uncle Joshua Satterfield and his spinster sister Harriet at the Elms, Victoria Park, Manchester. Agnes married Charles Sandars (1813–77) in 1851 and moved away from Manchester to live in the Midlands, but maintained contact with the Gaskells and the Winkworths.

Mary Rich, née Mackintosh (1789–1876), daughter of Sir John Mackintosh, lawyer and politician; wife of Claudius John Rich, East India Company representative in Baghdad. She was with her father in Paris on the eve of Waterloo, meeting the famous Mme Anne Louise Germaine de Staël (1766–1817), author of *Corinne* (1807) and *De l'Allemagne* (1810). Later Mary Rich was incarcerated in Baghdad with her husband; she also travelled to Bombay with him. She was part of the Wedgwood circle, and lived with Hensleigh and Frances Wedgwood from the 1830s. See especially *Letters,* pp. 212–3.

Mrs Mary Robberds, née Turner (1786–1869), Grosvenor Square, Manchester. Daughter of William Turner of Newcastle and wife of John Gooch Robberds (1789–1854), minister at Cross Street Chapel, Manchester 1811–54. William Gaskell was his colleague from 1828. Her brief 'Recollections of a long life' is printed in *Private Voices*, though she does not mention ECG.

Martin and Susanna Schunck (1789–1872; 1793–1884), merchant of Manchester, of naturalised German extraction. He founded the firm of Schunck, Mylius and Co., shipping agents and exporters, and was a Trustee of Cross Street chapel from 1854. He married Susanna Katharina, née Mylius; his sister Friederike married John Middleton Pickford. Antonio C. N. Gallenga (1810–95) married their daughter Juliet (1826–55) 12 July 1847; William Gaskell was to preach her funeral sermon on 30 September 1855. Her brother, Henry Edmund Schunck (1820–1903) was a distinguished research chemist and governor of Owen's College, where the Schunck Memorial Laboratories are named after him.

Salis and Julie Schwabe (1800–53; 1819–96). [Grace Schwabe in *Letters* is an error.] Salis and his brother Adolf were rich calico printers of German extraction, with business premises at Rhodes, Middleton, near Rochdale. The Salis Schwabes were patrons of the arts; famous musicians performed and stayed at their house in Crumpsall, North Manchester. After his sudden death at Glyn Garth, their country home in North Wales, his wife continued her cultural and philanthropic activities, notably with the firm's workforce, before retiring to Naples. Their first and third sons, Edward and Frederick, took over the family business; their second son, Colonel George Schwabe, married the daughter of Mrs Maria James. They had three daughters, the eldest daughter of whom was Harriet (b. c. 1838).

William and Emily Shaen (1822–87; 1822–87), of 8 Bedford Row till 1860, thereafter 15 Upper Phillimore gardens, London. William's father, Samuel Shaen (d. 1854), a prominent Unitarian of Crix, Essex, and his wife Rebecca, née Solly (1782–1858) had nine children, several of whom feature in ECG's correspondence. William Shaen married Emily Winkworth on 2 September 1851 (*Letters*, p. 159). As a solicitor, William represented ECG, notably over the legal challenge to *The Life of Charlotte Brontë* in 1857. He was on the Garibaldi Italian Unity Committee; 'the Clan', intimate friends guided by the Italian nationalist Giuseppe Mazzini (1805–72), used to meet at each other's houses c. 1850 (*L & M*, I. 300 n.)

George Smith (1824–1901), from 1846 the sole owner of the family publishing firm of Smith, Elder and Co., which by a combination of business acumen and sympathetic treatment of his authors, he developed into one of the great Victorian publishing houses. He published Jane *Eyre* in 1847 and all of Charlotte Brontë's subsequent novels, becoming her friend. On her death he commissioned ECG's *Life* (1857), after which he published her last major works, *Sylvia's Lovers* (1863), *Cousin Phillis* (1864) and *Wives and Daughters* (1865–6), the last two initially in the *Cornhill Magazine*, founded by him in 1860.

Emelyn Eldridge (d. 1894) **and William Wetmore Story** (1819–95), an expatriate American sculptor and poet with a studio at 43 Via di San Isidoro, Rome. The Storys, friends of Madame Mohl* and Charles Eliot Norton*, are indelibly associated with ECG's magical visit to Rome in 1857. 'I like the Storys very much ... [She is] much more like an Englishwoman than an American, with a full but nice figure, rather snub features, but a good complexion, animated eyes, and a quantity of beautiful hair, lively caressing manners. He is small and dark, with a pointed beard and a clever, mobile, humorous face, rather sensible than powerful' (Catherine Winkworth, *L & M*, II. 120).

William Turner (1761–1859), of Newcastle, minister of Hanover Square chapel 1782–1841. He was instrumental in founding the Newcastle Literary and Philosophical Society in 1793. One of the most distinguished Unitarian figures of his time, he was well known to both ECG's father and her husband. He lived with his youngest daughter Ann (1796–1851), eventually retiring to Manchester. See Stephen Harbottle, *The Reverend William Turner: Dissent and Reform in Newcastle upon Tyne,* Newcastle 1997; *EY,* Appendix C, 'Turner Family'.

Catherine and Susanna Winkworth, of The Polygon, Ardwick, Manchester; from 1850 Ferns Cottage, Alderley, Cheshire, etc. Their father Henry Winkworth (d. 1869), silk manufacturer, married (1) a daughter of Stephen Dickinson (d. 1841); (2) in 1845, Eliza, née Leyburne (c. 1799-c. 1893). Of his first marriage were born Susanna (1820–84), Emily (1822–87), Selina (1825–85), Catherine (1827–78) and Alice (by 1838-post–1878); and two sons: William (c. 1829–39), Stephen (1831–86, m. Emma Thomasson). The daughters took lessons from William Gaskell; ECG jokes about Susanna's interest in him. Susanna and Catherine, who remained unmarried and were deeply religious, distinguished themselves in the field of German theology, Susanna by translating the *Life and Letters of Niebuhr* and Catherine the *Lyra Germanica,* a highly significant work in the history of hymnody. They were later involved in promoting women's education. Emily married William Shaen*, and Selina, John Collie.

Susanna Winkworth's *Letters and Memorials of Catherine Winkworth* (completed by Margaret J. Shaen, daughter of William and Emily, and circulated privately, 2 vols, 1883–6) offers a highly detailed account of the lives of Catherine and Susanna, and provides a considerable insight into the situation of women of their class and circumstances. It is also an invaluable source of information about the life of ECG and her family from the 1840s. A greatly shortened and far less useful version, edited by Margaret J, Shaen in one volume entitled *Memorials of Two Sisters* (1908), has some additions, such as a brief character of Henry Winkworth's second wife, a bibliography and a short index.

INDEX

Relationships given without qualification are to Elizabeth Cleghorn Gaskell, née Stevenson. Literary works can be found under authors' names. Names and page numbers in bold indicate correspondents and letters in this edition. Note numbers are also supplied. Question marks after Christian names and surnames indicate uncertain identifications. Question marks after page references indicate uncertain identifications on that page.

Carleton College Library
One North College Street
Northfield, MN 55057-4097